THE STUDIA PHILONICA ANNUAL
Studies in Hellenistic Judaism

SBL

Society of Biblical Literature

THE STUDIA PHILONICA ANNUAL
Studies in Hellenistic Judaism

Editors
David T. Runia
Gregory E. Sterling

THE STUDIA PHILONICA ANNUAL
Studies in Hellenistic Judaism

Volume XXIV

2012

EDITORS
David T. Runia
Gregory E. Sterling

ASSOCIATE EDITOR
Sarah J. K. Pearce

BOOK REVIEW EDITOR
Ronald Cox

Society of Biblical Literature
Atlanta

THE STUDIA PHILONICA ANNUAL
Studies in Hellenistic Judaism

The financial support of

C. J. de Vogel Foundation, Utrecht
Queen's College, University of Melbourne
University of Notre Dame
Pepperdine University

is gratefully acknowledged

ISBN: 978-1-58983-697-6
ISSN : 1052-4533

The cover photo, *Ezra Reads the Law*, is from a wall painting in the Dura Europos synagogue and used with permission from Zev Radovan (www.BibleLandPictures.com).

Printed on acid-free, recycled paper conforming to ANSI/NISO Z39.48-1992 (R1997) and ISO 9706:1994 standards for paper permanence.

∞

THE STUDIA PHILONICA ANNUAL
STUDIES IN HELLENISTIC JUDAISM

Contributions should be sent to the Editor, Prof. G. E. Sterling, 409 Prospect Street, New Haven, CT 06511, USA; email: gregory.sterling@yale.edu. Please send books for review to the Book Review Editor, Prof. Ronald Cox, Religion Division, Pepperdine University, 24255 Pacific Coast Highway, Malibu, CA 90263-4352; email: rcox@pepperdine.edu.

Contributors are requested to observe the "Instructions to Contributors" located at the end of the volume. These can also be consulted on the Annual's website: http://www.nd.edu/~philojud. Articles which do not conform to these instructions cannot be accepted for inclusion.

The Studia Philonica Monograph series accepts monographs in the area of Hellenistic Judaism, with special emphasis on Philo and his *Umwelt*. Proposals for books in this series should be sent to the Editor, Prof. Thomas H. Tobin S.J., Theology Department, Loyola University Chicago, 1032 West Sheridan Road, Chicago, IL 60660-1537, U.S.A.; email: ttobin@luc.edu.

CONTENTS

NOTE. The editors wish to thank the typesetter Gonni Runia once again for her tireless work on this volume. They wish to express their thanks to Tamar Primoratz (Melbourne) for her assistance with the bibliography, and also to Sister Lisa Marie Belz OSU ABD, and Cambry Pardee, for meticulously proof-reading the final manuscript. As in previous years we are deeply grateful to our publisher, The Society of Biblical Literature, and to Leigh Andersen and Kathie Klein, for making the publication of the Annual possible.

ABBREVIATIONS

The abbreviations used for the citation of ancient texts and modern scholarly literature generally follow the guidelines of the Society of Biblical Literature as published in *The SBL Handbook of Style* (Hendrickson: Peabody Mass. 1999) §8.4. In addition to the abbreviations listed in the Notes to contributors at the back of the volume, please note the following:

BBB	Bonner biblische Beiträge
FC	Fathers of the Church. Washington D.C. 1947–
HUT	Hermeneutische Untersuchungen zur Theologie
LThK	Lexikon für Theologie und Kirche
NTTSD	New Testament Tools, Studies and Documents
OBO	Orbis biblicus et orientalis
RHR	Revue de l'histoire des religions
SBS	Stuttgarter Bibelstudien
ScEs	*Science et esprit*
SCI	*Studia Classica Israelica*
SEAug	Studia Ephemiridis Augustinianum
StPB	Studia post-biblica
StudTheol	*Studia Theologica*

The Studia Philonica Annual 24 (2012) 1–68

PHILO OF ALEXANDRIA
QUAESTIONES IN EXODUM 2.62–68:
CRITICAL EDITION*

JAMES R. ROYSE

Prolegomena

The remains of Philo's *Quaestiones et solutiones in Genesim et Exodum* exist in overlapping texts preserved in three languages.[1] The most extensive is the ancient Armenian translation (from the late sixth century), although even it is missing substantial portions of Philo's original work.[2] The ancient Latin translation (from the fourth century) preserves what seems to have been the original book 6 of *QG*, and contains twelve sections not found in the Armenian.[3] The original Greek of the *Quaestiones* has survived fragmentarily in many scattered places, but chiefly in two types of collections, the exegetical catenae and the florilegia.[4] Several hundred

---

* I would like to thank David T. Runia for his encouragement and advice concerning this project, and Gonni Runia for her invaluable assistance with the technical aspects of this article. I am also grateful for the comments and corrections provided by Gregory E. Sterling and an anonymous reader.

[1] See my "The Original Structure of Philo's *Quaestiones*," *SPh* 4 (1976–1977): 41–78, and "Philo's Division of his Works into Books," *SPhA* 13 (2001): 59–85, esp. 76–85. Details on various issues discussed below can be found in these two articles.

[2] The text with Latin translation is found in Johannes Baptista Aucher, *Philonis Judaei paralipomena Armena* (Venice: Typis coenobii PP. Armenorum in insula S. Lazari, 1826). On the date of the Armenian translation see Abraham Terian, ed., *Philonis Alexandrini de animalibus* (Chico, Calif.: Scholars Press, 1981), 6–9, and idem, ed., *Alexander* (PAPM 36 [Paris: Cerf, 1988]), 21–23.

[3] The text is found in Françoise Petit, ed., *L'ancienne version latine des Questions sur la Genèse de Philon d'Alexandrie* (2 vols.; TU 113—14; Berlin: Akademie-Verlag, 1973); on the dating, see 1:8–9.

[4] See Petit, ed., *Quaestiones: fragmenta graeca* (PAPM 33 [Paris: Cerf, 1978]), 13–31, and my *The Spurious Texts of Philo of Alexandria: A Study of Textual Transmission*

Greek fragments have been located within the Armenian translation, and three others within the Latin alone. A few dozen more appear to derive from portions missing in both Armenian and Latin, since they are more or less plausibly assigned to the *Quaestiones* but cannot be located within either ancient translation. And among the further hundred or so unidentified Greek fragments that are ascribed to Philo there may be yet further texts that derive from the *Quaestiones*.

The Greek fragments are typically brief, often consisting of merely a phrase or two. However, on occasion one finds longer portions, such as the two halves of *QE* 1.6 found in two different sources,[5] the entire section of *QG* 2.62 quoted by Eusebius, and citations of about one-half of *QG* 2.1–7 discovered in Athous Vatopedinus 659 and edited by Paramelle.[6]

However, one source stands out as a wonderful exception to all these remnants. In Vaticanus gr. 379 we find the continuous text of seven sections of the *Quaestiones in Exodum*, namely 2.62–68. This manuscript, dating from the fourteenth century, contains many of Philo's works, followed by some excerpts from Euclid, then a citation from *Her.* 167–173, and then *QE* 2.62–68.[7] The miscellaneous nature of these three concluding selections is puzzling, although there are some slight verbal connections among them. The excerpts from Euclid end with ἀλλήλοις ἐστὶν ἴσα, which may have been related by the scribe (or an ancestor) to the subtitle of *Her.* (περὶ

---

and Corruption with Indexes to the Major Collections of Greek Fragments (ALGHJ 22; Leiden: Brill, 1991), 14–58.

[5] See my "Philo's *Quaestiones in Exodum* 1.6," in *Both Literal and Allegorical: Studies in Philo of Alexandria's Questions and Answers on Genesis and Exodus* (ed. David M. Hay; BJS 232; Atlanta: Scholars Press, 1991), 17–27.

[6] Joseph Paramelle, with the collaboration of Enzo Lucchesi, eds. and trans., *Philon d'Alexandrie: Questions sur la Genèse II 1–7* (Cahiers d'Orientalisme 3; Geneva: Patrick Cramer, 1984). See my review in *SPhA* 1 (1989): 134–44.

[7] See PCW 1:xxv–xxvi (followed by G-G, #81), where, however, Cohn overlooks the citation from *Her.*, a discussion of which may be found in my "The Text of Philo's Quis rerum divinarum heres 167–173 in Vaticanus 379," *Theokratia* 3 (Jahrbuch des Institutum Judaicum Delitzschianum; Leiden: Brill, 1979), 217–23. The manuscript was described authoritatively by Robert Devreesse, *Bibliothecae Apostolicae Vaticani: Codices Vaticani Graeci* 2: *Codices 330–603* (Vatican City: Vatican Library, 1937), 73–74.

τῆς ἴσα καὶ ἐναντία λόγων αὐτοῦ), and the words ὄνομα κυρίου at *Her.* 170 may have been related to the selection from *QE.*[8]

In any case, some scribe, either that of the Vatican manuscript or that of an ancestor, decided to extract *QE* 2.62–68 from a manuscript of the *Quaestiones.* It may seem implausible that a fuller manuscript survived into the fourteenth century, but in fact there is some evidence that manuscripts of portions (at least) of the *Quaestiones* survived into rather late times. For example, a Greek fragment from *QE* 1.19 is contained in the catena on Luke that was compiled by Nicetas of Heracleia (Serranos) in Constantinople about 1080.[9] Nicetas mostly derived his material from the original texts, rather than from earlier compilations.[10] And so it seems likely that Nicetas copied the (otherwise unknown) fragment from *QE* 1.19 from a manuscript of the *Quaestiones.* Again, in a fourteenth century manuscript, Athous Vatopedinus 659, we find extensive excerpts from *QG* 2.1–7, and it seems likely that the scribe copied this material from a manuscript of the *Quaestiones* rather than from some previous collection of extracts. The extent of such manuscripts is completely unknown, but it seems probable that they would have each contained at least one entire book of the *Quaestiones.* The source of the extract in Vat. gr. 379 would have thus contained at least all of book 2 of *QE,* perhaps all of *QE* (however many books that may have been), or even conceivably all of both *QG* and *QE.* It is thus with a mixture of gratitude (for what we have) and regret (for what we might have had) that one contemplates what the scribe of this manuscript (or perhaps of some ancestor) had in his hands.

Of course, that fuller manuscript has doubtless perished, as did all the other Greek manuscripts that must have existed at one time or another of the *Quaestiones, De providentia, De animalibus,* and the various other lost works of Philo. For now we must be content with what Vat. gr. 379 has saved from oblivion.

This text of *QE* 2.62–68 provides an intricate discussion of the divine powers. This is a theme to which Philo returns repeatedly, notably in the fragment *Deo,* preserved only in the Armenian version,[11] as well as at *Cher.*

---

[8] "The Text of Philo's Quis heres," 218.

[9] The fragment is edited by Petit, PAPM 33:236–37.

[10] Joseph Sickenberger, *Die Lukaskatene des Niketas von Herakleia* (TU N.F. 7.4; Leipzig: J. C. Hinrichs, 1902), 75.

[11] See Folker Siegert, ed. and trans. *Philon von Alexandrien, Über die Gottesbezeich-*

27–28, *QG* 1.57, and other places.[12] But *QE* 2.62–68 preserves his most thorough discussion of this topic, presented as reflections on the significance of the Cherubim, as described in Exod 25:18–22 (25:17–21 LXX).[13]

Moreover, it seems certain that Vat. gr. 379, which I shall designate as V,[14] preserves a highly accurate, although not quite uncorrupted, text of these sections. At the very least, the close agreement with the Armenian throughout shows that the Greek of V is very close to the Greek that was read by the Armenian translators in the late sixth century. And the style of the text and its agreement with Philo's wording and thought found elsewhere show that the Greek is, with a few exceptions, as close to Philo's *ipsissima verba* as we are likely to find. Fortunately, the text of V is quite readable. The scribe makes liberal use of ligatures, but never (I believe) is the reading of V seriously in doubt. There is, though, some very slight damage to the top of the last few pages, where there is a thin vertical tear that extends through the center of the upper two or three lines. This tear is small enough that only one or two letters per line are affected, and sometimes another hand has rewritten those letters at the edge of the tear. But even at these places the original reading is never (again, as I believe) in doubt. However, see the note on 2.68 l. 39 below for the one place where the damage (from the tear and in the nearby area) is significant.

The scribe has also provided the title of the book from which these sections derive. Preceding *QE* 2.62 at Vat. gr. 379, f. 385ᵛ he writes: ἐκ τῶν ἐν Ἐξόδῳ ἤτοι Ἐξαγωγαὶ ζητημάτων καὶ λύσεων.[15] The dual designation for

---

nung *"wohltätig verzehrendes Feuer"* (*"De Deo"*): *Rückübersetzung des Fragments aus dem Armenischen, deutsche Übersetzung und Kommentar* (WUNT 46; Tübingen: J. C. B. Mohr, 1988). In his retroversion from Armenian into Greek and in his commentary Siegert provides many illuminating comments on the Greek and Armenian terms that are found in *QE* 2.62–68 as well.

[12] For some further references see Terian's note 7 in PAPM 34C:280–81.

[13] There is a substantial literature on Philo's doctrine of the divine powers; a recent work is by Cristina Termini, *Le potenze di Dio: Studio su δύναμις in Filone di Alessandria* (SEAug 71; Rome: Institutum Patristicum Augustinianum, 2000), who discusses our passage at 125–35.

[14] Note though that in PCW "V" is used for two manuscripts in Vienna.

[15] More precisely we find: ἐκ τῶν ἐν ἐξόδω ἤτοι ἐξαγωγαὶ ζητημάτων καὶ λύσεων. Mai prints the title in capitals, and edits the name of the Biblical book as ΕΞΟΔΩΙ ΗΤΟΙ ΕΞΑΓΩΓΑΙ. Tischendorf's transcript reads exactly as in the manuscript (but

Exodus is unusual; it combines the usual title (Ἔξοδος) with the title that Philo exclusively uses (Ἐξαγωγή).[16] That the latter term was used by Philo in the title of *QE* is confirmed by Eusebius, who refers (*Hist. eccl.* 2.18.1) to the books of *QE* as τῶν ἐν Ἐξαγωγαὶ ζητημάτων καὶ λύσεων, although he says a few lines later (2.18.5) that these books discuss Exodus (Ἔξοδος). We may, of course, infer that Eusebius is there simply reverting to his normal usage. Similarly, the *pinax* found in Vindobonensis theol. gr. 29 has the title τῶν ἐν Ἐξόδῳ ζητημάτων καὶ λύσεων.[17] I thus suppose that Philo's original title had simply Ἐξαγωγῇ (which Philo would of course have written as ΕΞΑΓΩΓΗ), and that the title in Vat. gr. 379 has disjoined that name of the book with the usual name, while also making a slight copying blunder (Ἐξαγωγαὶ for Ἐξαγωγῇ).

However, these sections, despite being the most extensive continuous portion of the *Quaestiones* in Greek and being so important for Philo's thought, have suffered an unsatisfactory fate at the hands of scholars. Even though they exist in a Greek manuscript of very high quality and in a very literal Armenian version, they have never been, as I would judge, properly edited. One might have expected to find them in Françoise Petit's excellent edition (in the PAPM series) of the Greek fragments of the *Quaestiones*. However, she argued that V, rather than containing fragments, is a (very limited) transcription from a continuous text of the *Quaestiones*, and so belongs to the direct transmission of Philo's works; thus its contents would be out of place in her edition.[18] Two smaller excerpts from these seven sections are preserved in the *Sacra parallela*, namely at 2.64 and 2.65, and these

---

without accents and breathings). Then Grossmann edits Ἐξόδῳ ἤτοι Ἐξαγωγῇ, and Tischendorf shifts to capitals and drops the iota subscripts by writing: ΕΞΟΔΩ ΗΤΟΙ ΕΞΑΓΩΓΗ. Harris, Marcus, and Terian do not, I believe, supply the title.

[16] It occurs four times (*Migr.* 14, *Her.* 14, 251, *Somn.* 1.117). See Naomi G. Cohen, *Philo's Scriptures: Citations from the Prophets and Writings* (Leiden: Brill, 2007), 29–33, who does not mention the title of *QE*.

[17] The precise writing is ἐξόδω; see PCW 1:xxxvi, and the photograph in David T. Runia, *Philo in Early Christian Literature* (Assen and Minneapolis: Van Gorcum and Fortress, 1993), facing p. 20.

[18] For her reasons for not including all of *QE* 2.62–68 in her edition, see her comments at PAPM 33:13 and 273, and Terian's comments at PAPM 34C:283–86. See also my review of the latter work at *SPhA* 10 (1998): 182.

are indeed printed by Petit along with the evidence of V.[19] But the bulk of the material found in V is not included.

What we have is that the Greek text of V is found in six separate publications, edited by Mai, Grossmann, Tischendorf, Harris, Marcus, and Terian. These editions present texts that are more or less different, where the text of V is often misreported or obscured. Moreover, the witness of the Armenian version has not been utilized to its fullest degree nor cited in a clear fashion. A survey of the publication history of these sections will show why a critical edition is still needed, and why even after six editions Runia could call the text "neglected."[20]

History of Editions

The first publication of these sections was by Angelo Mai in 1831.[21] In his preface Mai notes that he is republishing some other Philonic texts, and then states:

> Et quidem Philoni novum accedit nunc incrementum ex vaticano codice, septem scilicet de Cherubim quaestiones, ex eius amplo in exodum opere, quod nos graece desideramus. . . . Graeca fragmenta a me Romae nuper inventa cum armeniaco textu conspirant, immo eum saepenumero illuminant; sed et vicicissim ab eo lucem interdum accipiunt.[22]

Mai does not reprint Aucher's Latin translation of the Armenian, but provides his own Latin translation from the Greek. This *editio princeps* is disfigured by quite a few small blunders. Nevertheless, Mai's edition is here

---

[19]   PAPM 33:274–75.

[20]   David T. Runia, "A Neglected Text of Philo of Alexandria: First Translation into a Modern Language," in *Things Revealed* (ed. Esther G. Chazon, David Satran, and Ruth A. Clements; JSJSup 89; Leiden: Brill, 2004), 199–207.

[21]   Angelus Maius, ed., *Classicorum auctorum e Vaticanis codicibus editorum*, vol. 4 (Rome: Typis Vaticanis, 1831), 430–41. By the way, pdfs of the editions by Mai, Grossmann, and Tischendorf are available through Google Books.

[22]   Ibid., xii: "And now a new addition is made to Philo from a Vatican codex, namely seven questions on the Cherubim from his extensive work on Exodus, which we lack in Greek. . . . The Greek fragments recently found by me at Rome agree with the Armenian text, indeed repeatedly clarify it; but in turn they are sometimes clarified by it."

and there the most accurate of all, e.g., in writing τοῦ λεχθέντος at 2.66 l. 3, in including κύριον at 2.68 l. 25, a hardly negligible reading, and in writing καταρχὴν at 2.68 l. 39.

Unfortunately, Mai's edition went unnoticed by Grossmann, Tischendorf, and Harris. The first reference to it within the context of Philo studies (and perhaps at all) seems to have been by Schürer in 1886.[23] In that very year Harris published his edition. Indeed, the later editions by Marcus and Terian also make no reference to Mai's edition.[24] And so Mai's *editio princeps* has had no effect on the subsequent fate of the text for some 180 years, and the correct readings just cited were lost to Philonic studies.

Independently of Mai's work, as it seems, Tischendorf discovered the text in 1843. At that time Tischendorf was investigating manuscripts containing Philonic texts on behalf of C. A. F. Grossmann, who was planning a new edition of Philo.[25] Tischendorf communicated a transcript of the sections in V to Grossmann. And, *mirabile dictu*, this transcript is found today in the University of Leipzig library, where it forms part of Grossmann's papers, which were given to the library by Grossmann's son.[26] Since this transcript played a crucial role in the publication history of our text, I will report on it in some detail.

The collations that were provided to Grossmann now exist as four manuscripts in Leipzig, which are catalogued as Greek manuscripts 29, 30, 31, and 31ª.[27] The relevant one here is manuscript 30, where on ff. 253ʳ–

---

[23] See Emil Schürer, *Geschichte des jüdischen Volkes im Zeitalter Jesu Christi* 2 (2nd ed.; Leipzig: J. C. Hinrichs, 1886), 834 nn. 10 and 11; the same comments can be found in his *Geschichte des jüdischen Volkes im Zeitalter Jesu Christi* 3 (3rd ed.; Leipzig: J. C. Hinrichs, 1898), 491 nn. 11 and 12. See also now *SHJP* 3.2:820 n. 32. In the predecessor of the *Geschichte, Lehrbuch der neutestamentlichen Zeitgeschichte* (Leipzig: J. C. Hinrichs, 1874), 653 n. 1, Schürer cites the works of Grossmann and Tischendorf, but not that of Mai. Of course, Schürer's research in the years from 1874 to 1886 resulted in a vast enhancement of material on the works of Philo, including this reference to Mai.

[24] Petit simply notes the edition (PAPM 33:13 n. 1, erroneously citing pages "440–441" for 430–441), but has no occasion to refer further to Mai's work.

[25] See PCW 1:lxxxii for a brief report on Grossmann's preparations for this edition.

[26] The information reported here is based on my examination of these papers. I appreciate very much the cordial assistance of Dr. Christoph Mackert, Director of the Handschriftenzentrum of the Universitätsbibliothek at Leipzig.

[27] The first three are noted by Victor Gardthausen, *Katalog der griechischen Handschriften der Universitäts-Bibliothek zu Leipzig* (Leipzig: Otto Harrassowitz, 1898), 35–

256^r Tischendorf supplies a transcript of Vat. gr. 379, ff. 385–388.[28] This transcript (like all of Tischendorf's work in manuscripts 29 and 30, and in contrast with the careful writing of the other collators) appears to have been written very hastily and inelegantly. Indeed, I was often able to read what Tischendorf wrote only because I knew the text already from V itself and from the various editions, although the intended reader, Grossmann, evidently was able to cope (at least almost all of the time) with Tischendorf's script.

Nevertheless, the transcript is remarkably accurate, with only a very few corrections to what is written.[29] Following a common convention in

---

37. There they are called "Cod. Tischend. LX," "Cod. Tischend. LXI," and "Cod. Tischend. LXII," although, as noted by Gardthausen, MS 31 does not contain collations by Tischendorf. MSS 29 and 30 consist of collations by Tischendorf of Greek manuscripts that he examined in, respectively, Paris and Italy. As noted by Gardthausen (36), ff. 60^r–62^v of MS 30 consist of a collation by someone other than Tischendorf, evidently a French scholar who appends a note in French on f. 62^v. But unfortunately the signature on the note is hidden beneath the binding of the MS. MS 31 is a small notebook consisting entirely, as it seems, of collations by Henrich Ernest Poeschl of manuscripts in Vienna. Those three MSS (i.e., 29, 30, and 31) were given to the Library in 1888 by Grossmann's son (see Gardthausen, 37). Subsequently, in 1901 the Library received MS gr. 31^a, which is a small notebook containing collations in, I believe, a hand different from all the previous collators. This MS entered the Library after Gardthausen's catalog, and is thus uncatalogued; it was kindly called to my attention by Dr. Mackert. The first three manuscripts are listed (from Gardthausen's catalog) in G-G, ##280–82, although #282 (= MS 31) is said to contain "collations for Tischendorf" instead of "collations for Grossmann." (This error perhaps derives from PCW 2:i, where Wendland states of MS 31: "has collationes in Tischendorfii usum Henricus Ernestus Poesche confecit.")

[28] I was able to examine these pages at length in Leipzig, and then obtained excellent digital images of these pages, for which I thank the Leipzig Universitäts-bibliothek. Regrettably, the pages are bound in such a way that one or two or three letters are sometimes hidden at the inner margin. Thus the only conceivable discrepancies that could arise at such places would be spelling errors. Given the extraordinary accuracy throughout the transcript, I believe that such possibilities can be discounted.

[29] Copying a manuscript accurately is (*experto crede*) an extremely difficult task, and the multitude of errors in the manuscripts themselves and in the modern editions of manuscripts shows how easily mistakes arise. As a rule, only by repeatedly checking a transcript (preferably with some gap of time) is anything close to complete accuracy obtainable.

textual studies, Tischendorf omits most (but not quite all) accents and breathings. However, a comparison of this transcript and the text of V itself reveals that there is only one difference of any substance; namely, at *QE* 2.65 l. 5, where V has duplicated ταῖς at the end of a line, Tischendorf has written ταῖς only once. This is the sort of natural correction of an obvious blunder that we all make while reading (although a transcript should certainly cite it). Otherwise, Tischendorf departs from the text of V only in his rendering of *nomina sacra*. V writes the usual contracted forms θ̄ς̄ and κ̄ς̄ (and their inflected forms) everywhere that these words occur, except at 2.68 l. 25, where κύριον is written in full, since it there means "proper" or "appropriate" rather than "Lord."[30] V also writes π̄ρ̄ᾱ at 2.65 l. 3 (the only place that word occurs), but writes οὐρανοῦ *plene* at 2.64 l. 3 (its only occurrence). Tischendorf reproduces V's orthography except for writing:

> 2.62 l. 8: θεός for θ̄ς̄
> 2.64 l. 4: θεος for θ̄ς̄
> 2.65 l. 2: θεου for θ̄ῡ
> 2.65 l. 3: πατερα for π̄ρ̄ᾱ
>
> 2.67 l. 4: δωρηϕορων for δωρηϕορων (with superscript ο υ)
> 2.68 l. 6: θεου for θ̄ῡ
> 2.68 l. 22: θεος for θ̄ς̄

Relying on Tischendorf's report, Grossmann published the text in 1856.[31] Grossmann first prints the Latin of Aucher, and then the Greek of Vat. gr. 379. Further, there is a brief excerpt from Vat. gr. 746, which Grossmann assigns to the *Quaestiones et solutiones* on Num 15:32, but which in fact derives from *Mos.* 2.218.[32] There then follow a dozen pages of annotations, which discuss some textual issues and provide many parallels to Philo's comments.

---

[30] New Testament manuscripts sometimes make such a distinction; see the practices (by no means consistent) of 𝔓⁴⁶, 𝔓⁶⁶, and 𝔓⁷⁵ as discussed in my *Scribal Habits in Early Greek New Testament Papyri* (NTTSD 36; Leiden: Brill, 2008), 259 n. 333 (–260), 424 n. 120, and 650 n. 182 (–651).

[31] C. A. O. (C. A. F) Grossmann, ed., *Philonis Iudaei Anecdoton graecum de Cherubinis ad Exod. 25, 18* (Leipzig: Friedrich Fleischer, 1856).

[32] See PCW ad loc., where in the lower apparatus Cohn prints the text from the *Catena Lipsiensis*.

It is important to keep in mind that Grossmann was dependent on the report from Tischendorf, and had no direct acquaintance with V. But given the accuracy of Tischendorf's transcript, this was no great disadvantage. Unfortunately, though, what Grossmann printed differs here and there from what Tischendorf's transcript contains. One of these differences is at 2.68 l. 25, where he omits (from no discernible cause) the word κύριον, which is clearly present in V and in Tischendorf's transcript (as well as in Mai's edition). This error resulted in the loss of that word from all printed editions except Mai's.

Grossmann died in 1857, and in 1868 Tischendorf published the fruits of his Philonic studies, including the sections from Vat. gr. 379. Tischendorf explained his decision to publish this material on two grounds; first, Grossmann's publication had limited circulation, and further:

> Altera eaque gravior, quod verba Graeca parum curae ab editore nacta sunt, philosophiae illo quidem Philoneae curiosissimo atque scientissimo. Praeter leviora enim quae putantur, interpunctionem dico et accentuum spirituumque signa, quae tacite correximus, plura deprehendimus quae manum criticam postularent.[33]

It is striking that Tischendorf does not say that he had inspected V again, and does not indicate that he had retained a copy of his earlier transcript by which he could check Grossmann's edition. Rather, despite stating that Grossmann had presented the Greek with "insufficient care" ("parum curae"), it is clear that for his knowledge of V's readings Tischendorf (amazingly enough) relied entirely on what had been published by Grossmann.[34] Tischendorf corrected some minor matters, as he says, adds

---

[33] Constantinus Tischendorf, ed., *Philonea, inedita altera, altera nunc demum recte ex vetere scriptura eruta* (Leipzig: Giesecke and Devrient, 1868), xx: "The second and more weighty is that the Greek words received insufficient care from the editor, although he was most devoted to and knowledgeable of the Philonic philosophy. For besides matters that are considered trivial, such as punctuation, accents, and breathings, which I have tacitly corrected, we find many things that require a critical hand." See the fuller discussion at xix–xx.

[34] Ibid., 144–53. I had always been puzzled by the many inaccuracies in his presentation of such a short and legible text, given Tischendorf's justly deserved reputation in New Testament textual criticism for precision. Indeed, in his notes Tischendorf fails to comment on the actual readings of V, thus giving the impression that he had not really seen the manuscript, although he explicitly says (144 n. *): "Graeca exscripsimus ex cod. Vatic. 379 fol. 385 verso sqq." But these features of Tischendorf's

some conjectures and introduces a few errors of his own. The resulting publication is, of course, very similar to that found in Grossmann, even though it is by no means identical; e.g., Tischendorf omits εἰρήνης at 2.68 l. 9, thus creating confusion for the later editors. But the crucial point is that the errors committed by Grossmann in reproducing Tischendorf's transcript were simply repeated by Tischendorf in his publication.

Next, in 1886 appeared the very extensive collection of Philo fragments by Harris, who for *QE* 2.62–68 relied entirely on Tischendorf and Grossmann.[35] Since Harris depended on Aucher's Latin for his knowledge of the Armenian, and lacked a first-hand acquaintance with V, his textual notes often display some confusion.[36] For example, at 2.64 l. 10 Harris prints σπέρματα, and notes that Grossmann "gives" τέρματα. The reader would thus hardly divine that the latter is what V reads while the former is restored from the Armenian (as represented in Aucher's "semina") and is also supported by the fragment from the *Sacra parallela*, which Harris later prints but fails to relate to *QE* 2.64.[37] Again, at 2.68 l. 9, Harris follows Tischendorf in omitting εἰρήνης after δημιουργός, and adds in a note: "Gr. [viz. Grossmann] add εἰρήνης (rightly)." I would suppose that "rightly"

---

text and comments are explained by the fact that he was relying on Grossmann's edition, which in turn was based on Tischendorf's transcript.

[35] J. Rendel Harris, ed., *Fragments of Philo Judaeus* (Cambridge: Cambridge University Press, 1886; reprinted: Cambridge Library Collection-Religion; Cambridge: Cambridge University Press, 2012); *QE* 2.62–68 occur on pp. 63–68. Harris cites Grossmann and Tischendorf in his notes.

[36] In fact, despite the great service Harris rendered by collecting many Philo fragments from scattered places (see Schürer, *Geschichte des jüdischen Volkes* 3 [3rd ed.], 492), he makes no claim to be presenting a "critical edition." The opening line of his preface (v) reads: "This little book may perhaps be described most succinctly as scaffolding for the next edition of Philo." He might well have been dismayed that his report on *QE* 2.62–68 was still authoritative more than a century later.

[37] See Harris fragment 101.7. This text is also found in Mangey, 2:665.4, and Tischendorf (146) refers to it in connection with *QE* 2.64; a more explicit identification was made by Früchtel (see my "Further Greek Fragments of Philo's *Quaestiones*," in *Nourished with Peace* (ed. Frederick E. Greenspahn, Earle Hilgert, and Burton L. Mack; Chico, Calif.: Scholars Press, 1984), 148 and n. 26). I suppose that Harris was confused by what he found in Grossmann and Tischendorf, but without knowledge of V and the Armenian he had no way to resolve the issue.

means that the word should be added to the Greek from the Armenian, but V in fact has the word.

In 1953 Marcus presented a collection of the Greek fragments as an appendix to his translation (in the PLCL series) of the Armenian version of *QG* and *QE*.[38] This collection, while of great value, is constructed from the earlier collections of Harris, Wendland, Lewy, and a few others, without any investigation of the Greek evidence. On the other hand, Marcus was fully competent in Armenian, and makes many significant suggestions concerning the correspondence between the Armenian and the Greek fragments. But these suggestions are confined to footnotes, with (usually) no effect on the Greek that Marcus edits. Moreover, he makes different comments in his running notes on his translation and in the notes to the Greek fragments; thus, one needs to combine these comments in order to see what Marcus thought.

Since Marcus depends on Harris for 2.62–68, the confusions in Harris are repeated. At 2.64 l. 10 Marcus cites the Greek as having σπέρματα.[39] And at 2.68 l. 9 Marcus translates the Armenian as "the artisan of peace," and says that the "Greek frag. reads more briefly," i.e., without εἰρήνης, which Marcus tells us that Grossmann adds; but then in the appendix εἰρήνης occurs in the text.[40]

Finally, the full publication of the Greek of *QE* 2.62–68 within the PAPM series appeared in an appendix to the translation of *QE* by Terian in 1992, who prints the Greek and then cites in notes the Armenian readings that differ from the Greek.[41] In fact, for the Greek Terian seems to follow Marcus, although the exact source is not specified.[42] In any case, the confusions concerning the actual text of V that were cited earlier remain. At 2.64 l. 10 Terian prints σπέρματα without a note, since the notes discuss only the discrepancies with the Armenian and this Greek was in fact constructed to agree with the Armenian. Similarly, at 2.68 l. 9 Terian omits εἰρήνης from the Greek, and then tells us in a note that the Armenian adds it.

---

[38] PLCL Supp 2:179–263.

[39] Ibid., 2:111 n. c and 2:254.

[40] Ibid., 2:115 n. d and 2:255.

[41] PAPM 34C:283–86.

[42] See the *Leitfehler* at 2.66 l. 1.

Nevertheless, Terian's printed Greek is usually, naturally enough, the actual text of V, and thus of particular value are his comments on the discrepancies between the Armenian and the Greek, as well as his conjectures of the Greek that is presupposed by the Armenian at various places.

In his unpublished edition of the Greek fragments of Philo, Ludwig Früchtel cites these sections from Harris, with only a few revisions (mentioned in the notes below).[43] Further perceptive remarks on the Armenian may be found in a much neglected paper by Conybeare.[44] Also, there is the translation into English by Runia, who makes many valuable observations on the Greek text.[45] As he notes, his is the first translation of the Greek itself, rather than of the Armenian.[46] At about the same time Runia, noting that the neglect of this text had resulted in its not being covered by the TLG or *The Philo Index*, published a word index to the Greek text of these sections.[47] Runia utilized the text as found in Terian, and that text (like the text found in all the other editions) is very similar to the one presented here. But there are differences. Among other things, two of the five words that are not found elsewhere in Philo are not included here: καταρίθμησις and ὑπεμφαίνομαι (about which Runia expressed some doubt).

Despite the contributions of the scholars cited above, it is clear that this important text has indeed suffered neglect. Runia himself has noted that this text "badly needs to be edited once again, taking into account all

---

[43] On Früchtel's edition see my *Spurious Works,* 9.

[44] Frederick C. Conybeare, *Specimen Lectionum Armeniacarum* (Oxford: privately printed, n.d. [1891]), 8.

[45] "A Neglected Text."

[46] He correctly observes (ibid., 201 n. 10) that the translations of Marcus and Terian, while of course basically following the Armenian, import often without warning words or phrases or constructions found in the Greek fragments; thus "One can never be quite sure what they are translating." At least one knows that Aucher's translation of these sections (done five years before Mai's edition) was free of any influence from the Greek. By the way, Anna Sirinian, "'Armenian Philo': A Survey of the Literature," in *Studies on the Ancient Armenian Version of Philo's Works* (ed. Sara Mancini Lombardi and Paola Pontani; Studies in Philo of Alexandria 6; Leiden: Brill, 2011), 19 n. 48, incorrectly states that Aucher's Latin was "the basis" of Runia's English translation.

[47] "*Quaestiones in Exodum* 2.62–68: Supplement to *The Philo Index,*" SPhA 16 (2004): 229–34, supplementing Peder Borgen, Kåre Fuglseth, and Roald Skarsten, *The Philo Index* (Grand Rapids: Eerdmans; Leiden: Brill, 2000).

the details of the Greek and Armenian traditions."[48] The present edition is intended to give to these precious sections of Philo's work the attention that has long been their due.[49]

The Greek Text

The printed text is that of V, unless otherwise noted, except for matters of orthography. At 2.65 l. 5 I have corrected V's nonsense dittography, and (along with most or all other editors) have corrected the spellings at five other places: 2.62 ll. 3, 5; 2.66 l. 3; 2.67 l. 4; 2.68 l. 40. And at 2.62 l. 2 I have inserted ἤ against both V and Arm.

Apart from 2.62 l. 2 and the six obvious errors, I judge that the correct text is found, where V and Arm agree, in their common text, and where they disagree, in one or the other, most often in V. It is unfortunate that the common text of V and Arm at various points has often not been printed, and that, as we have seen, the actual readings of V have often been misreported.

Where V and Arm disagree, at thirteen places the Armenian preserves a superior reading: 2.63 l. 5, 2.64 l. 10; 2.66 l. 4; 2.68 ll. 1, 2, 6, 15, 19, 23, 26, 31, 33, 41. (Most of these have been approved by earlier scholars.) I have thus departed from the readings of V at a total of twenty places. But the Armenian has a corruption at twenty-five places: 2.62 ll. 2, 3, 3, 3–4, 5; 64 ll. 1, 7, 9; 65 ll. 4, 4; 66 ll. 7, 7, 12; 67 l. 1; 68 ll. 5, 20, 23, 30, 36, 38, 38, 38, 38, 39, 40. And these are apart from the minor retouchings and additions (such as of ἐστι). The superiority of V is, I believe, clear, although there are a few places where the readings of V may well be doubted (e.g., 2.66 ll. 10–11).

Appended to the edition proper is a collection of textual notes, which draw heavily upon the comments of the scholars cited above, although I have sometimes, perhaps foolhardily, disagreed with them. I trust that the reader will have the requisite information to make an independent judgment on controversial issues, although such judgments will often require

[48] Ibid., 230.

[49] In his prefatory remarks (2) Grossmann notes that of the many additions to Mangey's collection of Greek fragments, he presents our text first, "tum ab argumenti dignitate tum ab amplitudine membrorum prae ceteris commendabile."

knowledge of the wider area of equivalences between Greek and Armenian.[50] Naturally, these notes are not intended to provide a commentary on Philo's thought in these sections, but are directed toward issues relevant to establishing the text.

The Armenian Version

I have relied on Aucher's Armenian, but have made a few changes. For one thing, I have not attempted to reproduce his assortment of ligatures, most of which are often neglected in modern scholarly editions. I have written ***աւ*** for his *o*, which is a later writing; all the manuscripts that I have seen have ***աւ*** throughout, as do modern critical editions of Armenian texts. And I have removed the apostrophe before the preposition *ի*, except at the end of *QE* 2.68, q.v. Finally, I have revised his punctuation to accord with the Greek (and my understanding thereof). Otherwise, the text is as Aucher prints it except where noted. These further changes are to introduce readings found in the Armenian manuscripts that agree with the Greek, to correct errors or to make conjectures to bring the Armenian into agreement with the Greek when I suppose that a scribal error has occurred on the Armenian side. However, I have not, naturally enough, attempted to "correct" the Armenian translation by systematically providing more adequate equivalents for the Greek.

Through the courtesy of Professor Abraham Terian I have had access to photographs of several primary Armenian manuscripts. The witnesses cited here (all dating from the latter half of the thirteenth century) are:[51]

---

50 See the classic Armenian lexicon: Gabriēl Awetik'ean, Xač'atur Siwrmēlean, and Mkrtič' Awgerean [Aucher], ***Նոր Բառգիրք Հայկազեան Լեզուի*** (*Nor baṙgirk῾ haykazean lezui*) [New Dictionary of the Armenian Language] (2 vols.; Venice: San Lazzaro Press, 1836–1837; reprinted: Erevan: Erevan University Press, 1979–1981), cited as "NB." And for Philo there is Ralph Marcus, "An Armenian-Greek Index to Philo's *Quaestiones* and *De Vita Contemplativa*," *JAOS* 53 (1933): 251–82. The Armenian translation of Philo is cited from Aucher, *Philonis Judaei paralipomena Armena*; idem, *Philonis Judaei sermones tres* (Venice: Typis coenobii PP. Armenorum in insula S. Lazari, 1822); [Garegin Zarbhanalean], ***Փիլոնի Հեբրայեցՙոյ ճառք*** (*P῾iloni Hebrayec῾woy čaṙk῾*) [Works of Philo the Jew] (Venice: Mechitarist, 1892).

51 See the convenient listing and discussion in Terian, PAPM 36:30–39. It is to be regretted that the sigla for these manuscripts vary; for the first three I have adopted the letters used by Terian, and for the fourth (to which Terian doesn't assign a letter) I

A	Erevan 1500, dated 1282, written in two columns; QE 2.62–68 at ff. 476ʳ A l. 4 – 476ᵛ A l. 42.
D	Venice 1040, dated 1296, written in two columns and paginated; QE 2.62–68 at pp. 230 A l. 30 – 233 B l. 7.
E	Jerusalem 333, dated 1298, written in two columns; QE 2.62–68 at ff. 165ʳ B l. 11 – 167ʳ A l. 14.
L	Erevan 5239, dated 1274; QE 2.62–68 at ff. 139ʳ l. 10 – 142ᵛ l. 19.

Although there are few discrepancies of any weight with Aucher's edition,[52] I have provided the relevant results of my collations in the apparatus to the Armenian. I have not attempted to record every variation in the Armenian manuscripts. Frequently there are additions or omissions of the postpositive pronouns (sometimes called "articles") -*n*, -*d*, and -*s*. And there are many misspellings. However, I have attempted to report the additions, omissions, transpositions, and substitutions of entire words, although very few of these have any bearing on the relationship between the Greek and the Armenian. But on occasion there is some alternative reading that shows that Aucher's printed text is in fact a corruption from an earlier Armenian text that was closer to the Greek of V.

The Format of the Edition

Ultimately, I decided to present a trilingual edition, consisting of the critically established Greek text based on V, the Armenian text as revised from Aucher's edition, and my own English translation of the Greek. The inclu-

---

have followed Mercier. Note that Aucher's A is my D.

[52] Indeed, Terian states (PAPM 34C:283) concerning the apparatus that he provides to his printing of the Greek: "Les lectures diverses des manuscrits arméniens ne sont pas données dans l'apparat, puisqu'elles appartiennent à la tradition textuelle arménienne et n'offrent pas d'autres variantes significatives qui affecteraient notre compréhension du texte grec." But I believe that on occasion one can find readings in the Armenian manuscripts that are superior to those of Aucher, in the sense that they are closer to the Greek of V and thus (I would judge) closer to the original Armenian translation.

sion of the Armenian is justified by its crucial value for the establishment of Philo's text. I had initially planned to include Aucher's Latin because of its historical value; after all, for more than a century Aucher's Latin was the chief means by which the Armenian version of Philo's work reached scholars. But Professor Runia cogently observed to me that printing Aucher's nineteenth-century rendering of the Armenian into Latin in a critical edition is not entirely reasonable; after all, it is a modern artifact, and has no more textual weight than the modern translations into English, German, or French. Moreover, as my work developed, I chose to depart on occasion from Aucher's Armenian, and thus would have had to alter Aucher's Latin in order to coordinate the Armenian and Latin. But printing a modern revision of Aucher's Latin seemed even less appropriate. Thus, I have dispensed with Aucher's Latin, but added my own English translation. Nevertheless, whatever its shortcomings, Aucher's Latin has the virtue of being a very literal translation of the very literal Armenian, and it may thus serve as a guide to a language that remains very imperfectly known to most readers of Philo. And it is readily available in the PAPM volumes.

My decision to place the Greek on the left-hand page follows the tradition of the ancient Greek and Latin codices of the New Testament known as Codex Bezae (D [05] of the Gospels and Acts) and Codex Claromontanus (D [06] of the Pauline Epistles), where the Greek occupies the left-hand pages and the Latin the right-hand pages. We find the same placement of the original language on the left in the Loeb Classical Library editions.

Moreover, I have placed the material so that each section has its own pair of pages, except for the unusually long 2.68. This arrangement simplified some technical matters, and of course also makes reference between text and apparatus more convenient. But an unfortunate side effect is that occasionally some space goes to waste. Also, I have followed the practice of Früchtel in breaking up 2.68 into several sub-sections (although my divisions differ from his).

Of course, whatever the value, critical or aesthetic, of the arrangement on the page, my primary aim has been to provide the reader with all the relevant information concerning the textual transmission of this important text. Unless otherwise stated, the Armenian version supports, or is at least consistent with, the printed Greek. An apparatus is not the place to record all the discrepancies in earlier editions; the textual notes provide extensive documentation of the vicissitudes of these sections. However, where earlier scholars have suggested improvements to the text, I have attempted to cite the first. (This is sometimes Mai, even though later editors did not know of his work and thus often duplicated his conjectures.) And at a few particularly interesting places I have explicitly cited "V Arm" for a reading that the reader might find doubtful by looking at various editions.

In preparing the translation into English, I have aimed for literalness. Moreover, in order to represent the Greek as closely as possible, I have placed within parentheses those words that are not present in the Greek but are needed to have meaningful English. One frequent issue is how to express the implicit subject of the third-person singular verbs. As Marcus notes, λέγει (and similar terms) may have as subject God, Moses, or Scripture.[53] In order to avoid encumbering the translation with this choice at each point, I have opted for "Scripture," placed in parentheses since it is not explicitly expressed. In general, the reader will readily see my indebtedness to the translations by Marcus, Runia, and Terian.

---

[53] Cf. Oswald Spengler, *Der Untergang des Abendlandes* (Düsseldorf: Albatros, 2007 [originally published 1923]), 858: "Aus dieser metaphysischen Auffassung vom Wesen des heiligen Buches ergibt sich, daß die Ausdrücke „Gott spricht" und „die Schrift sagt" in einer unserem Denken ganz fremden Weise völlig identisch sind."

SIGLA

Gr = Greek
Arm = Armenian

Codices manuscripti graeci:[54]
V = Vaticanus gr. 379
Sacra paralleia:
C = Coislinianus 276
H = Hierosolymitanus S. Sep. 15
R = Berolinensis Phillippicus 1450
T = Thessalonicensis Vladaton 9

Codices manuscripti armeniaci:[55]
A = Erevan 1500
D = Venice 1040
E = Jerusalem 333
L = Erevan 5239

---

[54] I have had access to microfilms of all of these mss. through the kind assistance of the Institut de Recherche et d'Histoire des Textes, Paris. I have also examined C at the Bibliothèque Nationale. And I have studied V in detail at the Vatican Library and by means of photographs kindly supplied by the Vatican Library.

[55] I have had access to these mss. through photographs graciously made available by Professor Abraham Terian.

62   Τίνα τὰ Χερουβίμ;

Τὰ Χερουβὶμ ἑρμηνεύεται μὲν ἐπίγνωσις πολλή, <ἢ> ἐν ἑτέροις
ὄνομα ἐπιστήμη πλουσία καὶ κεχυμένη. σύμβολα δέ ἐστι δυεῖν τοῦ
ὄντος δυνάμεων ποιητικῆς τε καὶ βασιλικῆς. πρεσβυτέρα δὲ ἡ ποιητικὴ
τῆς βασιλικῆς κατ' ἐπίνοιαν. ἰσήλικες γὰρ αἵ γε περὶ τὸν θεὸν ἅπασαι   5
δυνάμεις, ἀλλὰ προεπινοεῖται πως ἡ ποιητικὴ τῆς βασιλικῆς· βασιλεὺς
γάρ τις οὐχὶ τοῦ μὴ ὄντος ἀλλὰ τοῦ γεγονότος· ὄνομα δὲ ἔλαχεν ἐν
τοῖς ἱεροῖς γράμμασιν ἡ μὲν ποιητικὴ θεός (τὸ γὰρ ποιῆσαι θεῖναι
ἔλεγον οἱ παλαιοί), ἡ δὲ βασιλικὴ κύριος (ἐπειδὴ τὸ κῦρος ἁπάντων
ἀνάκειται τῷ βασιλεῖ).   10

V, f. 385ᵛ l. 13–f. 386ʳ l. 2

---

2 τὰ Χερουβὶμ om. Arm codd.   ἢ addidi : ῇ add. Grossmann : om. Arm
3 ὄνομα : ὀνόμασιν Arm   καὶ om. Arm   σύμβολα : σύμβολον Arm   δυεῖν edd. (et
Arm) : δεῖν V   3–4 τοῦ ὄντος om. Arm   4 ὄντος ex ὄντως corr. V ut vid.   post δὲ
add. ἐστι Arm   5 τῆς βασιλικῆς om. Arm codd.   αἵ γε Terian Früchtel, αἵγε
Tischendorf Marcus (γε non exprimit Arm) : αἴτε V : ἄτε Grossmann : ai Mai
ἅπασαι V Arm (A E L) : om. Arm (D Aucher)   6 πῶς om. Arm   8 post θεός
add. καλεῖν Arm   9 καλεῖται add. post κύριος Arm (D E Aucher), ante κύριος
add. Arm (A L)

Զի՞նչ է քերովբիմն: **62**

<քերովբիմն> թարգմանի գիտութիւն բազում, յայլ
անուանս Հանճար մեծութիւն գեղեցալ. բայց նշանակ է երկուց
զաւրութեանցն, արարչականին, եւ արքունւոյ: Բայց երիցագոյն
5 է արարչականն <քան զարքունեանն> ըստ մտածութեան.
քանզի գուգահասակ են որ շուրջ զաստուածովն են ամենայն
զաւրութիւնքն, այլ յառաջ իմացեալ լինի արարչականն քան
զարքունեանն. քանզի թագաւոր ոք ոչ այնր որ ոչ ն է, այլ
այնր որ եղեալ ն է. եւ անուան Հասաւ ի սուրբ եւ յաստուա-
10 ծային գիրս արարչականն ատուած կոչիլ, քանզի զառնելն
դնել ասէին Հինքն. իսկ արքունեանն տէր կոչի, վասն զի
տէրն ամենեցուն ի նոքր կայ թագաւորին:

2 քերովբիմն addidi cum Gr   2–3 յայլ անուանս D E Aucher : յայլ յանուանս L,
յանուանս A   3 է om. A L   5 քան զարքունեանն addidi cum Gr   մտածութեան :
մեծութեան L   6 ամենայն A E L (= Gr) : om. D Aucher   8 զարքունեանն :
զարքունականն A L   10 զ- om. E   11 արքունեանն : արքունականն A L   տէր
կոչի D E Aucher : կոչի տէր A L

(**62**) What are the Cherubim?

The (word) "Cherubim" is interpreted as much knowledge, <or> elsewhere the name (is interpreted as) rich and diffused science. They are symbols of the two powers of the One who is, the creative and the kingly. The
creative (power) is older than the kingly (power) according to thought. For
all the powers around God are of the same age, but the creative is somehow thought of before the kingly; for someone is king not of what does not
exist but of what has come into being. And in the sacred writings the creative (power) has obtained the name "God," for the ancients said creating
was placing. And the kingly (power has obtained the name) "Lord," since
the lordship of all things is attributed to the king.

63   Διατί χρυσοῦ τορευτά;

Ὁ μὲν χρυσὸς σύμβολον τῆς τιμιωτάτης οὐσίας, ἡ δὲ τορεία τῆς
ἐντέχνου καὶ ἐπιστημονικῆς φύσεως· ἔδει γὰρ τὰς πρώτας τοῦ ὄντος
δυνάμεις ἰδέας ἰδεῶν ὑπαρχούσας καὶ τῆς καθαρωτάτης καὶ ἀμιγοῦς
καὶ τιμαλφεστάτης καὶ προσέτι τῆς ἐπιστημονικωτάτης οὐσίας μετα-   5
λαχεῖν.

V, f. 386ʳ ll. 3–10

---

2 post σύμβολον add. ἐστι Arm   τιμιωτάτης : τιμίας Arm   5 οὐσίας scripsi ex
Arm : φύσεως V

Ընդէ՞ր ոսկեղէն ճախարակեայ: **63**

Ոսկին նշանակ է պատուական ՀուԹեանն. իսկ ճախա-
րակեայն արուեստաւորին եւ Հանձարական բնուԹեանն: Քանզի
պարտ է զառաջինան զէին զաւրուԹիւնս տեսակս տեսակաց
5 զոյ եւ մաքրագոյն եւ անխառն, եւ պատուականագիւտին եւ
առ այսու եւս Հանձարագունի ՀուԹեանն յետոյ Հասանել:

---

4 զաւրուԹիւնս : բնուԹեանս A L

---

(63) Why are they (the Cherubim) engraved in gold?

The gold (is) a symbol of the most valuable substance, while the
engraving (is a symbol) of the artful and knowledgeable nature. For it was
proper that the primary powers of the One who is, being (as they are)
ideas of ideas, participate in the purest and unmixed and most precious
and moreover most knowledgeable substance.

64   Διατί ἐπ' ἀμφοτέρων τῶν κλιτῶν τοῦ ἱλαστηρίου τὰ Χερουβὶμ ἥρμοττε;

Τοὺς ὅρους τοῦ παντὸς οὐρανοῦ καὶ κόσμου δυσὶ ταῖς ἀνωτάτω φρουραῖς ὠχυρῶσθαι, τῇ τε καθ' ἣν ἐποίει τὰ ὅλα θεός, καὶ τῇ καθ' ἣν ἄρχει τῶν γενονότων. ἔμελλε γὰρ ὡς οἰκειοτάτου καὶ συγγενεστάτου   5
κτήματος προκήδεσθαι, ἡ μὲν ποιητικὴ ἵνα μὴ λυθείη τὰ πρὸς αὐτῆς γενόμενα, ἡ δὲ βασιλικὴ ὅπως μηδὲν μήτε πλεονεκτῇ μήτε πλεονε-κτῆται, νόμῳ βραβευόμενα τῷ τῆς ἰσότητος, ὑφ' ἧς τὰ πράγματα διαι-ωνίζεται. πλεονεξία μὲν γὰρ καὶ ἀνισότης ὁρμητήρια πολέμου, λυτικὰ τῶν ὄντων· τὸ δὲ εὔνομον καὶ τὸ ἴσον εἰρήνης σπέρματα, σωτηρίας   10
αἴτια καὶ τῆς εἰσάπαν διαμονῆς.

V, f. 386ʳ l. 10–f. 386ᵛ l. 1
ll. 9–11: τὸ εὔνομον — διαμονῆς· ἀνισότης — ὄντων:
R, f. 191ʳ (16) 16–18: τοῦ αὐτοῦ (scil. Φίλωνος, l. 13).
T, f. 249ᵛ A (4–5) 6–13: τοῦ αὐτοῦ (scil. Φίλωνος, f. 249ʳ B 21) ἐκ τῶν ἐν Ἐξόδῳ ζητημάτων.

---

1 ἱλαστηρίου : θυσιαστηρίου Arm   4 post ὠχυρῶσθαι add. αἰνίττεται Mai   7 μήτε πλεονεκτῇ om. Arm   9–11 τὸ εὔνομον — διαμονῆς ante ἀνισότης — ὄντων R T
9 πλεονέξια — ἀνισότης : ἀνισότης δὲ καὶ πλεονεξία R T (ἀνισώτης)   πλεονεξία et ἀνισότης : πλεονεξίᾳ et ἀνισότητι Arm   λυτικὰ : καὶ λυτικὰ R T (λυτηκὰ)   10 δὲ : om. R T   σπέρματα T Arm, σπέρμα R : τέρματα V   ante σωτηρίας add. καὶ R T
11 εἰσάπαν : εἰς ἄπαντα R, εἰς ἄπατα T

Ընդէ՞ր յերկոսին կողմանս սեղանոյն զքերովբիման պատ- 64
շաճէր:

զսահմանս ամենայն երկնի եւ աշխարհի երկուք եւ վերնա-
գոյն պահպանութեամբքն ամրացուցանէլ․ մի բստ այնմ, որով
5 առնէր գրզ,որ աստուած․ եւ մի բստ որում իշխան է եղելոցն:
Քանզի հանդերձեալ էր իբրեւ բնոանեզունի եւ ազգակցի
ստացուածոյ յառաջագոյն խնամ տանել․ արարչականն գի մի
լուծցին առ ի նմանէ եղեալք․ իսկ արքունեանն որպէս գի մի
ինչ առաւելեալ լիցի, աւրինակաւ առիթ եղեալ յաղթութեանն
10 նշանակաւ գ,ուգ,ութեանն, որով իրքն յաւէտանան․ քանզի
առաւելութեամբ եւ անգուգութեամբ, յարձակմունք պատե-
րազմին լուծանք են էիցն․ իսկ քաջաւրէնն եւ գ,ոյգ խաղաղու-
թեան սերմանք, փրկութեան պատճառք եւ յար հանապազ ն
կալոյ մնալոյ:

---

3 ամենայն A E L Aucher (= Gr) : om. D   երկնի D E L Aucher (= Gr) : երկրի A (=
γῆς)   5 որում D E Aucher : այնմ որ A L   6 իբրեւ D E L^{corr} Aucher (= Gr) : om.
A L*   8 արքունեանն D E Aucher : արքունականն A L

---

(64) Why did (Scripture) fit the Cherubim on both sides of the mercy-seat?

(This indicates that) the bounds of the entire heaven and cosmos are secured by the two highest guards, one according to which God made all things, the other according to which He rules those things that have come into being. For (each power) was meant to care for a most proper and closely related possession, the creative (power) so that the things that came into being through it should not be destroyed, the kingly (power) so that nothing would exceed or be exceeded, arbitrated by the law of equality under which things are eternized. For while excess and inequality (are) the occasions for war, destroyers of the things that exist, good order and equality are the seeds of peace, the causes of salvation and of continual survival.

65   Διατί φησιν· ἐκτείνει τὰς πτέρυγας τὰ Χερουβὶμ ἵνα συσκιάζῃ;

Αἱ μὲν τοῦ θεοῦ πᾶσαι δυνάμεις πτεροφυοῦσι, τῆς ἄνω πρὸς τὸν πατέρα ὁδοῦ γλιχόμεναί τε καὶ ἐφιέμεναι· συσκιάζουσι δὲ οἷα πτέρυξι τὰ τοῦ παντὸς μέρη· αἰνίττεται δὲ ὡς ὁ κόσμος σκέπαις καὶ φυλακτηρίοις φρουρεῖται, δυσὶ ταῖς [ταῖς] εἰρημέναις δυνάμεσι τῇ τε ποιητικῇ   5
καὶ βασιλικῇ.

V, f. 386ᵛ ll. 2–10

ll. 2–3: αἱ τοῦ θεοῦ — ἐφιέμεναι:

C, f. 60ᵛ (15) 16–18: (scil. Φίλωνος, l. 11) ἐκ τοῦ β̄ τῶν αὐτῶν (scil. τῶν ἐν Γενέσει ζητημάτων, ll. 11–12).

H, f. 74ʳ A (14) 15–18: τοῦ αὐτοῦ (scil. Φίλωνος, l. 9).

R, f. 106ᵛ (7) 7–8: (scil. Φίλωνος, l. 4) ἐκ τοῦ β̄ τῶν αὐτῶν (scil. τῶν ἐν Γενέσει ζητουμένων, ll. 4–5).

---

2 μὲν V (non exprimit Arm) : om. C H R   2–3 τῆς et ὁδοῦ V Arm C H : τὴν et ὁδὸν R   4 δὲ om. Arm   σκέπαις καὶ om. Arm   5 ταῖς | ταῖς V (solum ταῖς edd.), alterum seclusi

Ընդէ՞ր ասէ, ձգեսցէ զթևս քերովբիմն, զի Հովանի 65
արասցէ:

Աստուծոյ ամենայն զաւրութիւնքն թևաբոյս լինին. վերին
առ Հայրն ճանապարհի ցանկացեալք եւ բաղձացեալք: Իսկ
5 Հովանի առնելն զաւրքն թևոց զամենայնին մասունք. ստակէ
որպէս աշխարհս ծածկեալ լինի պահապանութեամբ երկուցն
ասացելոյք զաւրութեամբքն, արարչականաւն եւ արքունեաւն:

---

4 ցանկացեալք եւ բաղձացեալք D E Aucher (= Gr) : բաղձացեալք եւ ցանկացեալք A L   7 արքունեաւ ն D E Aucher : արքունականաւ ն A L

(**65**) Why does (Scripture) say: the Cherubim extend their wings so that
they overshadow (the mercy-seat)?

All the powers of God have wings, desiring and striving for the path
upward to the Father; they overshadow, as with wings, the parts of the
universe. (Scripture) indicates that the cosmos is guarded by protections
and guardposts, the two powers mentioned (earlier), the creative and the
kingly.

66   Διατί τὰ πρόσωπα τῶν Χερουβὶμ εἰς ἄλληλα ἐκνεύει καὶ ἄμφω πρὸς τὸ ἱλαστήριον;

Παγκάλη τίς ἐστι καὶ θεοπρεπὴς ἡ τοῦ λεχθέντος εἰκών· ἔδει γὰρ τὰς δυνάμεις, τήν τε ποιητικὴν καὶ βασιλικήν, εἰς ἀλλήλας ἀφορᾶν, τὰ σφῶν κάλλη κατανοούσας καὶ ἅμα πρὸς τὴν ὠφέλειαν τῶν γεγονότων   5
συμπνεούσας· δεύτερον ἐπειδὴ ὁ θεός, εἷς ὤν, καὶ ποιητής ἐστι καὶ βασιλεύς, εἰκότως αἱ διαστᾶσαι δυνάμεις πάλιν ἕνωσιν ἔλαβον· καὶ γὰρ διέστησαν ὠφελίμως ἵνα ἡ μὲν ποιῇ, ἡ δὲ ἄρχῃ. διαφέρει γὰρ ἑκά-τερον· καὶ ἡρμόσθησαν ἑτέρῳ τρόπῳ κατὰ τὴν τῶν ὀνομάτων ἀίδιον προσβολὴν ὅπως καὶ ἡ ποιητικὴ τῆς βασιλικῆς καὶ ἡ βασιλικὴ τῆς   10
ποιητικῆς ἔχηται. ἀμφότεραι γὰρ συννεύουσιν εἰς τὸ ἱλαστήριον εἰκό-τως· εἰ μὴ γὰρ ἦν τοῖς νῦν οὖσιν ἵλεως ὁ θεός, οὔτ᾽ ἂν εἰργάσθη τι διὰ τῆς ποιητικῆς οὔτ᾽ ἂν εὐνομήθη διὰ τῆς βασιλικῆς.

V, f. 386ᵛ l. 10–f. 387ʳ l. 5

---

1 τῶν Χερουβὶμ V Arm   3 τοῦ λεχθέντος V Arm (A E L) : τῶν λεχθέντων Arm (D Aucher)   ἔδει Arm edd. : εἴδει V   4 ἀλλήλας Mai ex Arm : ἀλληγορίαν V   6 ἐστι om. Arm   7 αἱ διαστᾶσαι δυνάμεις : τὴν διαστᾶσαν δύναμιν Arm   πάλιν ἕνωσιν om. Arm   8–9 ἑκάτερον om. Arm   10–11 ἔχηται om. et post βασιλικῆς "spectatrix sit" (Aucher) add. Arm   11 ante εἰς add. καὶ Arm   12 νῦν οὖσιν : συνοῦσιν Arm

Ընդէ՞ր դէմք քերովբիմացն ի միմեանց կողմ Հային, եւ 66
երկոքին ի Հաշտարանն:

Ամենաբարի իմն եւ վայելուչ է ասացելոցս կերպարան.
քանզի արժան էր թէ զաւրութիւնքն արարչականին եւ արքու-
5 նւոյն ի միմեանս կոյս Հայել, զանձանց իւրեանց զգեղեցկութիւնս տեսանելով, եւ միանգամայն առ ի յաւգտութիւն եղելոցն
ի միասին երկոցուն Հոգեչունչ առնելով: Երկրորդ, վասն զի
աստուած մի է արարիչ եւ թագաւոր, յիրաւի մեկնեալ զաւրու-
թիւն ընկալան. եւ քանզի մեկնեցան աւգտաբար զի մին առնիցէ
10 եւ միւսն իշխեսցէ: Քանզի զանազանեալ են, եւ յարմարեցան
միւսով եւս այլինակաւ ըստ անուանցն մշտնջենաւոր ընդ միմեանս Հարութիւն որպէս զի եւ արարչականն տեսուչ իցն իշխանա-
կանին եւ արարչականն արքունականն. զի երկոքին ի միմեանս
Հային եւ ի Հաշտարանն յիրաւի. քանզի եթէ ոչ էր այնոցիկ որ ի
15 միասին են Հատ աստուած, եւ ոչ գործեցեալ ինչ էր ի ձեռն
արարչականին եւ ոչ աւրինաւորեալ լինէր ի ձեռն արքունւոյն:

---

3 ասացելոյս A E L (= Gk) : ասացելոցս D Aucher　4–5 արքունւոյն D E L Aucher : արքունականին A　5–6 զգեղեցկութիւնս L (= Gk) : զգեղեցկութիւնն A D E Aucher　11 ըստ A L (= Gk) : ընդ D E Aucher　14 ի prius om. E

---

(66) Why do the faces of the Cherubim look at each other and both toward the mercy-seat?

The image of what is said is something excellent and fitting to God. For it was proper that the powers, the creative and the kingly, look at each other, understanding their beauties, and also conspiring together for the benefit of the things that have come into being. Second, since God, being one, is both Creator and King, the separated powers rightly again obtained unity. For indeed they were usefully separated, so that the one creates, the other rules. For each is distinct. And they have been joined together in another way through the eternal application of the names, so that the creative (power) is associated with the kingly (power) and the kingly (power) with the creative (power). For both (powers) are inclined rightly toward the mercy-seat; for if God were not merciful to the things that now exist, nothing would have been produced through the creative (power) and nothing would have been well ordered through the kingly (power).

67   Τί ἐστι· γνωσθήσομαί σοι ἐκεῖθεν;

Γνῶσιν καὶ ἐπιστήμην ὁ εἰλικρινέστατος καὶ προφητικώτατος νοῦς
λαμβάνει τοῦ ὄντος οὐκ ἀπ' αὐτοῦ τοῦ ὄντος (οὐ γὰρ χωρήσει τὸ μέγε-
θος), ἀλλ' ἀπὸ τῶν πρώτων αὐτοῦ καὶ δορυφόρων δυνάμεων. καὶ ἀγα-
πητὸν ἐκεῖθεν εἰς τὴν ψυχὴν φέρεσθαι τὰς αὐγὰς ἵνα δύνηται διὰ τοῦ   5
δευτέρου φέγγους τὸ πρεσβύτερον καὶ αὐγοειδέστερον θεάσασθαι.

V, f. 387ʳ ll. 5–15

---

1 σοι : ὑμῖν Arm   4 δορυφόρων edd. : δωρηφόρων V   5 ante ἐκεῖθεν add. ἐστιν
Arm

Զի՞նչ է, ծանուցայց ձեզ անդուստ: 67

Գիտութիւն եւ Հանճար լուսաւորագոյնն եւ մարգարէակա-
նագոյնն միտք ընդունին գէին. ոչ ի նմին իսկ յէէն, քանզի
ոչ տարցի գմեծութիւնն, այլ յառաջնոցն նորա եւ սպասաւոր
5 գաւրութեանցն: Եւ սիրելի է անդուստ յոգիան գալ Հասանել
ճառագայթիցն գի կարացէ ի ձեռն երկրորդ ճառագայթիցն
գերիցագոյնն եւ գճառագայթածեւագոյնն տեսանել:

———————————————

4 եւ D E Aucher : եւ ի A L

———————————————

(**67**) What is: I shall be made known to you from there?

The purest and most prophetic mind obtains knowledge and science of the One who exists not from the One who exists himself (for it [the mind] will not contain His greatness), but from His primary and ministering powers. And (it is) acceptable that the rays of light are carried from there to the soul, so that it is able to observe what is older and more splendid through the secondary light.

32 *James R. Royse*

68.1   Τί ἐστι· λαλήσω <σοι> ἄνωθεν τοῦ ἱλαστηρίου ἀνὰ μέσον τῶν
<δυεῖν> Χερουβίμ;

Ἐμφαίνει διὰ τούτου πρῶτον μὲν ὅτι καὶ τῆς ἵλεω καὶ τῆς ποιητικῆς καὶ πάσης δυνάμεως ὑπεράνω τὸ θεῖόν ἐστιν· ἔπειτα δὲ ὅτι λαλεῖ
κατὰ τὸ μεσαίτατον τῆς τε ποιητικῆς καὶ βασιλικῆς· τοῦτο δὲ τοιοῦτον   5
ὑπολαμβάνει νοῦς· ὁ τοῦ θεοῦ λόγος μέσος ὢν οὐδὲν ἐν τῇ φύσει
καταλείπει κενόν, τὰ ὅλα πληρῶν καὶ μεσιτεύει καὶ διαιτᾷ τοῖς παρ'
ἑκάτερα οἳ διεστάναι δοκοῦσι, φιλίαν καὶ ὁμόνοιαν ἐργαζόμενος· ἀεὶ
γὰρ κοινωνίας αἴτιος καὶ δημιουργὸς εἰρήνης.

V, f. 387ʳ l. 15–f. 388ᵛ l. 7

---

1 σοι addidi ex Arm   2 δυεῖν addidi ex Arm (D E L Aucher) : om. V Arm (A)
3 τούτου V Arm   5 καὶ βασιλικῆς om. Arm codd.   6 νοῦς Tischendorf cum
Arm : νοῦν V   post οὐδὲν add. καθόλου Arm   7–8 παρ' ἑκάτερα V Arm : παρ'
ἑκάτερᾳ Harris Marcus Terian   8 οἳ V Arm   9 post κοινωνίας add. ἐστι Arm
εἰρήνης V Arm

Զի՞նչ է, խաւսեցայց քեզ ի վերուստ ի Հախտարանէն ի 68.1
միջոյ երկոցունց քերովբիմացն:

Յուցանէ սովաւ նախ առաջին, զի Հախտականին եւ արարչականին եւ ամենայն զաւրութեանն գեր ի վերոյ աստուածու-
5 թիւնն է. եւ ապա, զի խաւսի դեկ ի միջոյն արարչականու-
թեանն <եւ արքունեանն>. եւ զայս այսպիսի իմն կարծեն
միտք: Աստուծոյ բանն իբրու զի ի դեկ ի միջոցին է ունչ ինչ
ամենեւին ի բնութեան թող ու ունայն, զամենայն լնլով եւ
միջնորդ լինի եւ դատաւոր երկոցունց կողմանց, որք ի միմէ-
10 անցն քեցեալ թուին, սէր եւ միաբանութիւն ընդրելով․ քանզի
միշտ Հասարակութեան է պատճառք եւ արարիչ խաղաղու-
թեան:

---

2 երկոցունց om. A   6 եւ արքունեանն addidi cum Gr   զայս D E Aucher : զի A
L   7 զի ի D E Aucher : զի A L

(68.1) What is: I shall speak <to you> from above the mercy-seat between the <two> Cherubim?

(Scripture) shows through this first that the Deity is above the gracious (power) and the creative (power) and every (other) power. Next, (Scripture shows) that He speaks in the very middle of the creative (power) and the kingly (power). The mind understands this as follows. The Logos of God, being in the middle, leaves nothing in nature empty, filling the whole, and mediates and arbitrates for those on each side, which appear to be separated, producing friendship and concord; for it is always the cause of community and the creator of peace.

68.2   τὰ μὲν οὖν περὶ τὴν κιβωτὸν κατὰ μέρος εἴρηται· δεῖ δὲ συλλήβδην   10
ἄνωθεν ἀναλαβόντα τοῦ γνωρίσαι χάριν τίνων ταῦτά ἐστι σύμβολα
διεξελθεῖν. ἦν δὲ ταῦτα συμβολικά· κιβωτὸς καὶ τὰ ἐν αὐτῇ θησαυρι-
ζόμενα νόμιμα καὶ ἐπὶ ταύτης τὸ ἱλαστήριον καὶ τὰ ἐπὶ τοῦ ἱλαστηρίου
Χαλδαίων γλώττῃ λεγόμενα Χερουβίμ, ὑπὲρ δὲ τούτων κατὰ τὸ μέσον
φωνὴ καὶ λόγος καὶ ὑπεράνω ὁ λέγων. εἴ τις <οὖν> ἀκριβῶς δυνηθείη   15
κατανοῆσαι τὰς τούτων φύσεις, δοκεῖ μοι πᾶσι τοῖς ἄλλοις ἀποτάξα-
σθαι ὅσα ζηλωτά, κάλλεσι θεοειδεστάτοις περιληφθείς.

V, f. 387ʳ l. 15–f. 388ᵛ l. 7

---

12   δὲ : γὰρ Arm   ante κιβωτὸς add. καὶ Arm   15 post ὑπεράνω add. τούτων
Arm   οὖν addidi ex Arm

 Արդ յաղագս տապանակին բստ մասանցն ասացեալ է. 68.2

բայց պիտի եւս միահամուռ վերստին առնուլ փոխանակ

15 գիտուն առնելոյ ոյց այսորիկ են նշանակ անցանել բանիւ.

քանգի էին այսորքիկ նշանականք. եւ տապանակն, եւ որ ի

նմա գանձեալ աւրէնքն էին, եւ ի վերայ սորա հաշտարանն, եւ

ապա ի վերայ հաշտարանին քաղդէացւոց լեզուովն ասացեալ է

քերովբիմ. եւ գեր ի վերոյ նոցա հանդէպ միջոցին ձայն եւ

20 բան. եւ գեր ի վերոյ նորա ասաւղն։ Արդ եթէ ոք ճշգրտապէս

կարասցէ հայել եւ իմանալ գսոցա բնութիւնս, կամ է ինձ

յայլոցն ամենայնէ հրաժարել, որ միանգամ նախանձելի են

ասուածատեսիլ գեղեցկութեամբ պատեալք։

---

14 եւս D E Aucher : եւ A L   19 նոցա A E L Aucher : սորա D   20 ասաւղ ն D^{mg}
Aucher : ասելով D^{txt} A E L   22 ամենայնէ D E Aucher : յամենայնէ A L

(68.2) The individual aspects of the ark have thus been stated. But one should proceed summarily from above and review for the sake of knowing of what things these are symbols. These are symbolic: the ark and the ordinances treasured within it and the mercy-seat upon it and on the mercy-seat what are called in the Chaldean language the Cherubim, and beyond these in the middle the voice and Word and on top He who speaks. <Then> if one can accurately understand the natures of these, it seems to me that one would renounce all other things that are sought, being captivated by their most godlike beauties.

68.3   σκοπῶμεν δὲ ἕκαστον οἷόν ἐστι. τὸ πρῶτον ὁ καὶ ἑνὸς καὶ μονάδος
καὶ ἀρχῆς ἐστι πρεσβύτερος. ἔπειτα <ὁ> τοῦ ὄντος λόγος, ἡ σπερμα-
τικὴ τῶν ὄντων οὐσία. ἀπὸ δὲ τοῦ θείου λόγου, καθάπερ ἀπὸ πηγῆς,   20
σχίζονται δύο δυνάμεις· ἡ μὲν ποιητική, καθ᾽ ἣν ἔθηκε τὰ πάντα καὶ
διεκόσμησεν ὁ τεχνίτης (αὕτη θεὸς ὀνομάζεται), ἡ δὲ βασιλική, καθ᾽
ἣν ἄρχει τῶν γεγονότων ὁ δημιουργός (αὕτη καλεῖται κύριος).

---

19 ἐστι V Arm   ὁ add. et λόγος scripsit Tischendorf (λόγος Arm) : λόγου V
20 ante οὐσία add. ὄντως Arm (recte?)   θείου V : ὄντος Arm   21 post σχίζονται
add. αἱ Tischendorf et Arm   23 ἄρχει Tischendorf cum Arm : αἱ ἀρχαὶ V
ὁ δημιουργός V : τοῦ δημιουργοῦ Arm codd.

25   Բայց ընդ միտ ածցուք զիւրաքանչիւր որակիսի ոք է. **68.3**
առաջինն, որ եւ քան զմին եւ քան զմիակ ն եւ քան զսկիզբն
է երիցագոյն. եւ ապա էին բան, սերմանական էիցն արդարեւ
էութիւն. իսկ յէն բանէ, իբր յաղբերէ, հերձեալ պատառին
երկու ն զաւրութիւնք. մի է արարչական, ըստ որում եղն
30 զամենայն ինչ եւ զարդարեաց արուեստագէտն, սա աստուած
անուանի. իսկ արքունականն, ըստ այնմ, ըստ որում իշխան է
եղելոցն արարիչ ն, սա կոչի տէր:

---

26 զսկիսմն D E Aucher : զսկիսքն A L   28 իբր D E Aucher : իբրեւ A L
31 է om. D*   32 արարիչ ն scripsi cum Gr : արարչին A D E L Aucher
(= τοῦ δημιουργοῦ)

(**68.3**) But let us examine what each (of them) is like. First (is) He who is older than the one and the monad and the beginning. Then (is) \<the\> Logos of Him who is, the spermatic substance of the things that exist. And from the divine Logos, as from a spring, two powers split off. The one is the creative (power), according to which the Craftsman placed and ordered all things, (and) this is named "God." The other is the kingly (power), according to which the Creator rules the things that have come into being, (and) this is called "Lord."

68.4 ἀπὸ δὲ τούτων τῶν δυεῖν δυνάμεων ἐκπεφύκασιν ἕτεραι· παραβλα-
στάνει γὰρ τῇ μὲν ποιητικῇ ἡ ἵλεως, ἧς κύριον ὄνομα εὐεργέτις, τῇ δὲ   25
βασιλικῇ ἡ νομοθετική, ὄνομα δὲ εὐθυβόλον ἡ κολαστήριος· ὑπὸ δὲ
ταύτας καὶ περὶ ταύτας ἡ κιβωτός· ἔστι δὲ κιβωτὸς κόσμου νοητοῦ
σύμβολον. ἔχει δὲ τὰ πάντα ἱδρυμένα ἐν τοῖς ἐσωτάτοις ἁγίοις συμβολικῶς ἡ κιβωτός, τὸν ἀσώματον κόσμον, τὰ νόμιμα ἃ κέκληκε μαρτύ-
ρια (τὴν νομοθετικὴν καὶ κολαστήριον δύναμιν), τὸ ἱλαστήριον (τὴν   30
ἵλεω καὶ εὐεργέτιν), τὰς ὑπεράνω τήν τε ποιητικήν, ἥτις ἐστὶ πηγὴ τῆς
ἵλεω καὶ εὐεργέτιδος, καὶ τὴν βασιλικήν, ἥτις ἐστὶ ῥίζα τῆς κολαστη-
ρίου καὶ νομοθετικῆς. ὑπερβάλλεται δὲ μέσος ὢν ὁ θεῖος λόγος, ἀνω-
τέρω δὲ τοῦ λόγου ὁ λέγων.

---

24 ante ἕτεραι add. αἱ Arm   25 κύριον V Arm   26 ἡ κολαστήριος Tischendorf
cum Arm : ἢ κολαστήριον V   29 ante τὰ add. καὶ Arm   30 τὸ ἱλαστήριον : ἡ ἵλεως
Arm   31 πηγὴ Mai ex Arm : πίστις V   33 ὑπερβάλλεται Terian ex Arm : ὑπεμφαίνεται V   34 post δὲ add. ἐστι Arm

Եւ ի սոցունց յայսցանէ յերկոցունց զաւրութեանց բուսան 68.4
այլքն. քանզի բուսանի առ արարչականին Հաշտականն, որոյ
35 իսկ անունն է բարեգործակ. իսկ արքունւոյն աւրէնադրականն,
որոյ անունն է դշկուղիդ սատակիչ. եւ ընդ սոքաւք եւ առ
սոքաւք տապանակն. եւ է տապանակն մառւոր աշխարհին
նշանակ. եւ ունի զամենայն ինչ Հաստատեալ զնիստս ի
ներքսագոյնան սրբոցն նշանակաւ տապանակն, զանմարմին
40 աշխարհն, եւ զաւրէնսն զորս կոչեաց վկայութիւնս, զաւ-
րէնադրականն եւ զսատակիչ զաւրութիւնն, զՀաշտականն,
զՀաշտն եւ զբարեգործականն, զզեր ի վերոյան զարարչականն,
որ է աղբիւր Հաշտականին եւ բարեգործականին, եւ զարքունեանն, որ է արմատ սատակողին եւ աւրէնադրականին. բայց
45 առաւելեալ է իբրու զի ի մէջ է աստուածային բանն. եւ
վերագոյն է քան զբանն, որ ասէն:

36–37 եւ առ սոքաւք om. E*   37 post տապանակն prius add. է E   45 առաւելեալ
է : երեւելի է Marcus (= ὑπεμφαίνεται)   եւ D Aucher (= Gk) : om. A E L   46 քան
զ- D Aucher : քանզի A E L   ante որ add. եւ A L

(68.4) And from these two powers have grown others. For beside the creative (power) sprouts forth the gracious (power), whose appropriate name is "beneficent," and beside the kingly (power sprouts forth) the legislative, whose correct name is the "punitive" (power). Under these and beside these is the ark; and the ark is the symbol of the intelligible cosmos. And the ark symbolically contains all things that are established in the innermost sanctuary: the incorporeal cosmos, the ordinances that (Scripture) has called "testimonies," (i.e.) the legislative and punitive power, the mercy-seat, (i.e.) the gracious and beneficent (power), and the (powers) on top, (i.e.) the creative (power), which is the source of the gracious and beneficent (power), and the kingly, which is the root of the punitive and legislative (power). The divine Logos, being in the middle, is superior, and above the Logos (is) He who speaks.

68.5 ἔστι δὲ καὶ ὁ τῶν κατειλεγμένων ἀριθμὸς ἑβδομάδι συμπληρού- 35
μενος· νοητὸς κόσμος, καὶ δυνάμεις δύο συγγενεῖς ἥ τε κολαστήριος
καὶ εὐεργέτις, καὶ ἕτεραι πρὸ τούτων δύο ἥ τε ποιητικὴ καὶ ἡ βασιλική, συγγένειαν ἔχουσαι μᾶλλον πρὸς τὸν δημιουργόν ἢ τὸ γεγονός· καὶ
ἕκτος ὁ λόγος καὶ ἕβδομος ὁ λέγων· ἐὰν δὲ ἄνωθεν τὴν καταρχὴν ποιῇ,
εὑρήσεις τὸν μὲν λέγοντα πρῶτον, τὸν δὲ λόγον δεύτερον, τρίτην δὲ 40
τὴν ποιητικὴν δύναμιν, τετάρτην δὲ τὴν ἀρχικήν, εἶτα δὲ ὑπὸ μὲν τῇ
ποιητικῇ πέμπτην τὴν εὐεργέτιν, ὑπὸ δὲ τῇ βασιλικῇ ἕκτην τὴν κολαστήριον, ἕβδομον δὲ τὸν ἐκ τῶν ἰδεῶν κόσμον.

V, f. 387ʳ l. 15–f. 388ᵛ l. 7

---

35 ἔστι om. Arm codd. (Aucher add.)   36 δύο : δι᾽ οὗ Arm   38 ἔχουσαι : ἔχει
Arm   πρὸς om. Arm codd.   ἢ : καὶ Arm   γεγονός : γένος Arm   39 ἕκτος :
ἕκαστος Arm   καταρχὴν V Arm : καταρίθμησιν Grossmann   40 εὑρήσεις om.
Arm codd.   τρίτην edd. : τρίτον V   41 ἀρχικήν Conybeare ex Arm : ἀρχήν V

Եւ ի հաշիւ անկելոցն <է> թիւ եաւթներեկ աւլցեալ. 68.5
մտաւոր աշխարհ, եւ զաւրութիւնքն ի ձեռն որոյ ագգակից են
սատակալդ ն եւ բարեգործակ. եւ այլ եւս երկու յառաջ քան
50 զստա արարչականն եւ արքունեանն ագգակցութիւն ունի
    առաւել <առ> արարիչն, եւ ագգ ն. եւ իւրաքանչիւրոք բանն.
    եւ եաւթներորդ որ ասեն. ապա եթէ ի վերուստ զսկիգբն
    արասցես, <գտցես> զստաւղ ն առաշին, եւ գբանն երկրորդ, եւ
    երրորդ զ արարչական զ աւրութիւնն, եւ չորրորդ զիշխանա-
55 կանն, ապա ընդ արարչականաւն հինգերորդ զբարեգործակ ն,
    իսկ ընդ արքունեաւն վեցերորդ զստակիչ ն, եւ եաւթներորդ
    զ 'ի տեսականգ ն աշխարհ:

---

47 է add. Aucher (= Gk)   49 եւս երկու D E Aucher : երկու եւս A L   51 առ
addidi cum Gr   52 զսկիգբ ն E (զսկիքբ ն A L): սկիքբ ն D Aucher   53 գտցես
addidi cum Gr   56 ընդ D E L^corr Aucher (= Gk) : om. A L*   արքունեաւ ն D E L
Aucher : արքունականն A   զստակիչ ն D Aucher : զստատկող ն A E L   57 գ 'ի L
(= Gk) : գ A : է գ 'ի D E , <է> գ 'ի Aucher

(68.5) And the number of the listed things is completed by the hebdomad: intelligible cosmos, and two related powers, the punitive and the beneficent, and two other (powers) prior to those, the creative and the kingly, having kinship to the Creator rather than to what has come into being, and sixth the Logos, and seventh He who speaks. But if you make the beginning from the top, you will find Him who speaks first, the Logos second, third the creative power, fourth the ruling (power), and then under the creative (power) fifth the beneficent (power), and under the kingly (power) sixth the punitive (power), and seventh the cosmos of the ideas.

Appendix: Supplementary Textual Notes

The line numbers refer to the Greek text. For convenience I have provided transliterations of the Armenian throughout. I have usually not provided precise references to the various editions and other works discussed above when they are simply "ad loc."

2.62:

2:     The Armenian has omitted (by haplography) the second occurrence of τὰ Χερουβίμ. I suspect that this as an error within the Armenian transmission, rather than an error of the translators.

2–3: Philo gives a slightly different interpretation of "Cherubim" at *Mos.* 2.97 (ἐπίγνωσις καὶ ἐπιστήμη πολλή), while at *Cher.* 21–28 he does not give such an interpretation, but has an extended discussion, culminating in the "higher view" (as at *Fug.* 100; *QG* 1.57, and here at *QE* 2.62) that the two Cherubim correspond to the two chief powers of God. Clement of Alexandria states that the term means ἐπίγνωσιν πολλήν (*Strom.* 5.35.6), and while this is sometimes taken as reflecting *Mos.* 2.97 (see the testimonium in PCW and Colson's note in PLCL), Clement's words are in fact identical with Philo's first interpretation here, and it seems simplest to suppose that *QE* 2.62 was his source.[56]

2–3: The second clause awkwardly follows the first. Grossmann added ῇ, and states (p. 13): "Post voc. πολλὴ insere ῇ, quae vox facile potuit praecedente -η absorpta excidere. Quam voculam nisi inserueris huilca oratio est, insertâ autem coagmentata et levis." He was followed by Tischendorf,[57] Harris, and Marcus, but not Terian. Runia compares the usage at *Fug.* 55, but notes that "the phrase [i.e. ῇ] is nowhere used for etymologies." He suggests that perhaps δέ, contrasting with μέν in the first clause, has fallen out. I hesitantly suggest that, as an easy error, ἤ was omitted (by haplography after πολλή). But there remains the difficulty at the beginning of the second clause, which will be discussed later.

In fact, there is a similar construction at *Deo* 6, where Philo gives two

---

[56] See Ludwig Früchtel, "Griechische Fragmente zu Philons Quaestiones in Genesin et in Exodum," *ZAW* 55 (1937): 114, who cites Philo from Aucher's Latin, not noting the extant Greek. See further Annewies van den Hoek, *Clement of Alexandria and his Use of Philo in the "Stromateis"* (VChrSup 3; Leiden: Brill, 1988), 132–33.

[57] He says of the phrase ῇ . . . κεχυμένη: "haec interpres Armenus non intellexit."

etymologies of the name "Seraphim."[58] Siegert retroverts the Armenian as: Σεραφὶμ ἑρμηνεύεται "τύποι" ἢ "ἔμπρησις."[59] The disjunction ἢ (corresponding to which the Armenian has *ьι ιμιπ* [*ew kam*]) at least gives a parallel to my conjecture. Indeed, a disjunction of etymologies is found for quite a few other names: *Leg.* 1.68 ("Geon," ἢ = *ιμιπ* [*kam*], with ὄνομα); 3.77 ("Noah," ἢ); *Fug.* 203 ("Shur," ἢ); *Mut.* 194 ("Dinah," ἢ); *Somn.* 2. 192 ("Sodom," ἢ); *QG* 2.65 and 2.77 ("Ham," *ιμιπ* [*kam*]; "Canaan," *ιμιπ* [*kam*]); 3.36 ("Pharan," *ιμιπ* [*kam*]); 4.23 ("Sodom," ἢ = *ιμιπ* [*kam*]), 4.31 ("Sodom," *ιμιπ* [*kam*]),[60] 4.72 ("Hebron," ἢ = *ьι ιμιπ* [*ew kam*]),[61] 4.83 ("Hebron," *ьι ιμιπ* [*ew kam*]), 4.161 ("Esau," ἢ = *ιμιπ* [*kam*] = "uel"), 4.171 ("Edom," ἢ = *ьι ιμιπ* [*ew kam*] = "siue"), 4.241 ("Hittite," *ьι* [*ew*], but Latin "siue").[62]

2–3:   For ἐν ἑτέροις ὄνομα (as found in V) the Armenian has *յայլ անուանս* (*yayl anuans*), which is translated as "in caetera nomina," "in other words," and "en d'autres termes."[63] We thus have an equivalence with ἐν ἑτέροις

---

[58]   The Armenian has "Cherub" (*քերովբէ* [*k'erovbē*]), but as both Maximilian Adler ("Das philonische Fragment De deo," *MGWJ* 80 [1936], 167) and Siegert (*Gottesbezeichnung*, 27 n. 65) observe, this must be an error; Philo wrote "Seraphim" (*սերովբէք* [*serovbēk'*]), or perhaps "Seraph" (*սերովբէ* [*serovbē*]), to which the Armenian is slightly closer. The term "Seraph" occurs in Philo only in this etymology and in the immediately preceding citation of Isa 6:1–2. (Grossmann, *Anecdoton*, 15–16, though, cites *Deo* 6 as an interpretation of "Cherubim.")

[59]   While I concur with this Greek, the Armenian for ἑρμηνεύεται there is *մեկնի* (*mekni*), rather than *թարգմանի* (*t'argmani*), as in l. 2. Both Armenian verbs occur frequently for etymologies, and both correspond to ἑρμηνεύω; see, e.g., *Leg.* 1.68, where the Armenian shifts from one to the other for the two occurrences of ἑρμηνεύω.

[60]   The etymologies of "Sodom" at *Somn.* 2.192; *QG* 4.23, and *QG* 4.31 are the same, and are presented as a disjunction. But at *Ebr.* 222 the same terms are conjoined with καί.

[61]   The Greek fragment has συζυγὴ ἢ ἑταιρία. At *Post.* 60 only συζυγή is given, while at *Det.* 15 we find συζυγὴ (δὲ) καὶ συνεταιρίς (the only Philonic occurrence of the last word).

[62]   See also *Congr.* 61 and *Somn.* 1. 41, where the two interpretations are presented with τοτὲ μέν . . . τοτὲ δέ.

[63]   The Armenian *յայլ անուանս* (*yayl anuans*) consists of the preposition *ի* (*i*) (written *յ* [*y*] before the vowel), the adjective *այլ* (*ayl*), and the noun *անուանս* (*anuans*), which is the accusative (= locative) plural of the noun *anuan*, which corresponds to ὄνομα. The *ի* (*i*) here, as frequently, corresponds to ἐν, and is used here (also as frequently) with the accusative (or locative) in Armenian (Hans Jensen, *Altarmenische Grammatik* [Heidelberg: Carl Winter, 1959], §344). The *այլ* (*ayl*) is actually the nominative singular form of the adjective "other" (frequently used for ἄλλος), but this form

ὀνόμασιν, as noted by Conybeare and Termini.[64] The editors do not comment on the discrepancy between V's ὄνομα and Arm's ὀνόμασιν. However, as Runia points out, Philo does not use ἐν ἑτέροις ὀνόμασιν,[65] but frequently uses simply ἐν ἑτέροις to mean "elsewhere," meaning either in Scripture or in Philo's own writings. In fact, this usage occurs thirty-seven times (besides *QE* 2.62): *Leg.* 1.51; 2.27, 2.35, 2.48; 3.4, 3.42, 3.65, 3.142, 3.186; *Sacr.* 67; *Det.* 103; *Post.* 26, 89,[66] 142; *Gig.* 48; *Deus* 77; *Conf.* 135; *Migr.* 131; *Her.* 50, 117, 123, 215; *Fug.* 58, 186; *Mut.* 98; *Somn.* 1.74, 1.168, 1.230; 2.222; *Dec.* 38, 101; *Spec.* 1.25, 1.104; 4.123; *Praem.* 113; *QG* 2.59; *QE* 2.10. The only place where it is not used to refer to another place in a writing is at *Somn.* 1.132, where it means "in other contests."[67]

At nine of these thirty-seven places the Armenian version is extant: At *Leg.* 1.51; 2.48; *Dec.* 38 it has յայլս (*yayls*), "in others." At *Leg.* 2.27, 2.35; *Spec.* 1.104 it has յայլսն (*yaylsn*), "in the others." We find at *Dec.* 101 յայլում տեղիս (*yaylum tełis*), "in other places," and at *QG* 2.59 յայլում վայրի (*yaylum vayri*), "in another place" or "dans un autre passage" as Marcus and Mercier have (Aucher "alibi"). And at *QE* 2.10 there is ոմանց (*omanc῾*), "by some" as Marcus has (Aucher "quibusdam," while Terian [rendering the Greek] has "ailleurs").[68]

---

is also used regularly with the nominative plural and with (as here) the accusative (= locative) plural (ibid., §425). Of course, the case is determined by the Armenian preposition ի (*i*), not by the Greek preposition ἐν.

[64] Termini, *Le potenze di Dio*, 126 n. 112.

[65] But ἑτέροις ὀνόμασι is found at *Deus* 60 and also (as it seems) at *Deo* 10 (see Siegert, *Gottesbezeichnung*, 31 l. 3), where the Armenian has այլով անուամբք (*aylov anuambk῾*), an instrumental plural; however, these two occurrences are not within the context of etymologizing.

[66] PLCL renders this "in other words." PCH and PAPM have more accurately "an anderer Stelle" and "ailleurs."

[67] The only textual variations that I find are: *Leg.* 1.51: ἑτέρῳ FL; *Post.* 142: ἑτέρῳ U (the sole manuscript; ἑτέροις is Mangey's conjecture); *Somn.* 1.132: ἑτέρῳ A^corr; *QE* 2.10: ἐν ἑτέροις om. Procopius.

[68] Such expressions also often occur where the Greek is lost. E.g., at *QG* 1.100 we have յայլսն (*yaylsn*), translated as "in other places," "dans d'autres passages," and "caeteris locis." At *QE* 2.14 there is յայլում վայրի (*yaylum vayri*), translated as "alias," "in another passage," and "dans un autre passage." And at *QE* 2.14 we find յայլում տեղի լոջն (*yaylum tełwojn*), rendered as "in another place," "ailleurs," and "alibi." It is likely that Philo wrote ἐν ἑτέροις at each place.

All of this evidence shows that ἐν ἑτέροις occurs frequently with little or no textual fluctuation, and that it is rendered more or less correctly and literally by the Armenian translators (only *QE* 2.10 may be a slight exception). I can only suggest that the translators were somehow misled by the awkward ἐν ἑτέροις ὄνομα (assuming that their text in fact had that Greek), and took the words as one phrase.

Of course, it is not at all clear what "elsewhere" would be referring to in our text. It is tempting to interpret the phrase as meaning "by others," or "in other interpretations," but Philonic usage seems to provide no support for such renderings.[69] Grossmann (p. 13) suggests that the reference is either to a lost work of Philo or to the passage at *Her.* 217: σύμβολον . . . μείζονος φύσεως . . . ἢ . . . κεχυμένη . . . συνυφήνασα. Although the only direct connection here with *QE* 2.62 is κεχυμένη, Grossmann pursues this topic at considerable length (pp. 13–16), and argues that the "higher nature" here is the wisdom of God, concluding that according to Philo the name of the Cherubim designates the wisdom of God.[70]

In any case, the construction of the second clause is awkward, and perhaps there has been some corruption, such as the loss of δέ, as Runia suggests (see further the preceding note).

3:     Although V reads δεῖν all editors agree in printing δυεῖν, the form of the dual as used by Philo (see also on 2.68 ll. 1–2 below). Only Grossmann reports V's actual reading, as found in Tischendorf's transcript.

3–4:   The omission by the Armenian of the equivalent of τοῦ ὄντος, which would be էին (*ēin*), seems unexplained; this omission is noted by Conybeare, Marcus, and Terian.

4:     Although unreported by earlier editors, V seems to have corrected an original ὄντως into ὄντος.

---

[69]   At *Cher.* 25 Philo introduces another interpretation of the two Cherubim with the phrase: καθ᾽ ἑτέραν ἐκδοχήν. At *Mos.* 2.98 "some" (τινες) are said to hold an alternative view of the Cherubim. And at *QG* 1.57 Philo introduces a second interpretation of the fiery sword with the words "there are some who say." The Greek is lost here, but the Armenian for "some" has ոմանք (*omank'*), which would correspond to τινες or ἔνιοι. But none of these texts is verbally close to *QE* 2.62. Fred Strickert, "Philo on the Cherubim," *SPhA* 8 (1996): 43, states of our passage: "it is also possible to read this as 'the name [is translated] among others . . .'," but does not give any parallels.

[70]   See p. 16: "His adductus argumentis statuere posse mihi videor, Cherubinorum nomine secundum Philonis interpretationem nihil aliud designari quam Sapientiam Dei per omnem rerum naturam intentam atque commeantem."

5:      As at 2.68 l. 5, the Armenian has omitted τῆς βασιλικῆς, evidently by a scribal leap: արարչ ակ֊անն քան գ արքու ն ե֊անն (*ararč 'ak<u>ann</u> k 'an zark 'u-ne<u>ann</u>*).

5:      For V's αἴτε Grossmann suggested ἄτε, but Tischendorf more plausibly read αἴγε (as an easy confusion in a majuscule ancestor), and he was followed by later editors, although Terian and Früchtel more correctly write αἵ γε. Mai had edited simply αἱ, no doubt by an oversight.

5:      Although the Armenian equivalent of ἄπασαι is omitted by Aucher, it is found in three of the four Armenian manuscripts cited here. It may have been omitted by a scribal leap: են ամենայն (*e<u>n</u> amenay<u>n</u>*). But its omission would also have been facilitated by the fact that it is frequently written as simply ա with a superscripted line.

8:      As Marcus notes, the Armenian has a doublet for ἱεροῖς.

8–9:   The Armenian has added forms of the equivalent of καλέω at two places; I consider these to be simply clarifying additions.

2.63:

1:      Where V has χρυσοῦ in the *quaestio* the Armenian has ոսկեղէն (*oske-lēn*), which is the adjective "golden," corresponding to χρύσεος (χρυσοῦς),[71] in contrast to the Greek's use of the noun "gold" in the genitive case. I suppose that the noun is correct, and that the Armenian shifted to an adjective, as we also find for χρυσοῦ at *Contempl.* 49.[72]

1–2:   Philo is here commenting on the final two words of the first part of Exod 25:17 (LXX): καὶ ποιήσεις δύο Χερουβὶμ χρυσᾶ τορευτά. For the final phrase B* has χρυσοτορευτα, and for the final word quite a few witnesses have τορνευτά. But precisely what is meant seems uncertain.[73] The Armenian has for both τορευτά (in the *quaestio*) and τορεία (in the *solutio*) the same word, ճախարակեայ (*čaxarakeay*), which literally means "turned."[74]

---

[71] *NB* 2:519B.

[72] But at *Prov.* 2.18, 18, 22, 27, the Armenian noun renders the Greek noun.

[73] See the comments by John William Wevers, *Notes on the Greek Text of Exodus* (SBLSCS 30; Atlanta: Scholars Press, 1990), 399, and Alain Le Boulluec and Pierre Sandevoir, *La Bible d'Alexandrie* 2: *L'Exode* (Paris: Cerf, 2004), 257–58. There is similar textual variation at Exod 25:30 and 25:36.

[74] See *NB* 2:165B on this and related words. The latter occurrence (in the *solutio*) has the suffixed -*n*, reflecting no doubt the article in Greek. The Armenian version of Exod 25:18 has: ոսկիս ճախարակեայս (*oskis čaxarakeays*), which would literally be "gold, turned," where both the noun and the adjective are marked as plural. This

Although Marcus seems to think that the Armenian correctly renders both words, Terian states that the Armenian of the *quaestio* corresponds to τορεία (as in l. 2) rather than to τορευτά. This seems to be a fine distinction. Apparently, τορευτός occurs in Philo only at *Her.* 216, while τορεία occurs only at *Contempl.* 49, where τορείαις is translated as ճախարակեայք (*čaxara-keayk῾*), the plural of the word at ll. 1–2.[75] *QE* 2.73 has an extended discussion of this "turning," but unfortunately no Greek survives.[76]

The fluctuation in the Greek at many of these places makes it difficult to be confident about the presumed meaning of the Armenian word. It seems to me likely that the Armenian simply failed to capture the distinction between these two Greek words.

2:     The Armenian adds (the equivalent of) ἐστί in order to have a verb in the opening clause.

2:     For τιμιωτάτης the Armenian has the ordinary adjective corresponding to τιμίας (see the translation by Marcus and the note by Terian).

4:     Terian states that the Armenian adds εἶναι after ἰδεῶν; however, the Armenian գոլ (*gol*), literally "to be," here seems to represent (not quite exactly) ὑπαρχούσας, which is not otherwise expressed.

5:     It seems not to have been noted previously that the Armenian here, էութիւն (*ēut῾iwn*), most likely renders οὐσίας rather than φύσεως.[77] Within only *Prov.*, *QG*, and *QE.*, there are fifty-four (other) occurrences of φύσις.[78] At fifty of these it is translated by բնութիւն (*bnut῾iwn*), and never by

---

reading is taken by the Göttingen LXX as supporting τορνευτά.

[75] Conybeare (*Philo about the Contemplative Life* [Oxford: Clarendon Press, 1895]), 168, reports that one manuscript has ճախարակեալք (*čaxarakealk῾*). A similar note is in the 1892 edition of Philo's works in Armenian, p. 19. We also find τορεύω at *Leg.* 3.104, διατορεύω at *Leg.* 3.88, and τορνεύω at *Post.* 104 (none of which is in Armenian).

[76] But Marcus and Terian state that Philo probably read τορνευτήν at *QE* 2.73, even though in the *quaestio* there we again find the same Armenian word that occurs twice in *QE* 2.63.

[77] In his "Index" Marcus cites "φύσις (?)" for *QE* 2.63, and in his translation says that the Greek "differs only slightly" from the Armenian, without giving details.

[78] To use *The Philo Index* we have to convert from the aberrant numbering of the sections of *Prov.*, and two of the references are to occurrences that are, according to the Armenian or Latin, not actually from Philo: *QG* 1.76; 4.195.9. (Petit prints in her lighter italic type.) And we add the occurrences at *QE* 2.63 l. 3, 2.68 l. 6, 2.68 l. 16.

48   James R. Royse

էութիւն (ēut'iwn).[79] This evidence alone makes it very unlikely that the
Armenian translators saw φύσεως at l. 5. Turning to οὐσία we find various
renderings of the sixteen (other) occurrences of οὐσία in Prov., QG, and
QE.[80] But seven times it is translated by էութիւն (ēut'iwn): QG 1.92; 2.15,
2.59, 2.59; 4.8; QE 2.63 l. 2, 2.68 l. 20.[81]

    The question is whether a Greek scribe wrote φύσεως for οὐσίας, or
the Armenian translators chose to shift from their regular rendering of
φύσεως. I see no explanation for the latter change, while the explanation for
the alteration in Greek is evident: a scribe was influenced by the occurrence of ἐπιστημονικῆς φύσεως a couple of lines earlier to write ἐπιστημονικωτάτης φύσεως here. I have consequently followed the Armenian and
emended the Greek.

2.64:

1:    As reported by Marcus and Terian, the Armenian translators have
slipped here in rendering ἱλαστήριον as "altar," i.e., սեղան (sełan), which
corresponds rather to θυσιαστήριον.[82] At 2.66 (twice) and 2.68 (thrice) we
find the correct հաշ ատարան (haštaran) for ἱλαστήριον.[83] Similarly, at 2.60

---

[79]   The other four occurrences are: Prov. 2.23, where բնիկ (bnik) renders φύσει;
Prov. 2.24, where for φύσιν the Armenian lacks a corresponding noun (Aucher conjectures the Armenian); Prov. 2:24, where νόμος φύσεως is translated by բնաւորեալ է
(bnaworeal ē), a related verbal construction; QE 2.25, where ի բուն (i bun) renders
φύσει. Also, at Prov. 2.15 the Armenian occurs where the Eusebian mss. have συνέ-
σεως, and Conybeare, Specimen, 9, conjectured φύσεως. See the parallels at Opif. 144;
Plant. 41; Her. 233; QG 2.62. Mangey (before the Armenian) suggested συστάσεως.

[80]   At QG 3.49 the occurrence is not in an actual fragment.

[81]   It is translated three times by նիւթիւն (niwt'iwn): Prov. 2:50 (first occurrence),
2:50 (second occurrence), 2.101; three times by գոյացուat'իւն (goyac'ut'iwn) at QG 2.12,
2.59, 2.59; once by բնութիւն (bnut'iwn) at QG 4.30; and once by the equivalent of αἰτία,
as Petit and Marcus note, at QG 3.38 (here we may suspect that the Greek has been
corrupted). And at Prov. 2.50 (third occurrence) the Armenian omits, as Conybeare
(Specimen, 9) observes, any equivalent of ἐκ τελείας οὐσίας.

[82]   See NB 2:705A. This is the rendering at Leg. 1.48, 48, and 50, although at Spec.
1.83, 285, 287, 290, 291, 293, and QG 1.62 բագին (bagin) is used for θυσιαστήριον. The
quaestio of QE 2.30 (not extant in Greek) cites the LXX of Exod 24:4, which has θυσιαστήριον, and the Armenian has սեղան (sełan). However, in the solutio both սեղան
(sełan) and բագին (bagin) occur, as they do also in QE 2.98–102; see Marcus's comment at PLCL Supp 2:150 n. a.

[83]   Marcus, "Index," says that հաշ ատարան (haštaran) occurs four times in QE 2.68
for ἱλαστήριον, and that հաշ ատակ ան (haštakan) occurs three times in QE 2.68 for ἵλεως.

(twice) and 2.61 (once), not preserved in Greek, we find Հաշտարան ʿhašta-
ran) for the LXX's ἱλαστήριον.

4:     The opening sentence of the *solutio* lacks a finite verb in both Greek
and Armenian. Thus, Aucher adds "(designat)," and Marcus adds "(This
indicates that)." But only Mai suggests emending the Greek, by adding
αἰνίττεται, as occurs, e.g., in *QE* 2.65 l. 4.[84] Often, of course, Philo does have
αἰνίττομαι or a similar verb (ἐμφαίνω is also frequent) in the opening sentence of the *solutio*, but by no means always; from among the places where
the Greek is more or less clearly preserved, see the following verbless
opening sentences: *QG* 1.21, 1.55; 2.3 (Paramelle), 2.11, 2.16, 2.41; 3.29; 4.67,
4.102, 4.202, 4.208; *QE* 2.9, 2.11, 2.20, 2.21.[85]

7:     The Armenian omits the equivalent of μήτε πλεονεκτῇ, probably by a
scribal leap, either in Greek (μήτε πλεονεκτῇ μήτε πλεονεκτῆται) or in Armenian (առաւելեալ է եւ մի առաւելեալ լիցի [aṙaweleal ē ew mi aṙaweleal
lic'i], or similar words).

8:     The phrase νόμῳ βραβευόμενα τῷ τῆς ἰσότητος in V is rendered as
what Aucher translates as: "symbolice concilians victoriam indicio pari-
tatis." I suppose that the equivalent of συμβολικῶς was simply a transla-
tional liberty.

8–9: Mai and Tischendorf's transcript correctly have διαιωνίζεται. However, Grossmann printed διαμονίζεται, which Tischendorf then emended to
διαιωνίζεται, referring to the Armenian, thus arriving at what he had earlier
transcribed. But he further questions, as does Runia, the passive use of this
verb; indeed, the TLG gives only two occurrences of the passive: διαιωνίζεται in Ps.-Athanasius, and διαιωνίζονται in Theodorus Studites. However,
the active occurs twelve times in Philo,[86] and the use of the passive here
seems perfectly appropriate and is accurately reflected in յաւէտանան
(yawētanan), which is the verb used to translate διαιωνίζοντα at *Dec.* 53.

He thus silently incorporates a textual correction; see the note below on 2.68 l. 30.

[84] He states: "Hoc verbum deerat etiam in codice quo utebatur armenius interpres antiquissimus."

[85] In most of these the Armenian adds a verb, but it also lacks a verb at *QG* 2.3,
2.11, 2.16, 2.41, and *QE* 2.20.

[86] The complete list can be found in Günter Mayer, *Index Philoneus* (Berlin and
New York: de Gruyter, 1974); the list in *The Philo Index* omits *Mos.* 2.125; *Spec.* 2.5,
2.56. Note further that the active of συνδιαιωνίζω occurs four times.

9–11: The citation in the *Sacra parallela* has transposed the two clauses, and has made some other adjustments as part of the process of excerpting. The text was edited (from codex R) by Mangey (2:665, #4), and Tischendorf then referred to that location. However, Harris (101, #7) printed the citation as unidentified, and says that it is assigned to *De ebrietate*. Similarly, Wendland prints the citation among the fragments of the lost book *De ebrietate*.[87] Eventually, the correct identification was published by Früchtel,[88] and then was made independently by Petit.

9:        The Armenian has shifted the case of πλεονεξία and ἀνισότης to the instrumental, as shown in all three translations.

10:       V's τέρματα is evidently an error for σπέρματα, which is found in the *Sacra parallela* (T, but R has σπέρμα) as well as in the Armenian. Already Tischendorf chooses σπέρματα, citing Mangey (2:665), where the citation of R is found.[89] However, Grossmann prints τέρματα with no note, while Mai prints it with the note: "Video armenium interpretem legisse σπέρματα. Lectionem tamen τέρματα non desero, quoniam Sophocles τέρμα τῆς σωτηρίας dixit [*Oed. col.* 725]."

11:       The *Sacra parallela* mss. clearly have διαμονῆς; however, in V it occurs in the top line of f. 386ᵛ, where the slight tear has removed the μ. Tischendorf indicates this in his transcript, and Grossmann accordingly cites the text in his n. 17 as "δια ονῆς," and says: "Litteram situ deletâ legendum: διαμονῆς. it. [= item] Arm. 2, 619." The reference is (interestingly enough) to the last page of Aucher's edition of *De Deo*. Now, διαμονῆς does not, of course, occur on that page, but "perseverationem" does, and the Armenian original (*ınkιեι* [*tewel*]) is retroverted by Siegert as διαμονήν. Grossmann, who betrays no knowledge of Armenian, evidently was led to this page by the "perseverandi" in Aucher's translation of *QE* 2.64 (which there translates *կալոյ մնալոյ* [*kaloy mnaloy*]).[90]

---

[87] *Neu entdeckte Fragmente Philos* (Berlin: Georg Reimer, 1891), 24, #9. On the confusion here see my "Further Greek Fragments," 148 n. 26.

[88] "Griechische Fragmente," 109.

[89] There (2:665, #4) Mangey prints ἔννομον, which is approved by Tischendorf. And Harris (101, #7) also edits ἔννομον. But R in fact has εὔνομον, as printed by Wendland, *Neu entdeckte Fragmente*, 24, #9.

[90] On the various Armenian renderings of διαμονή, see my review of Paramelle, *Philon d'Alexandrie: Questions sur la Genèse II 1—7*, 141–43; there should have been noted yet further examples at *Leg.* 2.8 and 96. (At the occurrence at *Spec.* 1.289 the Armenian has a lacuna.)

2.65:

2:     The citation in the *Sacra parallela* omits μέν since the excerpt does not extend to the subsequent clause with δέ. The text was edited (from codex R) by Mangey (2.656, #4), and then identified by Harris.

4:     The Armenian omits any equivalent of δέ, and as a result Aucher has taken αἰνίττεται with what precedes, thus punctuating and translating.

4:     The Armenian omits the equivalent of σκέπαις καί, as Terian notes. At *Contempl.* 24 σκέπη is rendered by *ձեղուն* (*jełun*), but at *Spec.* 1.83 and *Contempl.* 38 by *ծածկոյթ* (*cackoyt'*). Related to the latter word is *ծածկեալ լինի* (*cackeal lini*), the translation of φρουρεῖται here at 2.65. Although it is possible that a couple of words have been lost in transmission, it seems to me more likely that the Armenian translators did not attempt to capture the distinction between σκέπη and φυλακτήριον, and rendered that pair by only one word, *պահպանութիւն* (*pahpanut'iwn*), which is the singular of the word that occurs in the plural for φρουραῖς at 2.64.[91]

5:     V in fact reads ταῖς ταῖς, having duplicated the word at the end of the line (δυσὶ ταῖς | ταῖς εἰρημέναις).[92] Mai's edition prints only one occurrence, and Tischendorf's transcript also has only one occurrence; as a result the duplication is unknown to all editions.

2.66:

1:     The phrase τῶν Χερουβίμ is found in V (agreeing with the Armenian) and duly printed by Mai, Grossmann, Tischendorf, and Harris. But it is missing in Marcus's appendix (255), although in his note to the translation (112 n. a) he cites the Greek *with* the two words; thus the omission in the appendix must be a mere oversight. But the omission is also found in Terian's text, who then states that the Armenian adds the words.

3:     V reads τοῦ λεχθέντος, as found in Mai and in Tischendorf's transcript. But without comment Grossmann shifted to τῶν λεχθέντων, and all later editors followed him. Now, Aucher's Armenian also has the plural (*ասացելոցս* [*asac'eloc's*], Aucher's "dictorum"), and thus Grossmann might have been correcting the Greek to the Armenian (although a note to that effect would have been helpful). However, in fact three of the manuscripts

---

[91]   *NB* 2:589A gives φυλακή and τήρησις for its meaning.

[92]   This sort of error seems very tempting to some scribes; see my *Scribal Habits,* 441 and 493, on the scribe of $\mathfrak{P}^{66}$.

cited here have the singular, *ասացելոյս* (*asac'eloys*).[93] I think that there can be little doubt that the plural in Armenian is a corruption, and that the singular was the original translation of the singular in Greek.[94] By the way, in Philo's surviving Greek we find τοῦ λεχθέντος with no modified noun at four other places where we have the Armenian version: *Abr.* 29 (*ասացելոց* [*asac'eloc's*], plural), 174 (*ասացելոյն* [*asac'eloyn*], singular); *Spec.* 3.37 (*ասացելաս* [*asac'ealss*], plural); *QG* 4.228 (*ասացելոյն* [*asac'eloyn*], singular). The evidence, slight as it is, is thus evenly divided as to whether the Armenian preserves the singular number. On the other hand the Armenian consistently retains the plural at occurrences of τῶν λεχθέντων with no modified noun.[95]

3: V reads εἴδει, which is found in Tischendorf's transcript, and is edited by Grossmann. The other editors all print ἔδει, and the only one to comment on the word is Tischendorf, who says: "Grossm. per errorem manifestum εἴδει." Of course, εἴδει would be nonsensical here, and the Armenian corresponds to ἔδει. Probably the scribe of V carried over the initial ει- from the preceding εἰκών.

4: V reads εἰς ἀλληγορίαν, which hardly makes sense. Already Mai noted that the Armenian corresponds to εἰς ἀλλήλας, and approved that Greek. Grossmann printed εἰς ἀλληγορίαν with no comment, but Tischendorf emended to εἰς ἀλλήλας on the basis of the Armenian. Harris and Marcus follow that emendation, and both Conybeare and Terian note that the Armenian corresponds to εἰς ἀλλήλας.

5: Aucher edits the singular in Armenian for κάλλη, but one Armenian manuscript has the plural, which I suppose was the original translation (as at *Abr.* 159 and *Dec.* 26). On the other hand, for the Greek plural at 2.68 l. 17 all the Armenian manuscripts have the singular (as at *Contempl.* 78).

6: Terian reports that the Armenian omits ἐστι. A few words earlier the Armenian represents the participial phrase εἰς ὤν with the finite verb է (*ē*), and likely it was felt that another finite verb for ἐστι would be awkward.

---

[93] In each word the final letter is the suffixed "article."

[94] The closest parallels I have found to the words here are *Migr.* 117 (εἶδος τῶν λεχθέντων), and *Plant.* 40 (δεῖγμα τοῦ λεχθέντος), with which may be compared *Plant.* 61 (δεῖγμα . . . τῶν εἰρημένων). I see that Aristotle, *Top.* 134b31, has εἶδος τοῦ λεχθέντος.

[95] There are three such places where we have the Armenian: *Abr.* 188 (*ասիցելոց* [*asic'eloc's*], plural); *Dec.* 95 (*ասացեալսն* [*asac'ealsn*], plural); *Spec.* 1.308 (*ասացելոց* [*asac'eloc's*], plural).

7:      Marcus notes that the Armenian "either had a different text or mis-understood the original." while Terian observes that the Armeniar omits πάλιν ἕνωσιν. And in connection with ἕνωσιν Grossmann aptly refers to *Cher*. 29: τὴν τῶν ἀκράτων δυνάμεων σύνοδόν τε καὶ κρᾶσιν.[96]

8–9: Marcus and Terian observe that the Armenian has no equivalent of ἑκάτερον. It is possible that there was a transcriptional error (*ե՛ն* [en] being written by a scribal leap for *ե՛ն երկոքեան* [en erkokʿean]), but it seems to me more likely that the term was simply deemed superfluous here by the translators.

9:      For ἑτέρῳ τρόπῳ the Armenian has *միւսով եւս աւրինակաւ* (*miwsov ews awrinakaw*), which might be retroverted as ἑτέρῳ ἔτι τρόπῳ.[97] Ⴀerian, though, states that the Armenian adds καὶ after ἑτέρῳ. On the other hand, I suggest that the Armenian has simply rendered ἕτερος by *միւս եւս* (*miws ews*), as we find at *QE* 2.14.[98]

9:      Corresponding to κατά Aucher prints *ը նդ* (*ənd*), as found in D E, and which renders ὑπό thrice in 2.68. But A L have *ը ստ* (*əst*), which is the regular rendering of κατά.[99] The reading *ը նդ* (*ənd*) is probably an assimilation to the occurrence of that word three words later (see the next note).

10:     For προσβολήν the Armenian has *ը նդ միմեանս հարութիւն* (*ənd mimeans harutʿiwn*), which Aucher renders as "inter se connexionem."[100] Marcus thus states that the Armenian has added "to one another."[101] Nevertheless, I am inclined to think that the translators saw our Greek, and used *ը նդ միմեանս* (*ənd mimeans*) to represent the prepositional prefix.[102]

---

[96] *Anecdoton*, 19 n. 19.

[97] See Marcus, "Index," s.vv.

[98] This equivalence is also given at *NB* 2:282C.

[99] See Marcus, "Index," s.v.; this rendering occurs 15 times in *Prov*.

[100] The entire phrase is cited at *NB* 2:276B, s.v. *միմեանս* (*mimeans*), where the Greek equivalent is given as σύμπτωσις (not in Philo's Greek). The word *հարութիւն* (*harutʿiwn*), is not itself cited in the *NB*, but is apparently related to *հարկանեմ* (*harkanem*), which is glossed (*NB* 2:63B–64A) with τύπτω, πλήσσω, et alia.

[101] Support for such a view might be found in *ի միմեանս* (*i mimeans*) for εἰς ἄλληλα at *Prov*. 2.10.

[102] We find that same rendering at *Prov*. 2.100, where προσαράξει is translated as *ը նդ միմեանս բախելով* (*ənd mimeans baxelov*). The only other use of προσβολή in Philo for which the Armenian is extant is *Dec*. 147, which is translated in a manner completely unlike what we find here at l. 10.

10–11: The verb ἔχηται seems to me inappropriately vague to describe this relationship between the chief powers. The Armenian has, in place of this verb at the end of the clause, the phrase "is a watcher of" (տեսունչ իցէ [tesuč' ic'ē]) earlier.[103] (Aucher has "spectatrix sit," and Marcus "might be a spectator of." Terian seems to translate the Greek with "est associée à," but in the appendix gives σκοπεῖν for the Armenian, although a finite verb seems required.) I wonder if the Greek may be corrupted, but have no suggestion to make. (On the thought, see *Cher.* 29.)

11:	For συννεύουσιν the Armenian has ի միմեանս հային (*i mimeans hayin*), which Aucher renders as "se mutuo respiciunt." Marcus thus states that the Greek has omitted "at each other." However, in his earlier index, Marcus cites ի միմեանս (*i mimeans*) as representing συν- at *QE* 2.66, which can only be this place.[104] And this view seems to me more likely.

12:	For τοῖς νῦν οὖσιν the Armenian has այնոցիկ որ ի միասին են (*aynoc'ik or i miasin en*), which corresponds to τοῖς συνοῦσιν, as noted by Mai, Conybeare, Marcus, Terian, and Runia. Indeed, Runia aptly remarks that the Armenian translators were influenced by the earlier συννεύουσιν, and says: "The Greek reading is to be retained."

2.67:

1:	As noted by Terian, for σοι the Armenian has ձեզ (*jez*), which corresponds to ὑμῖν, instead of the singular dative form քեզ (*k'ez*). The other editors make no comment, despite Aucher's "vobis." Indeed, Marcus and Terian translate the Greek ("to thee" and "à toi") rather than the Armenian. There can be no doubt that the error is on the part of the Armenian translators; no LXX witness has ὑμῖν, which would hardly make sense here. (Philo does not elsewhere quote these opening words of Exod 25:21.)

3:	Terian says that the Armenian represents λαμβάνουσι instead of λαμβάνει. However, I would suppose that the Armenian uses the plural verb because the word for νοῦς, i.e., միտք (*mitk'*), is a plural, which is regularly used for the singular νοῦς. Similarly, at 2.68 l. 6 the Armenian renders νοῦς with միտք (*mitk'*) and has a plural verb. At both places Aucher renders both noun and verb in the singular.

---

[103] The Armenian word is a *nomen agentis* from the verb "to see." It occurs at Acts 20:28 and 1 Pet 2:25 for ἐπίσκοπος. That word occurs eleven times in Philo, but regrettably not in the works translated into Armenian.

[104] "Index," s.v. միմեանս (*mimeans*).

4:      V has δωρηφόρων, as edited by Mai. Tischendorf's transcript has that writing, with his corrections to the first two vowels written supralinearly; in the margin another hand (no doubt Grossmann's) has written δορυφό-ρων. In his edition Grossmann prints δρυφόρων, but evidently by error, since in his note 21 he writes δωρηφόρων, says "Lege: δορυφόρων," and has two references. The first is "2, 546, 32," which is the location in Mangey of *Legat.* 6, where we find: τῶν δορυφόρων αὐτοῦ [scil. τοῦ θεοῦ] δυνάμεων. The second is "Arm. 2, 172," which I have not found.[105] Tischendorf and later editors simply print δορυφόρων with no comment.[106]

2.68:

1–2:   The lemma in the Armenian has two words that are missing in V: σοι and δυεῖν. Marcus and Terian note the discrepancy. Runia says: "Philo sometimes abbreviates the biblical lemma he is quoting, so it is difficult to determine whether these words were originally present in this passage." But Marcus states that the two words are "found in LXX and Heb. [i.e., the MT]," and aptly notes that Philo cites this verse in two other places (*Her.* 166 and *Fug.* 101), and at each place has both σοι and δυεῖν (or δυοῖν). In fact, there is a third occurrence; in *Deo* 5 we find a citation of the same passage, which includes both "you" and "two," and which despite some minor differences in the Armenian is retroverted into the usual Greek text of Exod 25:21.[107] Moreover, within the LXX tradition σοι is omitted by only six manuscripts and δύο by only one.[108] In any case, at least "two" seems

---

[105]   This may be a garbled reference to, e.g., *QG* 4.2 (at Aucher, vol. 2, p. 242), where (near the beginning) we find սպասաւորակք զաւրութիւնք (*spasaworakk' zawru-t'iwnk'*), translated as "virtutes ministrae," "ministering powers," and "puissances servantes." (In Marcus's translation this is at PLCL Supp 1:270, the last line.) This would correspond to δορυφόροι δυνάμεις, as in *QE* 2.67, although at *QG* 4.2 we have the adjective in Armenian, for which *NB* 2:737B gives δορυφορικόν, citing this passage.

[106]   At *Deo* 4, in a similar context, the Armenian uses պաշտպան (*paštpan*), for which *NB* 2:598A gives only ὑπερασπιστής in Greek. Nevertheless, Siegert (no doubt correctly) retroverts it as δορυφόρος; see *Gottesbezeichnung,* 26 n. 49, and 71–73.

[107]   See Siegert, *Gottesbezeichnung,* 26 ll. 52–53, who does not comment on the discrepancies with the Armenian at *QE* 2.68.

[108]   The Göttingen LXX's citation of Philo at Exod 25:21 is inaccurate. Only the evidence from PCW is cited (by volume and page), but for that we find: "δυοιν Phil III 38 132ᵃᴾ; δυειν Phil III 132ᵗᵉ." However, Wendland prints δυεῖν at both places, following Pap, the Coptos Papyrus, at *Her.* 166 (PCW 3:38) and G at *Fug.* 101 (PCW 3:132). At *Her.* 166 all the codices (which do not include "Pap") have δυοῖν, and at *Fug.* 101

relevant to Philo's discussion; so it is implausible that Philo would have chosen to omit that. I thus find it more likely that the scribe of V (or an ancestor) made two easy slips in the lemma: omitting σοι after λαλήσω (σοι similar to σω), and omitting δυεῖν after τῶν (a leap from τῶν to δυεῖν). Consequently I have emended the Greek and included these words in the translation. (And I follow PCW in writing δυεῖν rather than δυοῖν as the form likely to have been preferred by Philo.[109])

3: Although Mai, Grossmann, and Tischendorf correctly printed διὰ τούτου (as in V), Harris printed διὰ τοῦτο, and he was followed by Marcus and then Terian. However, Früchtel wrote διὰ τούτου, and Marcus stated in a note "l. τούτου," although in his appendix he prints the Greek as διὰ τοῦτο with no comment. Indeed, Arm has *սովաւ* (*sovaw*), the instrumental form of "this," which seems rather to agree with διὰ τούτου.[110] And thus Marcus translates "by this" and Terian "par cela," renderings which seem to require διὰ τούτου, whereas διὰ τοῦτο would (I suppose) be "therefore," which hardly makes sense.

4–5: After λαλεῖ the Armenian has added *դէպ* (*dēp*), which Aucher translates as "quasi." Marcus suggests that this is the translators' way to indicate the force of the following superlative. In any case, it seems to be a peculiar addition.

5: As at 2.62 l. 5, the Armenian has omitted τῆς βασιλικῆς, evidently by a scribal leap: *արարչ ակ անն եւ արքունեանն* (*ararč'ak<u>ann</u> ew ark'une<u>ann</u>*).

6: V has written νοῦν after the verb, although the sense requires νοῦς, as found in the Armenian. Mai and Grossmann edited νοῦν, as found in Tischendorf's transcript. But in his edition Tischendorf corrected to νοῦς, and he was followed by the later editors.

---

the other codex (H) has δυοῖν. Thus, the citation should read: "δυειν Phil III 38te 132te; δυοιν Phil III 38ap 132ap." Regrettably, the selection from *Her.* found in Vat. gr. 379 begins a few lines after the citation of Exod. 25:21.

[109] See also Siegert, *Gottesbezeichnung,* 26 n. 52, and the note on 2.62 l. 3 above.

[110] However, elsewhere for διὰ τούτου we find *ի ձեռն սորա* (*i ježn sora*) at *Leg.* 2.38, 2.81, and *Dec.* 93, *ի ձեռն նորա* (*i ježn nora*) at *QG* 1.21, and *ի ձեռն այսորիկ* (*i ježn aysorik*) at *Abr.* 34 and *QG* 2.59 (where R, like Harris, shifts to τοῦτο). I cannot account for the discrepancy, but note that *սովաւ* (*sovaw*) occurs at *Leg.* 2.12 for ἐν τούτῳ. On the other hand, διὰ τοῦτο is usually rendered by *վասն այսորիկ* (*vasn aysorik*), sometimes by *վասն այնորիկ* (*vasn aynorik*), and sometimes in other ways.

6:     For the phrase μέσος ὤν the Armenian has ֆբրու զի ի դէպ ի միջոցʻին է (*ibru zi i dēp i mijocʻin ē*), which Aucher renders as "eoquod in medio est conveniente," and Marcus as "inasmuch as it is appropriately in the middle." Terian takes the addition to be of (the equivalent of) ἄτε.[111] But see *Prov.* 2.15, where δὲ καί is rendered as դէպ է զի (*dēp ē zi*), and *Prov.* 2.99, where դէպ լինի զի եւ (*dēp lini zi ew*) has no counterpart in Greek. I suppose that here at l. 6 the translators have simply introduced a circumlocution for the participial phrase, as they have at, e.g., *Prov.* 2.51 (πηγή τις ὤν = ֆբրու զի աղբիւր է [*ibru zi ałbiwr ē*]); *QG* 2.54 (χρηστὸς ὤν καὶ φιλάνθρωπος ὁ θεός = ֆբրու զի բարի է եւ քաղցր եւ մարդասէր հայրն [*ibru zi bari ē ew kʻalcʻr ew mardasēr hayrn*]);[112] *QG* 4.204 (μὴ ὤν ὑβριστής = ֆբրեւ ոչ թշնամանող [*ibru očʻ tʻšnamanoł*]).[113]

6:     After οὐδέν, rendered as often by ոչ ինչ (*očʻinčʻ*), the Armenian adds ամենեւին (*amenewin*), which would correspond to ἄπαν, καθόλου, ὅλως, and the like (see *NB* 1:68B), and which Aucher renders as "omnino." Although it is possible that such a word has dropped out of the Greek, I suppose that the Armenian translators have simply added a word for emphasis.

7–8:   While Mai, Grossmann, Tischendorf, and Früchtel write παρ' ἑκάτερα (as found in V), Harris edited παρ' ἑκατέρᾳ, and was followed by Marcus and Terian. In fact παρ' ἑκάτερα seems to be correct (unless ἑκάτερα were taken as a modifier), and is found sixteen times in PCW as well as at *Deo* 4 (in connection with which Siegert refers to *Abr.* 121, where we indeed find παρ' ἑκάτερα in a similar context, although the Armenian version there is quite different). Note that at *Deo* 4 the Armenian is the same as here at *QE* 2.68, but Siegert inserts δυεῖν.

8:     Mai and Grossmann correctly edit οἵ, as is found in Tischendorf's transcript. However, in his edition Tischendorf omits it, noting: "post ἑκάτερα apud Grossm. οἵ additur, quod locum habere nequit." The word is thus missing in subsequent editions. For what it is worth, the Armenian also has a relative clause at this point (որք . . . թուին [*orkʻ . . . tʻuin*],

---

[111] Terian then renders the phrase: "aussi longtemps que le Verbe divin est présent." Note that, for example, ἄτε is rendered at *Prov.* 2.31 as ֆբր զի (*ibr zi*), at *Prov.* 2.51 as ֆբրու զի (*ibru zi*), and at *Prov.* 2.110 as ֆբրու (*ibru*).

[112] Evidently the florilegia have changed the original πατήρ to θεός, and have expressed χρηστός with a doublet, as also at *Spec.* 3.6 (բար եւ լաւ [*bar ew law*]), in contrast to *Prov.* 2.27 (բար [*bar*] alone).

[113] Petit states (PAPM 33:207 n. 15): "ὡς mendose legit arm."

which corresponds to οἵ . . . δοκοῦσι), although the version often thus rewrites participial constructions.

9:     Mai and Grossmann correctly edit εἰρήνης, as is found in Tischendorf's transcript. But Tischendorf omits it with no comment, and thus no doubt simply by error. Harris deduced from the discrepancy between Grossmann and Tischendorf that Grossmann had added it to the Greek: "Gr. add εἰρήνης (rightly)." Marcus and Terian then follow Harris in believing that V omits the word.

11:     Although Terian states that the Armenian omits the equivalent of χάριν, I believe that it is represented by փոխանակ (*p'oxanak*), as Marcus also held.[114]

12:     It has not been previously noted that for δὲ the Armenian has քանզի (*k'anzi*), which corresponds to γὰρ (Aucher has "namque"). But δὲ seems to make better sense, as seen in the modern translations.

15:     Where V has ὁ λέγων, Aucher edits ասող ն, the later form of ասաւղ ն (*asawln*), and comments in a note: "Sic in marg. Ms. A. eodem calamo, ասող ն [*asōln*] (ut participium) recte; sicut et infra habetur: corrupte itaque in textu scriptum erat Mss. A. et C. ասելով [*aselov*] (ut gerundia)." Note that Aucher's A is my D; I have not seen his C (Venice 1334), but my A E L have the same reading. The participle (i.e., "the speaker") is also found for τὸν λέγοντα at l. 40, and Aucher is referring to that occurrence. But for ὁ λέγων at ll. 34 and 39 the Armenian has որ ասէն (*or asēn*), which is a relative clause with the suffixed article,[115] literally "he who speaks."

15:     V writes εἴ τις with no connective, as found in Mai, Tischendorf's transcript, and Grossmann. But in his edition Tischendorf writes εἰ δέ τις, and notes: "Grossm. δέ omittit." And later editors just follow him in writing δέ. However, the Armenian has արդ (*ard*), meaning "thus" or "so," which most often renders οὖν.[116] I have accordingly added οὖν, although I cannot account for its omission.[117]

16:     For κατανοῆσαι the Armenian has հայել եւ իմանալ (*hayel ew imanal*), which Marcus translates as "view and understand." But instead of seeing

---

[114] See "Index," s.v.

[115] See Jensen, *Altarmenische Grammatik*, 209 (§549).

[116] See Marcus, "Index," 257. At *Prov.* 2.23 արդ (*ard*) renders δέ, but there are ten places in the Greek fragments of *Prov.* where it renders οὖν.

[117] At *Cher.* 19; *Det.* 124; *Somn.* 1.44; and *Spec.* 4.79 we find εἴ τις οὖν.

this as a doublet, Marcus asserts that the Greek omits "and understand."[118]
I believe, though, that the presence of a doublet is confirmed by the following renderings: *Leg.* 2.81 (κατανοησάτω = *ի մխտ առց է և խմացի* [*i mit arc 'ē ew imasc 'i*]), *Leg.* 2.85 (κατανοήσω = *հայեցեալ տեսից* [*hayec 'eal tesic '*]); *Abr.* 73 (κατανοήσεις = *հասեալ իմացիս* [*haseal imasc 'is*]); *Prov.* 2.27 (κατα-νοεῖς = *հայիս տեսանել* [*hayis tesanel*]); *QG* 2.5 (κατανοεῖν = *հայել տեսանել* [*hayel tesanel*]).[119]

19:    V has ἐστι πρεσβύτερος, as found in Mai and Tischendorf's transcript, and in the Armenian. But Grossmann omitted ἐστι in his edition, and all later editors followed him.

19:    The final -ου of V's λόγου is written as a supralinear ligature that is not quite as clearly -ου as is found elsewhere (e.g., in the preceding τοῦ and the following λόγου). On the other hand, the scribe writes final -ς even superlinearly as separate letters (as in the preceding ὄντος), and Mai and Tischendorf's transcript both report λόγου. So that is doubtless the reading, but seems clearly incorrect, even though it is found in Mai and Grossmann. Tischendorf corrects to λόγος, as in the Armenian, and also inserts the definite article, thus arriving at the construction ὁ τοῦ ὄντος λόγος, as found at *Fug.* 110, 112; *Somn.* 2.237. (A slightly fuller form occurs at *QE* 2.122.) However, the Armenian (*էին բան* [*ēin ban*]) does not add the suffix *ն* (*n*), which would correspond to ὁ, although this could have easily been omitted after *բան* (*ban*).

20:    As Conybeare and Marcus remark, before οὐσία the Armenian has *արդարև* (*ardarew*), which would correspond to ὄντως. Thus, Aucher and Marcus translate with "vere" and "truly," respectively (but Terian chooses an adjective, "vraie"). Marcus suggests that the Armenian has mistakenly duplicated (more or less) the preceding ὄντος or ὄντων. On the other hand, I would be tempted to suppose that the Armenian is correct here, and that ὄντως has been omitted in the Greek (after ὄντων); but it seems that in his extant Greek Philo does not use that adverb in connection with οὐσία.[120] However, at *QG* 4.130 we find a similar phrase: *որ արդարև եութ 'եամբն լց 'oyc ' zamenayn* (*or ardarew ēut 'eambn lc 'oyc ' zamenayn*), which is trans-

---

[118]   But in his "Index," s.v. *իմանամ* (*imanam*), he takes the phrase as a doublet.

[119]   The Greek and Armenian are found in Paramelle, *Philon d'Alexandrie: Questions sur la Genèse II 1–7*, 150; on the equivalence see my review, 140.

[120]   But Plato does; see *Soph.* 248a11: τὴν ὄντως οὐσίαν; *Phaedr.* 247c7: οὐσία ὄντως οὖσα; and *Leg.* 891e8–9: τῆς ὄντως οὐσίας.

lated as "qui vera essentia implevit omnia," "who truly with His being fills all things," and "celui qui, par son essence, a vraiment tout remplit." Here Aucher has chosen an adjective. Marcus retroverts the crucial phrase as ὄντως τῇ οὐσίᾳ.

20: For θείου the Armenian has էն (ēn), which corresponds to ὄντος (perhaps the genitive of "the One who is"), as noted by Conybeare, Marcus, and Terian. Marcus suggests that the Armenian աստուածային (astuacayin) was abbreviated as ային (ayin), which was then misread. Alternatively, I suggest that the Armenian translators (or perhaps a scribe) assimilated the wording here to the wording in the preceding line.

21: After σχίζονται Tischendorf added αἱ, and he was followed by Harris and Marcus. Terian does not print αἱ, but notes that the Armenian adds it. (Naturally, Tischendorf could not have known that from Aucher's Latin.) In fact, the suffix ն (n), which often corresponds to the Greek definite article, is attached to the word for "two." Of course, as Tischendorf notes, αἱ could easily have been lost by haplography (σχιζονται αι). But Marcus, Terian, and Runia (calling the addition "unnecessary") translate without a definite article, and it seems to me that that makes better sense.

23: V reads αἱ ἀρχαί, as found in Mai, Tischendorf's transcript, and Grossmann. Tischendorf corrected to ἄρχει, which seems required by the sense, and is supported by the Armenian. The phrase καθ᾿ ἣν ἄρχει in relation to the kingly power is found at *Plant.* 86 and *Her.* 166 (and καθ᾿ ἣν ὁ πεποιηκὼς ἄρχει at *Fug.* 95), while καθ᾿ ἣν ἔθηκε in relation to the creative power occurs at *Conf.* 137; *Migr.* 182; and *Mos.* 2.99 (and κατὰ ταύτην ἔθηκε at *Spec.* 1.307).

23: Terian observes that the Armenian corresponds to τοῦ δημιουργοῦ. Aucher, in a note to his արարչին (ararč'in), adds in parentheses այսինքն յարարչէն (aysink'n yararč'ēn), i.e., "namely, from the creator." The point of this remark seems to be to inform the reader that the genitive արարչի (ararč'i), to which is suffixed ն (n), should be understood as an ablative, and so Aucher writes յարարչէն (yararč'ēn), which is formed from the prefix ի (i), the ablative արարչէ (ararč'ē), and the suffix ն (n). How Aucher understands this is made clear by his Latin: "princeps est factorum a creatore," i.e., "(the royal power) rules over the things made by the Creator." However, in the light of the Greek it seems probable that there has been a simple transposition of letters in the transmission of the Armenian: the translators wrote արարիչն (ararič'n), which corresponds precisely to ὁ δημιουργός. And I have thus emended the Armenian.

Marcus has misinterpreted Aucher's comment as meaning that there is a "variant," and translates Aucher's text in a footnote as that variant.[121] In the body of his translation Marcus has silently corrected the Armenian from the Greek. It is curious that no editor before Terian commented on the discrepancy between the Greek nominative and Aucher's "a creatore."

25:    V reads κύριον, as was edited by Mai and as is found in Tischendorf's transcript. The Armenian renders it with իսկ (*isk*).[122] However, Grossmann omitted κύριον, and the later editors all followed him. Although for the Armenian word Aucher has "proprium," no editor suggests that the lack of a corresponding Greek word is a textual difficulty. But a complication is that իսկ (*isk*) is also a conjunction, often rendering δέ.[123] That is evidently what Terian had in mind with his "aussi." Marcus omits the word in his translation, perhaps viewing it (in its sense of "autem") as superfluous, or perhaps following his Greek rather than the Armenian. In any case, with V's Greek before us, we can see that Aucher has the appropriate rendering.

There is no evident cause of Grossmann's omission (although the word is at the end of the line in Tischendorf's transcript). But there is no doubt as to the reading of V. The closest parallel I have found where both the Greek and the Armenian are extant is *Leg.* 1.75 (κύριον ὄνομα = իսկ եւ տէր աՆուՆ [*isk ew tēr anun*]), but there the Armenian has used a doublet. Another parallel is *Mut.* 14, where we find τὸ ἴδιον καὶ κύριον (scil. ὄνομα). Similarly, at *Deo* 4 we find աՆուՆ Նորա իսկ է եւ տէր (*anun nora isk ē ew tēr*), which Siegert retroverts as ὄνομα αὐτῷ ἐστιν ἴδιον καὶ κύριον. If this was the original Greek (as at *Mut.* 14), then the Armenian translators chose իսկ (*isk*) for ἴδιον and տէր (*tēr*) for κύριον when both words were present; note that the latter is the usual rendering of κύριος throughout the Armenian Bible as well as Philo. But it seems quite possible that the Armenian has a doublet at *Deo* 4, as at *Leg.* 1.75.

26:    V's (hardly intelligible) ἢ κολαστήριον is found in Mai, Tischendorf's transcript, and Grossmann (who prints κολαστήρεον). Tischendorf corrects

---

[121] PLCL Supp 2:116 n. i.

[122] See *NB* 1:868A, which cites for this word κύριον and "proprium." Note also that at *QE* 2.16 κυρίως is rendered as իսկապէս (*iskapēs*), an equivalence found at *NB* 1:868C (along with "proprie").

[123] See *NB* 1:868A–B, which cites δέ and "autem," and then further meanings. See also Marcus, "Index," s.v. In the Greek fragments of *Prov.* the word occurs 37 times, and 34 times renders δέ.

to ἡ κολαστήριος, as in the Armenian, and later editors follow him.

28–34: The enumeration of the various entities symbolically contained in the ark is confusing. A (naive) reading of Marcus's translation might result in the following list: (1) the incorporeal world, (2) the ordinances, (3) the legislative power, (4) the punitive power,[124] (5) the mercy-seat, (6) the propitious power, (7) the beneficent power, and then up above those (8) the creative power and (9) the royal power, and in their midst (10) the Logos, and above the Logos (11) the Speaker. But this count conflicts with the number seven that is later emphasized. In fact, items (3) and (4) are identical, and items (6) and (7) are identical; we simply have different names (and Philo uses yet others), as is made clear at ll. 25–26. Moreover, items (6) and (7) are subsumed under item (5), as is made explicit at *QE* 2.60. That (3) and (4) are subsumed under (2) is not, I believe, explicitly stated, but follows (more or less) from what Philo says at *QE* 2.59: the "testimonies" are related to the laws, i.e., to the legislative (= punitive) power. We thus arrive at a total of seven, as at the end of the section.[125] I have tried to punctuate the Greek and to arrange the English in accordance with this interpretation.

30:    Terian correctly observes that the Armenian corresponds to ἡ ἵλεως rather than to τὸ ἱλαστήριον, and Marcus reasonably judges that Հաշ տակ ան (haštakan) is an "obvious miswriting" of Հաշ տարան (haštaran).[126] Whether the error was made by the translators or by a later scribe is uncertain.[127]

31:    Where V has πίστις the Armenian has աղբիւր (ałbiwr), which corresponds to πηγή (Aucher "fons"), as noted by Mai, Conybeare, Marcus, and Terian (but not Grossmann, Tischendorf, or Harris). The word πηγή occurs

---

[124] I separate the legislative and the punitive, and the propitious and beneficent, since Marcus has "powers" at both places.

[125] See also the related enumerations at *Fug.* 94–95 and 100–101. By the way, the presence of ὁ λέγων at ll. 15, 34, and 39, and of τὸν λέγοντα at l. 40, surely removes any doubt about τοῦ λέγοντος at *Fug.* 95, as was expressed by Mangey and Wendland (see PLCL and PCH ad loc.)

[126] And he alters his "Index" appropriately; see the note on 2.64 l. 1 above.

[127] Note that Aucher's translation goes astray here; since another word that means ἡ ἵλεως follows, he (reasonably enough) translates only one. By the way, this other word, Հաշ տ (hašt), occurs there (2.68 l.31) and at 2.66 l. 12 for ἵλεως, while Հաշ տակ ան (haštakan) renders that Greek at 2.68 ll. 3, 25, and 32. I cannot account for the fluctuation. Similarly, for what would seem to be ἵλεως we have Հաշ տ (hašt) at *QE* 2.60 and 2.61 (once each), but then at 2.61 also Հաշ տարար (haštarar).

earlier (l. 20) and makes much better sense. Nevertheless, all editors have printed πίστις. In majuscules the words are similar (ΠΙCTIC for ΠΗΓΗ; imagine that the C is less rounded), and perhaps the scribe was influenced by the surrounding words (ἥτις ἐστὶ and τῆς) to write πίστις. I have thus emended the Greek. Runia, while approving πηγή, translates V's Greek.

33:     Where V has ὑπεμφαίνεται, which does not occur in Philo's Greek, the Armenian has աււաւելեալ եալ է (aŕaweleal ē), which is translated by Aucher as "excellit." Marcus states that the Armenian means "there is multiplied," but adds that it is "evidently a corruption" of երեւելի է (ereweli ē), which would mean "there appears." Presumably Marcus takes this as representing the meaning of ὑπεμφαίνεται. Following this conjecture he prints as his translation "appears." Terian follows Marcus and this conjecture (as it seems) by rendering the Armenian as "semble être." However, in his notes on the Greek text Terian states that the Armenian corresponds to ὑπερβάλλεται, although that does not seem to be the meaning found in his translation. But in fact the Armenian that is found in the manuscripts, աււաւելեալ եալ է (aŕaweleal ē), does correspond (as can be seen from Aucher's translation) to ὑπερβάλλεται. Furthermore, of the ninety-five occurrences of ὑπερβάλλω in Philo, eleven occur in portions of Philo that are translated into Armenian. At *Abr.* 267 it is not rendered.[128] At *Leg.* 1.58 it is rendered with գերազանցեմ (gerazanc'em).[129] At *Abr.* 252 and *QE* 2.105 it is rendered with զանցուցանեմ (zanc'uc'anem).[130] Finally, at seven passages (*Abr.* 40, 154,[131] 167, 194; *Spec.* 3.34, 3.45; *Prov.* 2.50) ὑπερβάλλω is translated by աււաւելում (aŕawelum).[132] So most likely the present passage is another example. Runia also approves of Terian's retroversion as making "much better sense," and accordingly translates as "has a superior position." But how the corruption

---

[128]   The word is omitted in Greek by the manuscripts except BEK.

[129]   This Armenian verb does not occur in Marcus's index, but the Armenian lexicon (*NB* 1:543B) glosses it with ὑπερβάλλω, ὑπερβαίνω, and ὑπερέχω. Marcus does note that the related abstract noun գերազանցութիւն (gerazanc'ut'iwn) occurs twice for ὑπερβολή in *QE* 1.6, an equivalence also found in *NB* 1:543C. (See further my "Philo's *Quaestiones in Exodum* 1.6.")

[130]   Marcus cites the second example, and the Armenian lexicon (*NB* 1:715A) glosses it with ὑπερβάλλω and προσυπερβάλλω.

[131]   CFGMP have ὑποβάλλει.

[132]   See *NB* 1:297C–298A, although ὑπερβάλλω is not given as an equivalent. Marcus's "Index" informs us that this verb translates πλεονεκτέω at *QE* 2.64.

to ὑπεμφαίνεται occurred is unclear; perhaps the scribe recalled ἐμφαίνει back at 2.68 l. 3, although that is a curious choice.

36: Where V has δύο the Armenian has *ի ձեռն որոյ* (*i jeřn oroy*), which corresponds precisely to δι᾽ οὗ, as Conybeare and Marcus note, and as we find at *Abr.* 262; *Dec.* 93; *Spec.* 1.81; *Prov.* 2.33.[133] (Aucher translates as "quatenus.") On the other hand, Terian states that the Armenian has the equivalent of διά. The error in the Armenian here must be due to the translators or to earlier Greek scribes, not to the Armenian scribes. (If the translators had translated δύο, they would have written *երկու* [*erku*], which could hardly have been corrupted into *ի ձեռն որոյ* [*i jeřn oroy*], whereas a misreading of δύο as δι᾽ οὗ is much more likely.)

38: Before *արարիչ ն* (*ararič῾n*) there is, as Terian notes, no equivalent of πρός. I suppose that a preceding *առ* (*ař*) has been omitted by scribal error.

38: As noted by Conybeare and Marcus, for ἤ the Armenian has *եւ* (*ew*), which regularly corresponds to καί. Indeed, for the phrase μᾶλλον ἤ we usually find *առաւել քան* (*arawel k῾an*), as at, e.g., *QG* 1.17; 2.2 (Paramelle), 2.16, 2.54, 2.54; 4.169, 4.191, 4.193; *QE* 2.18, 2.25, 2.38. Perhaps the error here is connected with the following writing of (the equivalent) of τὸ γένος.

38: For V's τὸ γεγονός, which seems clearly correct, the Armenian has the equivalent of τὸ γένος, as Conybeare, Marcus, and Terian observe. The identical error occurs at *Leg.* 2.17, where we find one Greek manuscript (A) supported by Arm in having γένος, as well as at *Her.* 206, where only Pap has γεγονός while γένος is read by the codices and N, and at *Praem.* 85, where H has γένος (followed by Turnebus) while the other manuscripts have γεγονός. Thus, it seems possible both here and at *Leg.* 2.17 that we have either a misreading by the Armenian translators or an earlier error by a Greek scribe that was present in the *Vorlage* of Arm.

39: Conybeare, Marcus, and Terian note that for V's ἕκτος (which is certainly correct) the Armenian has the equivalent of ἕκαστος. Again one can suppose either an error by the Armenian translators or an earlier corruption in the Greek.

39: At the top line of f. 388ᵛ V clearly has (or at least had) καταρχὴν, as edited by Mai, although the tear in the last folio has removed most of the χη. But it seems to me that the original reading can only have been καταρχὴν; the tear is hardly the width of one letter, and we can still see the lower

---

[133] It also translates δι᾽ ἧς at *Abr.* 71; *Spec.* 1.342; *QG* 1.51; 2.6 (Paramelle). (Note that Armenian has no distinctions of gender.)

left line of the χ and the right half of the η. The grave accent is written over the final ν, as is the scribe's custom. Three lines further down ἀρχὴν occurs (this is 2.68 l. 41, so accented), and one can readily compare that word with the remnants at line 1. Above the final ν with its accent the later hand has written χὴν again for the sake of clarity.

Besides the tear there is some further damage to the top of this last page, which has involved the loss of two letters. Immediately after καταρ-χὴν we read οιῆ for ποιῆ, with simply a blank area where the π stood. And immediately below that blank area is another one where the ω of πρῶτον once stood. I cannot account for the loss of these two letters, but I think that there can be no doubt that V originally had ποιῆ and πρῶτον. In his transcript Tischendorf ignores these two blank spaces and simply writes ποιῆ and πρωτον (*sic*, with accent and without). I suppose that he thought that it was obvious what the missing letters were, although it is also possible that these letters were lost after his examination. In any case, I will consider the readings ποιῆ and πρῶτον to be non-controversial.

But let us return to καταρχὴν. In his transcript Tischendorf writes "καταρ. . ν̀," and then adds "χη ?" in the margin. In fact he meant the two dots to represent the length (i.e. two letters) of the (mostly) missing text, for which he suggested χη. However, Grossmann seems to have interpreted the dots (not unreasonably) as simply indicating a lacuna, since at his note 32 he prints "την καταρ—ν ποιῆ," and comments: "Nisi me omnia fallunt, legendum est: καταρίθμησιν." His text, though, has καταριδμησιν [*sic*], without accent, which must be a misprint for καταρίθμησιν. This conjecture is based not on the (Latin translation of the) Armenian, but rather on the sense of the passage. Tischendorf then edits καταρίθμησιν with no comment, and he is followed by the later editors. Since no one seems ever to have questioned the appropriateness and Philonic origin of the phrase καταρίθμησιν ποιῆ, we might judge Grossmann's conjecture as having been an unqualified success.

However, let us look (finally) at the Armenian, which has զսկիզբն առասցես (*zskizbn arasc'es*).[134] This phrase is translated as "inchoabis," "make the beginning," and "débutez." Marcus's version is the most literal,

---

[134] Aucher prints սկիզբն (*skizbn*). However, three of the four manuscripts I have seen prefix զ (*z*), the sign of the accusative. And two of those three write զսկիսբն (*zskisbn*), which I take to be a slight phonetic miswriting.

since զսկիզբն (zskizbn) corresponds to ἀρχήν,[135] and արասցես (arasc'es) corresponds to ποιῇ.[136] One would thus suppose that the Armenian would be naturally retroverted to ἀρχὴν ποιῇ. However, with an eye on the Greek that he read in Harris, Marcus states: "The Armenian translator appears to have read καταρχήν instead of καταρίθμησιν, as in the Greek frag." Thus he arrives at the actual reading of V by a retroversion from the Armenian.[137]

And Marcus's retroversion is surely correct. Although *in abstracto* we might expect ἀρχὴν ποιῇ to be the origin of the Armenian, given our two choices here, there can be no hesitation: the Armenian supports καταρχὴν ποιῇ. And since that is the reading of V, that is the reading we adopt.

Unfortunately, neither καταρίθμησις nor καταρχή occurs in the extant Greek of Philo, although καταριθμέω occurs twenty-three times (and συγκαταριθμέω twice) and κατάρχω occurs twelve times.[138]

Further, it is interesting that Mai in his Latin has "initium numerandi feceris," while editing καταρχήν. Perhaps he intended to emend the Greek, but there is no note to that effect. Finally, an interesting parallel to QE 2.68 is found at *Abr.* 12: εἰ μέντοι καταριθμήσειέ τις ἀπὸ τοῦ πρώτου . . . εὑρήσει τέταρτον.[139] Perhaps this passage was in Grossmann's mind when he made his conjecture.

40:     As is seen in Aucher's translation, the Armenian lacks the verb "you will find," as is read in the Greek; Marcus and Terian place the verb from the Greek in parentheses. Here the Greek is surely correct, and we have an omission in the Armenian. The simplest explanation is that the Armenian at an earlier stage read արասցես գտցես (ara*sc'es* gtc'es) for ποιῇ εὑρήσεις,

---

[135] *NB* 2:721B, and Marcus, "Index," 278.

[136] *NB* 1:308B, and Marcus, "Index," 256 (s.v. առնեմ [aṙnem]); the Armenian is the subjunctive aorist. The Greek is (assuming that V's ποιῇ is correct except for the missing iota subscript) the middle/passive indicative (or subjunctive) form (see LSJ s.v., A.II.5), which can be paralleled by κατάλογον ποιεῖται at *Deus* 126, ποιεῖται τὴν ἀναφοράν at *Her.* 314, and ποιεῖται κατάλογον at *Abr.* 31. Further, three times in the *Letter of Aristeas* (134, 200, 235) we find middle forms of ποιέω governing τὴν καταρχήν.

[137] At the very least, this confirms *something* about the possibility of such retroversions. But here the presence of the prefix κατα- in the Greek was crucial.

[138] *The Philo Index* cites 13 occurrences, but at QG 1.96 it does not correspond to the Armenian, as Petit indicates (PAPM 33:78).

[139] Here καταριθμέω is rendered by the Armenian թուեմ (t'uem), as also at *Dec.* 160 and QE 2.20. For that Armenian *NB* 1:820B gives only ἀριθμέω as the Greek equivalent.

and the second word dropped out by a scribal leap.[140] In fact, in the Greek
that follows we have seven objects of εὑρήσεις (three with δύναμιν understood), and in the Armenian all seven corresponding terms are prefixed
with the particle զ (z), which marks them as being in the accusative case
(as Marcus notes); we thus have evidence that the translators originally
wrote a governing verb. But in the absence of the verb, Aucher shifts the
construction in his translation, so that all seven nouns in Latin are in the
nominative case. (See further the note on l. 43.)

41:    V has ἀρχήν, as printed by all editors. However, Conybeare pointed
out that the Armenian իշխանական (*išxanakan*), translated by Aucher as
"principativa," corresponds to ἀρχικήν, and Runia independently made the
same conjecture.[141] At *Abr.* 124 we find the latter word similarly used for
the power called κύριος, and likewise translated by իշխանական (*išxanakan*).[142] Further, at *Deo* 5 we find իշխանականի (*išxanakani*), the dative
form, which Siegert initially retroverted as ἀρχοντικῇ.[143] However, Runia
suggested that this should be ἀρχικῇ, which Siegert accepted.[144] So it seems
certain that ἀρχήν here should be emended to ἀρχικήν. V's error doubtless
arose as a leap from χ to the similar-sounding κ.

43:    After the rendering of ἕβδομον, Aucher has added in parentheses the

---

[140]   The only place in the Armenian version of Philo where I have found զոգես
(*gtc'es*) is *QG* 2.2 (Paramelle), where though the Greek has εὑρήσει, as is required by
the context; so presumably the Armenian has a simple error for զոգէ (*gtc'ē*).

[141]   At *NB* 1:864C we find both ἀρχοντικός and ἀρχικός for the Armenian word.
But Runia cogently notes that only the latter is a Philonic word, occurring 7 times
(apart from *QE* 2.68). Marcus, "Index," 265, cites ἀρχή (the reading of V) for the
Armenian word from our passage.

[142]   Runia, "A Neglected Text," 207, erroneously cites *Abr.* 99. At that place we
find ἀρχικώτερον used of virtue, and translated by the Armenian comparative իշխա-
նագոյն (*išxanagoyn*); see *NB* 1:864C, where *Abr.* 99 is the only passage cited. Note further that ἀρχικός also occurs at *Prov.* 2.31, in the phrase τοῖς ἀρχικοῖς τὰς φύσεις (Mras,
following manuscript I), referring to "men naturally fitted to rule" (Colson, who has
τοῖς τὰς φύσεις ἀρχικοῖς). However, here the Armenian has "istis naturam corpulentis"
(Aucher's translation in his note), which corresponds to τοῖς τὰς φύσεις σερκικοῖς
(Conybeare, *Specimen*, 12; Aucher suggests τοῖς φύσεις σαρκικοῖς) or to τοῖς σαρκικοῖς
τὰς φύσεις (which is closer to the Armenian and to Mras's text), where in any case we
have the dittography of a sigma.

[143]   *Gottesbezeichnung,* 26, l. 62.

[144]   Runia, Review of Siegert, *Gottesbezeichnung, VC* 43 (1989): 3; Siegert, *Drei
hellenistisch-jüdische Predigten* 2 (WUNT 61; Tübingen: J. C. B. Mohr, 1992), 360.

copula է (*ē*) to match his construction in Latin; two Armenian manuscripts also have the copula. The temptation to add the copula derives from the loss of the verb corresponding to εὑρήσεις earlier, although neither the scribes nor Aucher removed the seven occurrences of the particle զ (*z*). (See further the note on l. 40.)

43:    Aucher writes զ՚ի (*z'i*) for the concatenation of զ (*z*), the prefix that designates the accusative case, and ի (*i*), the preposition that here corresponds to ἐκ. Thus we have a literal rendering of τὸν ἐκ. On the other hand, the single word զի (*zi*) is a conjunction.

Claremont, California

The Studia Philonica Annual 24 (2012) 69–84

ALEXANDRIA IN PHARAONIC EGYPT:
PROJECTIONS IN *DE VITA MOSIS*

RENÉ BLOCH

Who was Philo of Alexandria? A short, but honest answer to this question would be: We don't really know.[1] In spite of the impressively large oeuvre of Philo of Alexandria, there is very little one can say for sure about his life and his activities. While Philo's extensive philosophical work allows for a fairly good assessment of his philosophical and theological ways of understanding Judaism, his biography—in a simple chronological, but also in an intellectual sense—is very difficult to grasp. Philo only rarely speaks of himself.

We do not even know the exact dates of Philo's life. He was probably, or so it is stated in the encyclopedias, born around 20 B.C.E. and died around 50 C.E. However, it is telling that much of the dating of Philo's life depends on when one wants to imagine a man of the ancient world turning gray. As is well known, at the beginning of his tractate *Legatio ad Gaium*, which deals with the Jewish embassy to the emperor Caligula in the late 30s of the first century C.E., Philo refers to himself as an old man (γέρων), who had turned gray (πολιός).[2] Philo's hair in *Legatio ad Gaium* is part of the very spurious DNA which might help us define Philo's life span more accurately.

Fortunately, Josephus in his *Jewish Antiquities,* approximately one generation after Philo, has a few lines on our Alexandrian philosopher.[3] The context of Josephus' remarks is again the Jewish embassy to the Roman emperor Gaius Caligula. However, there are some inconsistencies between

---

[1] This paper was presented to the Philo of Alexandria Group at the Annual meeting of the Society of Biblical Literature in San Francisco, November 21, 2011. A German version of this paper is appearing as a chapter in my book *Jüdische Drehbühnen: Biblische Variationen im antiken Judentum* (Tria Corda. Jenaer Vorlesungen zu Judentum, Antike und Christentum; Tübingen: Mohr Siebeck, forthcoming). I would like to thank Mohr Siebeck for allowing me to publish the English version of this chapter in *SPhA*.

[2] Philo, *Legat.* 1.

[3] Josephus, *Ant.* 18.257–260.

Philo's and Josephus's line-up of the Jewish team sent to Rome. According to Josephus, the embassy consisted of three men, according to Philo of five.[4] And while Philo nowhere explicitly confirms that he was the head of the Jewish delegation to Rome, Josephus does so.[5] Josephus also tells us that his brother Alexander, the father of Tiberius Julius Alexander whom we know from both Jewish and pagan sources[6], was an alabarch. What this title exactly stands for is a matter of controversy. It certainly was the title of a senior official, perhaps in the area of tax collection.[7] Even if it is sometimes stated too quickly that Philo came out of one of the very wealthy Jewish families of Alexandria, it is safe to state that Philo grew up in an established family in Alexandria. The very existence of his vast oeuvre indicates that he must have enjoyed financial independence.

Philo probably lived all his life in Alexandria, the intellectual center of Greek-speaking Judaism at the time. Occasionally he may have travelled—and lived up to what he states in the context of Abraham's departure from Ur: Men who have never travelled are like blind people.[8] On at least one occasion Philo visited the temple in Jerusalem.[9] That he was "very knowledgeable in the field of philosophy," as Josephus states, is the least one can say about his work.[10]

So far this is the familiar, barren *Curriculum vitae* of our author, as we know it.[11] However, it seems to me that we can learn more about Philo by taking a closer look at the representation of the most important figure in his work: Moses. I would like to argue that when writing about Moses, Philo has his autobiographical moments. We will start by looking at passages concerning Moses and/or Philo as "politicians," and then as philosophers.

---

[4] Josephus, *Ant.* 18.257; Phil. *Legat.* 370.

[5] Josephus, *Ant.* 18.259.

[6] Josephus, *Ant.* 20.100; Tacitus, *Hist.* 2.74.79. Cf. Gregory E. Sterling, "Tiberius Julius Alexander," in *The Eerdmans Dictionary of Early Judaism,* (ed. John J. Collins and Daniel C. Harlow; Grand Rapids: Eerdmans, 2010), 1309–1310.

[7] Daniel R. Schwartz, "Philo, His Family, and His Times," in *The Cambridge Companion to Philo,* (ed. Adam Kamesar; Cambridge: Cambridge University Press, 2009), 12.

[8] Philo, *Abr.* 65.

[9] As he mentions briefly in *Prov.* 2.64.

[10] As stated by Josephus, *Ant.* 18.259; οὐκ ἄπειρος ("not inexperienced") is a litotes and meant to underline Philo's great knowledge. Josephus uses the same phrase—with much less sympathy!—referring to his rival Justus of Tiberias (*Vita* 40).

[11] For a more detailed evaluation of the scarce sources on Philo's life cf. Schwartz, op. cit., and also the detailed attempt by Louis Massebieau et al., "Essai sur la chronologie de la vie et des œuvres de Philon." *RHR* 53 (1906): 25–64; 164–185; 267–289.

Moses and Philo as Politicians

It seems to me that between Philo's *De Vita Mosis* and his "political" tractate on the embassy to Caligula, the *Legatio ad Gaium*, there are thematic and linguistic parallels which allow us to draw conclusions about Philo's understanding of his role in the delegation, about his understanding of the Moses figure and not the least about the place of *De Vita Mosis* in Philo's oeuvre. As far as I can tell, these matters have not yet been studied in depth.[12]

Philo was probably not politically active for a long time. In *De specialibus legibus* 3.3 Philo mentions "a vast ocean of civic worries" which began to detract him from his philosophical studies. In that passage he is probably referring to the political turmoil in Alexandria in the late 30s.[13] It was then, in light of the suffering of his fellow Jews in Egypt that Philo felt obliged to get involved in politics and to speak up on behalf of the Jews at the court of the emperor. To some extent, then, Philo slipped into the role of Moses, who according to the biblical story only reluctantly—having seen the oppression of the Israelites and having been urged by God—stepped forward and talked to the emperor of *his* time, the Pharaoh. In a small delegation, together with his brother Aaron, Moses argued with the Emperor and fought for justice for his people.[14] Moses, too, would have preferred to stay out of this. According to Philo, when still in Midian and before his political involvement, Moses was very much committed to the study of philosophy.[15]

To prevent any misunderstandings: I am not trying to suggest that Philo was presenting himself as a *Moses redivivus*. Such an equation would surely have been perceived as outrageous—by his readers and by Philo himself—and certainly was not Philo's intention. In Philo's presentation,

---

[12] On *De Vita Mosis* cf. more recently: Sarah J. K. Pearce, "King Moses: Notes on Philo's Portrait of Moses as an Ideal Leader in the *Life of Moses*," in *The Greek Strand in Islamic Political Thought,* (ed. Emma Gannagé et al.; Mélanges de l'Université Saint-Joseph LVII; Beirut: Imprimerie catholique, 2004), 37–74; Brian McGing, "Philo's Adaptation of the Bible in His Life of Moses," in *The Limits of Ancient Biography,* (ed. Brian McGing and Judith Mossman; Swansea: Classical Press of Wales, 2006), 117–140; Louis H. Feldman, *Philo's Portrayal of Moses in the Context of Ancient Judaism* (Notre Dame: University of Notre Dame Press, 2007).

[13] For a different reading of *Spec.* 3.3 cf. Erwin R. Goodenough, *The Politics of Philo of Judaeus. Practice and Theory* (New Haven: Yale University Press, 1938), 66–68.

[14] Exod 3–4.

[15] Philo, *Mos.* 1.48. Feldman, *Philo's Portrayal of Moses*, 74, also notes this parallel between Philo and his Moses.

Moses is the unattainable ideal of piety and wisdom.[16] Moses is the "most pious" man who has ever lived,[17] the "perfect wise man," the only one to have tasted pure and "undiluted wisdom."[18] Moses's wisdom begins where Abraham's reached its peak.[19] Philo was not so presumptuous to equate himself with Moses, but he does admire Moses.[20] While he realizes that Moses is inaccessible due to his unique proximity to God, he is also—because of this very proximity—a landmark to be followed. As Philo writes in his *Life of Moses*: Moses is "a role model for those who want to imitate him" (παράδειγμα τοῖς ἐθέλουσι μιμεῖσθαι). "Happy," Philo continues, "are all those who imprint or strive to imprint that image in their souls."[21]

Now, Philo's Moses is obviously just that: *Philo's* Moses. Philo is, as I will show below, mirroring his philosophical ideals in his presentation of Moses. He felt tempted, it seems to me, to connect Moses's biography, as presented in the Torah, with his own. I would like to argue that *De Vita Mosis* can be read as a tractate in which Philo ponders on his own life and, especially, on what happened during the anti-Jewish riots in Alexandria. (It goes without saying that there are many other important aspects in *De Vita Mosis*).

In fact, there are some striking parallels between the description of the Jews' suffering in *Legatio ad Gaium* and *De Vita Mosis*: In both cases the Jews are treated as prisoners of war. In *De Vita Mosis* Philo describes the suppression of the Israelites as follows:

> So, then, these strangers, who had left their own country and come to Egypt hoping to live there in safety as in a second fatherland (ἐν δευτέρᾳ πατρίδι), were made slaves by the ruler of the country and reduced to the condition of captives taken by the custom of war (τούτους … ὁ τῆς χώρας ἡγεμὼν ἠνδραπο-δίζετο καὶ ὡς πολέμου νόμῳ λαβὼν αἰχμαλώτους), or persons purchased from the masters in whose household they have been bred.[22]

And in the context of the anti-Jewish riot in Alexandria Philo writes:

---

[16] See David Winston, "Sage and Supersage in Philo of Alexandria," in *The Ancestral Philosophy: Hellenistic Philosophy in Second Temple Judaism. Essays of David Winston* (ed. Gregory E. Sterling; BJS 331/SPLM 4; Providence: Brown University, 2001), 171–180.

[17] Philo, *Mos.* 2.192: ὁσιώτατον τῶν πώποτε γενομένων.

[18] Philo, *Mos.* 2.204: πάνσοφε, μόνος ἀμιγοῦς ἠκρατίσω σοφίας.

[19] Philo, *Post.* 174.

[20] Philo, *Sacr.* 50. Cf. Feldman, *Philo's Portrayal of Moses*, 74.

[21] Philo, *Mos.* 1.158–159 (transl. PLCL, slightly adjusted); cf. also *Virt.* 51 (Moses's "own life" as an "archetypal model"). Cf. Alan Mendelson, *Secular Education in Philo of Alexandria* (Cincinnati: Hebrew Union College Press, 1982), 63–64.

[22] Philo, *Mos.* 1.36 (trans. PLCL).

For treating us as persons, given over by the emperor to suffer the extremity of calamity undisguised or as overpowered in war (πολέμῳ κατακρατηθέντας), they worked our ruin with insane and most brutal rage. They overran our houses, expelling the owners with their wives and children, and left them uninhabited.[23]

In *De Vita Mosis*, Philo in his paraphrase of the biblical events in Egypt seems to plead on behalf of his fellow Jews in Alexandria. Biblical Egypt is described as the (second) fatherland of the Israelites, where the Israelites wanted to live in security. As is well known, in Philo's understanding Jerusalem is the *metropolis* or "mother city" of all the Jews, while their "fatherland" (πατρίς) is the place where they actually live.[24] Thus to Philo, Alexandria and Egypt at large, was certainly his fatherland.[25] Philo and the Israelites share the same fatherland.

The overseers of Egypt—at the time of Philo as well as at the time of Moses—were very brutal, inhumane, even bestial. Similarly, the overseers of the Israelites are "animals in human shape" (ἀνθρωποειδῆ θηρία).[26] In the *Legatio* we hear how the Egyptians with "animal rage" (θηριωδεστάταις ὀργαῖς) went off on the Jews.[27] Thus, the Egyptian overseers—in Roman as well as in Pharaonic Egypt—were both of "beastly furor." Philo describes the maltreatment of the Jews in both his own and in biblical times in identical words: they were "subjected to every kind of ill-treatment."[28]

There are also parallels between the villains Pharaoh and Caligula: both emperors share a tendency towards rage and injustice.[29] Both succeeded rulers who had some sympathies towards the Jews: Augustus and Tiberius on the one hand, and the previous Pharaoh of Joseph's time on the other.[30]

---

[23] Philo, *Legat.* 121 (trans. PLCL). Roger Arnaldez et al. in their French edition of *De Vita Mosis* (PAPM 22; Paris: Éditions du Cerf, 1967), 42 n. 4, also suspect an "allusion à la situation de sa propre communauté à Alexandrie," but do not elaborate on this observation.

[24] Philo, *Flacc.* 46.

[25] Cf. Carlos Lévy, "Mais que faisait donc Philon en Égypte? : A propos de l'identité diasporique de Philon," in *La rivelazione in Filone di Alessandria: natura, legge, storia : atti del VII Convegno di Studi del Gruppo italiano di ricerca su Origene e la tradizione alessandrina (Bologna 29–30 settembre 2003)* (ed. Angela Maria Mazzanti, Francesca Calabi; Verruchio: Pazzini, 2004), 295–312.

[26] Philo, *Mos.* 1.43.

[27] Philo, *Legat.* 121.

[28] Philo, *Mos.* 1.44: πάσας αἰκιζόμενος αἰκίας; *Legatio* 128: αἰκιζόμενοι πάσαις αἰκίαις.

[29] Philo, *Mos.* 1.45; *Legat.* 190.

[30] Tiberius always "acted with profound prudence" (*Legat.* 33: φρονήσει βαθείᾳ χρώμενος) and no one "was a greater master of thought or of language among those who were in the prime of life in his time" (142; transl. PLCL). In his eulogy on Augustus (*Legat.* 143–147), Philo does not hesitate to praise him for having hellenized the barbarians (§ 147).

Both, Caligula and the Pharaoh of Moses' time, are in their blindness unable to understand the aniconic regulations of the Jews: Caligula's insistence on the importance of visual representations of gods and himself is at the very core of the treatise *Legatio ad Gaium*. Similarly, for Philo's Pharaoh in *De Vita Mosis*, it is unthinkable, "since he was in diapers" that a God could be thought of without anything visual (ἔξω τῶν ὁρατῶν).[31]

These parallels may suggest, then, that Philo's description of the suffering of the Hebrews in *De Vita Mosis* should be read in the context of the anti-Jewish riot in 38 C.E. and the subsequent Jewish embassy to Rome. And indeed, one may even speculate that Philo was aware of the parallels between Moses's pleading with Pharaoh on behalf of the Israelites in Egypt and his own efforts on behalf of the Jews in Egypt at the palace of the Roman Emperor. The parallels—in content and in language—between Pharaonic and Roman Alexandria bring Philo's *Legatio ad Gaium* into the vicinity of Moses's "Legatio ad Pharaonem." In fact, in the *Legatio ad Gaium* there is a passage where Philo brings his own time, the suppression in 38 and the difficulties surrounding the embassy to Rome, into connection with the Bible: "Perhaps these things are sent to try the present generation, to test the state of their virtue and whether they are schooled to bear dire misfortunes (...)?"[32] In his answer to this question, Philo refers to earlier difficult times when God saved the people from hopeless and desperate situations.[33] Philo does not mention a specific biblical parallel, but for him the Exodus story would certainly be the most important reference for divine help and reliability.

As already mentioned, Philo nowhere explicitly states that he was the head of the Jewish delegation to Rome. This is only reported by Josephus. In the *Legatio*, Philo, who is rarely explicit about himself, mentions that because of his age and his good education he "seemed to have greater prudence."[34] Philo tries to be modest: the differences between him and his colleagues are due to his age, his education, and experience. Nevertheless, the two keywords mentioned in this brief self-presentation—prudence (φρόνησις) and education (παιδεία)—are also, and especially, characteristics

---

In the biblical story, too, the depiction of the "bad" pharaoh is built up on the positive image of his predecessor (Exod 1:8ff.). In *Mos.* Philo does not refer to the earlier, "good" pharaoh (mentioned, in a positive light, in *Ios.* 119–121).

[31] Philo, *Mos.* 1.88.

[32] Philo, *Leg.* 196 (transl. PLCL).

[33] Philo, ibid.: πολλάκις ἐξ ἀμηχάνων καὶ ἀπόρων περιέσωσε τὸ ἔθνος.

[34] Philo, *Legat.* 182: φρονεῖν τι δοκῶν περιττότερον.

of Moses—as we will see shortly in the context of the descriptions of Moses's and Philo's education.[35]

Philo slips into the role of Moses. This is also true for his lack of a predestined role as a leader of a political movement. As already mentioned, we can safely assume that Philo was not eager to leave his philosophical studies behind in order to take over a political role—desiring it as little as the biblical and Philonic Moses did with respect to his calling. Philo's Moses is aware of how unstable Fortune is and therefore remains modest in successful moments without seeking a leadership position.[36] It is only the suffering of the Jews in Egypt that forces him to do so. Philo may have seen his political role in a very similar light. The very fact that he does not mention that he was the leader of the Jewish delegation may point in this direction. Philo is not simply projecting himself into Moses, he is also just noticing certain parallels between his life and Moses' life as described in the Torah.

The observations made so far, especially the strong echoes of the political tensions in Alexandria in *De Vita Mosis*, also have implications for the difficult question of the dating of this treatise. Among the numerous works by Philo of Alexandria, *De Vita Mosis* is perhaps the tractate which is most difficult to categorize and its intentions have been a matter of great dispute. It certainly does not belong to the "Allegorical Commentary." Some have understood it as part of or an introduction to the "Exposition of the Law."[37] Some scholars have understood *De Vita Mosis* as an introductory tractate with an agenda of making Moses known to a larger audience.[38] Recent scholarship places *De Vita Mosis* among the apologetic and historical works—more *e negativo*, though, because the tractate does not really seem to be part of the "Exposition."[39]

I believe that the parallels between *De Vita Mosis* and *Legatio ad Gaium* could very well help us better understand the place and the role of *De Vita*

---

[35] Philo, *Mos.* 1.23–25.

[36] Philo, *Mos.* 1.30–31.

[37] Cf. Erwin R. Goodenough, "Philo's Exposition of the Law and His De Vita Mosis." *HThR* 26 (1933): 109–125 and more recently Gregory E. Sterling, "How Do You Introduce Philo of Alexandria? The Cambridge Companion to Philo," *SPhA* 21 (2009): 67–68 ("an introduction to the Exposition in particular"); James R. Royse, "The Works of Philo," in *The Cambridge Companion to Philo,* (ed. Adam Kamesar; Cambridge: Cambridge University Press, 2009), 47 ("there seems to be some relationship between the 'Exposition' and the *De vita Mosis*. It seems clear, on the one hand, that *De vita Mosis* is not properly part of the 'Exposition,' but on the other hand, it may have been intended as a kind of introduction to it").

[38] David T. Runia, "Philon von Alexandreia," in *Der Neue Pauly*, 9:852.

[39] Royse, "The Works of Philo," 47, 50.

Mosis in Philo's oeuvre. In the light of our discussion so far, I would like to suggest that Philo's *De Vita Mosis* and *Legatio ad Gaium* were written around the same time. If Philo was already an old man, as he claims, when he wrote the *Legatio*, *De Vita Mosis* cannot have been what it is often understood to be: an early introductory tractate to the Philonic oeuvre. *De Vita Mosis* is probably a late and mature work of Philo.[40] It is true that in this tractate Philo makes important general statements (e.g., on the Septuagint), but one does not have to be young to write what one might call an introduction to Judaism. Philo could also have written a work functioning as a general introduction at a later stage.

In addition to the parallels with the *Legatio*, there may be other signs in *De Vita Mosis* indicating that this tractate was written around the time of the political turmoil in 38 C.E. Philo's allegorical reading of the burning bush episode—the burning bush is a "symbol of those who suffered wrong"—may not only refer to the biblical suffering of the Israelites in Egypt, but also to the suppression in Philo's Alexandria.[41] Elsewhere in *De Vita Mosis* and in a more contemporary context Philo describes the Jews as a people "which has not flourished for a long time."[42]

I am not the first scholar to suggest a late dating of *De Vita Mosis*. In fact, Leopold Cohn had already done so more than a hundred years ago. Cohn suspected that the tractate originated from the "period of the political fights." Cohn's argument is rather different from mine, though. He reads the tractate as an apologetic text which in the light of these fights tried to defend Judaism.[43] More recently, Louis Feldman took a similar approach.[44] However, I see very little apologetics in *De Vita Mosis*. This is, as so often in Jewish-Hellenistic literature, much more an inner-Jewish dialogue (which

---

[40] If so, this would obviously mean that tractates where Philo refers to *Mos.* (*Virt.* 52; *Praem.* 53: cf. Sterling, "How Do You Introduce Philo of Alexandria?," 67) were written later.

[41] Philo, *Mos.* 1.65–70 (67: σύμβολον ... τῶν ἀδικουμένων).

[42] Philo, *Mos.* 2.43 (ἐκ πολλῶν χρόνων τοῦ ἔθνους οὐκ εὐτυχοῦντος/μὴ ἐν ἀκμαῖς).

[43] Leopold Cohn, "Einteilung und Chronologie der Schriften Philos." *Philologus Suppl.*7 (1899): 434: "In diese Zeit der politischen Kämpfe gehören wohl auch die Bücher *de vita Mosis*. Die für einen griechischen Leserkreis bestimmte Lebensbeschreibung des jüdischen Gesetzgebers war vermutlich die erste in der Reihe der apologetischen Schriften, zu deren Abfassung Philo zum Zwecke litterarischer Abwehr der Angriffe der Gegner gegen das Judentum sich entschloß."

[44] Feldman, *Philo's Portrait of Moses*, 61. Cf. also the classification by Royse, "The Works of Philo," 51: "The current consensus is that *De vita Mosis* belongs among the apologetic and historical works, although it certainly differs from the other works included here in its concentration on events of the distant past."

may still reflect non-Jewish discourses on Judaism) than some sort of counter-attack.

Moses and Philo as Philosophers

I suggest, then, that in addition to his explicitly historical tractates *Legatio ad Gaium* and *In Flaccum*, in *De Vita Mosis* Philo is also addressing the painful times in Alexandria during which he became the leader of the Jews. His role as leader of the Jewish delegation to Rome opened up an opportunity to follow along the lines of Moses, who at least to some extent seems to have been his *paradeigma*. Philo sees in Moses a mirror image of himself. Moses is an ideal that cannot be attained, but it remains the goal of Philo. Let us take a look at another theme where one can observe a similar process: Philo's identity as a philosopher. In this short paper I can only hint at a few aspects.

The biblical Moses can hardly be called a philosopher (even if he does have his moments of intense reflection). On the other hand, the image of Moses as philosopher is not one which Philo invented. It goes back to earlier Jewish-Hellenistic authors such as Pseudo-Eupolemus, Artapanus and Aristobulus. From the second century B.C. on, in Jewish-Hellenistic literature there was an opinion circulating that Moses was the first sage[45] or even the inventor of philosophy[46] *tout court*. Artapanus, in a catalog of Mosaic inventions which recalls a list of inventions connected with Prometheus,[47] adds philosophy to Moses's list of innovations. Moses had brought many useful things to humanity: "boats and devices for stone construction and the Egyptian arms and the implements for drawing water and for warfare, and philosophy."[48] Probably around the same time, Aristobulus, the first Jewish philosopher of whom we know, linked the Greek philosophers Pythagoras, Socrates and Plato to Moses.[49] At the time of Philo, then, the connection of Moses with philosophy was something of a cliché. However, as we are going to see, in Philo Moses the philosopher is a much more complex figure than in these earlier texts (of which we obviously have only excerpts).

---

[45] Pseudo-Eupolemus *apud* Eusebius, *Praep. ev.* 9.26.1.

[46] Clement, *Strom.* 1.23.153.4.

[47] Cf. Aeschylus, *Prom.* 442–506.

[48] Artapanus *apud* Eusebius, *Praep. ev.* 9.27.4 (trans. J.J. Collins, OTP).

[49] Aristobulus *apud* Eusebius, *Praep. ev.* 13.12.3–4.

Philo speaks through Moses. He profits from the old cliché of Moses as the philosopher and projects his own philosophical agenda onto Moses. *De Vita Mosis* is again a key text for this project. Moses' teaching stands for "true philosophy" (τῷ ὄντι φιλοσοφεῖν), which consists of the three elements "deliberation" (βούλευμα), "reason" (λόγος) and "action" (πρᾶξις) and leads to a happy life (εὐδαιμονία).[50] For this form of philosophy, Philo writes, the Sabbath is especially suited. As a matter of fact, Moses taught philosophy on the Sabbath.[51] And Philo sees himself very much in this tradition: "Even now this practice is retained, and the Jews every seventh day occupy themselves with the philosophy of their fathers, dedicating that time to the acquiring of knowledge and the study of the truths of nature."[52]

That Philo found himself walking along Moses's path can also be seen in connection with his presentation of Moses's early years. Philo sends Moses to school.[53] He describes in some detail the *paideia*, the education and training of Moses. Moses, in the version of Philo, enjoys a first class education, a "royal upbringing" (τροφὴ βασιλική).[54] Philo imagines an international education of Moses:

Teachers at once arrived from different parts, some unbidden from the neighbouring countries and the provinces of Egypt, others summoned from Greece under promise of high reward. But in a short time he advanced beyond their capacities; his gifted nature forestalled their instruction, so that his seemed a case rather of recollection than of learning, and indeed he himself devised and propounded problems which they could not easily solve. For great natures carve out much that is new in the way of knowledge; and, just as bodies, robust and agile in every part, free their trainers from care, and receive little or none of their usual attention, and in the same way well-grown and naturally healthy trees, which improve of themselves, give the husbandmen no trouble, so the gifted soul takes the lead in meeting the lessons given by itself rather than the teacher and is profited thereby, and as soon as it has a grasp of some of the first principles of knowledge presses forward like the horse to the meadow, as the proverb goes. Arithmetic, geometry, the lore of metre, rhythm and harmony, and the whole subject of music as shown by the use of instruments or in textbooks and treatises of a more special character, were imparted to him by learned Egyptians. These further instructed him in the philosophy conveyed in

---

[50] Philo, *Mos.* 2.212.

[51] Philo, *Mos.* 2.215: "for it was customary on every day when opportunity offered, and pre-eminently on the seventh day … to pursue the study of wisdom with the ruler expounding and instructing the people what they should say and do, while they received edification and betterment in moral principles and conduct" (trans. PLCL).

[52] Philo, *Mos.* 2.216: ἀφ' οὗ καὶ εἰσέτι νῦν φιλοσοφοῦσι ταῖς ἑβδόμαις Ἰουδαῖοι τὴν πάτριον φιλοσοφίαν (trans. PLCL). Philo speaks about the Jews in general, but he clearly shares this understanding of the sabbath.

[53] Philo, *Mos.* 1.20–26.

[54] Philo, *Mos.* 1.20.

symbols, as displayed in the so-called holy inscriptions and in the regard paid to animals, to which they even pay divine honours. He had Greeks to teach him the rest of the regular school courses, and the inhabitants of the neighbouring countries for Assyrian letters and the Chaldean science of the heavenly bodies. This he also acquired from Egyptians, who give special attention to astrology. And, when he had mastered the lore of both nations, both where they agree and where they differ, he eschewed all strife and contention and sought only for truth.[55]

This is a remarkable description of Moses's education. Arithmetic and geometry, rhythm, harmony, metrics, music, and astronomy: these subjects are part of the ancient educational canon, as described in particular by Plato. From the first century B.C.E. on, such a *Bildungskanon* was known as the *enkyklios paideia* (ἐγκύκλιος παιδεία) and this is the term which Philo uses here.[56] Philo's list of subjects is indeed reminiscent of those in Plato's *Republic*,[57] but above all it is probably based on Philo's own school days. We know that Philo, probably like most Jewish children of noble families in Alexandria, passed a thorough curriculum, as explained in his tractate *De Congressu Eruditionis Gratia* (*On the Preliminary Studies*).[58] There Philo looks back on his school days and lists three areas of study, two of which—geometry and music—were also part of Moses's education, as he has it in *De Vita Mosis*:

> For instance when first I was incited by the goads of philosophy to desire her I consorted in early youth with one of her handmaids, Grammar, and all that I begat by her, writing, reading and study of the writings of the poets, I dedicated to her mistress. And again I kept company with another, namely Geometry, and was charmed with her beauty, for she showed symmetry and proportion in every part. Yet I took none of her children for my private use, but brought them as a gift to the lawful wife. Again my ardour moved me to keep company with a third; rich in rhythm, harmony and melody was she, and her name was Music, and from her I begat diatonics, chromatics and enharmonics, conjunct and disjunct melodies, conforming with the consonance of the fourth, fifth or octave intervals. And again of none of these did I make a secret hoard, wishing to see the lawful wife a lady of wealth with a host of servants ministering to her.[59]

Philo's personal canon of subjects does not entirely agree with that of Moses. But Philo does generally not know of a conclusive definition of the

55 Philo, *Mos.* 1.21–24 (trans. PLCL).
56 Philo, *Mos.* 1.23.
57 Plato, *Resp.* 526d ff.
58 Cf. Mendelson, *Secular Education in Philo of Alexandria*, 26–27.
59 Philo, *Congr.* 74–76 (trans. PLCL).

enkyklios paideia,[60] and one can safely say that Moses and Philo are introduced into the same *kind* of education. Alan Mendelson, who has written an important book on Philo's secular education, explains Moses's Hellenistic education in *De Vita Mosis* with the apologetic intent of that work. According to Mendelson, Philo wanted to throw a bridge to his pagan readers by giving Moses a "classical" training.[61] This seems unlikely. Once more, one has generally overestimated the apologetic intent of this text. What is more important in Philo's parallel readings on Moses's and his own education is, again, his endeavor to present himself as a close follower of Moses and possibly also to convey a message to his Jewish readers: even Moses enjoyed a secular education!

In the center of Philo's *De congressu eruditionis gratia* is his interpretation of Abraham's relationship with the slave Hagar, who at the time of Sarai's infertility gives birth to a son (Gen 16). In Philo's allegorical reading Hagar stands for the basic education, for the *enkyklios paideia*, which ideally is only preparing for the occupation with the philosophical work:

> When Abraham is about to wed the handmaid of wisdom, the school culture, he does not forget, so the text implies, his faith plighted to her mistress, but knows that the one is his wife by law and deliberate choice, the other only by necessity and the force of occasion. And this is what happens to every lover of learning. ... For philosophy is the practice or study of wisdom, and wisdom is the knowledge of things divine and human and their causes. And therefore just as the culture of the schools is the bond-servant of philosophy, so must philosophy be the servant of wisdom.[62]

In his allegorical reading of Gen 16, Philo describes in a Jewish context the pagan model of philosophy which is introduced by means of a basic education, the *enkyklios paideia*. The ultimate goal, though, is always philosophy and by means of philosophy the achievement of wisdom (σοφία).[63] In the words of Plato, all other sciences are "only the overtures to the melody, which should actually be learned."[64] Philo's allegorical interpretation—Hagar being the stepping stone to philosophy—seems to follow a similar pagan allegory according to which a restriction to the subjects of the

---

[60] Cf. Monique Alexandre, *Philon d'Alexandrie. De Congressu Eruditionis Gratia* (PAPM 16; Paris: Éditions du Cerf, 1967), 34–35; Mendelson, *Secular Education in Philo of Alexandria*, 4.

[61] Mendelson, *Secular Education in Philo of Alexandria*, 64: "Especially if we assume that De Vita Mosis is an apologetic work, there is every reason for Philo to elaborate any points of contact between the experience of his audience and that of his protagonist. One of these points would be encyclical education."

[62] Philo, *Congr.* 73, 79 (trans. PLCL).

[63] Philo, *Congr.* 79.

[64] Plato, *Resp.* 531d: προοίμιά ἐστιν αὐτοῦ τοῦ νόμου ὃν δεῖ μαθεῖν.

enkyklios paideia would be equal to suitors of Penelope who would only want to amuse themselves with Penelope's maids.[65] As we have already seen, Philo describes this ideal form of a curriculum with respect to his own youth: the basic subjects are merely servants of philosophy.[66] And as for Moses, his training—as imagined by Philo—follows these very same lines: Moses, too, first passes the *enkyklios paideia*,[67] and only then devotes himself to the study of wisdom (φρόνησις).[68] Certainly: Moses is a student of a first rate "university," he attracts the international elite teachers, and this only in order to subsequently leave them behind.[69] Again: Philo cannot and does not claim to be Moses. But he has Moses agree with his education policy. As young men they were both taken by an enormous desire for education. Such a desire for education (παιδείας ἵμερον),[70] Philo says of himself, had always been deep in his soul. The same goes for Moses: he was, as a young man, zealous for education and culture (ἐζήλωσε παιδείαν)[71] and for "what was sure to profit his soul" (ἃ τὴν ψυχὴν ἔμελλεν ὠφελήσειν).[72] This is how Philo presents his Moses, and this is how he sees himself.

Philo's Moses learned the *enkyklios paideia* from his Greek teachers. But he also had Egyptian teachers: he learned hieroglyphs, astronomy, and mathematics from local teachers.[73] Interestingly, Philo mentions that Moses was introduced by Egyptian teachers into the symbols of the hieroglyphs. Philo goes so far as to refer in this context to the Egyptian veneration of animals—which otherwise is a very common topic of intellectual critique in Jewish Hellenistic (and also pagan) literature.[74] Here, however, the symbolic, that is, allegorical philosophy, taught by Egyptians, is important enough to make it part of Moses's curriculum. This Egyptian kind of philosophy, together with the Greek *enkyklios paideia*, is Moses's basic curriculum, his first degree, so to speak. It is true that for Moses this degree involves more

---

[65] On this metaphor cf. Harald Fuchs, "Enkyklios Paideia," *RAC* 5:382 and Alexandre, *De congressu*, 62–64.

[66] Philo, *Congr.* 74–76.

[67] Philo, *Mos.* 1.23: τὴν δ᾽ἄλλην ἐγκύκλιον παιδείαν Ἕλληνες ἐδίδασκον.

[68] Philo, *Mos.* 1.25.

[69] Philo, *Mos.* 1.21.

[70] Philo, *Spec.* 3.4.

[71] Philo, *Mos.* 1.32.

[72] Philo, *Mos.* 1.20.

[73] Philo, *Mos.* 1.23–24.

[74] Philo, *Mos.* 1.23. On Philo's presentation of Egypt cf. Maren Niehoff, *Philo on Jewish Identity and Culture* (TSAJ 86; Tübingen: Mohr Siebeck, 2001), 45–74 and Sarah J. K. Pearce, *The Land of the Body: Studies in Philo's Representation of Egypt* (WUNT 208; Tübingen: Mohr Siebeck, 2007), esp. 241–308, for a treatment of animal worship.

memorizing than actual studying,[75] but this is more of a Platonic stereotype than a negation of Egyptian learning. Philo, after all, was not obliged to include Egyptian teachers in Moses's curriculum, but he did. Very much like the Israelites who later took their pagan education with them when they left Egypt,[76] Moses does this already in his youth.

Recently Ekaterina Matusova showed in an article in the *Studia Philonica Annual* that in Philo's time Egyptian allegorical interpretation played a certain role in the intellectual discourse in Alexandria. Matusova writes, "By Philo's time Egyptian culture became in Egypt highly significant as a symbolical culture and the barbarian culture par excellence. This locates Philo in a special set of circumstances in which, when using the tradition of allegorical interpretation of *hieroi logoi*, he could not avoid clear allusions to the Egyptian context as paradigmatic for his approach."[77] If so, we see again to what extent Moses's education in Philo's *De Vita Mosis* is aligned with the intellectual education in Philo's own time.[78]

Philo's Moses passes—fast as a "horse in the field," as Philo has it[79]— the best possible curriculum of his time. He studies with both Egyptian and Greek professors; in the end, however, in his search for truth he finds his own way, leaving both behind.[80] This is very much Philo's understanding of Judaism: It surpasses the teachings of others, but it is, at the same time, very much dependent on foreign impulses.

Philo's Moses does not simply adhere the traditional, biblical role, nor does he merely adapt to the dominant Hellenistic (Egyptian-Roman) culture. But he creates for Moses—and for himself—a third, new approach.[81] Philo and his Moses take advantage of the education of their time, but in the end, they go their own ways. Philo is consistently trying to situate Jewish tradition in the context of contemporary philosophy and science: he

[75] Philo, *Mos.* 1.21.

[76] Philo, *Her.* 272–274.

[77] Ekaterina Matusova, "Allegorical Interpretation of the Pentateuch in Alexandria: Inscribing Aristobulus and Philo in a Wider Literary Context," *SPhA* 22 (2010): 34–35.

[78] However, Philo does not state that he himself studied the Egyptian tradition of allegorical interpretation.

[79] Philo, *Mos.* 1.22. For this proverbial expression cf. Plato, *Theaet.* 183d: calling Socrates to an argument is like calling cavalry into an open plain. Thus the proverb is on people who are invited to do something in which they excel. In *Mos.* 1.22 it is on people, like Moses, who as soon as they have "a grasp of some of the first principles of knowledge press forward like the horse to the meadow ."

[80] Philo, *Mos.* 1.24: "he surpasses them, without contention" (ἀφιλονείκως τὰς ἔριδας ὑπερβάς, τὴν ἀλήθειαν ἐζήτει).

[81] John M. G. Barclay's postcolonial reading of Josephus (*Against Apion* (Flavius Josephus, Translation and Commentary 10; Leiden: Brill, 2006)) could also be fruitfully applied with regard to Philo.

attempts to make sense of the paradoxes in Jewish tradition, while at the same time participating in Jewish and non-Jewish discourses.

The biblical plot of Moses growing up at Pharaoh's palace before returning to his Israelite parents' home invited an updated reading of such a double course of education.[82] The book of Exodus does not give us any information on Moses's education, but according to the Bible Moses's mother brought him to Pharaoh's daughter, and he became her son. To Jewish-Hellenistic authors the biblical story of Moses's exposure offered an attractive platform for a more detailed description of an ideal Jewish-Hellenistic education. In fact, Philo was not the first Jewish-Hellenistic author staging such a double education. In Ezekiel's *Exagoge* Moses more explicitly than in the Bible enjoys two kinds of education: first, through his mother, he receives a Jewish education;[83] second, at the Egyptian court the Egyptian princess introduces, Ezekiel writes, Moses into the Egyptian (or Hellenistic) *paideumata*.[84] In both examples, Ezekiel and Philo, the conviction, typical of Jewish Hellenism, that Judaism and Hellenism are not two separate entities, becomes fairly explicit. Philo is obviously much more detailed and concrete, and he adds philosophy to the mix. According to Philo, Moses did not invent philosophy, contrary to Artapanus who, as we have seen, had stated just that.[85] It is true that Philo, too, at times stresses the antiquity and originality of Jewish philosophy: Philo argues, for example, that the philosophical statement that virtue equals happiness is not an invention of pagan philosophy but of Moses.[86] Similarly, the Greek philosophers Heraclitus and Zeno did not come up with "new inventions" (εὕρεσις καινή), but simply used "old findings of Moses" (παλαιὸν εὕρεμα Μωυσέως)[87] or (in the case of Zeno) the "source of Jewish law" (ἀπὸ πηγῆς τῆς Ἰουδαίων νομοθεσίας).[88] But still: Philo nowhere claims the absolute originality of Jewish philosophy. On the contrary, he is very open about his own philosophical predecessors, especially Plato. But in the end, Philo, too, chooses his own path. Philo pursues the very same dialectics as his Moses does. He addresses different opinions of the philosophical schools of his time, but in the end he formulates his own philosophy.

---

[82] While Philo says very little about Moses's Jewish upbringing, there is no doubt that he took it for a given; cf. Mendelson, *Secular Education in Philo of Alexandria*, 26.

[83] Ezekiel, *Exagoge*, v. 35: γένος πατρῷον καὶ θεοῦ δωρήματα.

[84] Ezekiel, *Exagoge*, v. 37. Cf. on this passage René Bloch, "'Meine Mutter erzählte mir alles': Ezechiel *Exagoge* 34–35 und der Mythos." *Judaica* 61 (2005): 97–109.

[85] Cf. above p.81.

[86] Philo, *Mut.* 167–168 (Philo refers to Exod 4:14).

[87] Philo, *Her.* 214.

[88] Philo, *Prob.* 57.

We have been looking at very different aspects in Philo's oeuvre where Philo projects his opinions onto Moses. It is, of course, not unusual that an author has his main protagonist represent his main theses. In the case of Philo, it seems to me, one has so far underestimated how much this is the case with regard to Moses. Such a projection or even parallelization was to some extent literally offered to Philo because of biographic parallels between Moses and Philo: their Egyptian origins, their political roles in favour of the Jewish people against foreign, pagan powers, their roles as philosophers (in the case of Moses present early on in Jewish-Hellenistic literature) —there were several reasons why Philo could feel tempted to blend his presentation of Moses with autobiographical elements. I leave it open whether this should be read on the side of Philo as a sign of modest admiration for Moses or rather as some sort of preposterous hybris. Maybe a little bit of both. Philo's portrait of Moses in *De Vita Mosis* should in any case be taken into account in our search for the historical Philo. There is some sort of *Tagespolitik* in *De Vita Mosis*, which makes this treatise rather a late than an early text. And there are some autobiographic moments in *De Vita Mosis*. Both observations can help us grasp Philo a little better.

University of Bern

The Studia Philonica Annual 24 (2012) 85–105

PHILO'S UNIVERSALIZATION OF SINAI
IN *DE DECALOGO* 32–49*

TRENT A. ROGERS

Jewish self-understanding and religious observance were centered on the foundational event of God's revelation of his Law at Sinai. Many Jews understood this covenantal Law to be directed at a particular people, and the practice of this legal code made them distinct from their non-Jewish neighbors—not the least in the observance of dietary restrictions, mono-latry, and circumcision. Philo of Alexandria, however, seeks to explain how the uniqueness of the Law rests not in its exclusivity but in its universal applicability to all humans who accord their lives with the law of nature and reason.[1] Philo, writing in an Alexandrian Jewish community whose rights and privileges were quickly diminishing, seeks to explain the peculiarity of the Jewish Law to a larger Greco-Roman audience in his *Exposition of the Laws*.[2] In the *Exposition*, Philo explains that the particular Mosaic Law is the written equivalent to the law of nature that is accessible to all humans; the creation account shows that the Law is concordant with nature in having the same source, and even the patriarchs can live in accord

---

* I am grateful for the comments and suggestions of the Philo of Alexandria Group at the Society of Biblical Literature Annual Meeting 2011, editor Gregory E. Sterling, and the anonymous reviewers of *SPhA*. Thanks is especially due to Thomas H. Tobin, S. J. who read an earlier draft of this article and provided his keen comments.

[1] Jutta Leonhardt-Balzer, "Jewish Worship and Universal Identity in Philo of Alexandria" in *Jewish Identity in the Greco-Roman World: Jüdische Identität in der griechisch-römischen Welt* (ed. Jörg Frey, Daniel R. Schwartz, and Stephanie Gripentrog; AGJU 71; Leiden: Brill, 2007), 33, provides working definitions of particularism and universalism for Second Temple Judaism: "Universalism in the context of Judaism is the idea that the Jewish traditions—in whichever form—are relevant for the whole world. The opposite term is particularism, which in the same context would mean the view that they refer to the Jewish nation only." See also Ellen Birnbaum, *The Place of Judaism in Philo's Thought: Israel, Jews, and Proselytes* (BJS 290/SPLM 2; Atlanta: Scholars Press, 1996), 1–6.

[2] Maren R. Niehoff, *Jewish Exegesis and Homeric Scholarship in Alexandria* (New York: Cambridge University Press, 2011), 170, argues that in the *Exposition* "Philo addressed a wider, non-Jewish audience at a stage in life when he had already become involved in the political affairs which led to the embassy to Rome."

with the Sinaitic Law because they pursue reason. But Philo must explain how this universal Law could be transmitted to a very particular people. He must show how the Sinai event of one people's religious heritage is relevant for all peoples. In order to present a Law that is ethnically unbound and plausible to the larger Greco-Roman world, Philo omits the particularizing elements of the Sinai event and heightens the cosmic elements to transform the Sinai event of a particular nation into the potentially universal revelation of the truly existent God to all peoples.

1. De decalogo *in the* Exposition of the Laws

The literary location of Philo's Sinai narrative is broader than *De decalogo* as it fits into the larger grouping of Philo's treatises in the *Exposition of the Laws*.[3] Scholars agree that the *Exposition* is less technical and thus more accessible to a broader audience.[4] Erwin R. Goodenough is an early representative of those who think Philo's *Exposition* is directed to a Gentile audience: "The Exposition is thus more intelligible throughout when, in contrast with the writings designed for Jews, it is recognized to have been written for gentiles."[5] Emil Schürer goes as far as to label the *Exposition* as

---

[3] Most accept the sequence of the *Exposition* to be *Opif., Abr., (On Isaac), (On Jacob), Decal., Spec., Virt., Praem.* See for example Peder Borgen, *Philo of Alexandria: An Exegete for His Time* (NTSup 86; Leiden: Brill, 1997), 77. There is debate concerning the insertion of *Mos.* as the last of the biographies. In *Praem.* 1–3, Philo himself indicates this scheme of Moses' work: creation of the world, history, and Laws.

[4] For example, Niehoff, *Jewish Exegesis*, 184, notes that *Decal.* fits the more accessible tone of the *Exposition* with its general introductory questions ("Why was the Law given the in the desert?" "Why was the number of laws ten?" "What is the nature of the voice" "Why was the singular 'you' used?") that do not deal with technical textual issues and could have been raised by someone who had not even read the Jewish Law. The overall tone suggests "Philo's audience in the *Exposition* indeed seems to be more interested in the overall values and customs of Judaism rather than in intricate questions" (174–5). These observations lead Niehoff to conclude that a non-Jewish audience for the *Exposition* is more likely.

[5] Erwin R. Goodenough, "Philo's Exposition of the Law and His De Vita Mosis," *HThR* 26 (1933): 124; cf. Frederick H. Colson, *De Decalogo* PLCL, xiv; Valentin Nikiprowetzky, *De Decalogo* (Les Oeuvres de Philon D'Alexandri 23; Paris: Cerf, 1965), 29–32; Peder Borgen, "Philo of Alexandria: Reviewing and Rewriting Biblical Material," *SPhA* 9 (1997): 47–53. Birnbaum, *Place of Judaism*, 20, concludes that Philo might have multiple aims and audiences in mind in the *Exposition*: "Philo may have several aims in mind here: to reclaim the alienated Jews, educate less knowledgeable ones, assuage non-Jews who may be hostile, and appeal to those who might be interested."

the *"Delineation of the Mosaic Legislation for non-Jews."*[6] The literary features described in this article are explained best by positing a Greco-Roman audience for *Decal.* as a work within the *Exposition*. If Philo intends the *Exposition* to make accessible and plausible Jewish history, Law, and practice to a larger Gentile audience, he must make his argument in a manner that shows the universality and superiority of the Mosaic Law. He must also show how the Law given at Sinai, which is a part of Jewish history, is relevant for non-Jews.

2. *Philo's Description of the Law in* De decalogo

While the main focus of this article is to describe the manner in which Philo shapes the narrative events around Sinai, some discussion of his treatment of the Law is fitting because the phenomenon of universalization is at work in his treatment of both the Law and the narrative. It is Philo's desire to show the universal nature of the Law that drives his universalization of the narrative. Philo appeals to the congruence between the written Law of Moses and the law of nature, evidenced through the lives of the patriarchs, observations of animal relationships, and arithmology, to show that the Mosaic Law is applicable to non-Jews.[7]

Philo clarifies the connection between the patriarchs and the written Law in his opening: "Having related in the preceding treatises the lives of those whom Moses judged to be men of wisdom, who are set before us in the Sacred Books as founders of our nation and in themselves unwritten laws, I shall now proceed in due course to give full descriptions of the written laws."[8] For Philo, the lives of the patriarchs, who precede the giving of the Law, demonstrate that the Law extends beyond nationalistic practice because it can be practiced in accord with nature and wisdom. Peder Borgen argues, "On the concrete and nationalistic level the lives of the

---

[6] Emil Schürer, *The Literature of the Jewish People in the Time of Jesus* (ed. Nahum Glatzer; trans. Peter Christie and Sophia Taylor; New York: Schocken, 1972), 338. See also, Emil Schürer, *The History of the Jewish People in the Age of Jesus Christ (175 B.C. – A.D. 135)* (trans. rev. ed. Geza Vermes, Fergus Millar, and Martin Goodman; Edinburgh 1973), 3.840–1.

[7] J. H. A. Hart, "Philo of Alexandria," *JQR* 17 (1904): 82, makes the connection between Philo and the Stoic natural Law: "So, then, the life according to Nature which the Stoic philosopher preached was after all no more than the life of the law-abiding Jew."

[8] Philo, *Decal.* 1 (PLCL, Colson). Although the audience knows who the "men of wisdom" are, the discrete Jewish designations never appear in *Decal.*: Abraham, Isaac, Jacob/Israel, and Joseph. Aaron also receives no mention and the priests are only mentioned twice (*Decal.* 71, 159).

Patriarchs were the lives of 'the founders of our nation,' i.e. of the Jewish nation. On the general level of law and philosophy they were archetypes and in themselves unwritten laws."[9] Although it is important that the Jewish people have wise ancestors, the significance of the patriarchs is that their wise manner of living agrees with the wisdom of the Mosaic Law.[10] Moreover, the Law of Moses accords with natural law because the Law is received from God who is the Creator.[11] While another Second Temple Jewish work, *Jubilees*, indicates that the patriarchs had access to the Mosaic Law in the form of heavenly tablets and thus kept the Law through direct revelation, Philo intends to show that the Mosaic Law has broader accessibility and applicability.[12] Special revelation to specific men excludes non-Jews, but Philo's presentation of the Law as the same as the law of nature opens the possible practice of the Law to all people who live in accord with reason and nature.[13] Hindy Najman summarizes, "In Philo's view, the patriarchs exemplify the possibility of leading a virtuous life even if one does not have access to the written Law of Moses (*Abr.* 16)."[14] Appeal to the congruence between the Mosaic Law and the natural law removes some of the exclusive Jewishness of the Law because it can be lived partially through wisdom.

While the affirmation of the Mosaic Law's accordance with the natural or unwritten law allows the Law to pass beyond Jewish bounds, it also creates a potential problem for Philo. Philo must affirm that the best of Greek laws have some value in their accordance with the natural law if he wants to appeal to a Greek audience, but he must also show that they are deficient representations of the natural law. He accomplishes this mainly by advancing a positive argument for the greatness of the Mosaic Law. If written laws are seen by Greeks as less pure expressions of the natural law,

[9] Borgen, *Philo*, 71.

[10] See John W. Martens, *One God, One Law: Philo of Alexandria on the Mosaic and Greco-Roman Law* (Leiden: Brill, 2003), 86–90, who correctly notes that more than just being in accordance with the Law of nature, these wise men become unwritten laws that are determined by the law of nature.

[11] See Francesca Calabi, *The Language and the Law of God: Interpretation and Politics in Philo of Alexandria* (Atlanta: Scholars Press, 1998), 37–8.

[12] E.g., *Jub.* 6:17; 15:1; 16:28. See Peder Borgen, "Philo of Alexandria," in *Jewish Writing of the Second Temple Period: Apocrypha, Pseudepigrapha, Qumran Sectarian Writings, Philo, and Josephus* (ed. Michael E. Stone; CRINT sec. 2, vol. 2; Philadelphia: Fortress, 1984), 238, n.23; Hindy Najman, "The Law of Nature and the Authority of the Mosaic Law," *SPhA* 11 (1999): 61–2.

[13] On the natural law being the law of reason, see Philo, *Opif.* 172; *Prob.* 47–9; Najman, "Law of Nature," 62–3.

[14] Hindy Najman, "A Written Copy of the Law of Nature: An Unthinkable Paradox," *SPhA* 15 (2003): 60.

the Mosaic Law could also be of only relative worth as another imperfect expression of the natural law. That is, if other written laws are transcended by the natural law, would not the Mosaic Law also be transcended? Valentin Nikiprowetzky argues correctly that, for Philo, the written Law is not an imperfect representation of the natural law, but the natural law is a prewritten form of the written Law.[15] Thus Philo can affirm that the Greek laws point to the natural law, and the natural law is the same as the Mosaic Law; therefore, even the Greek laws point to the perfect expression of Law in the Mosaic Law.[16] John Martens concludes: "In taking over Greek views of the law, Philo particularized a universal view of the law, the law of nature, and universalized a particular law, the law of Moses."[17] It is only by

[15] Nikiprowetzky, *De Decalogo*, 133; cf. Martens, *One God*, 127; Hart, "Philo," 82; Najman, "Written Copy," 59. André Myre, S. J., "La Loi et Le Pentateuque," *ScEs* 25 (1973): 209–225, esp. 219–220, does not equate the two laws. While he argues for a strong connection between the two laws, he accords the Mosaic Law with a lesser status than the natural law.

[16] Philo can show the similarity of Greek laws and the Jewish Law while maintaining the superiority of the Jewish Law by explaining how the Jewish Law is the best promotion of the polis. The first tablet accords with the law of nature and proper philosophy, and the second tablet prevents the destruction of the polis. (6) Adultery is the greatest crime against the polis because it is founded in pleasure [*Decal.* 121], corrupts another's soul [§§123–4], destroys three families [§§125–7], and it leaves the children despised by both families [§§130–1]. (7) Murder is an offense against another person with a soul and robs the temple of God [§§132–4]. (8) The thief is an enemy of the polis (πόλεως ἐχθρός), and if the thief were strong enough, he would destroy the whole polis as his desire is only checked by his weakness [§§135–7]. (9) False witness destroys the legal system of the polis [§§138–41]. (10) All interstate wars spring from desire which is one of the four Stoic passions [§§142–53]. Thus, the Laws are cast in terms of philosophy and the polis, not in terms of covenant faithfulness and ethnic identity. Jutta Leonhardt, *Jewish Worship in Philo of Alexandria* (TSAJ 84; Tübingen: Mohr Siebeck, 2001), 286–92, compares Philo's works to Plato's *Laws* and argues "Philo describes the Torah as a Jewish constitution in the Hellenistic sense. This brings him close to the Greek descriptions of constitutions, and especially Plato's *Nomoi*, in which the philosopher attempts to design the ideal constitution by comparing the best aspects of a number of Greek states" (286). Moreover, Philo appeals to his audience through language appropriate to the contemporary Greco-Roman context. On the desert as a place of cleansing (*Decal.* 12–13), Maren Niehoff, *Philo on Jewish Identity and Culture* (Tübingen: Mohr Siebeck, 2001), 256, notes, "By thus associating Mosaic Law with health Philo has inscribed it into Nature and suggested its objective value." Niehoff explains that this way of presenting the Mosaic Law in terms health reflects a contemporary trend in Greco-Roman culture in which ethics was understood as treatment and a cure. In *Spec.* Philo explains how the Law is the best remedy both for mental and physical ailment. For example, indigestion is cured through the prohibition on gluttony (*Spec.* 4.100). For an explanation of the special Laws as Greek virtues, see Naomi G. Cohen, "The Greek Virtues and the Mosaic Laws in Philo: An Elucidation of *De Specialibus Legibus* IV 133–135," *SPhA* 5 (1993): 9–23.

[17] Martens, *One God*, 129.

affirming that the natural law is the Mosaic Law that Philo can both maintain its perfection and move it beyond the bounds of Judaism.

The theme of the revealed Law according to the natural law runs throughout *Decal.* in a number of manifestations. Arithmology indicates the significance of ten "to those who have eyes to see" (*Decal.* 26). That is, nature accords ten with a significance that is also echoed in the revealed Law, so that the perceptive, wise human understands the importance of the Ten Commandments.[18] This understanding of ten's significance is available through philosophical reflection as the appeal to Aristotle demonstrates (*Decal.* 30; cf. Aristotle, *Cat.* 4.I). Horst Moehring argues, "Arithmology allows Philo to stress two points: a. the cosmic and human order described by Moses is of universal validity...b. the order is represented most clearly and purely in Jewish Law, liturgy, and tradition; the Jewish religion is, therefore, the most 'natural' religion."[19] The ethical implications of the Law can even be witnessed in animals (*Decal.* 115–17). The manifestation of the Law in the natural world suggests that proper philosophical reflection would lead one to the acceptance of the Mosaic Law.[20]

In a few places, Philo moralizes particularly Jewish elements of the Law. While almost any audience would agree on the morality of prohibiting murder, obeying parents, and not stealing, a common invective against the Jews was their observance of the Sabbath. But Moses shows that the Sabbath should be devoted "to the study of wisdom" (*Decal.* 98). The Sabbath year teaches about community and equality (*Decal.* 162) and the year of Jubilee teaches about humanity and justice (*Decal.* 164). While Philo does not go into great detail about some of these Laws in *Decal.*, he defends the ones to which Gentiles most strongly object as promotions of virtue.[21]

---

[18] See Hindy Najman, *Seconding Sinai: The Development of Mosaic Discourse in Second Temple Judaism* (JSJSup 77; Leiden: Brill, 2003), 81; Najman, "Written Copy," 59–60.

[19] Horst M. Moehring, "Arithmology as an Exegetical Tool in the Writings of Philo of Alexandria," in *The School of Moses: Studies in Philo and Hellenistic Religion In Memory of Horst R. Moehring* (ed. John P. Kennedy; BJS 304/SPLM 1; Atlanta: Scholars Press, 1995), 176, see also 146.

[20] There are a number of allusions that Philo makes to contemporary philosophy to buttress his assertion of the universality of the Law. For example, the life as opposed to the good life (*Decal.* 17) is a distinction that Aristotle has already made in *Politics* 1. The rational soul of *Decal.* 33 draws on Plato's *Republic*. The depiction of God as the truly existent one (*Decal.* 8) is a Middle Platonic critique of Stoicism's assertion that all things are material. These allusions to contemporary Greco-Roman philosophy, while not developed in any length, appeal to the Greco-Roman audience not only in showing that philosophy properly leads to the Law but also to display Philo's learnedness.

[21] In general, Philo conceptualizes virtues in Platonic and Aristotelian terms. See Cohen, "Greek Virtues," 9–19.

As Philo presents the Law itself in a broader manner, he correspondingly describes the Sinai event as a universal transmission of Law.

3. *Philo's Omissions of the Septuagint's Particularizing Elements in* Decal. *32–49*

A comparison between the Septuagint with which Philo was working and his description of the theophany in *Decal.* alerts the reader to some remarkable, and it will be argued intentional, omissions.[22] While one does not expect a verbatim retelling of Exodus, the elements of the story that Philo omits pertain specifically to features of the Sinai narrative that tie it exclusively to the Jewish people. We cannot know unquestionably why Philo omits certain elements from the narrative, but it is significant that almost all reference to things that are particular to the Jewish people and Judaism are omitted. The fact that Philo omits from the Sinai narrative "Sinai," ethnic descriptions of the people, Jewish descriptions of God, and cultic and covenantal elements suggests that Philo's reworking of the narrative is a deliberate muting of especially Jewish elements. The purpose of the theophany, for Philo, is to secure the uniqueness of the Jewish Law given in a miraculous way from the true God just as the patriarchs showed the uniqueness of the Law as true representatives of the law of nature.[23]

3.1. *Omission of "Sinai"*

While the LXX frequently mentions the location of the giving of the Law as Mount Sinai (e.g., Exod 19:11, 16, 18, 20, 23), Philo avoids this designation.[24] Despite the significance of the Law and its prevalence in Philo's writing, he

[22] This article will also make some connections to Philo's depiction of Sinai in other treatises although the main focus of this article is on how the Sinai event functions in *Decal.* Considering the importance of Sinai as a foundational event for Israel, it is remarkable how little Philo deals with it. For Philo's treatment in other treatises, especially as the Sinai revelation relates to the Logos and the school of Moses, see Burton L. Mack, "Moses on the Mountaintop: A Philonic View," in *School of Moses*, 16–28.

[23] The theophany may show the superiority of the Decalogue both to Greco-Roman legal codes and the Jewish special Laws. For Philo, this special status of the Decalogue does not lessen the importance of the special Laws; rather, it secures their status in accordance with the heads of the Laws in the Decalogue. See Yehoshua Amir, "The Decalogue According to Philo," in *The Ten Commandments in History and Tradition* (ed. Ben-Zion Segal and Gersho Levi; Jerusalem: Magnes Press, 1990), 124–7.

[24] Samuel Sandmel, *Philo of Alexandria: An Introduction* (New York: Oxford University Press, 1979), 66, notes this oddity.

does not frequently mention the events of its giving in his treatises. We might, however, expect mention of Sinai where he deals with the event of giving the Law such as *Quaestiones et Solutiones in Exodum*. Here, Philo does designate the mountain as "Sinai" which translates inaccessible.[25] So why does Philo provide an extended explanation of the "Sinai" narrative in *Decal.* without mentioning Sinai? This muting of a specific name is a major move toward de-particularizing the events surrounding the giving of the Law. The mountain scene could accord with Greco-Roman conceptions of revelation at high places; for example, the Delphic oracle along with other revelatory mediums was on a mountain. The mountain is a well-accepted place of nearness to and revelation from a deity, but "Sinai" is specific to Israel. Removal of "Sinai" is a step in opening the Law to a broader audience.

3.2. *Omission of Jewish Descriptions of the People*

In Exod 19:1 and 2, the LXX designates the people as Israel; moreover the Law is addressed to a particular nation: "'This is what you shall say to the house of Iakob and report to the sons of Israel…you shall be for me a people special above all nations. For the earth is mine. And you shall be for me a royal priesthood and a holy nation. These words you shall say to the sons of Israel'" (Exod 19:4…6 NETS). These are undeniable ethnic identity designations that Philo mutes; rather, he prefers to use the more general "people" (λαός) who were gathered at Sinai.[26] Certainly λαός is prevalent in the LXX Sinai narrative, but Philo has omitted the particularizing designations by an ethnic group's forefathers (Jacob and Israel). This is especially pronounced when viewed alongside his Jewish contemporaries who emphasize the specific ethnicity of the people gathered at Sinai. For example, Josephus refers to the people as "Hebrews" (*Ant.* 3.77, 79, 84,

---

[25] *QE* 2.45, 47; cf. Josephus, *Ant.* 3.75, 76. Sinai can also be described as exceedingly high: Philo, *Mos.* 2.70; Josephus, *Ant.* 2.264; 3.76, 82; Pseudo-Philo 3.76. See the discussion of Philo's etymology of "Sinai" in Lester L. Grabbe, *Etymology in Early Jewish Interpretation: The Hebrew Names in Philo* (BJS 115; Atlanta: Scholars Press, 1988), 207–208.

[26] For a discussion of terminology for the Jewish people in Philo's works, see Birnbaum, *Place of Judaism*, 30–60, esp. 50–51. In *Decal.* Philo does describe the people gathered at Sinai with the generic "nation" but without any specific designation such as "holy nation": "The ten words or oracles, in reality laws or statutes, were delivered by the Father of All when the nation, men and women alike, were assembled together" (*Decal.* 32 [Colson, PLCL]). Philo broadens the description of God to include potentially all nations by describing God as the universal Father.

95).[27] Josephus emphasizes the particularity of the people through reference to Jewish figures: Adam, Noah, Abraham, Isaac, Jacob, and Moses son of Amaram and Jochabad (§§ 86–7). This brief retelling of Jewish history secures the Law to the particular people, the Hebrews. Again by omitting the phrase "my treasured possession out of all people," Philo omits a description of the people that creates two classes, Israel and everyone else. Philo likewise omits "holy nation."[28]

3.3. *Omission of Jewish Descriptions of God*

Along with the de-particularization of the covenant recipients, Philo's move toward a more universal presentation of the Sinai narrative also affects his portrayal of God. For example, Philo's first commandment does not include God's self-description as the God of Israel, "I am the LORD your God, who brought you out of the land of Egypt, out of the house of slavery" (Exod 20:2); rather, God is "the transcendent source of all that exists" (*Decal.* 52). Again Philo silences the covenantal and national overtones. Removal of the nationalistic overtones associated with God's self-identification as the deliverer from the Egyptians and redefining God in terms of Creator and True Existence place him within Greco-Roman categories for deity.[29]

3.4. *Omission of Covenantal and Cultic Elements*

At the beginning of God's communication with the people in the Exodus narrative is the covenantal context (Exod 19:5). Philo remains strangely

---

[27] Pseudo-Philo prefers the label "sons of Israel" (11.1, 5, 15), and emphasizes the close connection between this God and his people. Moreover, Pseudo-Philo nearly reproduces Exod 20:2–17 including the covenantal nature of the Law. Philo mentions the Sabbath which is practiced by "the Jewish nation" and he quickly shows how this practice accords with the events of creation, thus placing it within a universal, creation framework (*Decal.* 96–98' cf. 159 "Hebrews").

[28] Another element that Philo omits is the fear that the people felt. Josephus and Pseudo-Philo especially emphasize the theme of terror from the LXX .

[29] "God" is by far the most common designation, but a number of concepts, those not specific to Israel, are also prominent: Creator (41, 51, 61, 64, 69, 105, 107, 120, 155), truly existent One (8, 81), Father of all (32, 51, 64, 90, 105, 134), King (41, 61, 155, 178), eternal or uncreated One (41, 60, 64, 67, 120). A particularly Greco-Roman idea is present in God as Benefactor and Source of good (41, 81, 176). Philo occasionally has an extended description of God, and they all present a non-ethnic God: "highest and most august, the Begetter, the Ruler of the great World-city, the Commander-in-Chief of the invincible host, the Pilot who steers all things in safety" (*Decal.* 53 [Colson, PLCL]; cf. *Decal.* 41, 60, 155). For the fusion of Jewish traditions about God with Platonism, see Borgen, "Philo," in *Jewish Writings*, 264–6.

silent on the idea of covenant even though the Sinaitic covenant becomes an integral aspect of Jewish identity. Some of the strangeness of this silence is evident in comparison with Pseudo-Philo who puts more stress on the covenantal context than even the LXX does.[30] Removing the Law and the giving of the Law from the covenantal context suppresses God's providential care for this people, but this specifying meaning of the Law is exactly the kind of thing that Philo is suppressing in the Sinai event. In fact, "covenant" (διαθήκη) does not occur at all in *Decal.*[31]

With the muting of the covenantal aspects of Sinai, Philo also downplays some cultic aspects. The priests find little mention in *Decal.* although *Spec.* mentions the priesthood far more than any of his other treatises.[32] The LXX mentions the priests in Exod 19:22, 24 where the priests are a particularized group distinct from the people. Moreover, Philo does not mention Aaron, the high priest, even though the LXX says that he ascends Sinai with Moses. Philo can keep—probably must keep—Moses because he is not just the priest and mediator of the covenant but more importantly he is the paradigmatic, virtuous philosopher and lawgiver. The priests occur in *Decal.* 71 and 159, and neither of these occurrences attributes them any prominence. That the priesthood is important for Philo in his other works and is mentioned regularly in *Spec.* which follows and is connected to *Decal.* in the *Exposition* suggests that Philo intentionally subdues its prominence in *Decal.*[33] The difference in the presentation of the priesthood between *Decal.*

---

[30] Pseudo-Philo repeats Exod 19:1, but his treatment of 19:3–6 places greater emphasis on the particularity of the people and the specialness of the their relationship to God: "'I will give a light to the world and illumine their dwelling places and establish my covenant with the sons of men and glorify my people above all nations. For them I will bring out the eternal statutes that are for those in the light but for the ungodly a punishment'" (trans D. J. Harrington, "Pseudo-Philo," in *OTP* 2:318).

[31] Birnbaum, *Place of Judaism*, 144–52, notes the absence of "covenant" between God and humans in all the *Exposition*: "In this series, Philo presents the relationship between God and Biblical Israel as one that is accessible to any virtuous person" (152).

[32] One might question if *Spec.* fits into the broader corpus of the *Exposition* with *Decal.*, why does *Spec.* not seem as concerned to mute Jewish particularities? A number of factors probably contribute to this difference, but most significant is that Philo wants to defend and promote Jewish religious practice and the Jewish way of life. *Decal.* defends the Law as the most wise, rational, and natural Law because it can be proven to accord even with Greek understandings of wisdom, rationality, and nature. But it is important for Philo to maintain the need to observe the Law in the governance of one's daily life. He wants to defend the particular Jewish way of life, and he does this first by showing the Decalogue, the heads of the special laws, are proved true by other means.

[33] Jutta Leonhardt-Balzer, "Priests and Priesthood in Philo: Could He Have Done Without Them," in *Was 70 CE a Watershed in Jewish History? On Jews and Judaism before and after the Destruction of the Second Temple* (ed. Daniel R. Schwartz and Zeev Weiss with the collaboration of Ruth E. Clements; Leiden: Brill, 2012), 127–53, demonstrates the

and *Spec.* may be attributable to the different scopes of the works.[34] In *Decal.*, it is likely that he downplays the significance of the priesthood as yet another particularizing element of the covenant at Sinai, especially since the Jewish cultic singularity was a common Gentile criticism of Jewish practice.[35]

4. *Philo's Enhancements of the Septuagint's Language in* Decal. *32–49*

In addition to excluding elements of the Septuagint's Sinai narrative that limit it to the Jewish people, Philo emphasizes elements of the narrative that demonstrate the universal manner of the giving of the Law. He reads Exodus carefully and shows that the Law addresses individuals who are receptive to reason regardless of their ethnicity, and the cosmic elements of the theophany indicate both the greatness of the Law and that the transmission of the Law extends beyond a physical location. Philo's most elaborate description is that of the voice of God which he describes as a miraculous dictation to the souls of humans.

---

importance of the priesthood in Philo's thought. Drawing on the larger Philonic corpus, Leonhardt-Balzer shows that Philo views the Jewish people as the priests of the world and the high priest as representing both the nation and creation before God; thus, Philo's view of the priesthood is both universalizing and particularizing. Philo's avoidance of the priesthood in *Decal.* is likely due to both the general scope of *Decal.* and the particularizing aspects of the priesthood. Daniel R. Schwartz, "Philo's Priestly Descent," in *Nourished with Peace: Studies in Hellenistic Judaism in Memory of Samuel Sandmel* (ed. Frederisk E. Greenspahn, Earle Hilgert, and Burton L. Mack; Chico, Cal: Scholars Press), 155–71, concludes that Jerome's comment that Philo was from a priestly family is very probable; this makes it even more likely that Philo does understand the priesthood to play a significant role in Jewish life.

[34] Because *Decal.* discusses the Ten Commandments which are general introductions to the special Laws discussed in *Spec.*, the nature of the discussion can be more general. Due to the less specific nature of the Ten Commandments, they may also be more adaptable to universalizing and presentating the Jewish legal code and practice as desirable for non-Jews. But Philo still wants to uphold the specific Jewish practices as the proper expression of the soul responding to the Law; thus, having given a general, accessible, universalizing, and perhaps attractive introduction to the Law in *Decal.*, Philo can discuss some more specific issues of Jewish practice in *Spec.* Mention of Jewish things such as priesthood are unavoidable in the discussion of the Jewish way of life.

[35] Philo has no aversion to Aaron in *QE* 2.27 although he interprets Moses, Aaron, Nadab, and Abihu allegorically.

4.1. *The Recipients of the Law*

It was shown that Philo omits descriptions of the people that would classify them apart from a larger Greco-Roman audience. But more than just omission of the particular ethnic designations, Philo advances a positive argument that the people, or more properly persons, addressed at Sinai are not Jews but everyone who obeys the Law; obedience to the Law is a viable possibility even for those without the Law if they live in accord with nature and reason as the patriarchs demonstrate.

Philo reads the LXX carefully and notes that the imperatives—both those that are morphologically imperatives and future indicatives functioning as imperatives—are second person singular; thus, if one takes a very literal stance, the Law is addressed to individuals. And the addressees are not only Jews. Philo explains: "Each single person, when he is law-abiding and obedient to God, is equal in worth to the whole nation, even the most populous, or rather to all nations, and if we may go still farther, even to the whole world. And therefore elsewhere, when He praises a certain just man, He says, I am thy God, though He was also the God of the world."[36] The removal of the covenantal context of the Law has opened the door for Philo to attribute the address to those other than Jews. The recipients of the Law are redefined from the LXX account to be those individuals who are law-abiding and just. Jews are not excluded from these recipients of the Law, but they also do not have a position as recipients that excludes Greeks.

4.2. *The Miraculous Occurrences*

To describe the miraculous occurrences at Sinai, Philo draws on Exod 19:16: "And it happened on the third day, when it was toward dawn, sounds and lightning and a dark cloud were all occurring upon the mountain Sina; the sound of the trumpet was ringing loudly, and all the people were terrified" (NETS). To each of these elements, Philo attaches an additional description. The LXX describes the thunder as "sounds occurring" while Philo says that there were "clashes of thunder louder than ears could hold."[37] Philo heightens the language to demonstrate that the revelatory process superseded physical capacities. This serves as an indicator of something more than a sense-perceptible event. Moreover the "lightning occurring" of the LXX is

---

[36] Philo, *Decal.* 37 (Colson, PLCL).
[37] Philo, *Decal.* 44 (Colson, PLCL); cf. Pseudo-Philo, *LAB,* 11.4–5.

taken to be "flashes of lightning of surpassing brightness."[38] The sound of the unseen trumpet again points beyond the physical capacities of perception (*Decal.* 44). This trumpet also is unique in that it is heard at the farthest distance (*Decal.* 33) which is another indication that the giving of the Law supersedes the sense-perceptible world. The cloud then stands as a symbol of the distance spanned by the giving of the Law: there was "the descent of a cloud which like a pillar stood with its foot planted on the earth, while the rest of its body extended to the height of the upper air, the rush of heaven sent fire which shrouded all in dense smoke."[39] By enhancing the descriptions of the miraculous occurrences of the theophany, Philo has emphasized both the source of the Law and the realm of dictation and reception. The cloud symbolizes the spanning of the gap between heaven and earth as God transmits the Law. And the thunder, lightning, and trumpet all point beyond the sense-perceptible world.

The terms for noises that Philo chooses are somewhat different from the LXX, but he seems concerned to make a distinction between the voice of God (φωνὴ ἐκ τοῦ πυρός) and the sounds of the thunder (κτύποι βροντῶν) and the trumpet (ἦχος σάλπιγγος). The latter sounds, while miraculous and awe-inspiring, serve to indicate the greatness of God's voice and the Law proclaimed. In comparing the LXX and *Decal.*, one notices that Philo has tidied up the LXX language which uses φωνή to refer to God's voice (19:5, 19b; 20:18a), the thunder (19:13, 16a), and the trumpet (19:16b, 19a; 20:18b).[40] Rather than equate God's voice with another sound, such as the

---

[38] Philo, *Decal.* 44 (Colson, PLCL); cf. Pseudo-Philo, *LAB,* 11.4–5; Josephus, *Ant.* 3.80; Aristobulus 2.16.

[39] Philo *Decal.* 44 (Colson, PLCL). The cloud is a frequent Jewish symbol for the presence of God (Cf. Exod 13:21–22; 40:34–38; 1 Kgs 8:10–11; 2 Chr 5:13–14; Neh 9:12, 19; esp. Sir 45:4–5). Pseudo-Philo, *L.A.B.* 11.15, takes the cloud to represent God's presence; while Josephus, *Ant.* 3.79, only mentions the cloud in passing as Sinai itself is the place of God (*Ant.* 3.76). In *QE* 2.246, Philo explains the presence of the cloud for six days as representing a second birth for the prophet that exceeds his physical birth. Aristobulus makes explicit what Philo explains through the elevated language: "Therefore, it is clear that the divine descent occurred for these reasons: in order that the viewers might comprehend each of these things in a revelatory way—not that the fire consumed nothing, as has been said, nor that the trumpet blasts came into being without human activity or the use of instruments, but that God, without any aid, manifested his own majesty, which is throughout all things" (Aristobulus Fragment 2.17 translated by A. Y. Collins in *OTP* 2:839).

[40] The semantic range of φωνή becomes especially overlapping when multiple meanings occur in the same sentence. For example, Exod 19:16 uses φωνή both for thunder and a trumpet: ἐγίνοντο φωναὶ (thunder) καὶ ἀστραπαὶ καὶ νεφέλη γνοφώδης ἐπ᾽ ὄρους Σινα, φωνὴ (trumpet blast) τῆς σάλπιγγος ἤχει μέγα, καὶ ἐπτοήθη πᾶς ὁ λαὸς ὁ ἐν τῇ πορεμβολῇ. And then Exod 19:19 uses φωνή for both a trumpet and God's voice: ἐγίνοντο δὲ αἱ φωναὶ (trumpet blasts) τῆς σάλπιγγος προβαίνουσαι ἰσχυρότεραι σφόδρα, Μωυσῆς ἐλάλει, ὁ δὲ θεὸς

unseen trumpet or the loud thunder, Philo attributes the voice of God to the visible fire.

4.3. The Miraculous Voice in Decal. 32–35

Philo sandwiches this magnificent theophany on the mountain between two differing but complementary descriptions of God's voice at Sinai. If Philo continues to follow the sequence of the narrative in the LXX, *Decal*. 32–35 likely describes the voice in Exod 19:16–19. The comments on the Law intervene (*Decal*. 36–43; Exod 20:1–17), and then *Decal*. 46–49 address the voice in Exod 20:18. We will seek to answer why the voice receives such prominence and how Philo's explanation functions in *Decal*.

Philo questions if the Father of all gave the Law through a humanlike voice.[41] One of Philo's overarching suppositions is "God is not like humans" (*Decal*. 32).[42] This is a central anti-anthropomorphic tenet that governs the explanation of the voice.[43] Again the rejection of anthropomorphic qualities to God not only secures his uniqueness but also the

---

ἀπεκρίνατο αὐτῷ φωνῇ (voice of God). Philo seems to equate the trumpet blasts that are perceptible at the farthest distance with God's voice (*Decal*. 33; cf. Exod 19:19). With this intermixing, it is not entirely unwarranted for Philo to interpret φωνή in 20:18 as God's voice and the trumpet blast even though in the LXX the referents seem to be thunder and trumpet blast: Καὶ πᾶς ὁ λαὸς ἑώρα τὴν φωνὴν (God's voice) καὶ τὰς λαμπάδας καὶ τὴν φωνὴν (trumpet blast) τῆς σάλπιγγος καὶ τὸ ὄρος τὸ καπνίζον, φοβηθέντες δὲ πᾶς ὁ λαὸς ἔστησαν μακρόθεν. Philo expresses this conglomeration of ideas in *Decal*. 33: God wanted "an invisible sound to be created…which giving shape and tension to the air and changing it to flaming fire, sounded forth like a breath through a trumpet an articulate voice so loud that it appeared to be equally audible to the farthest as well as the nearest" (Colson, PLCL).

[41] In the closing sentence of *Decal*. 45, God's instruction to Moses is described as oracular instruction, χρησμῳδέω. Francesca Calabi, *Filoni di Alessandria: De Decalogo* (Pisa: ETS, 2005), 63–65 n. 64, points out that the private revelation Moses received at the burning bush was described in similar language (χρησμός; *Mos*. 71).

[42] Philo presses forward in his description of events and says that God, the Father of all (ὁ πατὴρ τῶν ὅλων; *Decal*. 8) delivered the Ten Commandments. Already Jewish literature, especially the Maccabean literature, had used similar phraseology to emphasize God's transcendence: Σὺ κύριε τῶν ὅλων ἀπροσδεὴς ὑπάρχων ("You Lord of everything, although needing nothing"; 2 Macc 14:35). Simon's prayer seems to express the Jewish conception of God: σὺ γὰρ ὁ κτίσας τὰ πάντα καὶ τῶν ὅλων ἐπικρατῶν δυνάστης δίκαιος εἶ ("For you, the Creator of all things and Governor of all, are a just Ruler"; 3 Mac 2:3; cf. 3 Macc 2:2 with emphasis on God's transcendence; 3 Macc 6:9). This subtle designation of God affirms his transcendence directly prior to the seemingly anthropomorphic description of God with the voice.

[43] John Dillon, *The Middle Platonists 80 B. C. to A. D. 220* (2nd ed.; Ithaca, N.Y.: Cornell University Press, 1996), 143, comments: "As the Stoics claimed for Homer, so Philo claims that any apparent inconsistencies or infelicities are simply signs by Moses to the intelligent reader that the passage is to be taken allegorically."

uniqueness of the Law. The occasion merited some miraculous event by God. At this point in the treatise Philo comments on Exod 19: "Now all Mount Sinai was wrapped in smoke, because the Lord had descended upon it in fire; the smoke went up like the smoke of a furnace while all the people were extremely astonished. And the voices/noises/blasts of the trumpet grew louder and louder, and Moses spoke, and God answered him in a voice" (Exod 19:18, 19 author's translation).

Philo takes this nondescript voice from the LXX and elaborates on its nature. In so doing, Philo seems to be participating in a larger Hellenistic Jewish discussion concerning the voice of God.[44] While previous and contemporaneous Jewish authors had noted the anomaly of seeing the voice of God with the interpretation that auditory and visual perceptions were merged, Yehoshua Amir argues that what is unique about Philo is that to explain this textual anomaly, he relies on the philosophy of his day.[45] What Philo does is merge an exposition of the biblical text with contemporary philosophy to show the concordance between the two as far as contemporary philosophy and science accord with truth in nature.

This voice is more harmonious than instruments and in a liminal state of not being soulless but also not having a soul and body like a living creature. Rather this sound is composed of the rational soul (ψυχὴ λογική). Philo makes a basic distinction of the soul into rational and irrational parts. The rational portion can be identified with the mind or intellect to which Philo refers in his conclusion of this section: "the hearing of the mind

[44] Ezekiel the Tragedian does not offer much description about the fire and voice Moses encounters at the burning bush, but he does combine the visual and auditory perception of the event, "'the place on which you stand is holy ground, and from this bush God's word shines forth to you'" (*Ezek. Trag.* 98–99 trans. R. G. Robertson in *OTP* 2:813; cf. *Ezek. Trag.* 246; *Pseudo-Philo, LAB,* 11.14). Josephus, *Ant.* 2.266, notes the enigma of the blazing fire at the burning bush without consuming or even charring the bush: "Moses was terrified at this strange spectacle, but was amazed yet more when this fire found a tongue, called him by name, and communed with him…" (*Ant.* 2.267, [Thackeray, PLCL]). In Josephus's description of God's voice at Sinai, he describes the miraculous transmission to the people even though he does not mention the anomaly of seeing the voice (*Ant.* 3.88–89). Philo describes the bush in *Mos.* 1.65–71. While he notes the textual anomaly of the bush not being consumed, he interprets the fire allegorically as a portent that the Jewish sufferers would not be consumed by their oppressors. Philo later mentions that the voice at Sinai gave "commands promulgated by God not through His prophet but by a voice which, strange paradox, was visible and aroused the eyes rather than the ears of the bystanders…" (*Mos.* 2.213, [Colson, PLCL]). Further, Philo describes the voice at Sinai: "the voice of God, and seen by the eye of the soul, he very properly represents as visible" (*Mig.* 48 [Colson, PLCL]; cf. *Mig.* 4, 46–49).

[45] Amir, "Decalogue," 136–148. Amir is helpful for understanding Philo in light of contemporary Stoic and scientific understandings.

(διανοία) possessed by God" (*Decal.* 35).[46] Here John Dillon says "Philo observes the normal [for Platonism and Middle Platonism] bipartite division of the soul, into rational (*logikon*) and irrational (*alogon*) parts."[47] That the voice belongs to the realm of the rational soul serves three purposes for Philo: (1) the realm of the rational soul is immaterial, so it avoids attributing physicality to God while maintaining his direct involvement in their dictation; (2) this type of voice, speaking to the souls of humans, is superior to physical hearing and thus elevates the Law itself in the miraculous manner of its reception; (3) reception of the Law is not dependent on one's ethnicity but on the rational nature of the soul.

First, Philo explains away the apparent anthropomorphism of God speaking by drawing on both the rational nature of the sound and an anomaly in the text. The unseen sound (ἠχώ here but subsequently φωνή) "which giving shape and tension to the air and changing it to flaming fire, sounded forth like the breath through a trumpet an articulate voice so loud that it appeared to be equally audible to the farthest as well as the nearest."[48] Philo appears to draw on a specific phrase in Exod 19:19 that can be interpreted as the sound progressively increasing (προβαίνουσαι ἰσχυρότεραι σφόδρα). Philo interprets the reception of this voice as "more illuminating in its ending than in its beginning."[49] Clearly physical voices, probably to be associated with the non-rational realm, do not increase in clarity with distance. This textual anomaly buttresses Philo's previous observation about the unique character of the voice. Because the voice belongs to the realm of the rational soul and Moses describes it in an anomalous way, a literal interpretation of the voice as a physical sound must be rejected. This is not to be understood as allegorical; rather it is an elaborate interpretation to deny the anthropomorphizing of God. In this argument, Philo participates in a broader rejection of anthropomorphisms attributed to God in both the Jewish and Greco-Roman settings.[50] Philo wants to show both that God is transcendent and that he is immanent

---

[46] It would be more tidy if Philo were to refer to the hearing of the mind as νοῦς, but Philo makes the same contrasting pair in *Decal.* 13.

[47] Dillon, *Middle Platonists*, 174. Dillon also notes (174 n.1) "Philo's concept of two opposed powers in the soul of man seems to have its closest parallels in post-Biblical Jewish literature, e.g. *Test.* XII *Patr. Ass.* I; 6; *Jud.* 20. Also in Qumran texts, I *QS* 3, 13ff.; 4, 15f."

[48] Philo, *Decal.* 33 (Colson, PLCL).

[49] Philo, *Decal.* 35 (Colson, PLCL).

[50] See John M. G. Barclay, "Snarling Sweetly: Josephus on Images and Idolatry," in *Idolatry: False Worship in the Bible, Early Judaism and Christianity* (ed. Stephen C. Barton; London: T&T Clark, 2007), 73–87. E.g., Xenophon, Frg. 23; Varro in Augustine, *Civ. Dei* 4.27, 31; 6.5–6; Cicero, *De Natura Deorum* 2.70–72.

enough to deliver the Law directly. His explanation of the voice provides such an explanation.[51]

Second, the unique constitution and reception of the voice speaking the Law supports Philo's implicit argument for the uniqueness of the Law. To simplify what Philo says, this rational voice speaks more directly to the soul than a physical voice. This voice creates a reception of a totally different kind, ἀκοὴν ἑτέραν πολὺ βελτίω τῆς δι' ὤτων ("another kind of hearing far better than the hearing through ears"; *Decal.* 35). Philo intimates that this sound should not be thought of as a conventional sound because it speaks to the souls of humans and not to their ears.[52] Physical hearing is a very imperfect sense, "but the hearing of the mind possessed by God makes the first advance and goes out to meet the spoken words with the keenest rapidity."[53] The mind of the hearer is "in-Godded" (ἔνθεος) so that the voice speaks directly to the soul. Moreover, the "in-Godded" mind is moved to initiate the meeting with God and goes out eagerly to meet the voice. Clearly this is no ordinary God or voice that speaks to the minds and souls of humans; therefore, the content of this voice must be altogether unique and special. The description of the voice is particularly important for Philo to highlight the uniqueness of the Laws.

Third, If Philo intends to argue that the Mosaic Law is the very same Law as the law of nature (evidenced through creation and the patriarchs) and thus open to non-Jews, he must show how the written manifestation of the law of nature is not inferior to the unwritten Law. Najman notes that the Greek conception of the law of nature is that it is not expressible in a written code and written expressions are necessarily inferior.[54] One of the

---

[51] Cf. Aristobulus in Eusebius *Praep. ev.* 8.10.17, who argues the miraculous events and especially the voice occurred "in order that the viewers might comprehend each of these things in a revelatory way—not that the fire consumed nothing, as has been said, nor that the trumpet blasts came into being without human activity or the use of instruments, but that God, without any aid, manifested his own majesty, which is throughout all things" (Adela Yarbro Collins, *OTP*, 2:839).

[52] Nikiprowetzky, *De Decalogo*, 135, distinguishes between the eye and ear of the soul and their corresponding receptions: "Il n'en demeure pas moins que, tandis que 'l'oeil de l'âme' designe le discernment et a des harmoniques surtout d'ordre noétique, 'l'oreille de l'âme' est l'appelation d'une activité qui intéresse particulièrement la volonte." See also Niehoff, *Philo on Jewish Identity and Culture*, 202.

[53] Philo, *Decal.* 33 (Colson, PLCL).

[54] Najman, "Law of Nature," 72, argues, "Mosaic Law was traditionally conceived of as authoritative because it was a sacred written tradition associated with the particular relationship between Israel and God, and with Israel's particular practices. Philo, however, was thinking and writing in a Hellenistic context that denigrated writing in favor of the unwritten, law of nature, and denigrated misanthropic particularity in favor of philanthropic universality." Cf. Najman, "Written Copy," 52–63; "Law of Nature," 55–73. In this

ways that Philo preempts this criticism is to show how the Mosaic Law is transmitted miraculously to the soul of the one living in accord with wisdom and nature. By heightening the language of thunder, lighting, and the trumpet, Philo indicates that this transmission of the Law exceeded the sense-perceptible world, and by the anomalous voice, Philo indicates that the transmission was to the rational souls of humans. Philo removes the importance of Sinai's location in Jewish history as he places the revelatory event beyond the sense-perceptible realm. This move not only secures the Law's uniqueness in that it can perfectly transmit the law of nature in a written form, but it also opens the recipients of the Law to all those who possess a rational soul. Moreover, Philo has made his argument about the universalization of Sinai in a way that can draw on the Middle Platonic philosophy of his day.

4.4. The Miraculous Voice in Decal. 46–49

Philo returns to his analysis of the voice from the fire, but here he is drawing on Exod 20:18. The flame in the revelation of the Ten Commandments becomes articulate speech to the people. From the blazing fire come words that were so clear ὡς ὁρᾶν αὐτὰ μᾶλλον ἢ ἀκούειν δοκεῖν ("that they seemed to see rather than hear them"; Decal. 46).[55] Philo arrived at this by noticing an anomaly in the text: Καὶ πᾶς ὁ λαὸς ἑώρα τὴν φωνὴν καὶ τὰς λαμπάδας καὶ τὴν φωνὴν τῆς σάλπιγγος καὶ τὸ ὄρος τὸ καπνίζον, φοβηθέντες δὲ πᾶς ὁ λαὸς ἔστησαν μακρόθεν ("And all the people saw/witnessed the sound/voice and the lightening and the sound/voice of the trumpet and the smoking mountain, and all the people were afraid and stood apart"; Exod 20:8). He rejects that the voice is a literal voice since God does not have speech organs. But this is not an allegorical interpretation because a close reading of the text reveals that the voice is seen, so Philo's interpretation is in some ways a very literal one that points to a different kind of speech. Moreover whatever God says is not in words, but he speaks in deeds (Decal. 47), so that one should not expect God to speak as humans speak. The speaking of God is perceived or "judged by the eyes rather than the ears" (Decal. 47). Nikiprowetzky notes this first reason for a different interpretation of the voice, the textual anomaly, but he adds that Philo as a well-informed reader

---

description, Philo also intends to counter any accusations of human origin (Cf. Josephus, C. Ap. 2.25).

[55] Nikiprowetzky, De Decalogo, 135, cautions that the main concern of this passage is not the visible words of God and may allude to Mig. 47; Ps 19:9; 119; 130.

of the LXX must also have thought about the creative speech of God as action. Simply put "God speaks and the world is created. To act, for God, is to speak."[56] Philo's purpose here seems to be to give an account of the textual anomaly as a rejection of an anthropomorphic interpretation. Moreover, he purposes to describe the miraculous giving and Giver of the Law in a way that shows the Law's uniqueness and divine reception in those who have purified themselves.

The significance of the voice coming from the fire does not rest only in its anti-anthropomorphic use for Philo. Rather, the fire is also something that functions symbolically (διὰ συμβόλου; *Decal.* 49).[57] The combination of the fire and the oracles of God indicates the purity of the commandments because they are refined by fire. But the fire also symbolizes something close to the allegory of the soul: "Since it is the nature of fire both to give light and to burn, those who resolve to be obedient to the divine utterances will live forever as in unclouded light with the laws themselves as stars illuminating their soul."[58] The intended symbolism is that the fire represents the Law.[59] It has either of two effects depending on the soul of the one receiving it: either it illuminates or burns. Also the Law symbolizes the stars that illuminate the souls of humans. Nikiprowetzky explains this well: "Humans carry within themselves a heaven where the practice of the Law enlightens the stars and it corresponds to the movements of the cosmic heaven … Intelligence as stars produces its own light as it has been able to lead them to the home of intelligible light."[60] The Law illuminates the soul of the rational human. Again the positive nature of the Law does not rest on the ethnic identity of the human, but on the soul submitting in obedience to the Law. Similarly the metaphor is drawn from the cosmic realm and does not reference anything specifically Jewish. This may also

---

[56] Nikiprowetzky, *De Decalogo*, 136, "Dieu parle et le monde est créé. Agir, pour Dieu, c'est parler." Elsewhere, Philo uses the speech as action explanation to describe how the wise man's words can be described as light (*QE* 2.44).

[57] It is interesting at this point that Philo does not distinguish between the heavenly fire and common fire as he does in *Mos.* 2.148. In *Mos.* 2.148, Philo seems to abandon the Middle Platonic notion of a four element universe and offers a more Aristotelian five-element universe (Cf. *Plant.* 1–8; *Det.* 154). Dillon, *Middle Platonists*, 171, offers a possible reconciliation.

[58] Philo, *Decal.* 49 (Colson, PLCL).

[59] See Nikiprowetzky, *De Decalogo*, 137. But Philo is likely drawing on the rest of Exodus also where the fire reveals God's glory, "Philon explique ainsi l'appearance de feu dévorant, que revet la gloire divine selon *Ex.* 24, 17" (Nikiprowetzky, *De Decalogo*, 138).

[60] Ibid., 137. L'homme porte en lui un ciel, où la pratique de la Loi allume des étoiles et qu'elle accorde aux mouvements du ciel cosmique…L'intelligence comme les astres entretient sa propre lumière, qu'elle a comme eux puisée au foyer de la lumière intelligible.

serve as an implicit apostrophe for the reader's self-examination. Philo argues that if the reader is virtuous, he or she will receive the Law. If the intended audience was Gentile, Philo is calling them to examine their response, whether it is obedient or rebellious.

5. *Conclusion*

As Peder Borgen has noted, Philo is "an exegete for his time" in his own social, political, and religious location.[61] Philo's location at the apex of the Jewish Alexandrian community, with its diminishing rights and prominence, compels him to craft *De decalogo* in a manner that is plausible and possibly even compelling to a larger Greco-Roman audience.[62] Philo shows that wise men antecedent to the Mosaic Law practiced the same, natural law. Similarly nature and the best of philosophy still point to the uniqueness of the Mosaic Law. Najman's conclusion is fitting "Only through the unique Sinai event does it become possible for the written Law of a particular nation to serve as the perfect copy of the unwritten law of nature."[63] But to universalize the Law for his Greek audience, Philo omits specific names, the covenant, and some of the cultic aspects of the Law. This muting of specifically Jewish elements promotes broader application of the Law as not being ethnically bound. Meanwhile Philo highlights the cosmic elements of the giving of the Law to show its divine delivery and reception. Philo spends the most time in his Sinai account describing the anomalous voice that he takes to be God speaking to the souls of rational humans (again, not exclusively Jews). Instead of warping the Exodus text, Philo reads it closely and provides an interpretation both that Moses, according to Philo, intended with his textual clues and that shows the universal applicability of the Mosaic Law. It is clear that Philo has no intent of presenting the Law in a universal manner that would compromise the distinctiveness and superiority of the Jewish Law, manner of living, and God. Rather, Philo is so intent on presenting the exceptionalness of the Jewish Law that he presents it in a way that is universally applicable. Borgen comments on this impulse in Philo, "Philo's extreme form of particularism risked ending up in a universalism where Jewish distinctiveness

---

[61] Borgen, *Philo*.
[62] See Niehoff, *Jewish Exegesis*, 169–85.
[63] Najman, *Seconding Sinai*, 105.

was in danger of being lost."[64] He presents the Law as proved true by nature and philosophy and shown to be unique by its divine and miraculous origins, but to universalize the Law Philo must hurcle the particularizing aspects of the Sinai narrative and transform Sinai into a truly universalizing event.

Loyola University Chicago

---

[64] Peder Borgen, "Philo of Alexandria," in *ABD* 5.341. It should also be noted that Philo's universalism can be read as an extreme particularism in which other nations abandon their practices and observe the Jewish Law because it is the legal code that accords perfectly with the law of nature and reason. Cf. *Mos.* 2.17–20, 43–4.

The Studia Philonica Annual 24 (2012) 107–127

ON THE CONFUSION OF TONGUES AND ORIGEN'S ALLEGORY OF THE DISPERSION OF NATIONS*

PETER W. MARTENS

I. *Introduction*

The story of the tower of Babel (Gen 11:1–9) elicited significant commentary in Jewish and Christian antiquity.[1] While the reception history of this short pericope demonstrates considerable diversity, there were also striking similarities among its early interpreters. In this article I examine Origen's extended allegory of Babel and explore whether it was indebted to Philo's earlier treatment of the story in his *On the Confusion of Tongues*. Portions of the Alexandrian Christian community of the second and third centuries received Philo's writings favorably and, as is well known, Origen was himself an admiring reader of Philo.[2] He referred to him a little more than a

---

* I would like to thank Ronald Cox for the invitation to present an earlier version of this paper at the Philo of Alexandria Group at the Society of Biblical Literature (San Francisco, 2011). I am also grateful for the close reading and formatting provided by my research assistant, Andrew Chronister.

Unless otherwise noted, I use the following translations: Philo, *On the Confusion of Tongues* (trans. Francis H. Colson and George H. Whitaker; PLCL 4; Cambridge, MA: Harvard University Press, 1958); Origen, *Contra Celsum* (trans. Henry Chadwick; Cambridge: Cambridge University Press, 1953). The Greek edition for the relevant sections of *Cels.* is: Marcel Borret, ed., *Origène: Contre Celse*, vol. 3 (SC 147; Paris: Cerf, 1969).

[1] For a discussion of ancient Jewish readings of Babel, see Christoph Uehlinger, *Weltreich und "eine Rede": Eine neue Deutung der sogenannten Turmbauerzählung (Gen 11,1–9)* (OBO 101; Göttingen: Vandenhoeck & Ruprecht, 1990), 9–290; Theodore Hiebert, ed., *Toppling the Tower: Essays on Babel and Diversity* (Chicago: McCormick Theological Seminary, 2004); Philip M. Sherman, "Translating the Tower: Genesis 11 and Ancient Jewish Interpretation" (Ph.D. diss., Emory University, 2008); Maren R. Niehoff, *Jewish Exegesis and Homeric Scholarship in Alexandria* (New York: Cambridge University Press, 2011), 77–86. The most extensive discussion of the tower of Babel and its place in intellectual history is Arno Borst, *Der Turmbau von Babel: Geschichte der Meinungen über Ursprung und Vielfalt der Sprachen und Völker* (6 vols.; Stuttgart: A. Hiersemann, 1957–1963). The discussion on Origen can be found in 1:235–39.

[2] On the reception of Philo in the Alexandrian church, see Attila Jakab, *Ecclesia Alexandrina: evolution sociale et institutionnelle du christianisme alexandrin, IIe et IIIe siècles*

dozen times in his surviving writings, and from these passages a distinct portrait of Philo emerges: he was one of Origen's "predecessors" in the allegorical interpretation of the law and prophets.[3] This favorable assessment of Philo has prompted scholars to search for additional passages in Origen's writings that suggest unannounced Philonic influence. Thanks to the careful work of Annewies van den Hoek, who builds upon the earlier work of David Runia, we now have a working descriptive catalogue of parallel passages between these two authors, with graded assessments of the likelihood of Origen's dependence on Philo.[4] Van den Hoek has identified six passages in Origen's corpus where he almost certainly drew upon *On the Confusion of Tongues*.[5] In only one of these, however, is Origen wrestling with his own interpretation of Babel;[6] in another case she sees a parallel, but no dependence.[7] In what follows I will attempt to correct and expand upon Van den Hoek's dossier, responding to her initial call for others "to work with, to elaborate on, to correct and to improve" her catalogue.[8]

Origen mentions the story of Babel (or "Confusion," as the Septuagint reads) only a handful of times in his surviving corpus.[9] However, in many of these passages he quickly hints at the same, provocative allegorical

---

(Bern: Lang, 2001), 53–64; Ronald E. Heine, *Origen: Scholarship in the Service of the Church* (Oxford: Oxford University Press, 2010), 31.

[3] The four places where Origen mentions Philo by name are: *Comm. in Gen.* (Karin Metzler, *Origenes: Die Kommentierung des Buches Genesis*, Werke mit deutscher Übersetzung 1/1 [Berlin: De Gruyter, 2010], D4); *Cels.* 4.51; *Cels.* 6.21; *Comm. in Matt.* 15.3. For a list of anonymous references to Philo (i.e. passages where Origen vaguely points to "one of our predecessors," etc.), see David T. Runia, *Philo in Early Christian Literature* (Minneapolis: Fortress Press, 1993), 161–3. On Philo's writings in Origen's library, see pp. 20–23, 157–8.

[4] Annewies van den Hoek, "Philo and Origen: A Descriptive Catalogue of Their Relationship." *SPhA* 12 (2000): 44–121. See the earlier work by David Runia on the relationship between Origen and Philo: Runia, *Philo in Early Christian Literature*, 158–63; idem, *Philo and the Church Fathers: A Collection of Papers* (VCSup 32; Leiden: Brill, 1995), 120–121; idem, "Filone e i primi teologi cristiani." *Annali di storia dell'esegesi* 14 (1997): 355–80.

[5] These passages rate an "A" or "B" for degree of dependence, where the grades signify certain dependency, or high probability of dependency, respectively. One passage is listed at "Philo and Origen," 113 ("A") and the other five at 114 ("B"). Note that van den Hoek also identifies two sets of parallel passages (*Cels.* 5.30//*Conf.* 68 and *Hom. in Gen.* 4.5//*Conf.* 134) neither of which suggests Origen's dependence on Philo (these merit a rating "C" or "D").

[6] Origen, *Cels.* 4.21, a passage discussed below in section III (passage #3).

[7] Origen, *Cels.* 5.30, a passage discussed below in section III (passage #6).

[8] Van den Hoek, "Philo and Origen," 48.

[9] I count eight references, relying on Jean Allenbach, et al., eds., *Biblia Patristica: Index des citations et allusions bibliques dans la littérature patristique, vol. 3: Origène* (Paris: Editions du Centre national de la recherche scientifique, 1980), 46.

interpretation. The lengthiest version, which will be the focus in the first part of this paper, occurs in his late work, *Against Celsus* (written ca. 248).[10] Here he proposes a labyrinthine interpretation of Babel, and several other related scriptural passages in his response to his interlocutor's scorn that this passage contained no hidden teaching. Origen's interpretation is particularly noteworthy since it echoes, but also develops in important ways, his teaching on the pre-existent state of souls that he had first articulated two decades earlier in *On First Principles*. It is a remarkable interpretation that plunges readers into arcane topics like the primordial fall of souls and their subsequent embodiment, the role of angelic powers in this process, and comparative religious, cultural and political themes. In the second part of this paper I will highlight the most striking resemblances I have been able to detect between Origen's account of Babel and what we find in Philo's *On the Confusion of Tongues*. There are a number of important similarities, and while not all reflect direct dependence, some likely can be attributed to Origen's firsthand awareness of Philo's treatise.

II. *Origen on the Dispersion of Nations*

In book 5 of *Against Celsus*, Origen responds at length to Celsus' claim in his *True Doctrine* (written ca. 178) that the story of Babel "hints at nothing [μηδὲν αἰνίσσηται]" and was, in fact, "obvious [σαφὴς]."[11] The larger context for Origen's ensuing allegory was Celsus' commendation of Jewish conservatism, a foil for the insurrectionist Christian movement. Celsus writes:

> Now the Jews became an individual nation, and made laws according to the custom of their country; and they maintain these laws among themselves at the present day, and observe a worship which may be very peculiar but is at least

---

[10] Note as well that the editors of the *Philocalia* (the fourth century anthology of Origen's writings) excerpted this passage (*Cels.* 5.25–32) for their volume. See Éric Junod, *Origène: Philocalie 21–27, Sur Le Libre Arbitre* (SC 226; Paris: Cerf, 1976), 21–3. For literature on this section of *Against Celsus*, see Jean Daniélou, *Origen*, (trans. Walter Mitchell; New York: Sheed and Ward, 1955), 224–37; Michel Fédou, *Christianisme et Religions Païennes dans le* Contre Celse *d'Origène* (Paris: Beauchesne, 1988), 516–30; Uehlinger, *Weltreich und "eine Rede,"* 260–265.

[11] Following H. Chadwick and M. Borret, who both attribute these two assessments to Celsus himself, though this interpretation has been disputed in the scholarship (see SC 136:232 n. 1). Celsus' account of the story of Babel is briefly discussed by Origen at *Cels.* 4.21 (SC 136:232.4–5) before his more expansive discussion in book 5. On Celsus' denial of an allegorical interpretation of the OT, see John Granger Cook, *The Interpretation of the Old Testament in Greco-Roman Paganism* (STAJ 23; Tübingen: Mohr Siebeck, 2004), 59–64.

traditional. In this respect they behave like the rest of mankind, because each nation follows its traditional customs, whatever kind may happen to be established. This situation seems to have come to pass ... because it is probable that from the beginning the different parts of the earth were allotted to different overseers, and are governed in this way by having been divided between certain authorities. In fact, the practices done by each nation are right when they are done in the way that pleases the overseers; and it is impious to abandon the customs which have existed in each locality from the beginning.[12]

In this extract Celsus argues that the Jews, like every other nation, have ancient customs that could be traced back to "the beginning" and the governance of their own "overseer" or "authority."[13] These customs obviously differ from other nations, but so long as people live in accordance with their ancestral practices (as the Jews do), they act correctly. It would be "impious," on the other hand, to abandon one's own established customs in favor of newer ones. A few sections later, Origen reveals how Celsus considered Christianity illustrative of this impiety: "I will ask them [i.e., Christians] where they have come from, or who is the author of their traditional laws. Nobody, they will say. In fact, they themselves originated from Judaism, and they cannot name any other source for their teacher and chorus-leader. Nevertheless they rebelled against the Jews."[14] Unlike the Jewish nation, Christianity was not a community following customs that could be traced back to a collaboration between a particular lawgiver and an overseer. Christians only became a distinctive community because they rebelled against the ancestral customs of the Jews.

Origen offers an extended response to Celsus' critique of Christian origins, ultimately reversing his conclusion and contending that the Christian community was *the most pious* among the nations.[15] Origen's counter-argument is nuanced. He agrees with Celsus that nations have customs that go back to "the beginning" and are associated with the administrative work of different overseers. However, he does not agree that piety or impiety are determined by whether people happen to be loyal to the particular

---

[12] Celsus cited by Origen, *Cels.* 5.25. See as well the continuation of Celsus' argument in *Cels.* 5.34.

[13] For other references by Celsus to these authorities, see *Cels.* 8.35, 8.53, 8.64 and 8.67. For discussion, see Chadwick, *Contra Celsum*, xix–xx.

[14] Celsus cited by Origen, *Cels.* 5.33. Also see *Cels.* 3.5 where Celsus presents Christianity as a "revolt against the [Jewish] community." Note, however, that in this passage Celsus turns this critique against the Jews, whom he chastises for their revolt against the Egyptians. Origen criticizes Celsus for his shifting views on the ancestry of the Jews in *Cels.* 5.26.

[15] See esp. *Cels.* 5.32 where Origen refers to Christians as "pious [ὅσιος]" for breaking their ancient customs (SC 147:94.19). [16] Origen, *Cels.* 5.33.

conventions of their own nation. Again, he agrees with Celsus that Christianity originated from Judaism: "Our 'chorus-leader and teacher,'" he writes of Jesus, "came forth from the Jews."[16] But this assent does not imply for him that Christians have begun to pursue novel customs. At the heart of Origen's response is an alternative narrative of the dispersion of nations.[17] As we will now see, his allegorical interpretation of the story about Babel plays a leading role in his attempt to subvert the claim that Christian customs were impious.

"Celsus seems to me to have misunderstood certain very mysterious truths about the division of the regions of the earth."[18] Thus Origen begins his rebuttal by turning to Moses, "the prophet of God," who explains how the peoples of the earth *truly* came to be distinguished from one another under the leadership of overseers or authorities. "[L]et us take the risk and give an account of a few of the more profound truths which have a mystical and secret conception [ἔχοντά τινα μυστικὴν καὶ ἀπόρρητον θεωρίαν] of the way in which different regions of the earth were divided from the beginning among different overseers."[19] Origen highlights two passages from the Pentateuch that mutually illumine one another and become the springboard for his alternative account of the hierarchy of nations and their customs.[20] The obvious passage is Gen 11:1–9. But what is conspicuous about this pericope is that it does not refer, at least explicitly, to overseers. Importantly, Origen cites a second passage, Deut 32:8–9, which his Septuagint rendered as follows: "When the Most High divided the nations, as he scattered the sons of Adam, he set the boundaries of the nations according to the number of the angels of God [κατὰ ἀριθμὸν ἀγγέλων θεοῦ]; and the Lord's portion was Jacob his people, Israel the lot of his inheritance."[21]

---

[17] Note, however, that Origen does not rely entirely on his exegesis of Babel to advance his critique of Celsus. He denounces the moral relativism insinuated by Celsus's praise for adherence to traditional customs. How can it be the case, Origen asks, that the practices done by each nation are right, so long as they agree with what their overseers assigned, if in fact these practices differ and sometimes contradict one another? He highlights the relativity of legal and religious practices among the Scythians, Persians, Taurians and Libyans, and concludes that for Celsus, "piety will not be divine by nature, but a matter of arbitrary arrangement and opinion" (*Cels.* 5.27). This argument continues through 5.28 and is briefly revisited in 5.36. Later at *Cels.* 5.34–35, Origen wonders how Celsus would reconcile his critique of Christianity with the fact that philosophers frequently teach people to abandon their traditional customs.

[18] Origen, *Cels.* 5.29.

[19] Origen, *Cels.* 5.28 (SC 147:84.19–22).

[20] He cites a third passage (Wis 10:5), but it does not factor into the subsequent discussion.

[21] As Origen cites this verse at *Cels.* 5.29 (SC 147:86.18–21). Origen was aware that the septuagintal reading was at odds with the Hebrew text in his day, where the phrase in

When Origen turns to the topic of the dispersion of the nations, not only here in *Against Celsus* but elsewhere in his corpus, he consistently informs his account of scattering in Gen 11 with these lines from Deut 32.[22]

How then did Origen allegorize this account of the dispersion of nations? He acknowledges that there is "much of a mysterious nature" with this theme, but offers his readers an important initial clue. The story of Babel concerns "the way in which souls became bound to a body (though not by reincarnation) [περὶ ψυχῶν οὐκ ἐκ μετενσωματώσεως εἰς σῶμα ἐνδου-μένων]."[23] This clue is intended to orient readers to the overarching theme of the ensuing allegory: his esoteric doctrine of pre-existent souls, their fall and subsequent embodiment, a position he first articulated roughly twenty years earlier in *On First Principles*.[24] Here in *Against Celsus*, however, Origen is not nearly as explicit about how the detailed allegory of Babel informs this esoteric doctrine. He prefers to hint at it, relying upon his readers "who have the ability" to "work out the meaning of the passage for themselves."[25] Moreover, as we will see below, the version of pre-existence sketched out in response to Celsus has a decidedly communitarian dimension. The impression Origen gives in several sections of *On First Principles* is that this doctrine concerned simply the fall of individual souls. Here in *Against Celsus* we encounter a modified version of pre-existence: it is also about the fall of communities of souls, or nations.

Origen begins his interpretation with the "whole earth" (Gen 11:1) having one language, before otherwise unspecified people began to move away from the east. He posits that all these primordial nations are using "one particular language, and as long as they agree with one another they continue using the divine language. And they remain without moving from the east as long as they pay attention to the things of light and of the effulgence of the everlasting light."[26] There are two hints here at his doctrine of the pre-existence of souls. The emphasis on the nations using

---

question read, "according to the number of the children of Israel." See the brief text-critical discussion at *Hom. in Num.* 28.4.1.

[22] The juxtaposition of Gen 11:1–9 and Deut 32:8–9 also occurs at *Comm. in Jo.* 13.331–332 and *Hom. in Num.* 11.4.4. On the importance of Deut 32:8–9, see *Princ.* 1.5.2 and 4.3.11.

[23] Origen, *Cels.* 5.29.

[24] Versions of this doctrine can be found esp. at *Princ.* 1.6.2; 1.8.1–2; 2.1.1; 2.6.3–6; 2.8.3–4; 2.9.1–2; 2.9.5–6. For two different interpretations of this evidence, see Henri Crouzel, *Origen*, trans. A. S. Worrall (Edinburgh: T&T Clark, 1989), 205–218 and Mark J. Edwards, *Origen against Plato* (Aldershot: Ashgate, 2002), 87–97.

[25] Origen, *Cels.* 5.29. He says he does not want this teaching to be "cast before an uneducated audience" (5.29) lest he betray the secret oracles of God. On the "esoteric/ exoteric" distinction in Origen, see Heine, *Origen: Scholarship in Service of the Church*, 222–6.

[26] Origen, *Cels.* 5.30.

one language, and continuing to do so while they remain in harmony with one another, points to God's initial creation of souls. These, Origen insists, were all made equal with one another and existed harmoniously by engaging in the same activity, the contemplation of God and God's Son.[27] The references to people remaining in the east and paying attention to the "effulgence of the everlasting light" are allusions to the attentiveness of pre-existent minds to the Son of God, whom Origen associates here, as elsewhere, with light.[28]

But when some of these people "move themselves from the east and pay attention to things foreign to the east, they find "a plain in the land of Shinar" (Gen 11:2) which means 'a shaking of teeth,' as a symbol of the fact that they have lost that by which they are nourished, and they dwell there."[29] Already Gen 11:2 (and not the attempt to build a city and tower later in 11:3–4) refers to the primordial fall. The important clue is the reference to paying attention to things "foreign to the east," by which Origen signifies the moment when minds ceased their contemplation of God (or God's Word). According to his account of the pre-existent fall, these fallen minds subsequently became joined to bodies, and it is this association with materiality to which the subsequent sections in *Against Celsus* about the building of the city and tower seem to allude.[30] "Then they desire to collect material things and to join what cannot naturally be joined to heaven ...."[31] The allusion here is likely to the linking of minds with bodies. Elsewhere Origen refers to minds being placed in bodies with similar language: it was a laborious task that required "bring[ing] together two somewhat opposing natures into one composition."[32]

At this point, Origen effortlessly appends Deut 32:8–9 (where God scatters the nations and appoints them to angels) to his reading of Babel.[33] He writes:

[27] For example, see Origen, *Princ.* 2.9.2 and 2.9.6.

[28] See Origen, *Cels.* 5.33. See also *Comm. in Jo.* 1.158–181 and *Princ.* 1.2.9–11.

[29] Origen, *Cels.* 5.30.

[30] See Origen, *Princ.* 2.9.1–2; 2.9.6. Also *Cels.* 4.40.

[31] Origen, *Cels.* 5.30.

[32] Origen, *Comm. in Jo.* 13.327 (Origen, *Commentary on the Gospel According to John, Books 13–32* [trans. Ronald E. Heine; FC 89; Washington, D.C.: Catholic University of America Press, 1993], 138). Note in this passage (13.326–333) Origen's further speculations about distinct angelic and divine roles in the dispersion of nations. Not only do the angels bear responsibility for the languages and locales of the nations, they are perhaps also responsible for embodying fallen souls, whereas God takes direct responsibility for embodying Israel. See below for more on this distinction between angelic and divine roles.

[33] Origen will develop the Jewish idea that each nation is under an angel in what follows. For literature on early Christian and Jewish angelology, see: Friedrich Andres, *Die*

> And each one [i.e., nation], in proportion to the distance that they moved from the east, whether they had travelled far or a little way ... is handed over to angels who are more or less stern and whose character varies. Under them they remain until they have paid the penalty for their boldness. And each one is led by angels, who put in them their native language, to the parts of the earth which they deserve. Some are led to parched land, for example; others to country which afflicts the inhabitants by being cold; and some to land that is difficult to cultivate; others to land that is less hard ... .[34]

Origen is not forthcoming about the identity of these angels who are "more or less stern and whose character varies."[35] What *is* clear is that they bequeath nations their own languages. Elsewhere we learn that Gen 11:7—"Come, let us confound their language"—is about God speaking to angels.[36] These angels also allot nations to the regions of the earth that justly correspond to the degree by which they fell away "from the east." Finally, Origen refers to the punishment that these angels mete out.[37] This punishment, however, involves more than disagreeable climate or topography. Origen deftly moves to Rom 1, where Paul refers three times to God "giving up" or "handing over" humanity to sinful practices (the verb παραδίδωμι is used in Rom 1:24, 26 and 28). What is particularly helpful for Origen is that this language of "giving up" coincides with his own account of God divesting himself of the direct rule of the nations and handing them over to other, fallen overseers. Moreover, Rom 1 conveys the sort of punishment that Origen thinks the nations endure under their angelic masters: "on account of their sins," he writes, the nations "were given over [παρεδό-θησαν] 'to a reprobate mind' [Rom 1:28] and 'to passions of dishonour'

Engellehre der griechischen Apologeten des III Jahrhunderts (Paderborn: Druck und Verlag von Ferdinand Schöningh, 1914); Erik Peterson, "Das Problem des Nationalismus im alten Christentum." *TZ* 7 (1951): 81–91; Jean Daniélou, "Les sources juives de la doctrine des anges des nations chez Origène." *Recherches de science religieuse* 38 (1951): 132–37; idem, *The Angels and Their Mission According to the Fathers of the Church* (trans. David Heimann; Westminster, MD: Newman Press, 1957); Joseph Turmel, "Histoire de l'angélologie des temps apostoliques à la fin dun Ve siècle." *Revue d'histoire et de littérature religieuses* 3 (1989): 299–308; Michael Mach, *Entwicklungsstadien des jüdischen Engelglaubens in vorrabbinischer Zeit* (TSAJ 34; Tübingen: Mohr Siebeck, 1992).

[34] Origen, *Cels.* 5.30 (trans. Chadwick, 287, slightly modified). For a similar passage, see *Princ.* 2.9.3.

[35] See Daniélou, *Origen,* 229–33, for a helpful discussion of this problem. Important parallel passages include: *Princ.* 3.3.2–3; *Hom. in Luke* 12.4; *Cels.* 8.36.

[36] See Origen, *Comm. in Jo.* 13.331 and esp. *Hom. in Num.* 11.4.4.

[37] These nations remain under the angels until they have "paid the penalty for their boldness." Twice in the immediately following paragraphs Origen refers to these angels receiving their subjects "for the purpose of punishment [ἐπὶ κολάσει]" (*Cels.* 5.31 and 5.32).

[Rom 1:26] and 'to impurity in the lusts of their hearts' [Rom 1:24],[38] in order that by being sated with sin they might hate it … ."[39] Here a crucial point in Origen's argument emerges: the punishments that the angelic overseers administer to the nations are not Celsus's vaunted ancestral customs, but more often than not, sinful practices.

Origen resumes his account of the primordial dispersion, picking up the theme of Israel's election in Deut 32:8–9. This passage creates intertextual tension for him since it suggests that God did not scatter Israel, only the nations, whereas the Babel episode speaks sweepingly of "the whole earth" moving away from the east. Origen resolves this dilemma by reminding his readers that not everything at the level of the letter in Scripture is true: the story about Babel expresses both "something true in its literal meaning and also indicates some secret truth."[40] His strategy is to offer an interpretation that explains, first, the sense in which Israel was not scattered (against the literal sense of Gen 11:1–9); and next, the sense in which Israel joined the "whole earth" in this dispersion (with the literal sense of Gen 11:1–9).

There are some people who indeed "have preserved the language from the beginning, who, because they have not moved from the east, continue in the east and with the eastern language."[41] Here Origen is alluding, as he elsewhere says more explicitly, to the Hebrew language.[42] He continues: "And let [the reader] understand that only those have become the Lord's portion and His people, who are called Jacob; Israel has become the lot of his inheritance. They alone are under the charge of a ruler who has not received his subjects for the purpose of punishment like the others."[43] Origen strikingly rewrites the narrative of universal dispersion in Gen 11 with an eye to Deut 32:8–9. Not only is Israel excluded from the experience of Babel, its refusal to leave the east in the primordial world serves as

[38] Christoph Uehlinger thinks these expressions in Rom 1 are taken allegorically by Origen to refer to the punishing angels (*Weltreich und "eine Rede,"* 262, n. 33). While this interpretation is possible, it seems to be a particularly strained way of referring to angels. More likely, I think, is that Origen is referring, with Paul, to the actual sinful practices that pervade the nations.

[39] Origen, *Cels.* 5.32. For a parallel passage where Origen reflects at greater length on the redemptive quality of being "sated with sin," see *Orat.* 29.13. Jean Daniélou helpfully notes the mirroring in Origen's thought between the pre-existent fall of souls due to being sated with *the good*, and the return of these souls because they were sated with evil (*Origen,* 221).

[40] Origen, *Cels.* 5.31. The same sentiment about the literal and allegorical meanings of Gen 11:1–9 is expressed earlier at *Cels.* 4.21

[41] Origen, *Cels.* 5.31.

[42] Origen, *Hom. in Num.* 11.4.4.

[43] Origen, *Cels.* 5.31.

justification for its unique status as God's elect nation, a story that begins in Gen 12. In other words, it *merited* this status as the Lord's own, distinct from the other nations that were scattered and assigned to angelic punishment.[44]

Yet Origen is aware of exile. He proceeds to weave the subsequent story of Israel into the same allegorical reading of Babel that he outlined for the nations above.

> [I]n the society of these people who are assigned to the Lord as the superior portion[,] sins were committed which at first were tolerable and of such a character that they did not deserve to be utterly forsaken ... And let [the reader] realize that this happened for a long time, and that a remedy was always applied, and at intervals they turned back. Let [the reader] perceive that in proportion to their sins they were abandoned to those beings [i.e., angels] who had obtained other countries. At first, after they were punished and had paid the penalty to a small extent, and having been as it were chastised, they returned to their native land. And let [the reader] see how later they were handed over to sterner rulers, the Assyrians and then the Babylonians, as the scriptures would call them. Then let [the reader] notice that although remedies were applied[,] nevertheless they sinned still more, and on this account were scattered in the other parts by the rulers of the other nations who carried them off.[45]

Origen explicitly locates the vicissitudes of Israelite history in his narrative of fallen angelic overseers. The sins of the Israelite people ultimately led to their dispersion because their ruler, God, forsook them and handed them over to the angelic overseers of other nations. Thus the situation, prior to the advent of Jesus, was that all nations, even the Jews, were removed from God's direct care and allotted to angels under whom they served punishments proportionate to their misdeeds.[46]

---

[44] In addition to intertextual tension with Gen 11:1–9, Deut 32:8–9 also created theological tension for Origen. This passage had to be interpreted in such a way that it did not present Israel as receiving unmerited favor from God. If this were the case, it would suggest to Origen either that God had acted arbitrarily; or worse, it would have reinforced the Valentinian teaching of determined natures, where election was nothing more than the unjust predetermination of one nation to privilege, while all others were excluded from it (*Princ.* 2.9.5–7). Jean Daniélou comments insightfully and colorfully: "The logic of Origen's system is once more in evidence, here, with its insistence that you always get the conditions you deserve. Gone is the idea that when God chose Israel as his special portion he was simply exercising his sovereign freedom, the idea that his choice of a sinful people had nothing behind it but a gratuitous outpouring of divine love. Instead, the choice God made of Israel is represented as a reward for loyalty in the midst of universal apostasy. The spirit of the prophets is stifled by the spirit of the Pharisees" (*Origen*, 236).

[45] Origen, *Cels.* 5.31 (trans. Chadwick modified).

[46] See Origen, *Hom. in Jer.* 12.3.2 for a very similar integration of Israelite history into this allegorical reading of Babel.

At this point in his interpretation Origen turns to Christianity. He has gone to great lengths to discredit Celsus' notion that it is laudatory simply to adhere to one's own customs. As we have seen, the two passages on dispersion, combined with Rom 1, are central to Origen's argument since they help him recast national customs (at least some of them) as sinful practices. Now he takes the final step in his response by pointing to the Christian community whose laws he thinks ought to be followed. Fascinatingly, he does not leave the two Pentateuchal passages on dispersion behind to make this next claim. Rather, Origen presents the church's emergence as a reversal, in several ways, of this narrative of dispersion. First, whereas God originally *scattered* sinful nations through the world, the Christian community is a *gathering* of dispersed peoples. "Each one of us has come," Origen writes, to the church; "all the nations are coming to it."[47] In a scholion on the book of Genesis, he explicitly presents the nascent church as it was depicted in the Acts of the Apostles—where harmonious believers were of one heart and soul (Acts 4:32)—as the corrective to the nefarious plurality of Babel.[48] Second, whereas in the beginning God *bequeathed* fallen nations to angelic forces, the ecclesial ingathering occurs because God is *divesting* the angels of their subjects, with the result that this church is restored to direct rule under God. It is God, the supreme overseer, Origen writes, who "is far more powerful than the others, since he has been able to take chosen men from the portions of all the others, and to deliver them from the beings who had received them for the purpose of punishment."[49] And third, whereas the nations were handed over to *sinful practices*, the church is governed by *corrective customs*, i.e. "better and more divine laws."[50] When

---

[47] Origen, *Cels.* 5.33 (see as well *Hom. in Jer.* 12.3.3).

[48] Metzler, *Die Kommentierung des Buches Genesis*, E27. According to Christoph Uehlinger, Origen was the first Christian author to present the unity of the church as the corrective of Babel (*Weltreich und "eine Rede,"* 264). Perhaps, however, this move was already anticipated in the *Shepherd of Hermas* (a text Origen knew—see *Princ.* 1.pref.4; 1.2.3; 2.1.5, etc.) where the church is presented as the tower that unifies the nations into one thought, mind, faith and love (9.17.4). Arno Borst claims, however, that Origen was the first Christian author to make the link between Babel and Pentecost explicit (*Der Turmbau*, 236).

[49] Origen, *Cels.* 5.32. Origen also attributes the defeat of angelic forces to Jesus. Jesus is "the most powerful being, 'delivering us from this present evil world' [Gal 1:4], and from 'the rulers of this world who are coming to nought' [1 Cor 2:6]" (*Cels.* 5.32). To reinforce the legitimacy of Jesus's role in the conquest of the nations, Origen refers his readers to the prophecy spoken in Ps 2:8, where God addressed Jesus: "Ask of me, and I will give thee nations for thine inheritance and the uttermost parts of the earth for thy possession" (*Cels.* 5.32; see also *Comm. in Jo.* 13.333). For more on this theme, see Daniélou, *Origen*, 226–32.

[50] Origen, *Cels.* 5.32.

God annexes peoples to himself, he does so that he "might appoint laws for them and show them a life which they should follow, his purpose being to lead them on to the end to which he led those of the earlier nation who did not sin."[51]

Origen singles out two of the traditional practices of the nations that Celsus implicitly endorsed when he recommended that people follow the customs they had inherited from their divine overseers: warfare and idolatry. Both are intimately linked to what transpired at Babel. The church, Origen stresses, is a community of peace-makers, a clear contrast to the cacophony of Babel. "No longer do we take the sword against any nation, nor do we learn war any more, since we have become sons of peace through Jesus who is our author instead of following the traditional customs, by which we were 'strangers to the covenants.'"[52] It is also a community that rejects idolatry, so that the gathered nations now say with the prophet Jeremiah, "our fathers have inherited lying idols, and there is none among them that sends rain [Jer 16:19]."[53] Origen has chosen this scriptural passage carefully. Idolatry is "inherited," and thus Celsus was correct: it *was* a traditional practice. Yet Origen immediately adds that this practice was hardly commendable. Nor was it traditional in the deepest sense. Babel symbolized, after all, the nations abandoning their former, *truly* traditional way of life: the attentive contemplation of God and his Son. It was the nations who moved away from this pristine ideal and thus became mired in idolatry. The church, however, moves toward this ideal, and so while distinctive, and perhaps even disruptive, against the immediate horizon of Greco-Roman society, against the broadest horizon, only it is truly traditional, truly original. It is in the church, Origen says, where the nations re-direct their focus on God and his Son—the Light from the "east"—that they paid attention to in the original primordial world. In the space of a few lines, he stresses this new focus in worship: "Each one of us has come 'in the last days,' when our Jesus came ... to the Word far above every word, and to the house of God." Or again: "[W]e exhort one

---

[51] Origen, *Cels.* 5.31.

[52] Origen, *Cels.* 5.33.

[53] Origen, *Cels.* 5.33. Note Origen making Celsus' divine overseers complicit in idolatry at *Cels.* 5.10.

another to the worship of God through Jesus Christ, which has shone out in the last days."[54] The church and its constitutive practices represent God's intent of creating a community that aims for the beginning, restoring the practices of that pre-existent "earlier nation who did not sin."[55]

Origen's elaborate interpretation of the dispersion of nations (Gen 11:1–9; Deut 32:8–9) serves as a rebuttal of Celsus' general claim that people do what is right so long as they follow the primordial customs ordained by their national overseers. It also addresses the more specific claim that Christianity, because it has rebelled against traditional Jewish customs, was impious. As we have seen, these dispersion pericopes allow Origen to position the scattering of the nations against the backdrop of the primordial fall. Not simply have the nations fallen and been assigned to fallen angels, but they have also been given over to sinful customs. Origen thus turns Celsus' general claim on its head. "For we see it as *pious* to break 'customs which have existed in each locality from the beginning.'"[56] While these customs ought not be followed, the laws and way of life of the church *should* be followed. Through a creative reversal of these same dispersion narratives, Origen contends that Christian customs ought to be followed precisely because they are not derived from a fallen angelic overseer who was assigned to punish a nation. Rather, they are derived directly from the supreme overseer, God, under whom all nations at one point lived in the primordial, prelapsarian world. While this Christian way of life admittedly takes its start from the recent Jesus, Origen does not accept Celsus' insinuation that this way of life is novel. It is, rather, commensurate with the way of life of that "earlier nation who did not sin," and thus it is the Christian community that is fundamentally traditional. So Origen concludes: "it is impious *not* to cast oneself upon him who appeared and proved himself to be purer and more powerful than all rules."[57]

---

[54] Both citations from Origen, *Cels.* 5.33. On worship of the Logos, also see *Cels.* 5.35. Note as well the possibility that Origen's critique of idolatry might have been inspired, or at least reinforced, by the similar critique in Rom 1, a passage he refers to in the preceding lines.

[55] Origen, *Cels.* 5.31.

[56] Origen, *Cels.* 5.32. The original claim by Celsus, that it was "impious" to break these customs, was cited at *Cels.* 5.25.

[57] Origen, *Cels.* 5.32.

III. *On the Confusion of Tongues and Origen's Allegory of Babel*

How, if at all, does Origen's elaborate exegesis of Babel depend upon Philo's even more extensive allegory in *On the Confusion of Tongues*? In its broadest contours, it is important to acknowledge that these authors offer very different readings of this pericope. The focus in Philo's allegory is less political and more psychological, attending to the disharmony within each person. The solution to this problem is, of course, not the advent of Jesus or the alternative society of the church, but as J. O'Leary proposes, a *koinonia* grounded in the philonic *logos* and the philosophy of Moses.[58] There are, however, some notable similarities between their respective allegories. In what follows I will highlight seven parallel passages, beginning with the two that most clearly suggest Origen's dependence upon Philo.

1. Philo and Origen's interpretations of Gen 11:7 are conspicuously similar. To whom is God speaking ("Come, let *us* go down ...")? Philo thinks it is clear that God is speaking with "some persons whom He treats as His fellow-workers [τισιν ὡς ἂν συνεργοῖς αὐτοῦ],"[59] or a few sections later, his "lieutenants [τοῖς ὑπάρχοις]."[60] He notes that God is surrounded by "numberless powers (δυνάμεις) ... among them are included those who punish (αἱ κολαστήριοι)."[61] A few lines later, Philo notes that there are angels who serve these powers as well, and that this collective group is responsible for the "punishments of the wicked [τὰς ... κατὰ πονηρῶν κολάσεις]."[62] After a brief reflection on the contributing role of angels in exacting punishment, Philo turns to Gen 11:7 and attributes the "us" to them in particular: while the wicked deserve to be punished by God's powers, "He decreed that it should be exacted by others," which in this context can only appear to mean the angels.[63]

---

[58] Joseph S. O'Leary, "*Logos* and *Koinonia* in Philo's *De Confusione Linguarum*," in *Origeniana Octava: Origen and the Alexandrian Tradition (Papers of the 8ᵗʰ International Origen Congress, Pisa, 27–31 August 2001)*, vol. 1 (ed. Lorenzo Perrone; Leuven: Leuven University Press, 2003), 245–73. For additional commentary on Philo's treatise, see the prefatory essay and supplementary notes in Jean Georges Kahn, *De confusione de linguarum* (PAPM 13; Paris: Cerf, 1963); Uehlinger, *Weltreich und "Eine Rede,"* 153–72; P. Sherman, "Translating the Tower," 275–350.

[59] Philo, *Conf.* 168.

[60] Philo, *Conf.* 179.

[61] Philo, *Conf.* 171 (translation modified).

[62] Philo, *Conf.* 180 (PLCL translation modified).

[63] Philo, *Conf.* 182. Jean Daniélou, "Les Sources Juives," thinks Philo is speaking of angels (135), as do Whitaker and Colson in the explanatory note ("a") in PLCL 4:110. For more on the "powers" in Philo, see Cristina Termini, *Le potenze di Dio: Studio su δύναμις in Filone di Alessandria* (Rome: Institutum Patristicum Augustinianum, 2000).

Angelic punishment is important for our purposes. As noted above, Origen repeatedly uses the same language for the punishment of nations (κόλασις) and attributes it, as Philo appears to do, to the angels. Philo also understands punishment in terms that echo Origen's later discussion. He is eager to associate only the good with God, whereas the subordinate powers are associated with the less seemly: punishment, destruction and evil.[64] As we have seen, Origen too makes this distinction when he demarcates the Jews who "alone are under the charge of a ruler who has not received his subjections for the purpose of punishment like the others [i.e. nations]."[65] Moreover, both authors fashion punishment as remedial. Philo speaks of angelic punishment as "not a thing of harm or mischief, but a preventive and correction of sin,"[66] and a little later, as "salutary for the human race."[67] Origen also speaks of punishment in this way: it is a disciplining [παιδεύω] or remedy [θεραπεία] designed to turn people back to God.[68] Finally, there is no earlier Christian author who sees Gen 11:7 as a dialogue between God and the angels.[69] Thus this exegetical decision, which he shares with Philo but no earlier Christian author, combined with several overlapping features in their respective understandings of angelic punishment, suggest Origen's dependence upon Philo.

2. But perhaps the most striking parallel occurs when these two authors reflect on the theme of peace. For Philo, a life corrective of Babel is oriented toward the *logos*: they who "honour one father, right reason [τὸν ὀρθὸν λόγον], reverence that concert of virtues ... and live a life of calmness and fair weather."[70] The link between peace and the *logos* finds (as we have seen) a distinct Christological echo in Origen. Christians have become "sons of peace through Jesus" who does not try to control the world through warfare, but rather through the "word [λόγος] of his teaching."[71] Moreover, it is conspicuous that Philo contrasts polytheists from those who live at peace with the *logos*. Those "who affiliate themselves to that evil thing called polytheism, who take in hand to render homage some to this deity,

---

[64] Philo, *Conf.* 180–181. This disassociation of certain tasks from God runs from *Conf.* 171 to 182.

[65] Origen, *Cels.* 5.31.

[66] Philo, *Conf.* 171.

[67] Philo, *Conf.* 182.

[68] Origen, *Cels.* 5.31–32.

[69] Note also that both Origen and Philo link the "let us" of Gen 11:7 with Gen 1:26 (Philo, *Conf.* 168–169 and Origen, *Comm. in Jo.* 13.331).

[70] Philo, *Conf.* 43.

[71] Origen, *Cels.* 5.33 (trans Chadwick, 290). Perhaps there is additional significance to Origen using the singular, "*word* of his teaching," and not the plural, *words*, which would be associated with Babel.

some to that, are the authors of tumult and strife at home and abroad, and fill the whole of life from birth to death with internecine wars."[72] Origen moves in a similar direction, identifying a commitment to peace as well as a resistance to idolatry as the two features of the church that made it corrective of Babel.[73] Finally, just as Origen juxtaposed the church that lives at peace with the church that is at the same time militant against opposing spiritual forces,[74] so too does Philo embrace this tension: "For it is the nature of men of peace that they prove to be men of war, when they take the field and resist those who would subvert the stability of the soul."[75] The clustering of four different themes in these respective interpretations of the Babel narrative—peace, the *logos*, idolatry and warfare—strongly suggests Origen's dependence on Philo.[76]

The five sets of passages that follow also share notable similarities, though in each case it is less likely that Origen was actually dependent on Philo's earlier reflections on Babel.

3. In her aforementioned article, van den Hoek noticed that both authors discussed the similarities between the story about Babel and the Homeric myth of the sons of Aloeus. While she rates the passage in *Against Celsus* a "B" for likely dependence upon Philo, I am not inclined to see borrowing here.[77] Philo opens his treatise with the critique of otherwise anonymous interlocutors who wonder how people can speak of the Mosaic law "as containing the canons of absolute truth [τοὺς ἀληθείας κανόνας]" when "your so-called holy books contain also myths [καὶ μύθους περιέχουσιν] which you regularly deride when you hear them related by others."[78] Philo then refers to the resemblance between Babel and the story of the sons of Aloeus that might be used to demonstrate that Moses not only integrated a myth into his law, but also did so poorly since no one

---

[72] Philo, *Conf.* 42 as well as later at 144.

[73] Origen, *Cels.* 5.33.

[74] Note the reference in Origen, *Cels.* 5.32, to Jesus "delivering us from this present evil world" (Gal 1:4) prior to the discussion of the peaceful church in *Cels.* 5.32. This theme of the church both peaceful and militant is discussed in Daniélou, *Origen*, 233–5.

[75] Philo, *Conf.* 43.

[76] On clustering as a sign of dependence, see Van den Hoek, "Philo and Origen," 47.

[77] Van den Hoek, "Philo and Origen," 48.

[78] Philo, *Conf.* 2. The charge of myth in Gen 11:1–9 is raised again later in *Conf.* 6 and 9. Some think fellow Jews make this critique (Richard Goulet, *La philosophie de Moïse: Essai de reconstitution d'un commentaire philosophique préphilonien du Pentateuque* [Paris: J. Vrin, 1987], 227 and Niehoff, *Jewish Exegesis and Homeric Scholarship*, 77–78); on the other hand, the reference to the "so called holy books" might suggest pagans, as would Philo's description of his opponents as those "who cherish a dislike of the institutions of our fathers and make it their constant study to denounce and decry the Laws" (*Conf.* 2).

who accepts the "view of philosophers" could believe a tower would reach the heavens.[79] Philo has no clear response to this critique.[80]

Interestingly, Celsus later raises a similar criticism: that Moses "corrupted the story about the sons of Aloeus when he composed the narrative about the tower."[81] Celsus, however, seems less concerned than Philo's critics with the problem of a myth underlying the story of Babel. Rather, his critique centers on the familiar argumentative strategy in antiquity, where dependence on a prior authority connoted inferiority.[82] Origen's reply is that "the story about the tower recorded by Moses is much earlier than Homer and even than the invention of the Greek alphabet" and, thus, that the reverse is more likely true: Homer borrowed from Moses.[83] There are two reasons why, I think, Origen's reference to this Homeric myth should not be considered an instance of dependence upon Philo. First, there is nothing to suggest that Origen would have even broached this topic were it not for Celsus's critique—he only discusses the Homeric myth because *Celsus* prompted him to do so. And second, while Origen offers a response to the critique that this myth was similar to the story of Babel, Philo does very little (if anything) with it.

4. Philo reports that his accusers say the confusion of languages was "effected as a remedy for sin [ἐπὶ θεραπεία ... ἁμαρτημάτων], to the end that men should no longer through mutual understanding be partners in

---

[79] Philo, *Conf.* 4–5. This is the story of Otus and Ephialtes, the sons of Aloeus, the tallest men on earth, who were killed by Apollo for attempting to stack three mountains on top of one another to make a path into the heavens (Homer, *Il.* 5.385–387; *Od.* 11.305–320). Philip Sherman thinks Philo is relaying this example from the list his critics provided, though this is not entirely clear—he might be supplying it himself (Sherman, "Translating the Tower," 291–2). For a detailed analysis of the Tower exegesis by Philo's anonymous interlocuters, with an emphasis on their indebtedness to Aristotelian and Alexandrian scholarly practices, see Niehoff, *Jewish Exegesis and Homeric Scholarship*, 77–92.

[80] So also Sherman ("Translating the Tower," 296). Uehlinger thinks that Philo denies the similarities between the stories, but it is not clear to me that he does (*Weltreich,* 260 and n. 23).

[81] Origen, *Cels.* 4.21 (see also Niehoff, *Jewish Exegesis and Homeric Scholarship*, 93–94). Celsus makes this criticism of Moses's antiquity with respect to Homer elsewhere: *Cels.* 1.19–21; 3.59; 4.21; 4.41–42; 4.31; 6.7; 6.15.

[82] On this theme of borrowing, see Arthur J. Droge, *Homer or Moses? Early Christian Interpretations of the History of Culture* (HUT 26; Tübingen: J.C.B. Mohr, 1989); Peter Pilhofer, *Presbyteron Kreitton: Der Alterbeweis der jüdischen und christlichen Apologeten und seine Vorgeschichte* (WUNT 2.39; Tübingen: Mohr [Siebeck], 1990); and G. R. Boys-Stones, *Post-Hellenistic Philosophy: A Study of its Development from the Stoics to Origen* (Oxford: Oxford University Press, 2001), 176–202. See as well Marcel Borret, ed., *Origène: Contre Celse*, vol. 2 (SC 136; Paris: Cerf, 1968), 232 n. 3.

[83] Origen, *Cels* 4.21.

iniquity."[84] As we have noted, Origen sees the dispersion of nations and the acquisition of new languages as an instrument of restorative punishment, and also uses the term *therapeia*.[85] It seems unlikely, however, that we are uncovering a case of dependence on Philo's report. Celsus conveys a similar interpretation, that the confusion of languages happened for the "purification of the earth [ἐπὶ καθαρσίῳ τῆς γῆς]."[86] More plausible is that we are uncovering independent witnesses to a common and widespread interpretation of the story.

5. Philo interprets the line that the earth was "one language and one voice" (Gen 11:1) to refer to the "symphony of evil deeds great and innumerable."[87] This prompts him several sections later to reflect on "the most wonderful" symphony of all, "that united universal symphony in which we find the whole people declaring with one heart, 'All that God hath said we will do and hear' [Exod 19:8]."[88] Origen will also identify a later biblical episode as a foil for the experience at Babel. Both he and Philo gravitate toward the mountain motif, though instead of presenting the nascent Jewish community at Mt. Sinai as the antitype, Origen presents the church as the new Zion. Unlike that ancient city with its tower in Gen 11 that sought (but did not actually) reach the heavens,[89] the church is an authentic city—a "Zion," "Jerusalem"—that reaches up to the heavens. Origen draws upon the imagery of Isa 2:2–4 to speak of the church as the "visible mountain of the Lord," built "on the tops of the mountains," and "above the hills."[90] If Origen had folded the Sinai motif into his interpretation as well, then a strong argument could be made for dependence. But as it stands, the mountain theme is the only link between these interpretations, and this appears too thin to suggest Origen's dependence on Philo.

6. There are broad similarities between Philo and Origen's respective interpretations of the departure from the east and settling in the plain of Shinar (Gen 11:2). For Philo, this verse is to be read as follows: "Now all who have wandered away from virtue and accepted the starting points of

---

84 Philo, *Conf.* 9.
85 Origen, *Cels.* 5.31.
86 Origen, *Cels.* 4.21 (trans. Chadwick, 197).
87 Philo, *Conf.* 15.
88 Philo, *Conf.* 58.
89 Note Origen's telling insertion of "they suppose" into the quote from Gen 11:4: "Come, let us make bricks … to build a city and a tower, 'the top of which,' as they suppose, 'will reach to heaven" (*Cels.* 5.30).
90 Origen, *Cels.* 5.33. See as well *Hom. in Jer.* 12.3.3 where, after narrating the consequences of Babel, Origen turns to the church which is "enrolled in heaven where there is Mount Sion and the city of the living God, the heavenly Jerusalem."

folly, find and dwell in a most suitable place, a place which in the Hebrew tongue is called Shinar and in our own 'shaking out.' For all the life of the fools is torn and hustled and shaken, ever in chaos and disturbance, and keeping no trace of genuine good treasured within it."[91] As we have seen, Origen interprets the departure from the east as the primordial nations' abandonment of their contemplation of God. With Philo, he etymologizes Shinar as "shaking," and refers it to the shaking of teeth, "a symbol of the fact that they have lost that by which they are nourished."[92] On the surface, the fact that Origen and Philo offer the same etymology would seem to point to dependence. However, etymologies were often widely known and could also have been drawn from other sources, including *onomastica*.[93] Thus it is unlikely that this etymology suggests Origen's dependence on Philo.[94] Both authors admittedly see the movement from the east and the settling in Shinar as the abandonment of something good. Yet this is a highly abstract resemblance, confirmed by Philo who identifies this good with the soul's virtue and by Origen's rather different association of it with God.

7. Finally, Philo sees in the tower a symbol of "arguments of impiety and godlessness."[95] The only clear reference to the tower that I have found in Origen's corpus interprets it similarly: he equates Celsus' "false opinions" and "ideas contrary to the truth" with the city and tower of Gen 11 that need to be torn down.[96] While these interpretations of the tower are similar, I suspect there is no dependence here. It is clear from the Babel pericope that the tower was something to which God was opposed, and so it would hardly be surprising that two religious scholars with strong philosophical interests should identify false or impious thoughts as the referent of this allegory.

[91] Philo, *Conf.* 68–69.

[92] Origen, *Cels.* 5.30.

[93] For Philo's knowledge of these see Lester L. Grabbe, *Etymology in Early Jewish Interpretation: The Hebrew Names in Philo* (BJS 115; Providence: Brown University, 1988).

[94] See as well, Runia, *Philo in Early Christian Literature*, 181–2 (esp. his references to Nicholas de Lange). Van den Hoek, "Philo and Origen," 46, writes: "[E]tymologies were regarded with skepticism until certain standards were met. Since etymologies are very common and widespread, they are by themselves inadequate to prove a relationship between two specific authors. If an etymology, however, occurred in combination with an allegorical interpretation, then there was more solid ground to see a connection." Van den Hoek grades this particular etymology as a "C/D" (50) for degree of dependence, where C signifies a possible relationship between the two authors, but that it cannot be proven. D signifies a commonplace and, thus, that there is no evidence for dependence (ratings explained on 46–7).

[95] Philo, *Conf.* 114. Also see *Conf.* 125; 132–133 and *Somn.* 2:283–286.

[96] Origen, *Cels.* 4.1.

IV. *Conclusion*

Origen's allegory of the dispersion of nations turns out to be a crucial piece to the larger puzzle of his doctrine of pre-existence and fall. It certainly complicates the customary scholarly picture that this doctrine concerned individual souls—Origen was evidently willing to extend it to apply to communities of souls, or nations. Perhaps even more interesting are the ramifications of this doctrine for his comparative religious and political thought: the statuses of nations with their varied customs and religious traditions, all seem to trace back ultimately to this murky, pre-existent world. Origen's "communitarian" version of pre-existence certainly merits further study. Part of this includes the relationship between his account of dispersion and Philo's earlier treatment of the theme in *On the Confusion of Tongues*.

Origen was an enthusiastic reader of Philo and, as I have already demonstrated elsewhere, kept a keen eye on him when wrestling with the enigmatic opening chapters of Genesis.[97] While Origen's allegory of Babel is ultimately configured very differently from Philo's, he took several passages from *On the Confusion of Tongues* as suggestive hints for his own interpretation. Van den Hoek already recognized this, and in her descriptive catalogue identified two parallel passages between this Philonic treatise and Origen's later reflections on the dispersion of nations. According to this catalogue, one of these (the Homeric myth of the sons of Aloeus) was an instance of dependency; the other (the etymology of Shinar) should be considered a parallel with a low likelihood of reliance on Philo. In this paper, however, I have demonstrated that Origen's account of Babel suggests an even greater resemblance with Philo's *On the Confusions of Tongues*. I have modified van den Hoek's descriptive catalogue by expanding the list of parallel passages from two to seven. Of these seven parallel passages, five share similarities that are not striking enough to suggest dependency (#3–7 above).[98] Concerning the two remaining sets of parallel passages (#1–2), I have maintained that they ought be considered instances

---

[97] For his reliance on Philo for interpreting other difficult passages in Genesis, see my article, "Origen's Interpretations of the 'Garments of Skins' (Gen 3:21)," in *Esoteric Readings of Genesis 1–3* (ed. Susanna Scholz and Carolina Vander Stichele; Leiden: Brill, forthcoming 2012).

[98] As argued above, I agree with van den Hoek in placing the etymology of Shinar in this category. However, the story of the sons of Aloeus ought to be located here as well, since Philo merely mentioned it, whereas it was actually Celsus who prompted Origen to refer to, and then comment upon, the story. The three other parallel, but independent, passages were not recorded in van den Hoek's catalogue.

of dependency, since within each set there are several noticeable terminological and thematic resemblances. While they are not listed in van den Hoek's dossier, their presence in Origen's corpus would be difficult to explain were it not for his prior awareness of Philo's treatise. Of course, in neither of these two passages does Origen refer to, let alone cite, Philo. Yet as Origen says elsewhere, Philo was an interpreter from whom he was happy to take a "cue [ἀφορμή]" as he pursued his own exegetical work.[99] The dependencies that I have highlighted in this paper reflect this sort of admiring, but also unconstrained and imaginative, use of Philo.

Saint Louis University

---

[99] Origen, *Comm. in Matt.* 10.22.

The Studia Philonica Annual 24 (2012) 129–133

SPECIAL SECTION

PHILO AND ROMAN IMPERIAL POWER

INTRODUCTION

SARAH J. K. PEARCE

The rule of the emperor Gaius (37–41 c.e.) witnessed two fundamental crises for the Jews of the Roman Empire: in 38, a massive outbreak of violence against the Jews of Alexandria, accompanied by measures attacking Jewish institutions and political status in the city, presided over by the prefect of Egypt, Aulus Avilius Flaccus; and, within the year, as Philo discovered through his embassy to Gaius on behalf of the Alexandrian Jews, the emperor's plan to erect a statue in the Jerusalem Temple. Philo's interpretation of these events is set out in the treatises *In Flaccum* (*Flaccus*) and *De Legatione ad Gaium* (*Legatio*), originally part of a larger—now lost—series of works on the experiences of the Jews under Gaius. While Philo's exegetical works have been mined for evidence of his political attitudes, implicitly expressed, it is only in the *Flaccus* and the *Legatio* that he deals explicitly with the subject of Roman power. In the *Legatio*, in which Philo expounds the moral decline of Gaius, he draws attention to the positive treatment experienced by Jews under earlier emperors, contrasting their benevolence and wisdom with Gaius's malice and folly. On this basis, Philo's overall view of Roman rule has generally been judged as positive, with the dysfunctional Flaccus and Gaius the exceptions to the rule.[1] Even Erwin R. Goodenough, who detected Philo's animosity towards Roman rule within his exegetical works, saw in the *Flaccus* and the *Legatio* Philo's attempt to "fish with skill in the troubled waters of imperial politics,"

---

[1] See now the valuable comments by Katell Berthelot in "Philo's Perception of the Roman Empire," *JSJ* 42 (2011): 166–187.

portraying a positive account of what a good Roman ruler might be, for the attention, as Goodenough argued, of Gaius's successors.[2]

Presented for the first time in a panel on "Philo and the Roman World," organized by the Philo of Alexandria Group at the Society of Biblical Literature Annual Meeting, Atlanta, 21 November 2010, the three essays in this special section offer new readings of Philo's construction of Roman imperial power in *Flaccus* and the *Legatio*. Joshua Yoder explores Philo's portrayal of the eponymous subject of *Flaccus*. Philo's chief purpose in this work is not in doubt: for his role in presiding over the persecution of the Jews by their enemies in Alexandria, Flaccus's exile and execution, commanded by the emperor Gaius, represent "an indubitable proof that the help which God can give was not withdrawn from the nation of the Jews."[3] This is a lesson in divine providence, in which Flaccus must play the role of villain, justly punished for his crimes. But, Yoder argues, Philo's characterization of the prefect is complex and, indeed, in some respects subverts the portrait of Flaccus the villain by describing him in terms that would elicit sympathy for the prefect.

Yoder highlights two key aspects of Philo's "sympathetic" portrait of Flaccus, which provide a kind of framework to the tale of villainy within. Firstly, Philo's dramatization of the prefect's surrender to grief at the loss of the emperor Tiberius and other friends, and his despair over his own security on the accession of Gaius, explains Flaccus's loss of control, both of himself and of Egypt. Until this point, Flaccus had ruled Egypt with the appearance, at least, of excellence in the control of his subjects, proved by his suppression of the Alexandrian clubs.[4] Philo's treatment of Flaccus's fall may also be seen as inviting sympathy: where Philo has often been seen as gloating over the prefect's fate, Yoder underlines Philo's account of the Alexandrian Jews whose prayer thanks God for deliverance from their enemies, but also proclaims that they do not rejoice in their punishment, "for we have been taught by the holy laws to have human sympathy."[5] This "mixed" portrait of Flaccus, Yoder suggests, reveals something of Philo's ambivalent approach to Roman power. Roman prefects are capable of excellent rule, as Flaccus once was, but those like him who pervert their office by persecuting and not benefiting their subjects, will in accordance with God's plan, be removed by the emperor. In this sense, representatives

---

[2] Erwin R. Goodenough, *An Introduction to Philo Judaeus* (Oxford: Basil Blackwell, 1962), 60; cf. also Goodenough's *The Politics of Philo Judaeus: Practice and Theory* (Hildesheim: Georg Olms Verlagsbuchhandlung, 1967).

[3] *Flacc.* 191 (PLCL).

[4] *Flacc.* 1–17.

[5] *Flacc.* 121 (PLCL).

of Roman power may be seen as "benefactors." But, at the same time, this is hardly a ringing endorsement of Roman rule. Neither Tiberius nor Gaius, I would argue, appears in control of events; Tiberius's failure to stick by his own judgment of Gaius, and not that of his advisers, foreshadows the passivity of Flaccus, an error which, in Gaius, brings to power "the implacable enemy of all human beings," and, in the case of Flaccus, unleashes chaos in Alexandria.[6] Moreover, as Yoder rightly concludes, Philo's portrayal of Flaccus also underscores the materialistic and illusory qualities of political office, a delusion of true power as acknowledged at the end of the tale by a penitent Flaccus.[7] Is this perhaps, as Yoder suggests, not just a judgment about the compromised nature of the political life in general, but a "critique of the idea that Roman rule is a form of benefaction," and perhaps that, like the repentant Flaccus, Philo sees Roman benefactions as "essentially hollow and self-serving"?

Daniel Schwartz offers new insights into Philo's interpretation of the violence in Alexandria in 38 c.e. through a comparison with the historian Josephus's account of the same events, focusing on *Jewish Antiquities* Book 18. In contrast with Philo, Josephus gives relatively little attention to the sufferings of the Alexandrian Jews under Flaccus. This should not surprise us, argues Schwartz, given Josephus's situation: Josephus was a year-old infant in 38; he was a Jerusalem priest, not an Alexandrian; and, in the main context in which he mentions the *stasis* in Alexandria (*Ant.*18.257–260), his primary concern is with the emperor Gaius and his attempt to put a statue in the Jerusalem Temple. Schwartz's fresh approach to the translation of Josephus's brief comments in *Ant.* 18.257 suggests that Josephus introduces the case of the persecution of Alexandria's Jews as an illustration of Gaius's self-deification and impiety, delusions which led to his plans for the Temple.

According to Schwartz's analysis, Josephus differs from Philo's judgment of events on three distinctive points. 1) Josephus makes no judgment about who was responsible for the troubles in Alexandria, while Philo blames non-Jews and highlights the destruction by Judean Jews of a makeshift shrine to the imperial cult in Jamnia—not mentioned by Josephus—as background to Gaius's attack on the Jerusalem Temple. 2) Philo fights for the defense of both political and religious rights in Alexandria, while Josephus casts the dispute only in terms of the Jews' right to practise their ancestral customs, reflecting his perspective as a Judean Jew and his positive evaluation of Roman citizenship, showing little concern over whether

---

[6] *Flacc.* 13.
[7] *Flacc.* 164–165.

Alexandrian Jews could be or wanted to be Alexandrian citizens. 3) In his account of the crisis of 38, Philo never calls the Jews' enemies "Greeks," deliberately avoiding giving any impression that the Alexandrian Jews were in conflict with those with whom they identified on a cultural level as the other of the barbarian world; Josephus, by contrast, happily designates the Alexandrian Jews' enemies as "Greeks," reflecting and identifying with a Roman perspective in which "Greek" might be used as a pejorative designation for the lightweight and corrupt. The comparison shows the very different foci at the heart of interpretations of 38 c.e. according to Philo and Josephus, reflecting Philo's preoccupation with the fate of Alexandria's Jews, and Josephus's concern with the story of Gaius and Jerusalem. At the same time, Josephus's construction of events reveals by contrast with Philo a distinctively Roman outlook, which relativizes the value of Jewish local patriotism in Alexandria and has no hesitation in casting "Greeks" as the enemies of the Jews.

Finally, Erich Gruen challenges the substance of Philo's portrayal of Gaius in the *Legatio* on two fundamental fronts: Philo's account of Gaius's profound hatred of the Jews; and of the emperor's desire to promote a sense of his own divinity. Approaching Philo's narrative as a "collection of implausibilies," Gruen begins with Philo's insistence on Gaius's hatred of the Jews. In Philo's scheme, this hatred is prompted by the Jews' exceptional rejection of Gaius's divinity on principle, a hatred which, together with the emperor's claims to divinity, encourages the Jews' enemies in Alexandria and Jamnia to attack them and their institutions, and leads to Gaius's decision to prepare the installation of a statue in the Jerusalem Temple. As Gruen emphasizes, nothing in the classical sources even hints at Gaius's campaign of hatred against the Jews, and, indeed, this theme, so fundamental in the *Legatio*, is not mentioned at all in *Flaccus*. Even in the *Legatio*, however, Philo neither explains the origin of Gaius's hatred nor interprets it: it is, argues Gruen, "a mere Leitmotif for Philo's drama" of the conflict between virtue and vice.

As to the other fundamental theme of the *Legatio*, the emperor's obsession with the idea of his own divinity, Gruen highlights the contrast between Roman authors such as Suetonius and Dio who treat Gaius's impersonations of the gods as a joke, and Philo's very different Jewish perspective on such behavior as "deadly serious—not to mention seriously deadly." Given the absence of evidence for official acknowledgment of the imperial cult in Italy, what was Gaius trying to do with a statue in the Jerusalem Temple? The statue in question, according to Philo's evidence, was to have represented Jupiter or Gaius as Zeus Epiphanes; building on established practice in the Roman East, Gaius was perhaps aiming not at punishing Jews but rather at encouraging ways to show devotion to the imperial power, introducing Jupiter or Gaius as Zeus as a temple-sharing divinity with the God of the Jews. Gaius made a mistake. He did not intend to declare war on the Jews. Why then, as Philo has it, did the emperor persist in his plans for a statue in the Temple, even after the forces of piety and good reason had persuaded him otherwise, plans that were halted only by his assassination? According to Gruen, the one certainty in the *Legatio*'s "mass of uncertainties" is that the emperor did not intend to carry on with his plan: he commanded that the Temple be respected, and that, in areas bordering Jerusalem, the offerings of non-Jews to the imperial cult not be violated. Philo's interpretation of the emperor's command as a sign of his real intentions—to promote conflict between Jews and non-Jews and to further the cause of the statue in the Jerusalem Temple—are nothing more than speculation about the inner-workings of Gaius's mind. On this reading, there is no real basis for Gaius's supposed hatred of the Jews. His policy towards the Jerusalem Temple was a misjudgment, not an act of aggression. That conclusion coheres, to some extent, with Philo's judgment of Gaius as among the "microwits,"[8] his manifestation of hatred towards the Jews, as Philo presents it and perhaps as he himself experienced it, an irrational hatred for which no explanation can be offered.

All three studies in this section focus on questions about what is at the heart of the two treatises in which Philo explicitly deals at length with representatives of Roman imperial power, and open up new possible ways of reading aspects of Philo's interpretation of that power, as mediated by prefects and emperors. Our authors also underline the always complex task of reading Philo and his intentions, and the challenges of understanding Philo's attitude towards Roman power in particular. While these essays make no pretense at attempting to define Philo's interpretation of Roman power in general, their findings offer little by way of evidence for a positive evaluation of or identification with Roman rule on Philo's part.

University of Southampton

---

[8] *Legat.* 163.

The Studia Philonica Annual 24 (2012) 135–147

CALIGULA, THE IMPERIAL CULT, AND PHILO'S *LEGATIO*

ERICH S. GRUEN

Jewish experience in the early Roman Empire was not always a smooth and untroubled one. But one event stands out with high drama and great notoriety. It represented a terrifying, memorable, and, in many ways, inexplicable act on the part of the imperial power: the emperor Gaius Caligula's order to install a statue in the Temple in Jerusalem. The episode left a deep impression upon Philo, a contemporary of this shattering decision, who recounted it at length in his *Legatio ad Gaium*. The account, fascinating and frustrating, presents numerous problems, only a few of which can be addressed here—and even fewer solved.[1] But they do afford a valuable avenue for an assessment of Philo as a historian and the nature of his narrative.

A summary of the relevant text is in order.[2] Two fundamental motifs run through Philo's interpretation of events: Gaius's virulent hatred of Jews and his insatiable desire to demonstrate and broadcast his divinity. The two incentives combined when the emperor issued instructions to place a statue of himself in the Temple. A particular incident provided the pretext. Recent gentile immigrants to Jamnia, a city of mixed population, sought to

---

[1] For some discussions of the subject, see John P. V. D. Balsdon, *The Emperor Gaius* (Oxford: Clarendon Press, 1934), 135–140; Arnold H. M. Jones, *The Herods of Judea* (Oxford: Clarendon Press, 1938), 196–203; E. Mary Smallwood, "The Chronology of Gaius' Attempt to Desecrate the Temple." *Latomus* 16 (1957): 3–17; Emil Schürer, *The History of the Jewish People in the Age of Jesus Christ*, vol. I (rev. ed. by Geza Vermes and Fergus Millar (Edinburgh: T&T Clark, 1973), 394–397; E. Mary Smallwood, *The Jews under Roman Rule* (SJLA 20; Leiden: Brill, 1981), 174–180; Per Bilde, "The Roman Emperor Gaius (Caligula)'s Attempt to Erect his Statue in the Temple of Jerusalem." *StudTheol* 32 (1978): 67–93; Anthony A. Barrett, *Caligula: the Corruption of Power* (London: Batsford, 1989), 188–191; Daniel R. Schwartz, *Agrippa I* (TSAJ 23; Tübingen: Mohr Siebeck, 1990), 18–23, 77–89; Monika Bernett, *Der Kaiserkult in Judäa unter den Herodiern und Römern* (WUNT 203; Tübingen: Mohr Siebeck, 2007), 264–287. And see the valuable text and commentary of the *Legatio ad Gaium* by E. Mary Smallwood, *Philonis Alexandrini, Legatio ad Gaium* (Leiden: Brill, 1961).

[2] Philo, *Legat.* 184–346.

ingratiate themselves with the emperor by setting up a makeshift altar of brick, a deliberate affront to the Jewish inhabitants. As expected, the Jews tore it down. Word reached Herennius Capito, procurator in the region, who sent off a report to Rome. Caligula, after prompting from his most dubious advisers, the freedman Helikon and the actor Apelles, reacted with over-kill. He would teach the Jews a lesson. Instead of the paltry altar in Jamnia, he would set a statue in the holy sanctuary itself in Jerusalem. And he would make his statement quite unequivocally. The princeps gave orders by letter to P. Petronius, governor of Syria, to take half his army, two full legions, to implement this directive.[3]

Petronius was caught in a bind. He could hardly disobey a direct mandate from the emperor, especially one convinced of his divinity who would brook no opposition. Yet he also knew that Jewish resistance would be ferocious and horrific, not only from those dwelling in Judaea but from the countless multitudes in the diaspora, thereby setting off a conflagration that could be overwhelming. The legate had one piece of good luck. Caligula did not send a statue from Rome nor did he demand that one already available in Syria be transported to Jerusalem. This allowed Petronius to commission a new work of art from expert craftsmen in Sidon, providing a welcome respite and giving time for reflection and reconsideration. The Roman governor called upon Jewish leaders and appealed to sweet reason. Much better to yield on this issue than to risk massacre. Of course, the priests and elders would not hear of it. No compromise was possible with so fundamental a principle at the very core of their existence and identity. A vast multitude of Jews descended upon Petronius' headquarters in Phoenicia, unarmed but defiant, ready to lay down their lives, men, women, and children alike, rather than suffer the unspeakable horror of the Temple's defilement.[4]

Instead of pushing matters to the brink, Jews requested of Petronius that he permit them to send an embassy to Rome, thus to dissuade the emperor of his purpose. Petronius declined the plea but, being a reasonable and sympathetic man, said that he would write a letter to the emperor himself. The missive advised Caligula to delay his purpose. Since harvest time approached, why run the risk of Jews burning the crops and ravaging the land, especially as Caligula planned a trip to the Near East with his vast entourage which needed to be fed and housed in style? The arrival of the letter in Rome sparked a fit of rage. The emperor fumed at his appointee's insubordination. He fired off a letter in return, one that concealed his fury,

[3] Philo, *Legat.* 198–207.
[4] Philo, *Legat.* 209–238.

couched in pleasant and encouraging tones, but reiterating his desire to have the statue installed as soon as possible. Disaster still seemed inevitable.[5]

A fortuitous or providential event then intervened. Agrippa I, grandson of Herod, a friend and successful courtier of Gaius who had recently been awarded rule over much of the land of Palestine, was in Rome when matters came to a head. The emperor informed him of his decision and denounced Agrippa's fellow Jews as being the only nation to deny his divinity. Agrippa, stunned and shocked in disbelief, fell into a coma.[6] After recovery, he could not face Caligula but wrote him a long letter, recounted in Philo's text. The king outlined Jewish loyalty to Rome, including sacrifices on behalf of the emperors, and detailed Roman favors over the years to Jews, including support for and handsome gifts to the Temple. And he made clear the deep significance of attachment to ancestral traditions which keep the Temple inviolate, expressing readiness to give up all possessions and life itself rather than witness its desecration.[7]

The emperor greeted this letter with mixed response. He retained his wrath toward the Jewish nation, the one people who refused to recognize his divinity. But he made the key concession to his friend Agrippa. Gaius rescinded his order to Petronius and sent a letter that terminated any further action that might undermine the authority of the Temple. The letter, however, contained an added clause that bound the Jews in turn. Anyone in the areas near Jerusalem who wished to set up altars, shrines, images, or statues in honor of the emperor should be allowed to do so. If Jews should seek to prevent this, Petronius had full authority to punish them or to send them to Rome for punishment.[8]

That would seem to settle the matter. But not quite. Caligula shortly thereafter regretted his compliance, resurrected his earlier decision, and directed the construction of a new colossal image in Rome to be shipped by sea and erected surreptitiously before the Jewish people realized what was happening. This would involve transformation of the Temple into a shrine dedicated to Gaius himself.[9] So ends the narrative, somewhat abruptly and

---

[5] Philo, *Legat.* 239–260.

[6] Philo, *Legat.* 261–269.

[7] Philo, *Legat.* 270–329. Solomon Zeitlin, "Did Agrippa Write a Letter to Gaius Caligula?" *JQR*, 56 (1965/6): 22–31, doubts that such a letter could have been written in the fashion presented in Philo's account. But this rests on his presumption that Gaius was a maniacal believer in his own divinity and that Agrippa would not have dared use the language attributed to him.

[8] Philo, *Legat.* 331–334.

[9] Philo, *Legat.* 337, 346.

disconcertingly, as Philo returns to his discussion of the *legatio* on behalf of the Alexandrian Jews. As we know, the plans for the Temple did not materialize because Gaius conveniently died before they could be implemented. We know this, however, not from Philo but from Josephus—whose account is still more problematical. That will not be treated here.[10] We stick to Philo. He provides us with more than enough problems.

Why should Caligula have a deep-seated hatred of Jews? What would prompt immigrants to Jamnia to provoke Jews by setting up an altar to the emperor? How provocative really was that? Was it enough to justify destroying the altar and defying the emperor? Did this deed suffice in turn to rouse the fury of Gaius to such an extent that he ordered a statue to be placed in the Temple, an altogether unprecedented act? And to implement it, did he require the force of two Roman legions, removing half the garrison of the province of Syria? Would P. Petronius, governor of the province, drag his feet, risk the wrath of the emperor, and become weak-kneed at the idea of diaspora Jews coming from all over the Mediterranean and from beyond the Euphrates to encircle his troops and assault them? Was it a heavenly blessing that Gaius did not send an already constructed statue but gave Petronius time to arrange for a new one, thus providing respite for reconsideration? Did a huge throng of Jews show up in Phoenicia, baring their throats, and persuade Petronius to alter the resolve of his sovereign? Did Agrippa fortuitously happen to be in Rome at this crucial moment, in time to dissuade Caligula from his dastardly deed? Did the emperor, having reversed himself at the importuning of his friend, then reverse himself again almost immediately thereafter, and order a new statue to be enshrined secretly in the Temple?

It is not impossible, I suppose, that any individual piece in this plethora of puzzles could be explained to someone's satisfaction. Indeed few of the pieces have even been challenged, in the face of Philo's contemporary testimony. Yet the collection of implausibilities should surely give us pause.

This lengthy portion of Philo's narrative is patently theatrical, over-dramatized, and replete with embellishments and imaginings. The portrait of the princeps as obsessed with his own divinity and driven by a ferocious hostility to Jews underpins the entire exposition. Philo fits events into that structure and has the characters behave in accordance with that motif.

---

[10] Josephus, *War* 2.184–203; *Ant.* 18.256–309. See the comparisons of Philo's and Josephus's accounts in the works listed above, n. 1. See also Steve Mason, *Flavius Josephus, Judean War 2* (Flavius Josephus: Translation and Commentary, Volume 1B; Leiden: Brill, 2008), 156–168. For chronological discrepancies between them and efforts to reconstruct the chronology, see Balsdon, *Gaius,* 19–24; Smallwood, "The Chronology," 3–17; Bilde, "The Roman Emperor Gaius," 89–92; Schwartz, *Agrippa I,* 78–80.

As preamble to the story, Philo offers a long rehearsal of Gaius's extravagant behavior. He likened himself to the gods and heroes, dressed up as Heracles, Dionysus, or the Dioscuri, appeared in public as Hermes with staff, cloak, and sandals, as Apollo with sun rays on his head, bow and arrows in one hand and images of the Graces in the other, or as Ares with sword, helmet, and shield.[11] And animosity to the Jews is traced to the fact that, while all the other nations of the world acknowledged his divinity, the Jews alone rejected it out of principle and devotion to their own supreme deity. Hence the emperor determined to wage a great war against that people.[12] In a brief digression on the events in Alexandria, Philo observes that the enemies of the Jews there felt that they could attack them with impunity because of the well known hatred of the emperor toward that people.[13] The allegation comes just before the story of the statue, a suitable frame for Philo's narrative. The impulse for installing an image in the Temple is Caligula's drive to be acknowledged as a god, to appropriate the Temple for his ends, and to inflict grievous injury upon the recalcitrant Jews.[14] Like the Alexandrians, the gentile immigrants to Jamnia were also spurred to action by the knowledge of Gaius's unrelenting hatred of Jews and insatiable desire for deification. Hence, the setting up of the brick altar seemed a logical ploy, guaranteed to stir Jewish reaction, and then imperial retaliation. The whole scheme was concocted by the procurator Capito, just waiting his opportunity to report on events—and to exaggerate them—in a message to the emperor.[15] Just how Philo could have known this is beyond comprehension. But it suited his scenario of a building clash between a tyrannical monarch and a pious people whom he was determined to oppress.

The villainous ruler and his despicable advisors are juxtaposed in the tale with the admirable Petronius. The legate, while wary of Caligula's fury, respected the values of the Jews, moved by their piety and commitment to principle, impressed by the vast numbers who turned up and declared their determination to die for their beliefs, and even somewhat schooled, if we credit Philo, in Jewish philosophy and religious traditions.[16] The stark contrast between the virtuous and the wicked in Philo's morality tale is further punctuated by histrionics. The Jews who gathered in multitudes to make their case to Petronius came in structured groups of children, adults,

---

11 Philo, *Legat.* 75–97.
12 Philo, *Legat.* 114–119.
13 Philo, *Legat.* 133.
14 Philo, *Legat.* 198.
15 Philo, *Legat.* 201.
16 Philo, *Legat.* 245.

and the elderly of both sexes, with weeping, wailing, and smiting of breasts. They exposed their throats and insisted that no Roman armies were needed. If the order for the statue were not rescinded, the Jews would voluntarily commit mass suicide, each family slaughtering its own members, and bathing themselves in their own blood. The theatrical character of all this is expressly asserted by Philo himself who states that it would require the language of the tragic poets to describe the tragic sufferings that they faced.[17] Equally histrionic is the scene in which Agrippa receives the news of Caligula's decision to erect the statue. The king now turned a variety of colors from deep pale to fiery red in a matter of seconds, suffered a violent seizure in every part of his body, collapsed into a coma, and had to be carried off in a stretcher. He lay unconscious for a day and a half, and then took a few more days for recuperation before he realized where he was and what was happening. That did not, however, prevent him from ordering a writing tablet and composing a long, windy letter to the emperor in hopes of deflecting his purpose.[18]

Philo's tale, in short, is shaped around his message: a clash between virtue and vice, the devout Jews stand up to the anti-semitic despot, the reasonable Roman governor delays the emperor's design, and the pious Jewish prince dissuades him from it. Caligula, according to Philo, was still hatching evil schemes to the end, but, as his readers knew, the emperor's own death guaranteed that they would come to naught.

None of this means that Philo created the story out of whole cloth. But it certainly counsels caution about purported motives and unfulfilled intentions that the author ascribes to the princeps. Did Gaius Caligula conduct a campaign against the Jews? Nothing in the classical sources drops a hint on that score. Indeed the absence of evidence here merits emphasis. The whole episode of the statue goes unmentioned apart from a single line in Tacitus's *Histories*. The Roman historian observes that, when ordered by Gaius to set up an image in the Temple, Jews preferred to take up arms, an uprising terminated only by the death of the emperor.[19] He certainly did not get this from Philo, nor from Josephus, neither of whom speaks of armed rebellion, only passive resistance. Suetonius and Dio ignore the whole episode. It hardly counted as a matter of high importance to Rome. Of course, we cannot tell what Tacitus might have said about it in the missing portion of the *Annales* that recounted Gaius's reign. But the idea of an embittered

---

[17] Philo, *Legat.* 233–235.

[18] Philo, *Legat.* 261–276. The contrived character of Philo's picture of Agrippa here is recognized by Bilde, "The Roman Emperor," 83–86. See also Schwartz, *Agrippa I*, 85–87.

[19] Tacitus, *Hist.* 5.9.

hatred toward the Jews is difficult to fathom. What motive would there have been? Even in the *In Flaccum*, where Philo deals in detail with the riots in Alexandria, he lays no blame at the doorstep of the emperor. Caligula's one act of significance in that treatise was to remove the offending Roman prefect, Avillus Flaccus, from office, a deed that can only have been welcomed by Jews.[20] The fearsome hostility toward that nation appears only in the *Legatio* where it receives no origin, explanation, or interpretation. It is a mere Leitmotif for Philo's drama.

The aspiration to divinity, of course, receives much more play in the ancient sources. Philo dwells on the emperor's penchant for imitating gods and demi-gods, dressing in their garb, and brandishing their accoutrements. He ascribes it to Gaius's lunatic drive for superhuman ascendancy.[21] Other authors go further in describing his extravagant impersonations of divinity. In the accounts of Suetonius and Dio Cassius, Caligula not only paraded about in the costume of gods like Jupiter, Apollo, or Dionysus but clothed himself as Juno, Diana, or Venus. No sexual discrimination here. He employed wigs, false beards, and various female accessories, sported a trident or a thunderbolt or the hunting equipment of Diana. And the sacrifices he ordered in his honor were equally excessive. No rams, oxen, or pigs; instead, flamingos, peacocks, and pheasants, exotic imports rather than homegrown products.[22]

Far from seeing these acts as a serious claim on divinity, however, the sources reckon them, for the most part, as comic publicity stunts.[23] They stand on a par with Gaius placing himself next to a statue of Jupiter and asking an onlooker to declare which of the two is the greater.[24] Or his challenge to Jupiter: "either raise me up or I'll raise you up."[25] Or his declaration of having had intercourse with Selene, the moon-goddess.[26] Or

---

[20] Philo, *Flacc.* 109–115; cf. *Flacc.* 5.

[21] Philo, *Legat.* 75–97.

[22] Suetonius, *Cal.* 22, 52; Dio, 59.5–8; Donna Hurley, *A Historical and Historiographical Commentary on Suetonius' Life of C. Caligula* (American Classical Studies 32; Atlanta: Scholars Press, 1993), 81–91, 186–189; David Wardle, *Suetonius' Life of Caligula* (Collection Latomus 225; Brussels: Collection Latomus, 1994), 203–217, 336–341.

[23] Cf. Balsdon, *The Emperor Gaius*, 160–162; Barrett, *Caligula*, 146; Aloys Winterling, *Caligula: Eine Biographie* (Munich: C.H. Beck, 2003), 144–152. Ittai Gradel, *Emperor Worship and Roman Religion* (Oxford Classical Monographs; Oxford: Oxford University Press, 2002), 146–149, takes them more seriously as expressions of status. Cf. also Hurley, *A Historical Commentary*, 186–188; Wardle, *Suetonius' Life of Caligula*, 205–208; Manfred Clauss, *Kaiser und Gott: Herrscherkult im römischen Reich* (Munich: K.G. Saur, 2001), 89–94.

[24] Suetonius, *Cal.* 33.

[25] Suetonius, *Cal.* 22.4; Dio, 59.28.6. Cf. Seneca, *De Ira*, 1.20.8–9.

[26] Dio, 59.26.5, 59.27.6.

his creation of a mechanical contrivance which, whenever lightning and thunder came from the sky, would send off his own answering peals.[27] All of this seems more like mockery of the gods than emulation of them. Philo, writing from a Jewish perspective, presented such behavior as deadly serious—not to mention seriously deadly. The classical authors took a more sardonic view. Suetonius lists Gaius's rivalry with Jupiter among his practical jokes.[28] And Dio reports an incident in which a Gallic shoemaker, having witnessed the emperor dressed as Jupiter and delivering oracular pronouncements, burst into laughter. When Caligula confronted him and asked "what do I seem to you?," the shoemaker replied, "one big piece of nonsense." And the man got off scot-free.[29] One might observe also that nothing in the inscriptions, coinage, or archaeological evidence in Italy shows any trace of official acknowledgment of Gaius's divinity.[30] This hardly looks like a determined effort to compel worship as a god. Rather, a wicked sense of humor.

Why then seek to impose his worship upon the Jews, which neither of his predecessors had dreamed of doing? Or did he? Not exactly. It is worth observing—what is rarely noted—that the statue designated for the Temple was apparently not one of Gaius at all but one of Jupiter. Philo states this explicitly on two separate occasions.[31] And when he speaks of the emperor's intentions for the Temple, he alleges that it would be named for him as representing the new Zeus Epiphanes.[32] Not that this would make it any easier on the Jews. But it may take the episode outside the context of the emperor's supposed obsession with his own divinity. Whatever the situation in Rome, the imperial cult or cults in the east had strong roots dating from the Augustan era, indeed even earlier, on the initiative of the easterners themselves. The association of the emperor with a divinity housed in an eastern shrine would not itself be surprising.[33] Gaius may

---

[27] Dio, 59.28.6.

[28] Suetonius, *Cal. 33: inter varios iocos.*

[29] Dio, 59.26.8–9.

[30] Gradel, *Emperor Worship*, 149–159, interprets the literary testimony to mean that the cult to Gaius in Rome was private rather than public.

[31] Philo, *Legat.* 188: ἀνδριάντα ... Γάιος προσέταξε Διὸς ἐπίκλησιν αὑτοῦ; *Legat.* 265: ἐμοῦ κελεύσαντος ἐν τῷ ἱερῷ Διὸς ἀνδριάντα ἀνατεθῆναι.

[32] Philo, *Legat.* 346: μετεσχημάτιζεν εἰς οἰκεῖον ἱερόν, ἵνα Διὸς Ἐπιφανοῦς Νέου χρηματίζῃ Γαῖου. On Gaius and Jupiter, see Smallwood, *Philonis Alexandrini*, 315–316. C. J. Simpson, "The Cult of the Emperor Gaius," *Latomus* 40 (1981): 492–501, sees the relationship as one of rivalry, at least in Rome.

[33] Stefan Weinstock, *Divus Iulius* (Oxford: Clarendon Press, 1971), 304; Mary Beard, John North, and Simon Price, *Religions of Rome* (Cambridge: Cambridge University Press, 1998), 348–363.

have been a little more active in this regard than his predecessors. According to Dio, he directed that the temple to Apollo being constructed at Miletus should embrace him as well.[34] This could help to promote a more consistent and uniform mode of expressing loyalty to the crown among the subjects of the eastern Mediterranean.[35]

Might not Gaius have thought simply of extending this practice to Judaea, of having Jupiter or Gaius in the guise of Jupiter share the holy shrine of Jahweh? Temples to Roma and Augustus, of course, already stood in Palestine, the fruit of Herod's collaboration with Roman authority.[36] Agrippa I himself represented not only Caligula but even his sisters on the coinage of Caesarea Philippi.[37] If expansion of the imperial cult were to be general policy in the east, exemption for the Jews could cause serious difficulty for that nation itself since it would only stir resentment against them by other peoples in that part of the world.[38] Establishing some form of the imperial cult in Jerusalem did not entail, from the Roman point of view, suppression of the worship of Yahweh, indeed it was quite compatible with it. From the Jewish perspective, of course, the conjunction was impossible and anathema, thus prompting the stark drama depicted by Philo. The directive by Gaius, however, need not have been aimed at punishing Jews but at promoting paths to pay homage to the imperial power.

Such promotion might help to explain the affair at Jamnia. Philo, of course, accounts for it by word having reached the Jamnians of Gaius's passion for deification and his deep malevolence toward Jews.[39] The second point is highly dubious. But the first is not without some basis, if one understands it as response to messages, direct or indirect, from Rome encouraging acts of reverence to the emperor as expressions of loyalty and unity. The erection of a modest altar was a perfectly reasonable show of such allegiance. That it represented a deliberate provocation of Jews, antici-

---

[34] Dio, 59.28.1–2.

[35] On the imperial cult as a means of expressing allegiance and gratitude, see Keith Hopkins, *Conquerors and Slaves* (Sociological Studies in Roman History 1; Cambridge: Cambridge University Press, 1978), 197–242; Simon Price, *Rituals and Power: The Roman Imperial Cult in Asia Minor* (Cambridge: Cambridge University Press, 1984), *passim*; J. E. Lendon, *Empire of Honour: The Art of Government in the Roman World* (Oxford: Clarendon Press, 1997), 160–172. And see the recent collection of essays by Jeffrey Brodd and Jonathan L. Reed, *Rome and Religion: A Cross-Disciplinary Dialogue on the Imperial Cult* (SBLWGRWSupp Series 5; Atlanta: Society of Biblical Literature).

[36] See the recent and thorough study of Bernett, *Der Kaiserkult*, 28–170, with extensive references to bibliography at 1–15.

[37] Bernett, *Der Kaiserkult*, 271–272, 284–285.

[38] Cf. Josephus, *War*, 2.193–194.

[39] Philo, *Legat.* 201.

pating forceful reaction, and then retaliation by Rome, the flames fanned by the Roman procurator, is part of Philo's schema, but carries little plausibility for historical reconstruction. Why should Jews have found this makeshift shrine offensive? They were not being asked to worship at it. At most, a group of extremists, showing their zeal for the faith, pulled it down, and the whole episode was exaggerated in the report to Rome, as Philo himself acknowledges.[40] It strains credulity to believe that this minor incident in Jamnia triggered a momentous decision to violate and desecrate the sacred Temple in Jerusalem, an event that barely left a trace in the classical sources—which had few kind words for Gaius Caligula. It is much easier to conclude that the depth and force of Jewish reaction to the introduction of the imperial cult into Jerusalem was unforeseen, a miscalculation by the emperor rather than a retribution.

A critical question arises. Could Caligula possibly have been ignorant of the likely consequences of his order for a statue in the Temple? Does not the command to Petronius to bring half of the Syrian garrison to Palestine imply the anticipation of massive rebellion by the Jews? Perhaps. Yet no such Jewish rebellion had ever surfaced in the past. When opposition rose to the offensive acts of Pontius Pilate, it was passive resistance, the baring of throats and the willingness to perish for principle.[41] The same sort of demonstration occurred, as we have seen, in the appeal to Petronius. It is noteworthy too that Jewish leaders sought permission for an embassy to the emperor so that they could make their case and explain their commitment to tradition. This gesture implies both that they felt the need to instruct Gaius about Jewish beliefs and obligations of which he was otherwise ignorant and that they did not regard him as an implacable foe.

Why then did Petronius mobilize two legions? No easy answer to that. One might note, however, that there was more going on in the region than just the anticipated shipment of a statue. Tension and conflict within the Herodian house, itself no novel feature, became increasingly problematic in these years. Herod Antipas, the tetrarch in Galilee, had recently fought an unnecessary war with the Nabataeans, suffering a grievous defeat and forcing the Romans to intervene, with only mixed success. The Parthians

---

[40] Philo, *Legat.* 202. Bilde, "The Roman Emperor," 74–75, considers this a serious act of disloyalty, justifying strong Roman reaction. A comparable view in Schwartz *Agrippa I*, 80–83, who goes further to see the act at Jamnia as representing a fundamental clash between Jewish principles and the interests of the Roman empire. Cf. Barrett, *Caligula,* 190–191; Bernett, *Der Kaiserkult,* 278–280. Are we to imagine then that no other gentiles in Judaea ever set up offerings without incurring the fearsome wrath of the Jewish populace who regarded it as violating the sanctity of the holy land?

[41] Josephus, *War,* 2.169–177; *Ant.* 18.55–62.

still loomed across the Euphrates, and Antipas's involvement in negotiations with them drew the ire of Vitellius, the Roman governor of Syria, thus rendering Antipas's situation precarious and throwing the whole region into potential peril. Rivalry between Antipas and his nephew Agrippa soon came to a head. Caligula, shortly after accession to the throne in 37, awarded territories to Agrippa in Palestine and accorded him the title of king which had been denied to Antipas. Reports came back to Rome, fostered by Agrippa, about alleged collusion between Antipas and the Parthians. Antipas lost his tetrarchy and went off into exile, his region now also granted to Agrippa.[42] This can only have intensified friction in the homeland. And it may also explain why Agrippa, after only a short sojourn in his new kingdom, soon found himself back in Rome. Antipas's former subjects may not have given the new king a warm welcome, the Nabataeans remained recalcitrant across the Jordan, and Parthian power always posed a potential menace. Further, the episode in Jamnia demonstrated that raw nerves existed among some Jews and gentiles even in the heartland. If Caligula wished to extend the imperial cult and underscore Roman religious authority in so volatile a region, it was prudent to have a large army at the ready.[43] Its mandate, one might surmise, was to assure order and stability and to intimidate possible dissidents, not to punish Jews.

A final question. If Caligula's purpose were to extend the imperial cult as a symbol of uniform Roman rule in the east and the stability of the empire, why did he persist in this aim in the face of a determined opposition that could only undermine that stability? The answer is that he did not persist. That may be the one reasonable certainty in this whole morass of uncertainties. On Philo's own showing, Agrippa's plea to the emperor dissuaded him from his aim of setting a statue in the Temple. Gaius sent a letter to Petronius countermanding his previous order and directing him to take no action that might subvert the sanctity of the Jewish Temple.[44] This, of course, does not fit readily with Philo's portrait of the tyrannical monster. Hence, he has Gaius make the decision grudgingly and reluctantly, out of admiration for Agrippa's candor, while continuing to harbor deep resentment against the Jews.[45] Philo had put a similar spin upon the emperor's earlier letter to Petronius praising the governor for his sound policy and for his meticulous caution in preparing for future

---

[42] For the circumstances and course of events, see the summaries in Jones, *The Herods*, 176–203; Smallwood, *Jews under Roman Rule*, 183–193. More detailed analysis in Schwartz, *Agrippa I*, 53–74.

[43] Cf. Bernett, *Der Kaiserkult*, 280.

[44] Philo, *Legat.* 333.

[45] Philo, *Legat.* 331–332.

developments. But he adds that Caligula simply masked his real anger at Petronius with this friendly exterior and waited his opportunity for retaliation.[46]

The second letter, after instructing the legate to refrain from any offensive measures against the Jews, concluded with an admonition. If persons in the areas bordering on the metropolis of the Jews should wish to set up altars, shrines, images, or statues on the emperor's behalf, they should be free to do so, and Petronius was enjoined to punish those who sought to obstruct them.[47] That was a perfectly reasonable addendum. The princeps encouraged such expressions of loyalty and would not wish them to be interfered with, as some Jews had done at Jamnia. The Jewish Temple was to be respected, and Jews in turn should respect the religious offerings of their neighbors to the emperor. An appropriate quid pro quo.

Philo, however, does not leave it at that. He surmises the real—and insidious—motives of the scheming Caligula. Such an injunction, he supposes, would inspire gentiles all over the area to erect countless numbers of such offerings, thus provoking Jews to tear them down everywhere, affording the emperor his desired pretext to penalize the offenders and revive his order for a statue in the Temple.[48] Philo may have had access to good sources for the letters themselves. But he had no access to the interior of Caligula's mind. His comments on the emperor's diabolic motives and intent were part of the artistic construct.

Even that was not enough for Philo. In his vision the embittered and fearsome tyrant repented of his own repentance. Why wait for others to provide a pretext? He issued orders for another statue, this a colossal one of bronze and gold, to be fashioned in Rome, then shipped secretly to Jerusalem, where it would be installed, and then discovered only as a *fait accompli*.[49] Philo abandons the story there. Of course, nothing of the sort ever happened. The very idea of erecting a colossal statue in the Temple without anyone's knowing about it until after it occurred is preposterous. Nor would the Jewish reaction be any less violent and vociferous afterward than before. Philo simply could not leave the tale with a generous act on the part of Caligula. So he imagined a more wicked one in the offing. The testimony of the letters is a safer guide. The rest is concoction.[50]

[46] Philo, *Legat.* 259–260.
[47] Philo, *Legat.* 334.
[48] Philo, *Legat.* 335.
[49] Philo, *Legat.* 337.
[50] For similar skepticism about this last project of Gaius, see Bilde, "The Roman Emperor," 87–88. As is well known, Josephus conceived an even more dramatic conclusion to the whole affair. He has Gaius change his mind and send a blistering letter to Petronius,

It has not been my intent to whitewash Caligula or to turn this eccentric megalomaniac into a benevolent despot of sweet reasonableness. But insofar as the statue episode has been taken as an exemplary instance of despotic lunacy, stemming from irrational hatred of Jews and consuming passion for divinity, it might be prudent to take a more measured view. Gaius's supposedly virulent anti-semitism has no obvious basis and nowhere receives explanation, and his spread of the imperial cult may owe more to eastern policy than maniacal self-absorption. But Philo had a tale to tell. And his portrait did much to shape the tradition. The philosopher-historian conveyed a vivid narrative with dramatic force, driven by loathing for the emperor who had mocked and summarily dismissed his embassy on behalf of the Alexandrian Jews. He may have obtained some reliable information, including accounts of the correspondence between Gaius and his appointee in Syria. But imputed motivation and purported objectives were a different matter. Philo divined them to suit his portrait. They do not qualify as responsible reportage. And it is high time to question their authority.

University of California, Berkeley

---

demanding that the governor pay for his insubordination by committing suicide. But, by a great act of providence, the letter was slightly delayed and reached Petronius only after word came of the emperor's death; Jos. *BJ*, 2.203; *Ant.* 18.302–309. It was a breathtaking "nick-of time" tale. God had intervened to spare the virtuous and destroy the vicious. Cf. Bilde, "The Roman Emperor," 88–89. Schwartz, *Agrippa I*, 87–88, is prepared to believe it. Similarly, Bernett, *Der Kaiserkult*, 283–284.

The Studia Philonica Annual 24 (2012) 149–166

PHILO AND JOSEPHUS ON THE VIOLENCE IN ALEXANDRIA IN 38 C.E.

DANIEL R. SCHWARTZ

In 38 C.E. there was an eruption of violence between Jews and non-Jews in Alexandria. It is described at length in Philo's *In Flaccum*, which takes the story to its specific end: the arrest, humiliation, and execution of Avillius Flaccus, the Roman governor of Egypt whom Philo blamed for colluding, or worse, in the violence. But it also served as the background for a longer story, for in the wake of the violence both sides sent delegations to Gaius Caligula in Rome. Philo was a member of the Jewish delegation, apparently its head,[1] and recounted its story in his *Legatio ad Gaium*. These two books constitute the main sources for these events.

Josephus, in contrast, devotes very little attention to these events. He reports them, in their chronological context, in *Ant.* 18.257–260, and we may assume he had them in mind, along with other events, in his general statement in *War* 2.487–489 that there was "always" *stasis* between the Jews and the natives in Alexandria since the days of Alexander and the Ptolemies and under the Romans as well. Josephus makes that general statement as his introduction to his detailed account (*War* 2.490–498) of the new outbreak of such clashes in Alexandria in 66 C.E., but that account makes no specific reference to the events in the days of Gaius. Josephus does allude briefly to the violence under Gaius at *Ant.* 19.278, just prior to introducing an edict by Claudius to the Alexandrians, and he has Claudius allude to it in the course of that edict as well (§284).[2]

---

[1] So Josephus, *Ant.* 18.259. On Philo as a communal leader see esp. Ellen Birnbaum, "A Leader with Vision in the Ancient Jewish Diaspora: Philo of Alexandria," *Jewish Religious Leadership: Image and Reality* (2 vols.; ed. Jack Wertheimer; New York: Jewish Theological Seminary, 2004), esp. 1.60–64.

[2] For the assumption that the document cited by Josephus is not authentic, but rather a Jewish composition (or Jewish version of a Roman original), see my *Agrippa I* (TSAJ 23; Tübingen: Mohr [Siebeck], 1990), 100–5. Cf. Miriam Pucci Ben Zeev, *Jewish Rights in the Roman World: The Greek and Roman Documents Quoted by Josephus Flavius* (TSAJ 74; Tübingen: Mohr Siebeck, 1998), 304–326.

That Josephus does not devote much space to the Alexandrian events of 38 C.E. is not very surprising. While Philo was an Alexandrian, an adult at the time of the events, witness to them, and personally involved in them and in their aftermath, Josephus (who was born in Jerusalem only a year before the events in question) was none of the above. Moreover, Josephus had another story to focus on in the days of Gaius, namely, that emperor's attempt to erect a statue in the Temple of Jerusalem—to which Josephus devoted most of the next fifty paragraphs (*Ant.* 18.261–309). Indeed, that was a story that directly affected Josephus's home town, which was the Jews' capital city, and we may understand that, in his eyes, the Alexandrian events were at most something of a sideshow—or, as we shall see, a catalyst. One way or the other, the fact that Josephus ascribed them relatively little importance emerges clearly not only from the brevity of his account in *Antiquities* 18 but also from the way he ignored Alexandria at the opening of *Antiquities* 19. There Josephus begins his account of the assassination of Gaius, at the hand of Romans in Rome, by explaining that Gaius had exhibited his hubris and his madness to all the subjects of Rome and not only toward the Jews of Jerusalem and wherever they lived[3]—but makes no reference at all to the Alexandrian events.

Nevertheless, it frequently happens that the opportunity to compare one source's account of a given episode with that of another is useful, apart from whatever information it supplies, insofar as it points out roads not taken and thus leads us to notice points of view of the other source that otherwise might have been taken for granted and, therefore, escaped notice. In this brief study I will focus upon Josephus' main account of the Alexandrian events, as limited as it is, in *Antiquities* 18.257–260, first showing that his point of view is very different from Philo's and then underlining three aspects of Philo's account that are pointed up by the comparison with Josephus's version.

I. *Differing Points of View*

To begin with we must realize that Josephus's account has a focus totally different from Philo's. For Philo, the story is about the Jews of Alexandria. For Josephus, in contrast, the story is about Gaius. This emerges not only from the great amount of space that Josephus devotes to Gaius versus the Jews of Judaea in *Antiquities* 18 and to Gaius' death in *Antiquities* 19, but

---

[3] Ἰουδαίους τοὺς ἐν Ἱεροσολύμοις καὶ τοὺς ὁπόσοι τῇδε οἰκοῦσιν—not "and throughout Judaea," as translated by Louis H. Feldman in the Loeb Classical Library edition.

also from three points concerning the translation of the opening of Josephus's text about the Alexandrian events (*Ant.* 18.257) and one about what Josephus does not discuss in that account.

1. *Three Points about the Translation of Ant. 18.257*

These points all relate to the way Josephus links the Alexandrian story to his comments in §256 about Gaius, a paragraph that serves as a transition from the lengthy preceding story concerning Herod Antipas (§§240–255). According to §256, Gaius, although he began his reign by ruling "high-mindedly" (μεγαλοφρόνως),[4] eventually let the great extent of the empire go to his head and, ignoring the Deity, became so arrogant that he stopped considering himself a mere human and ruled in all matters in a way that dishonored the Deity (καὶ τὰ πάντα ἐπ᾽ ἀτιμίᾳ τοῦ θείου πολιτευεῖν ἦρτο). What does the Alexandrian story have to do with that?

1. According to the traditional division of Josephus' *Antiquities* and usual translations of §257, the answer is: "nothing." Josephus does not explicitly point to any relation between Gaius's delusions and the Alexandrian events. Indeed, according to the traditional division of *Antiquities*, §257 opens a new chapter, the eighth chapter of Book 18. As the Epitome puts it, after ch. 7 dealt with "how Herod, upon making a trip to Rome, was banished, and how Gaius presented his tetrarchy to Agrippa," §257 opens a new section about something else entirely: "the civil strife of the Jews and Greeks in Alexandria and the dispatch of delegates by both groups to Gaius."

The lack of connection between the two stories is especially evident in Matthieu and Herrmann's French translation of *Antiquities* 18, in which ch. 7 ends before the end of a page and ch. 8 begins on the next page with a new heading and no words of transition.[5] Translators who print the text continuously, similar to the way it was transmitted in antiquity, respond, in contrast, to the normal and legitimate expectations of readers that, when things are so juxtaposed, some relation be established between them. Namely, while Matthieu and Herrmann, who separated the units one from another, rendered §257 as "Des troubles s'élevèrent à Alexandrie entre la colonie juive et les Grecs," offering a fresh start with no coordination with

---

[4] Note that the same word appears twice at the very end of the Antipas narrative (in §§254–255), thus allowing readers to slide comfortably from one story to the next despite the fact that they deal with very different topics.

[5] *Œuvres complètes de Flavius Josèphe*, IV (ed. Théodore Reinach, trans. G. Mathieu and L. Herrmann; Paris: Leroux, 1929), 177.

the preceding story, those who print the stories one after another all insert a word of coordination: Whiston offered "There was *now* a tumult arisen at Alexandria," Clementz gives *"Unterdessen* war zu Alexandria zwischen den dort wohnenden Juden und Griechen ein Streit entstanden," and Feldman gives *"Meanwhile,* there was civil strife in Alexandria between the Jewish inhabitants and the Greeks."[6]

It was perfectly natural for editors and translators to think that the relationship of the stories was chronological, for that is the basic organizing principle of the *Antiquities.* Many stories in *Antiquities* are indeed linked to that which precedes them by "then," "about that time," "not long after," or the like; in *Antiquities* 18, for example, see §§39, 63, 65, 80, 106, 109, 126, etc. However, my first point about the translation of *Ant.* 18.257 is that the Greek text in fact includes nothing like that, nothing that corresponds to "now," "unterdessen," or "meanwhile."

That indicates, however, that Josephus assumed we would realize that the new event was, somehow, part and parcel of the preceding narrative. Were that not the case, were the two stories juxtaposed *only* because of their chronological proximity, Josephus probably would have said so, opening the new story (§257) with "at the same time" or the like. Compare, for example, Josephus's practice near the end of *Ant.* 11, where he interrupts a story in full swing at §303 and inserts §§304–5 about a completely different topic, only to return at §306 to the story he had interrupted at §303. Josephus introduces §304 with "at that time" because otherwise readers would not know what that extraneous report was doing there, then he reverts to the main story without any such words at the outset of §306, since the contents make clear that it is the direct continuation of §303. This is very common and totally logical (compare the openings of Gen 38 and 39!), and if Josephus did not use any such words pointing out temporal

<hr />

[6] *The Genuine Works of Flavius Josephus, the Jewish Historian,* II (trans. William Whiston, revised Samuel Burder; Boston: Walker, 1849), 90; *Des Flavius Josephus Jüdische Altertümer,* II (trans. Heinrich Clementz; Berlin-Wien: Harz, 1923), 550; LCL *Josephus,* vol. 9 (ed. Louis H. Feldman; London: Heinemann, 1965), 153. In all three citations, the emphasis is my addition. For a later edition of Whiston's translation, see below, n. 9. For a similar and nearby case, note that at §310, where Josephus begins the next chapter (ch. 9) of Book 18, again with a new episode with nothing coordinating it with the preceding story, Whiston and Feldman add "now" and Clementz opens "Um diese Zeit," while Matthieu and Herrmann, who again begin the chapter on a new page again have—therefore—no need to add anything of the kind. Josephus in fact connected §310 with the preceding narrative thematically, not chronologically, by the simple use of καί, which links this story with that of the troubles in Judaea under Gaius: "*Also* the Jews of Mesopotamia, and especially those who reside in Babylonia, were afflicted by terrible suffering…"

coordination at 18.257 that means he assumed readers would realize they are still reading the same story.

2. Note, moreover, that in further contrast to Whiston, Clementz, and Feldman, who use "was" (there *was* now a tumult," "war"...ein Streit entstanden," "there *was* civil strife"), the Greek does not offer such a finite verb.[7] Rather, it uses a genitive absolute, στάσεως ... γενομένης. That means, however, that Josephus does not mean to report the fact of the dispute in Alexandria for its own sake, as if one could end a unit after that information.[8] Rather, he reports it as the occasion for the dispatch of delegations to Gaius.[9] This seemingly minor grammatical point indicates that just as in §256, so too in our §257 Gaius is still the topic—the same conclusion indicated by our preceding point (the lack of temporal coordination). That is: Although Josephus is telling us something about Alexandria, the structure of §257 makes it clear that Josephus is telling the story *as part of his account of Gaius*. That is why no temporal connection was needed.

3. Finally, note that the reason the translations I cited posit a chronological relationship between §256 and §257 is because they rightly expect an author to posit some relationship between them but failed to notice that he did so by introducing §257 with the words Καὶ δή, which indicate another relationship between the stories. Namely, that opening explicitly indicates, I believe, that the story begun in §257 *is meant to illustrate the generalization* about Gaius' arrogant self-deification that Josephus offered in §256. That this is so is something I learned from Louis Feldman himself, more than twenty years ago, when I asked him about his Loeb translation of *Ant.* 19.332. There, after §331 reported that Agrippa was very pious, §332 opens as follows: Καὶ δή τις ἐν τοῖς Ἱεροσολύμοις ἀνὴρ ἐπιχώριος. In contrast to Whiston, who simply offers a more or less literal translation ("However, there was a certain man of the Jewish nation at Jerusalem"), Feldman opened his translation with a whole additional sentence: "Here is a supreme example of his character. A native of Jerusalem named Simon...."

---

[7] In this case Matthieu and Herrmann deviated the same way as the others ("s'élevèrent").

[8] As various translations do, with this or that degree of finality: Clementz uses a comma + "und," Matthieu/Herrmann—a semi-colon; Whiston—a colon; and Feldman went the whole way, inserting a period.

[9] This is reflected faithfully (apart from the addition of the opening "now") in Arthur Richard Shilletto's 1889 revision of Whiston (available in *Flavius Josephus: The Second Jewish Commonwealth* [ed. Nahum N. Glatzer; New York: Schocken, 1971], 419): "Now a tumult having arisen at Alexandria between the Jewish inhabitants and the Greeks, three ambassadors were chosen out of each party that were at variance, who came to Caius." So too Abraham Schalit's 1963 Hebrew translation (*Flavii Josephi Antiquitates Judaicae, in linguam hebraicam vertit...Libri XI-XX* [Jerusalem: Bialik Institute, 1963], 305 [in Hebrew]).

In response to my inquiry Feldman sent me, as is his generous wont, a list of examples of Josephus's use of Καὶ δή to introduce a clear example building upon, or illustrating, a foregoing generalization—what Liddell-Scott-Jones renders as *"and what is more,* adding an emphatic statement; *actually."*[10] But if so, if we return to our *Antiquities* 18.257 we should, I believe, prefer to open it as follows: "Indeed, (this is shown by what happened) when, after there was civic strife in Alexandria between Jews and Greeks resident there, three delegates chosen by each side came to Gaius. For there was ..." This means that the whole story is presented, by Josephus, as growing out of, and illustrating, his report in §256 that Gaius had begun to relate to himself as superhuman and as a god, and therefore showed disrespect to the true God.

Thus, three points about the translation of §257 all show that, for Josephus, his story is one about Gaius' arrogant self-deification, with the Jewish issue in Alexandria being only some grist for *that* mill, to illustrate *that* generalization.

2. *What Josephus Does Not Mention*

There is a remarkable disjunction in Josephus's narrative, between his opening report in §257a about Jewish-Greek *stasis* in Alexandria, on the one hand, and the continuation, beginning in §257b, on the other hand, which says not a word about issues between Jews and Greeks in Alexandria and focuses only on the divine honors to be conferred upon Gaius. Were the Alexandrian events the focus of this report, Josephus should have told us what happened in Alexandria and what engendered those events, probably presenting the matter apologetically and making it clear that it was the Greeks who attacked the Jews—as he does elsewhere. Thus, for example, in *War* 2.487 he clearly says that there was "always" civic violence among the local Alexandrians "against the Jews"; and when, in *Ant.* 19.278, he admits that the Jews started the violence at the beginning of Claudius's reign in 41 c.e., he takes the trouble to excuse them, at some length, by underlining just how much they had suffered at the hands of the Alexandrians in the days of Gaius. In our *Ant.* 18.257, however, Josephus simply has the Jews and Greeks of Alexandria involved in *mutual* strife (στάσεως ... γενομένης Ἰουδαίων ... καὶ Ἑλλήνων); he invests no effort in explaining what the issue was or who was responsible—issues that are so important for Philo. This

---

[10] LSJ 384, s.v. δή, IV, 4. See also Henry St. J. Thackeray and Ralph Marcus, *A Lexicon to Josephus*, II (Paris: Geuthner, 1934), 132, s.v. δή (3): "and what is more," "and actually," "and went so far as to."

again shows that for Josephus the story is not about the Jews of Alexandria; the whole episode is just an example illustrating Josephus's basic claim that Gaius arrogantly desired divine honors, and thus a springboard for Josephus's next long narrative, about the statue-in-the-Temple affair.

In concluding this section, I would simply add that Josephus's story in *Ant.* 18.257–260 is important not because it tells us about the Jews of Alexandria but because it tells us about Gaius's self-deification, the theme announced in §256, is bolstered by various other points as well:

1. At §260 Josephus ends his Alexandrian story by having Philo encourage the Jews to be of good heart because Gaius had now begun to fight against God Himself—which was the point of §256 as well.

2. At §261 Josephus draws the practical conclusion from the story, and it does not concern Alexandria. Rather, the Alexandrian story functions for Josephus as that which awakened Gaius's anger against the Jews and brought him, therefore, to order the erection of a statue of himself in the Temple of Jerusalem.

3. At §§306–9, in concluding the story of Gaius's attempt to erect the statue, Josephus explains that the emperor's death was the result of God's anger because Gaius had dared to consider himself an object of worship. No mention of Alexandria.

4. The fact that the next book of *Antiquities* opens with a long account of the death of Gaius and ends with an account of the sudden death of Agrippa I *because he accepted divine honors* (*Ant.* 19.344–350) underlines just how central that theme was for Josephus.

II. *Three Comparisons of Josephus's and Philo's Accounts of the Alexandrian Events*

Josephus's relative lack of interest in the sufferings of the Jews of Alexandria is a point of some interest from a few points of view. In the present context, I will pursue it to three comparisons with Philo's account, three points about Philo's account that seem not to have received much attention.

1. *Judaeans or Alexandrian Jews—who was to blame?* Josephus, as noted, made no effort here to assign guilt for the Alexandrian violence, contenting himself with the assertion that the mutual violence drew the conflict to the emperor's attention, but has Gaius's decision to erect the statue in the Temple of Jerusalem derive from his resentment at the Jews' refusal to worship him, which became apparent in his interview with the Jewish delegation from Alexandria. Philo, in contrast, clearly blames the non-Jewish Alexandrians for the violence in Alexandria, clearly refrains from

portraying the Alexandrian violence as the reason or background for the troubles in Judaea, and to a significant extent blames Judaean Jews for the problems in Judaea. The latter is the import of his story, at *Legatio* 197–203, of how Gaius's decision to defile the Temple was his reaction to the Jews' destruction of an altar in his honor in Jamnia. True, the way Philo tells the story the real villains are, of course, the Jews' hostile neighbors in Jamnia, who deliberately provoked the Jews by building the altar, and the emperor Gaius himself, whose reaction to the Jamnian event is presented as grossly disproportionate. However, the Jamnians' and the emperor's hostility was a given, and what Philo's story boils down to is that even if the altar erected in Jamnia violated the sanctity of the Holy Land (*Leg.* 202), destroying it amounted to playing into the hands of their enemies and engendering a worse problem.[11] That is, Philo's story is one of violent Jews in Judaea, who lacked *savoir faire* and brought imperial wrath down upon the Jews—thus engendering a major threat both to the Temple and to peace in Judaea, and also making the work of Philo's own delegation to Rome, on behalf of the Jews of Alexandria, all the more difficult. Josephus, in contrast, does not mention the Jamnian affair at all.

Thus, with regard to the Jews' troubles both in Alexandria and in Judaea, Philo and Josephus are at opposite poles. The Alexandrian Jew blames Alexandrian non-Jews for the troubles in Alexandria and Judaean Jews for their troubles in Judaea, while the Judaean Jew makes no effort to clear the Alexandrian Jews of responsibility for their troubles in Alexandria but makes Gaius's anger at the Alexandrian Jews when they appeared before him in Rome the point of departure for his attack upon the Temple. Here, it seems, we have evidence of competition between Judaean Jews and Alexandrian Jews: in the pressure-cooker of real troubles created by the onset of Roman rule in general, and by Gaius's policies and personality in particular, Jews of each center of the Jewish world would rather blame those of the other for their troubles.[12]

---

[11] To some extent my understanding of Philo's position derives from my assessment that such a spiritual person as Philo was not overly concerned about the sanctity of the Holy Land; "it cannot be over-emphasized that Philo has little or no concern for Palestine" (Samuel Sandmel, *Philo's Place in Judaism: A Study of Conceptions of Abraham in Jewish Literature* [augmented edition; New York: Ktav, 1971], 116). See my "Philo, His Family, and His Times," *The Cambridge Companion to Philo* (ed. Adam Kamesar; Cambridge: Cambridge University Press, 2009), 24–31.

[12] This is quite reminiscent of the way the Alexandrian author of 3 Maccabees makes Ptolemy's anger at the way he was treated in Jerusalem the reason for his decision to persecute the Jews of Egypt. In general, on competition between Alexandria and Jerusalem in 3 Maccabees, see Noah Hacham, "The Third Book of Maccabees: Literature, History and Ideology" (PhD. dissertation, The Hebrew University of Jerusalem, 2002).

2. *Did the Jews of Alexandria want Alexandrian citizenship?* A second contrast between Josephus's and Philo's accounts of the Alexandrian troubles seems equally to reflect differing Judaean and Alexandrian perspectives. Namely, it is clear that, for Philo, the Jews' troubles in Alexandria were subsumed under two separate and parallel titles: both their political status and their religious rights were in danger. The double-pronged nature of the threat is explicit at *In Flaccum* 53:

> When, then, Flaccus had seized our houses of prayer, not leaving even their name, and thought that the attempt against our laws prospered, again he turned to another (ἐφ' ἕτερον) exploit, the destruction of our polity, so that, our ancestral customs and participation in political rights, to which our life was anchored, cut off, we might undergo the direst misfortunes, having no cable to which to hold on for safety. (trans. Herbert Box)

But the same duality is obvious elsewhere as well, especially at *Legatio* 191–195, where Philo says that the news of Gaius's order to erect a statue in the Temple of Jerusalem convinced the Alexandrian Jewish ambassadors to Rome to give up pursuing "both (ἀμφοτέρων) of the objects on account of which they were sent" (§195) and turn to the defense of the Temple. The two objects of their original mission were, as the preceding paragraphs make clear, the defense of their synagogues and of their status as citizens of Alexandria.[13] And it is almost as obvious in *Legatio* 371 as well, where it looks like the final sentence, about the Jews' "specific laws/customs (*nomima*) and their general rights (*dikaia*) vis à vis each individual city," refers to the same two areas of controversy.

Josephus, in contrast, makes in *Ant.* 18.257–260 no reference to either issue, as we have seen, instead allowing his narrative to focus on Gaius's claim of divine honors. Now I will add that even when Josephus does relate, in Book 19, to the question whether the Jews were to be called "Alexandrians," in the context of the troubles in the days of Gaius, it turns out that the issue is, for Josephus, not political but only religious: the only practical issue addressed by Claudius, according to Josephus, is the Jews' right to follow their own customs (ἔθη –§§283, 285) and not to be forced to violate their ancestral religion, *threskeia* (§283, 284). Although the historical survey in the opening of his edict does relate to the question of political rights and status, when Josephus's Claudius becomes practical he makes no reference to them.[14]

This seems to me to be a very important distinction between Philo and Josephus, one with two dovetailing explanations. Although he does at

---

[13] On the translation of §§191–195, see the appendix to this article.
[14] See Pucci Ben Zeev, *Jewish Rights*, 316.

times refer to the issue (*Ag. Ap.* 2.38–41; *Ant.* 12.121) Josephus does not seem to care much about the question whether Alexandrian Jews were, or could become, citizens of Alexandria; Philo did. Josephus's attitude fits what we would expect from Josephus's Roman point of view, first of all. For Romans, Alexandria was far away, Alexandrians were not all that respectable,[15] and any citizenship apart from Roman citizenship was not very important anyway. But it also fits Josephus's Judaean perspective. For just as it was difficult for a Judaean, not to mention an erstwhile priest of Jerusalem who grew up in the shadow of the Temple and whose class drew its status from its role in the Temple, to relate seriously to the notion of another type of Jewish house of worship,[16] so too was it difficult for Judaeans to respect the dual loyalties of Jews of the Diaspora. Indeed, just as in the twentieth century it was so difficult for an Israeli scholar like the late Aryeh Kasher to accept Victor Tcherikover's assumption, based on his experiences in Russia and Germany, that Jews might want to be citizens of Alexandria,[17] so was it, in the first century, difficult for ancient Judaeans like Josephus to understand, or accept, that Jews resident in Alexandria might want to be citizens of that city. Roman citizenship he could understand, for Rome was universal; but why be an Alexandrian? Must it not be the case that all the Jews of Alexandria, or of elsewhere in the Hellenistic Diaspora, really wanted was the right to live according to their own ancestral laws, which amount to what we call the Jewish religion? That was certainly important for Josephus, and he emphasizes it constantly in his writings, especially *Antiquities*.[18]

---

[15] Sarah J. K. Pearce, *The Land of the Body* (WUNT 208; Tübingen: Mohr Siebeck, 2007), 61, n. 80.

[16] On Josephus's lack of interest in synagogues, see Arnaldo Momigliano, "What Flavius Josephus Did Not See," in idem, *Essays on Ancient and Modern Judaism* (ed. Silvia Berti; Chicago: University of Chicago Press, 1994), 70–71.

[17] Aryeh Kasher, *The Jews in Hellenistic and Roman Egypt: The Struggle for Equal Rights* (TSAJ 7; Tübingen: Mohr [Siebeck], 1985), viii–ix, 263. Cf. the review by Hans G. Kippenberg in *JSJ* 17 (1986): 255–256, "…spiegelt seine These auch etwas vom modernen judischen Selbstverständnis wider: dem Streben nach Eigenstaatlichkeit nämlich, das die judische Geschichte im 20.Jh. bestimmte […] Mir scheint, der Verfasser lehnt aus (nicht explizierten) Gründen Assimilation ab und thematisiert sie daher auch nicht im historischen Material des antiken Judentums."

[18] See especially Shaye J. D. Cohen, *Josephus in Galilee and Rome: His Vita and Development as a Historian* (Columbia Studies in the Classical Tradition 8; Leiden: Brill, 1979), 144–151; Bernd Schroeder, *Die "vaterlichen Gesetze": Flavius Josephus als Vermittler von Halachah an Griechen und Römer* (TSAJ 53; Tübingen: Mohr [Siebeck], 1996); and Gunnar Haaland, *Beyond Philosophy: Studies in Josephus and His* Contra Apionem (Dr. theol. diss; MF Norwegian School of Theology, 2006), 47–53.

3. *Were the villains "Greeks?"* A third point underlined by the contrast of Josephus's account to Philo is that the latter does not call the Jews' opponents "Greeks." Josephus quite consistently does: in *Ant.* 18.257 he says the *stasis* was between Jews and "Greeks"; at *War* 2.487–489 he clearly states that the issue and the incessant conflicts in Alexandria, from the days of Alexander to his own, were between Jews and Greeks (§§487, 489); and his report of the violence there at the time of the outbreak of the Judaean rebellion states that it was between Jews and "Greeks" (§§490, 492). Philo, in contrast, never identifies the Alexandrian villains as Greeks. The word "Hellene" never appears in *In Flaccum*, and although it does appear three times in the *Legatio*, it never designates the Alexandrian villains. Rather, Philo uses it only in the stock phrase "Greeks and barbarians," which he uses when he wishes to refer to all of humanity (*Leg.* 145, 162, and 292); in that pair, of course, "Greeks" have the higher and better valence. That same contrast, between Greeks and barbarians, is very important to Philo; indeed, it appears another several times in *Legatio*, using not *Hellenes* but, rather, *Hellas* or *Hellenikos*—§§8, 83, 141, 147. But as for the Jews' enemies in Alexandria—Philo never calls them "Greeks." Josephus, as we saw, consistently does.

This point is especially impressive insofar as Philo evidently had no other name with which he was comfortable as a designation of the Jews' enemies in Alexandria. True, now and then he refers to them as "Alexandrians" (*In Flaccum* 23, 78, 78, 80; *Legatio* 120, 162, 164, 170, 172, 183, 194). Frequently, however, readers of Philo's two historical works, and especially of the *Legatio*, may well share my impression that there are simply too many subject-less verbs in the third-person plural concerning actions perpetrated against the Jews by unidentified villains. That this is so is well demonstrated, I think, by the contrast between the strange Greek and the sensible English of Edith Mary Smallwood's edition and translation of the *Legatio*:[19] in §124–133, the paragraphs that focus on the Alexandrian violence, Philo's Greek never mentions "Greeks" but Smallwood's English does, four times: §§124, 130, 132, 133. Again, Smallwood did the same later in the *Legatio* as well, at §§152, 173, and 202. This indicates not only Smallwood's well-founded belief, that the others, who persecuted the Jews, were called "Greeks"—a point made explicit by Josephus (as noted above) and also by a papyrus or two[20]—but also her good sense that the continuous use

---

[19] Edith Mary Smallwood, *Philonis Alexandrini Legatio ad Gaium* (2nd ed.; Leiden: Brill, 1970).

[20] See Koen Goudriaan, "Ethnical Strategies in Graeco-Roman Egypt," *Ethnicity in Hellenistic Egypt* (ed. Per Bilde et al; Studies in Hellenistic Civilization 3; Aarhus: Aarhus

of "they" without antecedent can become tedious, even unbearable, and, at times, even confusing, especially in accounts of intense interaction between two groups.

But Philo, of course, knew how to write. So, I suggest, if he did not call Greeks "Greeks," preferring to leave us with a text that is at times tedious, unbearable, or even confusing, it was either because he did not *want* to be more explicit, or because, psychologically, he *could* not.[21] I suspect that anyone who wants to understand Philo here might well draw on the experience of modern German Jews, who often speak of their persecutors of the 1930s and 1940s as "Nazis" or "they" but find it difficult to call them "Germans." For German Jews to call their persecutors "Germans" would have amounted to admitting that they themselves were not Germans. But that would be very difficult, for they grew up knowing they were Germans, and that it was honorable to be Germans. As Victor Klemperer put it in a 1942 entry in his diary:

> Den schwersten Kampf um mein Deutschtum kämpfe ich jetzt. Ich muß daran festhalten: Ich bin deutsch, die andern sind undeutsch.[22]

Similarly, in understanding Philo's avoidance of "Greeks" for his persecutors we should revert to the point, mentioned above, that Philo repeatedly refers to Greeks in the *Legatio* in the context of the standard contrast of Greeks and barbarians (§§145, 162, and 292), just as he uses *Hellas* and *Hellenikos* in that same contrast.[23] In general, moreover, it is of course clear that, for Philo, the Greeks were the measure of respectability.

University, 1992), 98, n. 62, referring to *CPJ* II, no. 156b, col. 2, l. 35 and, perhaps, no. 158a, col. 3, l. 19.

[21] For a similar case, compare *Ant.*11.326–347 where, apart from the opening and closing paragraphs that do name Jaddua, Josephus tediously avoids naming the high-priest and rather uses "the high priest" or "the high priest of the Jews" or the like—because, I believe, he did not want to explicitly replace the name supplied by his source. See my "On Some Papyri and Josephus's Sources and Chronology for the Persian Period," *JSJ* 21 (1990): 187–189.

[22] "I'm now engaged in the most difficult struggle for my Germanism. I must hold onto this: I am German, the others are un-German." Victor Klemperer, *Ich will Zeugnis ablegen bis zum letzten: Tagebücher 1942–1945*, II (8th ed., ed. W Nowojski; Berlin: Aufbau, 1996), 83–84 (my translation; cited by Susanne Heim, "The German-Jewish Relationship in the Diaries of Victor Klemperer," *Probing the Depths of German Antisemitism: German Society and the Persecution of the Jews, 1933–1941* [ed. David Bankier; New York: Berghahn, 2000], 316). See also Lawrence Birken, "Prussianism, Nazism, and Romanticism in the Thought of Victor Klemperer," *German Quarterly* 72 (1999): 33–43; at p. 37 Birken cites, inter alia, Klemperer's contrast (*Ich will Zeugnis ablegen*, 2.189) between the German police, who were always polite, and the Gestapo.

[23] *Leg.* 8, 83, 141, 147. So too elsewhere in Philo.

For Josephus, in contrast, the picture is much more complex. As Tessa Rajak demonstrated in her survey of Josephus's usage of "Greeks,"[24] while he too uses the pair "Greeks and barbarians" to mean "everyone,"[25] his views about them tend much more to the other pole. Just as we should expect from a non-Greek writing in Rome, he is willing to use "Greeks" with a pejorative twang or worse and to bespeak standard Roman anti-Greek slurs; reference to Nikolas Petrochilos's *Roman Attitudes to the Greeks* (1974), to Luke's reference in Acts 17:21 to the Athenians who had nothing better to do than sit around and blather about words all day (for a serious Roman attitude, contrast Acts 18:14–15!), or to Plutarch's *Life of Cato the Elder* (chs. 12, 22–23), will suffice. Josephus lived in such a context and identified with it,[26] and if his last work, *Against Apion*, was directed against the Greeks,[27] the same attitude can also be found in his earlier works as well. Moving back from *Against Apion*, we come first to Josephus's *Vita*, which includes at §40 a stereotypical reference to Greeks as verbose liars; then to the *Antiquities*, where Greeks figure as corrupt anti-Jewish troublemakers in Rome who subverted Roman justice (*Ant.* 20.182–183); and finally to his earliest work, the *War*—where the reference to the Alexandrian Greeks as perpetual anti-Jewish troublemakers, in *War* 2.487ff., goes together well with such other passages as 2.266–67 (Greek-Jewish *stasis* in Caesarea), 7.43–53 (Greek-Jewish *stasis* in Caesarea and Antioch), and 1.13 (Greek historians typically neglect the truth).

To understand Philo's stance, we should compare his usage concerning "Greeks" to what is indicated by a well-known papyrus of 5 or 4 B.C.E. (*CPJ* II, no. 151) which shows that when a Jew named Helenos, applying to the Roman governor of Egypt for an exemption from the poll-tax imposed

---

[24] Tessa Rajak, "Ethnic Identities in Josephus," in: eadem, *The Jewish Dialogue with Greece and Rome: Studies in Social and Cultural Interaction* (AGJU 48; Leiden: Brill, 2001), 137–146.

[25] Or "everyone apart from Jews" (Rajak, ibid., 139, referring to *War* 5.17 and 6.199). Numerous other references to Josephus' use of this phrase are assembled by Raimondo Bacchisio Motzo, *Ricerche sulla letteratura e la storia giudaico-ellenistica* (ed. Fausto Parente; Roma: Centro editoriale internazionale, 1977), 628.

[26] For Josephus's self-identification as a Roman, see esp. Martin Goodman, "Josephus as Roman Citizen," *Josephus and the History of the Greco-Roman Period: Essays in Memory of Morton Smith* (StPB 41; ed. Fausto Parente and Joseph Sievers; Leiden: Brill, 1994), 329–338, and Gunnar Haaland, "Josephus and the Philosophers of Rome: Does *Contra Apionem* Mirror Domitian's Crushing of the 'Stoic Opposition'?," *Josephus and Jewish History in Flavian Rome and Beyond* (JSJ Supplement 104; ed. Joseph Sievers and Gaia Lembi; Leiden: Brill, 2005), 309.

[27] And Porphyrius indeed used "To/Against the Greeks" as its title; Menahem Stern, *Greek and Latin Authors on Jews and Judaism* (3 vols.; Jerusalem: Israel Academy of Sciences and Humanities, 1980), 2:442.

upon lowly "natives" (the *laographia*), identified himself as an "Alexandrian," someone insisted that be changed to "Jew of Alexandria."[28] That change illustrates well the issue at hand: as Helenos put it, he ran the risk of being deprived of his native country (τῆς ἰδίας πατρίδος στερηθῆναι), what the Germans called being *ausgebürgert*. That is tragic enough; it seems that Helenos had grown up knowing he was an Alexandrian, and proud of not being one of the despicable natives, and now he saw himself losing all of that, and even being required to reflect that loss in his appeals about it to the relevant authorities.

But "Alexandrian" was—like "citizen of Germany"—a term with specific meaning, pertaining to citizenship, something with measurable implications, such as tax liability. "Greek" (like "German") was different, a more nebulous, cultural term. What is indicated by Philo's strangely obscure style, which avoids naming the Jews' enemies as "Greeks," is that if by the days of Gaius and Claudius the Jews of Alexandria were forced to battle, formally, about their right to be called "Alexandrians," they had no need to debate their right to be called "Greeks" and, indeed, Philo avoided giving any opening for such a debate.[29]

True, the Jews of Alexandria went on struggling to be called "Alexandrians." Thus, for example, Jews claimed that Claudius agreed that the Jews had been "called Alexandrians" since the earliest days (19.281).[30] But even Philo realized that it would be a "struggle" to get Gaius to believe that (*Leg.* 194), and his account of his delegation's hearing before Gaius indicates just how lost that cause was, just as Claudius himself, in his papyrus letter to the Alexandrians, specifically relates to the Jews as non-Alexandrians, as strangers in the city.[31] Accordingly, although they did go on arguing about it, Philo nevertheless allowed himself, now and then, to use "Alexandrians" to denote the Jews' enemies in that city (*In Flaccum* 23, 78, 78, 80; and *Legatio* 120, 162, 164, 170, 172, 183, 194).[32] Indeed, as Ellen Birnbaum has shown, he even tended at times to equate the Alexandrians who opposed the Jews with Egyptians, and thus to denigrate them.[33] But what our comparison

[28] See Joseph M. Modrzejewski, *The Jews of Egypt: From Rameses II to Emperor Hadrian* (Philadelphia: Jewish Publication Society, 1995), 164–165.

[29] As Goudriaan notes ("Ethnical Strategies," 85), "Philo never formulates himself so as to contrast Jews and Greeks directly." Cf. below, n. 34.

[30] See above, n. 2.

[31] *P. London* 1912 = *CPJ* II, no. 153, col. V, line 95.

[32] Note, however, that—contrary to many translations—Philo does not go so far as to admit in *Legatio* 194 that the Jews' struggle to remain "Alexandrians" was hopeless. See the appendix.

[33] Ellen Birnbaum, "Philo on the Greeks: A Jewish Perspective on Culture and Society in First-Century Alexandria," *SPhA* 13 (2001): esp. 48–52.

with Josephus has pointed up is that Philo was not willing to go so far as to give up on "Greek" as well. He was not willing to assert that "Greeks" could be so despicable, or to admit that Jews were not a type of Greeks[34]— and he was willing to preserve that fundamental pillar of the cultural notions with which he grew up even at the price of leaving some obscurity in his prose.

Thus, to summarize, even a brief comparison of Josephus's and Philo's accounts of the Alexandrian Jewish violence in 38 C.E., and of the ensuing embassy to Rome, points up, apart from the differing focuses of the two accounts (Josephus focusing upon Gaius vs. God, Philo focusing upon Jews vs. Greeks in Alexandria), three differences between the points of view of an Alexandrian Jew and those of a Judaean turned Roman:

- if any Jews had to be blamed, if only for lack of *savoir faire* in dealing with wicked people who were powerful, each preferred to blame Jews from the other center;
- if an Alexandrian Jew took the quest for Alexandrian citizenship seriously, a Judaean-Roman one did not, no more than a priest of Jerusalem took Alexandrian synagogues seriously; and
- if Alexandrian Jews assumed that being a Greek was something quite respectable and found it difficult to portray Greeks as villains, a Judaean-Roman Jew could easily differ on both counts.

***

---

[34] See Joseph J. Modrzejewski, "How to be a Jew in Hellenistic Egypt?," *Diasporas in Antiquity* (BJS 288; ed. Shaye J.D. Cohen, Ernest S. Frerichs; Atlanta: Scholars, 1993), 65–92. This does not, however, prevent Philo from expressing some competition between Jews and Greeks (see Birnbaum, "Philo on the Greeks," esp. 46–48); that amounts to a competition of one type of Greeks with Greeks of other types.

*Appendix: On the Structure of Philo, Legatio 191–195
and the Translation of ἄλλως in §194*

In considering the contrast between Philo's refusal to term his persecutors "Greeks" and willingness to term them "Alexandrians," which, I suggest, bespeak his insistence that the Jews of Alexandria were "Greeks" and recognition that they were involved in a struggle to be called "Alexandrians," for a moment I thought that *Legatio* 194 clearly stated that the latter struggle was a lost cause. That was because I was using Smallwood's translation of the passage, where Philo sets out the thoughts of the Alexandrian Jewish ambassadors to Gaius after they heard of his plan to erect a statue in the Temple of Jerusalem: "How can it be right and proper to struggle *vainly* to prove that we are Alexandrians, when over our heads hangs the danger threatening the whole civic position of the Jews at large?"[35] Indeed, that is the standard translation of Philo's ποῦ γὰρ ὅσιον ἢ θεμιτὸν ἄλλως ἀγωνίζεσθαι ..., found in translations by Hans Lewy ("ohne Aussicht auf Erfolg weiter zu kämpfen"[36]), Francis H. Colson ("vainly striving"[37]), Friedrich Wilhelm Kohnke ("fruchtlos den Kampf...zu führen"[38]), André Pelletier ("que nous dépensions en vain tant d'efforts"[39]), and Aryeh Kasher (*lashāv*[40]).

However, although that translation is widespread, it seems to me that another is preferable. Note, first of all, that although ἄλλως can mean "in vain" in classical Greek,[41] it appears to be difficult to document that meaning in later Greek: It does not show up in lexica to Polybius, papyri, Josephus, Plutarch, or New Testament Greek, and my check (with the help of Mayer's *Index Philoneus*) of all the forty-plus occurrences of ἄλλως in Philo did not find even one that means "vainly." I did, however, note several cases in which Philo uses the adverb, in the sense of "furthermore," to introduce the second of two arguments that both point to the same conclusion; thus, for some examples, *Eternity of the World* 98; *Special Laws* 3.50, 90 and 4.163, 171. Indeed, at *Special Laws* 3.90 Colson (Loeb) actually

---

[35] Smallwood, *Philonis Alexandrini Legatio*, 102 (my italics).

[36] *Philon von Alexandrien: Von den Machterweisen Gottes* (trans. Hans Lewy; Berlin: Schocken, 1935), 47.

[37] *Philo*, X (LCL; Cambridge, Mass.: Harvard University, 1962), 101.

[38] In: *Philo von Alexandria: Die Werke in deutscher Übersetzung*, VII (ed. Leopold Cohn et al.; Berlin: De Gruyter, 1964), 225.

[39] André Pelletier, *Legatio ad Caium* (PAPM 32; Paris: Cerf, 1972), 205

[40] In: *Philo of Alexandria: Writings*, I (ed. S. Daniel-Nataf; Jerusalem: Bialik Institute and Israel Academy of Sciences and Humanities, 1986), 106 (in Hebrew).

[41] Liddell-Scott-Jones cites a case in Homer and notes that that sense is frequent in tragedy and comedy.

translates "another consideration is." That seems to be what is meant here, as the following two points show: (a) §§191a and then—using ἄλλως—194a give two neatly matched rhetorical questions from principle, in each case following it with practical considerations that point in the same direction, so "furthermore" would be a natural way to link the two questions; and (b) the opening of §195 explicitly confirms this understanding of the passage. I shall detail these two points.

a. §191a and §194a offer two neatly matched rhetorical questions from principle

   i. §191a poses the first rhetorical question:
ἐξέσται δὲ προσελθεῖν ἢ διᾶραι τὸ στόμα περὶ προσευχῶν τῷ λυμεῶνι τοῦ πανιέρου—literally, "will it be allowed to approach, with regard to synagogues, him who desecrates that which is most sacred, or to open one's mouth to him about synagogues?" Note that the verb is impersonal; "we" are not mentioned.[42] That is, the question is not whether *Philo's delegation will be allowed* (by Gaius or his doorkeepers) to approach him. Rather, the rhetorical question is a matter of principle—*whether anyone would or should be allowed* (even if it were possible!) to approach Gaius and speak to him about synagogues, since he is the would-be defiler of something more holy (the Temple of Jerusalem) and combating that plan should take precedence.[43]

   Next, §§191b-193 offer three practical considerations in support of the obviously negative response to the opening question from principle. Philo first points out, in §191b, that probably Gaius would not agree to see them anyway, for if he ignores the Temple he certainly will show no regard for synagogues. Then, in the second and third places (§§192–193), Philo focuses upon two terrible practical consequences that would follow if perchance (εἰ δὲ καὶ γένοιτο) Gaius did nevertheless allow them a hearing: it would get the delegates killed, and it would bring upon them the reprobation of their fellow Jews, who would think they were selfish insofar as they had pursued their own local interests instead of those of the whole Jewish people.

   ii. Then §194a poses the second rhetorical question:
ποῦ γὰρ ὅσιον ἢ θεμιτὸν ἄλλως ἀγωνίζεσθαι, δεικνύντας ὡς ἐσμὲν Ἀλεξανδρεῖς, οἷς ὁ περὶ τῆς καθολικωτέρας πολιτείας ἐπικρέμαται κίνδυνος

---

[42] Contrast Colson and Smallwood, who both render "Shall we be allowed...?"

[43] Perhaps Pelletier's translation means that: "Pourra-t-on approcher, pourra-t-on ouvrir la bouche ...?"

τῆς Ἰουδαίων: "For is it, *furthermore*, pious or proper,[44] for those for whom a danger is hanging over the more general civic body of the Jews, to struggle to demonstrate that we are Alexandrians...." Obviously, in this case too the answer is "no."

In §194b Philo then juxtaposes, to that argument from principle, a practical consideration in support of that same argument, namely, that it would not help to deal with the Jews' Alexandrian issue as long as the main problem was unresolved. For in that case the Jews would still have to fear that the desecration of the Temple would lead to an imperial order to abolish the name of the entire nation.

b. *§195 draws the conclusion from the two rhetorical questions*

§195 opens with Ἀμφοτέρων οὖν: "If, therefore, both of the purposes for which we were sent are gone ..." Here, obviously, "both" refers to the issue of the synagogues, addressed in §§191–193, and to the issue of citizenship, addressed in §194, introduced by ἄλλως as parallel to the first one.

But the conclusion that "both" in §195 refers to the two issues discussed in §§191–194 entails the conclusion that ἄλλως in §194 means "furthermore," *for otherwise readers will likely fail to realize that the preceding lines discussed two topics.* That this is so is indicated quite impressively, in my opinion, by the fact that of the six translators listed above (notes 35–40), who took ἄλλως in §194a to mean something else, "vainly," all but the one (Lewy) who has no footnotes at all felt the need to include a footnote on "both" in §195, explaining what the two topics are—as if otherwise readers would not know.[45] But Philo was a better writer than that and—as opposed to his treatment of "Greeks"—had no reason to be obscure here. That is, §195 indicates explicitly that it follows upon two parallel arguments—linked by ἄλλως—"furthermore." As noted above, this usage corresponds to that at *In Flaccum* 53 and *Legatio* 371 where, too, Philo relates to these two separate issues in tandem.

The Hebrew University of Jerusalem

---

[44] For this sense of *themiton*, see Frederick W. Danker (ed.), *A Greek-English Lexicon of the New Testament and Other Early Christian Literature* (Chicago: Chicago Univ., 2000³), 449, s.v. *themitos*: "pertaining to being appropriate or right, with implication that the thing so described is not a matter of codified law but unwritten procedure based on custom and awareness of the transcendent, *allowed, permitted, right.*"

[45] In this connection, I will note that although the five apart from Lewy all explain, in their footnotes, that the two issues alluded to §195 are religious rights and civic rights, Smallwood and Pelletier, who note that the former is set out in §191, erroneously state that the latter is set out in §193. In fact, as we have seen, §193 is still finishing up the practical support of the first argument, that began §191. The second argument begins only in §194.

The Studia Philonica Annual 24 (2012) 167–182

SYMPATHY FOR THE DEVIL?
PHILO ON FLACCUS AND ROME

JOSHUA YODER

Philo's treatise on Aulus Avillius Flaccus, prefect of Egypt 32–38 C.E., describes Flaccus's mistreatment of the Jewish community of Alexandria during the anti-Judean[1] riots of 38, and his subsequent arrest, exile and execution. The point of the story is clear enough: Flaccus's fate at the hands of the emperor Gaius demonstrates God's providence, which manifests itself both in the just punishment meted out to Flaccus and in the resulting vindication of the Jews of Alexandria who suffered from his depredations. In order to play his role in the narrative, Flaccus must fit the part of a villain justly punished, and Philo's portrait of him accomplishes that. However, this does not exhaust the range of Philo's portrayal of Flaccus. In some parts of the narrative Philo characterizes Flaccus as misguided or manipulated, and even betrays some sympathy for him. In this essay I trace the contours and progression of Philo's characterization of Flaccus and consider what this multivalent portrayal suggests about Philo's view of Rome in general.

Philo's first words, δεύτερος μετὰ Σηιανόν, introduce Flaccus the villain, presenting the governor as the successor to Sejanus in "the plot against the Jews."[2] Philo must exert some energy to make that characterization stick: Flaccus did not have the power and influence of Sejanus, but only limited, local authority. Accordingly, Philo claims that Flaccus not only struck those he could reach "with severe injuries" (ἀνηκέστοις κακοῖς) but also, by

---

[1] I use "Judean" and "Jew" more or less interchangeably, favoring "Jew" or "Jewish" when speaking of the ethnic group in general, "Judean" when speaking of specific individuals or groups.

[2] διαδέχεται τὴν κατὰ τῶν Ἰουδαίων ἐπιβουλήν. In *Legatio* Philo makes a vague reference to Sejanus's "attack" (ἐπίθεσις), his desire "to destroy (ἀναρπάσαι) the nation," and unspecified false accusations directed against the Judeans living in Rome (§160). These accusations apparently endangered Judean diaspora populations far and wide: Philo represents Tiberius as interceding with the provincial governors on their behalf after discovering that the accusations were false or at least grossly inflated (§161). See E. Mary Smallwood, ed., *Philonis Alexandrini: Legatio ad Gaium* (Leiden: Brill, 1961), 243–5.

making up in artifice (διὰ τέχνης) for what he lacked in power, extended his attack to all Jews everywhere. Philo's subsequent comment that "those of a tyrannical nature to whom strength is not available accomplish their designs by underhanded dealings" suggests that Flaccus is both devious and disposed to tyranny, nicely rounding out the portrait of a hostile and treacherous antagonist (*Flacc.* 1).

Upon entering the narrative proper the picture changes considerably. Before narrating Flaccus's plots and attacks, Philo will describe his first five years in office during which he displayed "countless signs of excellence."[3] When at length he turns to his account of Flaccus's misdeeds, Philo offers yet another view of Flaccus, this one more nuanced than the flat characterizations of him either as an exemplary governor or as a deadly and deceitful Jew-hater. Philo describes how Flaccus "began to let loose and slacken everything" (ὑφιέναι καὶ χαλᾶν ἤρξατο τὰ πάντα) after the death of Tiberius and the accession of Gaius (*Flacc.* 9).[4] Here we have not a malicious tyrant, but a man losing his grip.

In this narrative of Flaccus's decline, Philo's interest in dramatic presentation overshadows his interest in placing Flaccus in the worst possible light.[5] Philo emphasizes Flaccus's closeness to Tiberius (*Flacc.* 9), and thus the emotional impact of the emperor's death. He describes in exaggerated terms Flaccus's expression of grief at the death of the emperor and his shock and horror at news of Gaius's murder of his friends and allies. Most tellingly, Philo artfully arranges his narration of Flaccus's political setbacks in such a way that the three successive blows that Flaccus receives—the death of Tiberius, the death of Gemellus, and finally the death of Macro—make the maximum impact on the reader. After each of the first two misfortunes, Philo assures his reader that Flaccus still retained some grasp on sanity, some narrow hope—only to narrate the next disaster. Moreover, between the death of Gemellus and the death of Macro, Philo interposes an account of the succession and of Macro's role in it (§12–13), thus drawing out the narrative and delaying the third and final blow. With the death of Macro, Philo relates, Flaccus lost his last vestiges of hope (§16). Again Philo the dramatist is at work—in point of fact Flaccus still has an intercessor, Lepidus, as we learn later in the narrative (§151).

---

[3] Or so it seemed - ὅσα τῷ δοκεῖν (*Flacc.* 2).

[4] Pieter van der Horst, *Philo's Flaccus: The First Pogrom* (PACS 2; Leiden: Brill, 2003), 100, links this description to the image of a charioteer losing control of his horses common in discussions of rulership since Plato (cf. *Resp.* 566d2).

[5] On *Flaccus* as "mimetic historiography," see Martin Meiser, "Gattung, Adressaten und Intention von Philos *In Flaccum*," *JSJ* 30 (1999): 420–22. Cf. Daniel Schwartz, "On Drama and Authenticity in Philo and Josephus," *SCI* 10 (1989–90): 113–120.

Philo's dramatization of Flaccus's situation and feelings subverts his portrait of Flaccus the villain, because it cannot help but engender sympathy for the governor. The more grim Flaccus's plight is made to appear to the reader, the more understandable his plunge into weakness and despair and his failure to keep up with his public responsibilities (*Flacc.* 15). The more Philo dramatizes Flaccus's grief and fear, the more the reader is led to empathize. To be sure, Flaccus is hardly a model of philosophical equanimity in the face of misfortune.[6] But neither can Philo's exaggerated depiction of the governor's emotions be safely taken as meant to mock or to condemn.[7] Elsewhere Philo ascribes such a display of grief to one of his heroes, Jacob, at the false report of Joseph's death (*Ios.* 22–23), and his description of Flaccus's horrified reaction to the bad news from Rome bears resemblances to his description of his own embassy's reaction to news of Gaius's plans for the Jerusalem temple (*Legat.* 189; cf. the reaction of Agrippa I, 266–67). This is not satirical writing, but dramatic writing, and the dramatization of Flaccus's plight works at cross-purposes with the narrative's goal of presenting Flaccus as a hateful and ruthless schemer. Philo does not write like an author bent on casting his subject in the worst possible light.

Flaccus as Puppet and Pawn

Philo's account of Flaccus's turn to the dark side brings him no closer to this goal. He describes a change of policy springing from two causes: the hopelessness of the governor's situation[8] and a decline in his reasoning capacity (*Flacc.* 18).[9] It is desperation that brings Flaccus to turn to his

---

[6] Abraham provides a model of appropriate mourning: βραχέα τῷ σώματι ἐπιδακρύσας θᾶττον ἀπανέστη τοῦ νεκροῦ (*Abr.* 258; cf. §§256–260). Philo apparently favored a moderate expression of grief—gentle weeping, but no loud lamentations. One might compare Agricola's response to news of the death of his infant son: he doesn't make a display of fortitude, but neither does he lament excessively (*quem casum neque ut plerique fortium virorum ambitiose, neque per lamenta rursus ac maerorem muliebriter tulit*; Tacitus, *Agr.* 29).

[7] A suggestion made by Maren Niehoff, *Philo on Jewish Identity and Culture* (Texts and Studies in Ancient Judaism 86; Tübingen: Mohr Siebeck, 2001), 133–135. Cf. van der Horst, *Flaccus*, 100.

[8] He is ἐν ἀμηχάνοις δὲ καὶ ἀπόροις, "a very strong expression for a hopeless situation in which one sees no way out whatsoever" (van der Horst, *Flaccus*, 106–7, citing as parallels *Abr.* 175; *Spec.* 4.127; *Legat.* 178).

[9] ἅμα τῇ τοῦ λογισμοῦ πρὸς τὸ χεῖρον μεταβολῇ. According to Francesca Calabi, "It seems necessary to resort to a pathology to explain behavioural changes. Herein lies an affinity with other works of the Hellenistic period such as 3 Maccabees, where often

former enemies for a way out, and loss of his former acuity that keeps him from seeing through their duplicity (§§18–19).[10] Philo attributes Flaccus's actions to motives that, while not admirable, are far from the hostility and hatred that Philo evoked in the introductory lines.

Philo makes it clear at this stage that Flaccus's anti-Judean policies are not his own but dictated by his new councilors. He "subscribes" (συνεπιγράφεται) to their schemes. He is said to become completely subjected to the worst of his subjects and the influence of the common mob that they represent. He is "as dumb as a mask on stage,"[11] bearing only the title of authority, his presence required only to keep up appearances while his councilors devise and execute their plans (*Flacc.* 18–20). This image severely limits Flaccus's agency, making him nothing but a rubber stamp. Flaccus the victim has become Flaccus the deceived and manipulated accessory; it is Flaccus's so-called friends who are portrayed as malicious and crafty, the authors of "most disadvantageous proposals" (§19).[12] This is far from the

---

wicked behavior is attributed to great personages as a result of the loss of mental faculties" ("Theatrical Language in Philo's *In Flaccum*," in *Italian Studies on Philo of Alexandria* [ed. Francesca Calabi; Leiden: Brill, 2003], 101). However, in this case Flaccus's behavior is not a direct result of mental derangement but an indirect result—his desperation and loss of acuity make him vulnerable to deception and false promises. At this point in the narrative his behavior is not so much wicked or deranged as foolish and motivated by the desire for self-preservation at any price.

[10] Philo uses the expression ἐσφάδαζε. In Philo the verb is usually associated with strong emotion: frustration, impatience and/or helplessness. It denotes a rapid movement of the body that can be rendered with "to struggle," "to shudder," "to chafe" or "to writhe," depending on the context (cf. *Cher.* 36; *Ebr.* 121; *Mig.* 156; *Abr.* 1.257; *Mos.* 1.170; *Spec.* 3.44, 81; *Virt.* 30, 128; *Praem.* 140; *Prob.* 39; *Flacc.* 162, 180; *Legat.* 184).

[11] A rather literal translation of κωφὸν ὡς ἐπὶ σκηνῆς προσωπεῖον (*Flacc.* 20). Herbert Box renders the phrase "mute stage character" (*Philonis Alexandrini In Flaccum* [London: Oxford University Press, 1939]). Francis H. Colson (PLCL) and van der Horst (PACS) render it as "masked dummy." προσωπεῖον is, properly speaking, the mask, not the character, though it can represent the latter by metathesis (André Pelletier, *In Flaccum* [PAPM 32; Paris: Cerf, 1972], 182–3). Pelletier takes the phrase κωφὸν προσωπεῖον as a technical term for a mask without a hole for the mouth, reserved for characters without a speaking part (see his discussion 182–4), by analogy with the phrase κωφὸν πρόσωπον, used as a technical term by Cicero (*Att.* 13.19). The syntax of Philo's sentence works against this, however. Another way of understanding the phrase takes Flaccus to be a mask through which others speak. In the absence of direct evidence for κωφὸν προσωπεῖον as a *terminus technicus*, I prefer to understand Philo's phrase in this sense, which fits the syntax more naturally. Either interpretation is appropriate to the point Philo wishes to make: Flaccus is an accessory, brought along for the sake of appearances, bearing authority in name only (ἕνεκα προσχήματος αὐτὸ μόνον παραλαμβάνοντες ἐπιγεγραμμένον ὄνομα ἀρχῆς). On Philo's use of language and images derived from the theater in *Flaccus* see Calabi, "Theatrical Language."

[12] εἰσηγούμενοι μὲν ἀλυσιτελεστάτας γνώμας.

Flaccus who lies awake at night inventing new plots against the Jews, whom we will meet later in the narrative (*Flacc.* 101).

The arrival of King Agrippa I proves to be an occasion for Philo to demonstrate that Flaccus's "madness" (ἀπόνοια) was "practiced more from instruction than by nature" (*Flacc.* 25).[13] He describes Flaccus's associates playing upon his insecurity and vanity to "incite" him (ἀνηρέθιζον) to jealousy (§§29–31). Even so, the governor does not dare show his sentiments openly; it is his private expressions of hostility that encourage the masses to publically show contempt (§33).[14] By evoking a Flaccus acting by instruction rather than by nature, Philo once again draws a different picture of the governor than he did in the introduction, where he implied that Flaccus had a tyrannical nature.

As the actions of the mob grow more serious, Philo continues to portray Flaccus as an accessory to rather than originator of the events. His lack of response to the insults, culminating in the mockery in the gymnasium (*Flacc.* 34–40), makes him an accessory to them. The crowds call for erecting images in the prayer-houses knowing that they have purchased the governor's complicity (§41), leading Philo to call Flaccus παλίμπρατος, "bought and sold."[15]

Only after the installation of images in the prayer-houses (*Flacc.* 43) does Philo begin to shift from a portrait of "Flaccus the puppet" to "Flaccus the tyrant." Philo now characterizes him as "lending a hand (συνεχειρούργει) to each wrong-doing," even using his "greater authority" to "rekindle the civil strife with fresh additions of evil" (§44).[16] Flaccus has now taken the lead, encouraging the hostility of the mob rather than just pandering to it. When Philo describes Flaccus's first overt action against the Judeans, the promulgation of a decree prejudicial to their status in Alexandria, he does not scruple to make Flaccus the agent of what the crowds have done: "Since, therefore, the unlawful enterprise seemed to him to be going well, having seized our prayer-houses and having not even left the name behind

---

[13] ἐκ μαθήσεως τὸ πλέον ἢ φύσεως ἐπιτετηδευμένην. It is not clear to me what sort of "madness" one can be "instructed" to "practice." Others have seen the difficulty as well. Box (*In Flaccum*) translates "loss of all sense," Pelletier (PAPM) "une folie," Colsor (PLCL) "infatuation," and van der Horst (PACS) "insanity." Insanity seems too strong here, unless not meant literally: whatever ἀπόνοια is, it is something that can be inculcated and practiced, and thus does not indicate complete mental derangement.

[14] Philo leaves open the possibility that Flaccus himself incited the mob.

[15] On παλίμπρατος see the notes in van der Horst (*Flaccus*, 134) and especially Box (93), with accompanying citations.

[16] ἀπὸ μείζονος ἐξουσίας ἀναρριπίζειν καινοτέραις ἀεὶ κακῶν προσθήκαις τὴν στάσιν ἠξίου.

(μηδὲ τοὔνομα ὑπολιπομένῳ), again he proceeded to another thing, the abrogation of our citizenship (πολιτεία)" (§53).

Calling this decree "a profession of tyranny" (τυραννίδος ἐπάγγελμα), Philo goes on to say, "then to the two first things he added a third as well."[17] The two first things evidently refers to the desecration of the prayer houses and the anti-Judean decree. Philo now implies that these two can be counted side by side as crimes of Flaccus. But just as the installation of images was not something Flaccus himself did, this third act, the plundering of Judeans' houses, is an act of the mob, not of the governor (*Flacc.* 53–54). Flaccus's responsibility seems to lie in the fact that the marauders perceived he would do nothing to hinder or punish them: Philo speaks of them as "having received amnesty (ἄδειαν)" (§55). Yet here too Flaccus is subsequently made the agent of the act in an elliptical way: "Flaccus, having broken in and robbed everything..."[18] As a result he can now be described as a "worker of enormities" (μεγαλουργός) and "originator of new abuses" (καινῶν ἀδικημάτων εὑρετής) (§73).

When Flaccus proceeds to the punishment of the Judean leaders, Philo admits that Flaccus metes out these beatings to please the crowd, "intending by this to win them over to what he had in mind" (*Flacc.* 82).[19] Even so, Philo claims that the act is "a proof of no small malice" (οὐ μικρᾶς δεῖγμα κακονοίας) on the governor's part as well (§78).[20] As his narrative progresses, Philo keeps up this rhetoric. He dubs Flaccus's order to search the Judeans' houses for arms a "second plan of spoliation" (δευτέρα γὰρ ἐπινοεῖται πόρθησις) (§86), thus linking this seemingly more innocuous action to the earlier violent plundering of Judean residences and businesses. To Philo, Flaccus's hostile intent is clear—to "range the mass of the soldiery against us" (τὸ στρατευόμενον πλῆθος ἡμῖν ἐπιτειχίσαι) (§86). The search

---

[17] εἶτα δυσὶ τοῖς προτέροις καὶ τρίτον προσέθηκεν.

[18] πάντα δὲ διορύξας καὶ τοιχωρυχήσας ὁ Φλάκκος.

[19] ταύτῃ νομίζων ἐξοικειώσασθαι μᾶλλον αὐτὸν εἰς ἅπερ διενοεῖτο. It is unclear exactly what things Flaccus had in mind. Erich Gruen interprets this as an indication of Flaccus's desire to pacify the crowds. "Here the author has it right. The prefect and the Alexandrians had different objectives" (*Diaspora: Jews Amidst Greeks and Romans* [Cambridge, Mass.: Harvard University Press, 2002], 59). This cannot be what Philo intends, however. It is more likely that he is alluding to Flaccus's desire for popularity with the crowds.

[20] It may be that the "proof" of Flaccus's malice lies in the fact that he chose to inflict a commoner's punishment on these distinguished Jews, rather than in the fact of punishment itself, for which Flaccus doubtless had some explanation. Philo never hints at the nature of the charges against these leaders.

testifies to the "relentlessness" (ἀποτομίας) of Flaccus and the crowds," from which even the Jewish women are not exempt (§95).[21]

Thus, from his depiction of Flaccus's despair and consequent vulnerability to manipulation, Philo has now returned to a portrait of Flaccus as a full-fledged villain whose actions spring from his own hostility toward the Jews rather than his complicity in the actions of others. Philo positions as the culminating misdeed and the turning point in the narrative Flaccus's failure to forward the Judeans' acclamation to the new emperor Gaius (*Flacc.* 97–101). Though chronologically prior to the riots, this act allows Philo to show Flaccus the villain in all his glory. He is the sole agent and he acts with hypocrisy and dissimulation. Moreover, by maneuvering to incite animosity for the Jews in the emperor himself, Flaccus craftily extends his reach to Judeans across the empire.

Thus the chronological dislocation in the narrative allows Philo to end his account of Flaccus's government of Alexandria where he began with the Flaccus depicted in the opening lines: an enemy acting with malice, by artifice rather than openly, acting to surpass the limited authority of his position in order to harm all Jews everywhere, and thus truly a worthy successor to Sejanus. It is this Flaccus whose downfall will serve as vindication for the Judean community of Alexandria.[22] Philo concludes, "Are these not the actions of one who has long lain awake at night and has carefully considered the plot against us, and not one in desperation acting rashly with some ill-timed impulse and lapse of reason?" (*Flacc.* 101). The rhetorical question explicitly contradicts Philo's earlier representation of Flaccus.[23]

---

[21] BDAG glosses ἀποτομία with "severity." The expression ἀποτομία θεοῦ is used twice in Rom 11:22. The word is used by Philo also in *Spec. Leg.* 2, 94. Box (*In Flaccum*) translates "atrocity" ("a plot of the atrocity of…"), van der Horst (PACS), with Colson (PLCL), "ruthlessness" ("a deliberate plot, due to the ruthlessness…"). Both give the word a negative connotation that it does not necessarily have. The literal translation, "a plot of the severity of Flaccus and of the crowds…" does not make good sense. The force of the genitive may be that the plot illustrated the severity or relentlessness of Flaccus and the crowds. In any case, in this context the word does suggest a deep and ongoing hostility.

[22] This view of Flaccus is continued in the next sentence: "But God… countering his flattering words and subtleties meant to cheat, and the council-chamber of his lawless mind, in which he was scheming against us… soon provided an opportunity for our hope not to be falsified" (*Flacc.* 102). The sentence emphasizes Flaccus's dishonesty, lawlessness and malice. A further such comment is in §107.

[23] Philo's break from chronological order creates some breaks in logic. The incident must have taken place soon after Gaius's accession to the throne, which Philo marked as the end of Flaccus's "good period" and the beginning of his decline. Yet according to Philo, Flaccus had already been plotting against the Judeans for a long time. Furthermore, the Jews apparently already believed that Flaccus was hostile to them and would not permit them to send an embassy directly (van der Horst, *Flaccus*, 188, also notes this problem).

But it seals in the mind the picture of Flaccus that Philo wishes his reader to take into the second half of his narrative.

Flaccus's Arrest and Punishment

Philo does not maintain this picture of Flaccus through the rest of his narrative, however. Once he has begun his account of Flaccus's arrest and punishment, his efforts at illustrating Flaccus's hostility and malevolence cease. When Flaccus is arrested at the home of a host, he is not drunk or misbehaving himself, but in the act of offering a toast and "being congenial" to the other banqueters (*Flacc.* 113).[24] Philo does not depict him as surrounded by swarms of slaves—quite the opposite: the modesty of his retinue allows his pursuers to arrest him easily. At the moment of arrest, he simply appears hapless—he is "struck dumb by consternation" (§114).[25]

Indeed, when Philo describes the slanders that Isidoros had instigated against Flaccus at an earlier point in the governor's career (*Flacc.* 138–145), his portrait of him is entirely positive. In fact, the account seems designed to exonerate Flaccus from any suspicion of blame in the incident. Not content merely to state that the accusations were groundless (§139), Philo portrays the disbelief and outrage of the general public and has the perpetrators freely confess to being paid, both in a private interrogation and before the public, confirming their story with specific details and reasonable proofs (§§139–143). The sympathy of the entire city is with Flaccus; Isidoros must flee not because the governor desires vengeance, but because the crowds are calling for his death (§144).[26] Flaccus himself is a model of clemency: he bears no grudge, but is concerned only with the peace of the city, which he imagines is assured now that the troublemaker has departed of his own accord.[27] This account not only betrays no

---

Richard Barraclough concludes that "the ascription to Flaccus of premeditated anti-Jewish action is a reading back from the events…" ("Philo's Politics: Roman Rule and Hellenistic Judaism," *ANRW* 21.1:417–553 [New York: de Gruyter, 1984], 463–64). Sandra Gambetti, *The Alexandrian Riots of 38 c.e. and the Persecution of the Jews: A Historical Reconstruction* (JSJSup 135; Leiden: Brill, 2009), 20–21, suggests a reason other than the governor's bad graces for the expectation that Flaccus would not grant permission for an embassy.

[24] φιλοφρονούμενος seems a quite positive word. His host is a freedman of Tiberius— once again reminding the reader of Flaccus's link to Tiberius, an emperor Philo depicted elsewhere as friendly toward the Jews.

[25] ὑπ᾽ ἐκπλήξεως ἀχανὴς γίνεται.

[26] Philo even implies that Isodoros himself had a guilty conscience (ἕνεκα τοῦ συνειδότος, §145).

[27] He does not "waste any time on him" (οὐδὲν ἐπ᾽ αὐτῷ περιειργάζετο, §145).

animosity toward Flaccus, it is positively partisan in the governor's favor. Its presence here, in the midst of Philo's account of how the governor got his just desserts, is remarkable.

Philo has been accused of displaying a certain amount of *Schadenfreude* in his account of Flaccus's demise.[28] However, there are several clues that he does not intend his readers to receive the account in a vindictive spirit. As noted (and dismissed) by F. H. Colson, Philo has the Alexandrian Jews insist in their prayer of thanksgiving that they do not rejoice in the downfall of their enemies (*Flacc.* 121). Philo also signals his own attitude when he describes people coming to watch Flaccus on his way to exile at Andros: only the ignoble look on with malice; the rest sympathize (συναλγήσοντες), for their habit is to take a lesson (σωφρονίζεσθαι) from the fates of others (§154).[29]

Nor does Philo go out of his way to make Flaccus an unsympathetic character in the midst of his sufferings on Andros. To be sure, his frenzied behavior does nothing to impress the reader with his ἐνκράτεια, but it also indicates the extremity of his mental suffering.[30] Flaccus convicts himself of "being soft" in being unwilling to take his own life (*Flacc.* 179),[31] but attributes this to destiny which is saving him for more punishments to come. Philo has Flaccus confess his wrongdoings and acknowledge that he is being punished justly (§§170–179), a device calculated to add credibility to Philo's accusations against the governor, but also one that hints at penitence.[32]

---

[28] Notably, Colson writes in his introduction in the Loeb edition, "He gloats over the misery of Flaccus in his fall, exile, and death, with a vindictiveness which I feel to be repulsive" (301). For a critique of this position see Valentin Nikiprowetzky, "*Schadenfreude* chez Philon d'Alexandrie?" in *Études Philoniennes* (Paris: Cerf, 1996), 97–109.

[29] Philo's vivid narration of Flaccus's final days is motivated by the need to demonstrate that Flaccus is fairly repaid for the misery that he caused, for "reciprocal punishment is the clearest proof of divine πρόνοια" (Matthew Kraus, "Philosophical History in Philo's *In Flaccum*," SBLSPS 33 [1994]: 477–494, 493). On the parallels between Flaccus's fate and that of the Alexandrian Jews, many of which Philo himself points out (§§115, 170–175, 189), see Nikiprowetsky, "*Schadenfreude*," 103–108 and esp. Richard Alston, "Philo's *In Flaccum*: Ethnicity and Social Space in Roman Alexandria," *Greece and Rome* 44 (1997): 166.

[30] Again, note a parallel in *De Iosepho* (16): when Judah finds that Joseph has been sold, "he cried out and wailed, and, tearing his clothes, staggered up and down like a madman, striking his hands together and tearing out his hair" (ἐβόα καὶ ἐκεκράγει καὶ τὰς ἐσθῆτας περιρρηξάμενος ἄνω καὶ κάτω καθάπερ ἐμμανὴς ἐφέρετο τὰς χεῖρας κροτῶν καὶ τὰς τρίχας τίλλων).

[31] μαλακίζομαι πρὸς θάνατον. One could read as passive: "I am being softened up for death," but the reference to suicide in the following phrase suggests the middle form.

[32] See Meiser, "Gattung, Adressaten und Intention," 428–429 on the speech as an aspect of the typical "Rede des gezüchtigten Gottesfeindes;" cf. Pelletier, *Flaccum*, 16–19.

Philo on Rome

Philo has a clear motive for portraying Flaccus as a hateful figure who acts deliberately and maliciously. Flaccus must be the consummate arch-villain, because he bears all the crimes against the Jews in his person, and thus his punishment represents a proof of divine providence and the vindication of the Judeans of Alexandria. The more sympathetic part of the portrayal is less obviously motivated, and I suspect that it betrays reflections of Philo's real perspective on events. When it suits his purpose, Philo claims that Flaccus cherished animosity towards the Jews over a long period of time. But his own account undermines this claim, and in fact holds clues that during the majority of his term Flaccus must have been well-regarded by the Judean population of Alexandria.

Philo provides a rationale for his glowing account of Flaccus's first five years in office (*Flacc.* 7) that is reasonable but not entirely satisfying. Desire to make such a rhetorical point does not seem an adequate motive to invent a period of excellent governance out of whole cloth.[33] At the least we are justified in presuming that Philo did not conjure such sunshine to cover up extreme discontent. However exaggerated and stereotypical the account, its inclusion suggests that the Judeans of Alexandria had few complaints with Flaccus prior to his last year in office. Philo must concede this fact, and explain why a governor with whom the Judeans maintained acceptable relations for the majority of his term suddenly turned on them. Thus the highly rhetoricized account of Flaccus's first five years, followed by the equally dramatic account of his unraveling.

The likelihood of good relations between the Judean community and the governor finds further support in Philo's report of Flaccus's measures to dissolve the clubs.[34] That such a policy is not sheer fantasy on Philo's part is suggested by the fact that Isidoros was influential in many of these associations (*Flacc.* 136–137), the same Isidoros who organized protests against the governor. Though Philo claims the protests were motivated by payments, one may conjecture that their real origin lay in the discontent of

---

[33] The stock figure of the virtuous ruler who degenerates into tyranny may also play a role. Van der Horst calls attention to *Legatio* 8–13 on the first period of Gaius's rule (98). There too the depiction has some basis in reality, reflecting a period of optimism at the beginning of the new regime. See Smallwood, *Legatio*, 168–9. On various conventional explanations for the change in character of such figures, see Christopher Gill, "The Question of Character-Development: Plutarch and Tacitus," *CQ* 33 (1983): 469–87.

[34] Barraclough ("Philo's Politics," 462 n. 390) points out the parallel in Pliny, *Ep.* 10.96, where we learn of Trajan's suppression of similar groups in Bithynia.

the members of these associations.[35] Philo has nothing good to say about these clubs (*Flacc.* 4),[36] and his view may well reflect the majority opinion of the Judean population. The defensive account that Philo gives of the uproar is quite well explained if it was the associations that were the bone of contention. The sympathies of the author are clearly with the governor in this conflict.

There are other clues as well. Philo claims that at first Flaccus only carried out his anti-Judean policy covertly, displaying bias against the Judeans in legal disputes and denying them audience with him (*Flacc.* 24). His account assumes that prior to this time the Judeans had not experienced Flaccus as biased in this way and that they were accustomed to having access to the governor when necessary. In addition, Philo's rhetoric suggests he shares Flaccus's political allegiances: like Flaccus, he sides with Tiberius and his "true offspring" and views Gaius, the "adopted offspring," as a threat (*Flacc.* 8–13). As previously noted, Philo and his embassy experienced feelings very similar to Flaccus's during their own confrontation with the emperor (*Legat.* 189). Under different circumstances, Flaccus's fate at Gaius's hands might have won him a great deal of sympathy from Philo.

Viewed objectively, Flaccus's behavior as reported by Philo does not strike one as the result of simmering hostility or the deeds of one who wished to bring incurable evils upon one segment of the Alexandrian population. Flaccus promulgates an edict defining the Judean Alexandrians as non-citizens, sends his troops to search for weapons in the Judean community, and punishes a certain number of Jews who Philo claims were innocent. The mocking, the rioting, the despoiling, the desecrating and the killing were all done by others. The bulk of the rhetorical work of *Against Flaccus* lies in demonstrating the governor's complicity in the events and in representing his actual deeds in the worst possible light.[37] Philo himself may not have regarded Flaccus as the chief villain of the affair. He may

---

[35] For an account of the riots that is particularly sensitive to the shifting conditions of power among political factions, see Werner Bergmann and Christhard Hoffman, "Kalkül oder 'Massenwahn'? Eine soziologische Interpretation der antijüdischen Unruhen in Alexandria 38 n. Chr.," in *Antisemitismus und jüdishe Geschichte. Studien zu Ehren von H. A. Strauss* (ed. R. Erb and M. Schmidt; Berlin: Wissenschaftlicher Autorenverlag, 1987), 15–46.

[36] Cf. *Spec.* 4.46–47.

[37] Indeed, it is not clear how much responsibility Flaccus really bore for the events at Alexandria. See Gruen, *Diaspora*, 54–83, who concludes, "[Flaccus's] tenure collapsed through ineptitude rather than malice." Gruen argues that the disorder in Alexandria ultimately brought about Flaccus's recall. However, the violence apparently never became so serious that Flaccus had to call in the legions (compare Josephus, *War* 2.494). For another explanation see Adrian N. Sherwin-White, "Philo and Avillius Flaccus. A Conundrum," *Latomus* 31 (1972): 820–28.

have felt more animosity toward the anti-Judean Alexandrian leaders. Had Isidoros, Lampo, and Dionysios met their end soon after the Alexandrian riots, *Against Flaccus* might never had been written.

What can we deduce from such a mixed and ambiguous portrait of a Roman governor about its author's attitude toward Rome? Despite the condemnation of Flaccus's mistreatment of the Judeans, Philo's account of Flaccus's "good" years implies that it is possible to be a "good" Roman governor of Egypt. The author has an opinion about what constitutes good governance, and can point to at least one individual who has closely conformed to that ideal. Furthermore, it is implied that a "good" Roman governor will benefit the Judean population of Alexandria by restraining the lawless and violent element of the population. Thus although the author understands that Roman governors can behave brutally and unjustly, he does not imply that the Roman regime will invariably be rapacious, brutal, and cruel.

Indeed, Philo portrays the power of Rome as a force for good in the provinces, working to discourage and curtail misrule by individual governors. Though some governors do pervert their office into tyranny, on their return to Rome they can count on a reckoning before a judge who will show them no partiality (*Flacc.* 105–106).[38] In the case of Flaccus the authorities did not even wait until his term had ended (§107). In this way, Philo depicts gubernatorial misconduct as an aberration from the norm, contrary to the wishes of the emperor. He can thus represent Rome and its emperors purely as "benefactors" (§§48, 74, 103).[39]

Nevertheless, there are indications that Philo's appreciation for Roman rule was not unalloyed. Not only does Philo acknowledge the reality that Roman officials can be corrupt and abusive, he also subtly points to cracks in the façade of his idealized portrait of a competent Roman governor. Referring to Flaccus's "dignified bearing," Philo remarks that "vanity is most advantageous for a ruler" (ἄρχοντι δὲ λυσιτελέστατον ὁ τῦφος, *Flacc.* 4). Vanity, τῦφος, always has a negative connotation elsewhere in Philo. By

---

[38] For a more realistic view see Peter A. Brunt, "Charges of Provincial Maladministration under the Early Principate," *Historia* 10 (1961): 189–227.

[39] The same dynamic is visible in Philo's critique of other Roman officials who persecuted the Jews: Sejanus (*Legat.* 159–161) and Pilate (*Legat.* 299–308). See Mireille Hadas-Lebel, *Jerusalem Against Rome* (trans. Robyn Fréchet; Interdisciplinary Studies in Ancient Culture and Religion 7; Leuven: Peeters, 2006), 372–79. These figures may have been the topic of their own treatises, perhaps part of a larger work of which *Against Flaccus* was a part (as is suggested by the reference to Sejanus in *Flaccus* 1.1). The emperor Gaius is shown to have pursued a radically different policy than did his predecessors Augustus and Tiberius, who did not share his insanity and arrogance (*Legat.* 298–318).

using the term here, Philo insinuates that even Flaccus's good years as governor were marred by pride and empty glory. By making the remark in the form of a general maxim, Philo links this critique to what he says elsewhere in his *oeuvre* about the political man, whose good intentions have no stability because he puts a premium on wealth and physical safety (cf. *Somn.* 2.11).

In the person of Flaccus, Philo offers a critique of the idea that Roman rule is a form of benefaction. Philo is aware of the status and honor to be derived in Roman society from political office and from the demonstration of able governance in the provinces. He alludes to Flaccus's pride at receiving the appointment to Egypt and his grandiose display of his good fortune along the way to his province (*Flacc.* 152). Given this reality, even a relatively honest governor was not likely to be purely disinterested. Just as governors could reap financial rewards from corrupt practices, governors could reap glory and reputation from being thought honorable and excellent.[40] But Flaccus's good conduct is shown to be hollow, discarded when it no longer benefits him. At base, he is a political opportunist. Could it be that Philo views Roman benefactions in general in the same way—as essentially hollow and self-serving?[41]

After Flaccus arrives at his place of exile, he behaves like a madman, and cries out in a kind of mockery of an aretalogy (*Flacc.* 163):[42]

> I am Flaccus, until a short time ago the governor of the great city—or multitude of cities—Alexandria, prefect of that most blessed country, Egypt, to whom so many thousands of inhabitants turned, who had among his subjects many

---

[40] See, e.g., Cicero's glowing reports of his own behavior as proconsul of Cilicia (e.g., *Att.* 5.16.3; 5.17.2; 5.20.6, 5.21.5) and his admonitions to his brother Quintus on the importance of his *integritas* to the family's reputation (*Quint. fratr.* 1.1). For an overview of the dynamics of honor involved in office-holding, see Jon E. Lendon, *Empire of Honour: The Art of Government in the Roman World* (Oxford: Clarendon, 1997), 176–222, esp. 191–94 on the importance of performance.

[41] It is noteworthy that Plutarch, in his *Lives*, characterizes his Roman subjects as arrogant, ambitious, and boastful more frequently than his Greek subjects (e.g., *Comp. Arist. Cat.* 5.2–4; *Comp. Nic. Crass.* 3.6–7; *Comp. Alc. Cor.* 1.3; 3.1-2; 4.5–6; 5.1; *Comp. Ages. Pomp.* 2.2–3; *Comp. Dem. Cic.* 2.1-3). I owe this insight to one of my readers.

[42] According to Kraus ("Philosophical History," 490) the aretalogy begins < ἐγώ *name* εἰμί > followed by a list of virtues in the articular position. The content [of Flaccus's lament] also mirrors [that typical of] the aretalogy, which includes the god's tutelary relations to specific places, powers, worshippers and "glorious array." Flaccus's speech describes his rule over Alexandria, his control of armies and ships, his many subjects, and his grand escort. In my view, van der Horst (*Flaccus*, 231) is correct to critique Kraus's conclusion that "Flaccus is one of God's 'forces,'" but the link to the aretalogy form still stands, serving to underscore the simultaneous arrogance and emptiness of Flaccus's former pretensions.

forces of infantry, cavalry, and navy, not a mere number but as excellent as can be, who on going out each day was attended upon by myriads.

Philo's language, while appropriate for a prefect of Egypt, also points beyond itself. Alexandria can properly be called a μεγαλοπόλεως, or even a πολυπόλεως if one considers the many different ethnic communities that make up the city. But the choice of words also conjures Rome as ruler of many peoples and claimant to world-wide rule: Philo elsewhere uses the term "μεγαλόπολις" for the universe, and the unusual locution "πολύπολις," inserted as a complement, he uses only here.[43] The reference to military forces is also appropriate—the prefect of Egypt commanded legions—but the picture of numerous units of infantry, cavalry and navy brings to mind the many forces at Rome's disposal. The image of myriads turning to the governor for succor recalls the role of the emperor as benefactor and subject of appeal.[44] Altogether, the description of Flaccus's former stature bears revealing comparison to Philo's description of the "unspeakable good fortune" enjoyed by the emperor Gaius at the beginning of his reign (*Legat.* 9).[45]

Yet the purpose of Flaccus's outburst is not to lament the extent of his losses—rather, it is to reveal what he has learned from his experience (*Flacc.* 164–165). In a thoroughly Platonic fashion, Flaccus recognizes that his former prosperity was an illusion, "the shadow of things, not things themselves." The sudden departure of all those things in which he had placed confidence and considered "brilliant" has revealed them to be insubstantial illusions, shadows now banished by the light of truth.[46] The unspoken corollary to this statement, as we know from both Platonic and

[43] See David T. Runia, "Polis and Megalopolis: Philo and the Founding of Alexandria," *Mnemosyne* 42 (1989): 405, a reference I owe to van der Horst (*Flaccus*, 231). The suggestion that the term πολύπολις is inspired by the many different ethnic communities living in Alexandria is Runia's, and while I find this explanation cogent, I do not think it was the only inspiration for Philo's use of this unusual word.

[44] For details of these activities, see Fergus Millar, *The Emperor in the Roman World* (Ithaca, N.Y.: Cornell University Press, 1977), 465–549, especially 465–77 on their ideological dimensions. The perceived accessibility of the emperor allowed him to play a "symbolic role as the source of justice for individual subjects" (549). Cf. the words Seneca places in Nero's mouth in *De Clementia* 1.2: "from my utterance peoples and cities gather reasons for rejoicing" (Basore [LCL]).

[45] In connection with *Legatio* 9 we should also recall Philo's description of Flaccus's confiscated wealth: "For his taste for things ornamental was quite exceptional... everything had been carefully selected for its elaborate workmanship, his cups, clothes, coverlets, utensils and all the other ornaments of the house, all were of the choicest" (*Flacc.* 148, Colson [PLCL]).

[46] On the transitory nature of wealth and pride as proof of their unreality cf. *Spec.* 1.25–27.

Stoic philosophy, is that virtue is what is real and the source of true lasting happiness.[47] But Flaccus has favored the illusions over the path of virtue, and he has realized his mistake too late.

It is odd that the "mad" Flaccus talks so much sense. Perhaps Philo meant to represent him as an oracle of the gods, or to relate his "corybantic frenzy" to a sudden perception of the truth.[48] It may be as well that Philo is making a connection with a madman who appeared earlier in the narrative: Carabbas, whose phony regalia can now be recognized as a symbol of the phoniness and emptiness of Flaccus's own former pretensions (*Flacc.* 36–39).[49] Philo has reminded us that in his journey into exile Flaccus has retraced the route he travelled on his way to Egypt; thus "the cities which then saw him putting on airs and displaying the weight of his good fortune might see him again, covered with dishonor" (*Flacc.* 152).[50] On his outward journey, the equivalence between Carabbas's rags and Flaccus's pomp would have been visible only to one who sees truly. On his return journey, their equivalence is visible to all.

Philo's reluctance to provide unambiguous praise even for the excellent Flaccus should remind us that however much Philo may have welcomed the advantages of Roman rule, he cannot have felt unequivocal appreciation for its trappings of wealth, power, and preeminence. He could harbor sympathy, even respect, for a Roman governor, but his view of the political life, though not entirely cynical, ranks it as second best, always compromised, and always prone to cultivate the worst parts of the soul. The political man is always adding what is superfluous to what is necessary, what is false to what is true, and pride (τῦφος) to life (βίος) (*Somn.* 2.47). With the reference to τῦφος in his description of Flaccus's "good period," Philo hints at what is to come, and alludes to the compromised position of even the best rulers.

Philo's multifaceted and ambivalent portrait of Flaccus evokes a sense of ambivalence about Roman rule. On the one hand, he is careful to depict the Judean community as grateful for its benefits. On the other hand, he

[47] Kraus is correct to insist that one cannot separate Philo the historian from Philo the philosopher, and in particular that politics is "essentially intertwined" with virtue and epistemology—that is, Philo's understanding of the nature and character of true perception ("Philosophical History," 477–480; cf. 488–490 for his explication of the philosophical underpinnings of Flaccus's soliloquies on Andros).

[48] According to Kraus, the metaphor is "consistently used by Philo to describe the mystical ascent of the intellect" ("Philosophical History," 489, and n. 60 for examples).

[49] Gambetti points out that the beggar suddenly elevated to king made an apt symbol for Agrippa I (*Riots*, 159–60).

[50] ἵν' αἱ τότε θεασάμεναι πόλεις αὐτὸν μέγα πνέοντα καὶ τὸν ὄγκον τῆς εὐτυχίας ἐπιδεικνύμενον πάλιν θεάσωνται μεστὸν ἀτιμίας.

recognizes the potential for the ruler to turn against the Judean community —the benevolence of a Roman governor is not something one can take for granted. On the one hand, he recognizes the possibility of excellence in a Roman governor. On the other hand, his recognition of the pride, vanity and materialism bound up with rulership inevitably erodes his enthusiasm. Philo's view of Roman rule, as of the political life in general, can best be described neither as "appreciative" nor "hostile," but as "cautious" and "hesitant."

University of Notre Dame

The Studia Philonica Annual 24 (2012) 183–229

BIBLIOGRAPHY SECTION

PHILO OF ALEXANDRIA
AN ANNOTATED BIBLIOGRAPHY 2009

David T. Runia, Katell Berthelot, Albert C. Geljon,
Heleen M. Keizer, Jutta Leonhardt-Balzer, José P. Martín,
Sarah J. K. Pearce, Torrey Seland

2009[1]

R. Alciati, 'Monachesimo come tempio: il cantiere di Cassiano nuovo Chira,' *Adamantius* 15 (2009) 246–269, esp. 255–258.

John Cassian (4th/5th cent.) dedicated his monastic *Institutiones* to Castor, bishop of Apt (in France), comparing himself in the preface to the artisan Hiram employed by king Salomon (here Castor) in the construction of the Temple (cf. 1 Kings 5). Reference to Salomon, Hiram and the Temple is found in Origen, for whom the Temple represents the Church. Philo gives an elaborate allegorical interpretation of the Temple (image of the intelligible universe) but does not speak about its being built by Salomon/Hiram; instead, he dedicates much attention to Moses and the latter's role in the construction of and cult in the Tabernacle. (HMK)

---

[1] This bibliography has been prepared by the members of the International Philo Bibliography Project, under the leadership of D. T. Runia (Melbourne). The principles on which the annotated bibliography is based have been outlined in *SPhA* 2 (1990) 141–142, and are largely based on those used to compile the 'mother works,' R-R, RRS and RRS2. The division of the work this year is as follows: material in English (and Dutch) by D. T. Runia (DTR), A. C. Geljon (ACG) and S. J. K. Pearce (SJKP); in French by K. Berthelot (KB); in Italian by H. M. Keizer (HMK); in German by Jutta Leonhardt-Balzer (JLB); in Spanish and Portuguese by J. P. Martín (JPM); in Scandinavian languages (and by Scandinavian scholars) by T. Seland (TS). Once again this year much benefit has been derived from the related bibliographical labours of L. Perrone (Bologna) and his team in the journal *Adamantius* (studies on the Alexandrian tradition). Other scholars who have given assistance this year are Manuel Alexandre Jr, Giovanni Benedetto, Ellen Birnbaum and Maren Niehoff. My research assistant in Melbourne, Tamar Primoratz, again helped me with various tasks. This year yet again I am most grateful to my former Leiden colleague M. R. J. Hofstede for laying a secure foundation for the bibliography through his extremely thorough electronic searches. However, the bibliography remains inevitably incomplete, because much work on Philo is tucked away in monographs and articles, the titles of which do not mention his name. Scholars are encouraged to get in touch with members of the team if they spot

M. ALEXANDRE JR, 'Philo of Alexandria and Hellenic *Paideia*,' *Euphrosyne* N.S. 37 (2009) 121–130.

Philo was not only a devoted Jew but he was also very familiar with Greek culture, as appears from his writings. He had studied the seven disciplines that were part of the ἐγκύκλιος παιδεία. His commentaries are based on the techniques of classical rhetoric. He uses an accurate technical vocabulary, and employs several types of persuasive discourse. Like Plato, he makes a distinction between true, philosophical rhetoric and false, sophistic rhetoric. True rhetoric can help the wise man to refute the specious arguments of the sophists. In his conclusion, Alexandre underlines two points: (1) Philo's education was deeply immersed in the classical tradition of rhetoric; (2) this rhetorical tradition formally and aesthetically inspired the elaboration of his discourse. (ACG)

C. ANDERSON, *The Ambiguity of Nature: Philo of Alexandria's Views on the Sensible World* (diss. Cambridge 2009).

The dissertation was prepared at the University of Cambridge under the supervision of Prof. Markus Bockmuehl. It has now been published under a different title as *Philo of Alexandria's Views of the Physical World*, WUNT 2.309 (Tübingen 2011). See the review by D. T. Runia of this edition elsewhere in the present volume. (DTR)

C. ARRUZZA, 'Le refus du bonheur,' *Revue de théologie et de philosophie* 141 (2009) 261–272.

In Origen's thought, it is likely that it is negligence (ἀμέλεια), i.e. a kind of laziness in contemplating God, and not satiety (κόρος) in the contemplation of the Good, that must be seen as the first cause of the fall of rational creatures which results in living in the world of sense-perception, of which Origen vaguely speaks in *De principiis*. This article examines the notion of negligence, by analyzing biblical and philosophical sources, notably Philo of Alexandria, as well as the meaning that must be attributed to it in the light of the theodicy elaborated by Origen in more general terms. In his reflection on this theme, Origen may have been influenced by the representation of Cain in Philo's treatises *Sacr.* and *Det.*, insofar as Cain was lazy in giving thanks to God for the fruits of the earth. Another Philonic treatise that may have inspired Origen is *Somn.*, in which the well of Genesis 28:10–11 is connected with depth of knowledge and the continuous effort that is required to acquire it, in opposition to laziness and negligence. (KB)

J. M. G. BARCLAY, 'Grace Within and Beyond Reason: Philo and Paul in Dialogue,' in P. MIDDLETON, A. PADDISON and K. WENELL (edd.), *Paul, Grace and Freedom: Essays in Honour of John Kenneth Riches* (London 2009) 9–21.

---

omissions (addresses below in 'Notes on Contributors'). In order to preserve continuity with previous years, the bibliography retains its own customary stylistic conventions and has not changed to those of the Society of Biblical Literature used in the remainder of the Annual. Investigations are still in progress in relation to the possibility of making an online version of the Bibliography which will cover the entire history of Philonic scholarship, including the material included in G-G.

This article compares Philo's and Paul's view on God's blessing and election of a people without apparent reason. In *Leg.* 3.65–106 Philo discusses biblical figures—for instance, Noah, Melchizedek, Abraham—who are blessed by God without there being an apparent cause for it. In his explanation, Philo points to the soul-character or nature that is recognized by God and accounted worthy of grace. In Rom 9:6–18 Paul is very close to Philo in treating examples of persons who are chosen by God. Paul argues that the choice is determined by God's will. Paul would criticize Philo for discovering a hidden reason in the nature of the persons, as if there is a correspondence between the human subject and divine grace. Philo would object that Paul has not revealed the real, if hidden, reasons for God's choices in election. (ACG)

C. Batsch, 'Identité inclusive, identité exclusive: Alexandrie et Qoumrân, deux stratégies d'identité juive dans l'empire romain,' in N. Belayche and S. C. Mimouni (edd.), *Entre lignes de partage et territoires de passage — les identités religieuses dans les mondes grec et romain.* Collection de la Revue des Études Juives 47 (Leuven 2009) 195–211.

In this article, the author rejects all the models of Jewish identity that involve an artificial opposition between 'universalism' and 'particularism.' Just as for any other social group in Greek and Roman Antiquity (ἔθνος, γένος, etc.), the common identity of ancient Jews was mainly described in terms of birth and education. Judaism added to these two widely held criteria the centrality of its monotheist cult in the Jerusalem Temple. Two very different Jewish communities, Qumran and Alexandria, added other principles to this pattern: in Alexandria it was the claim for a specific πολιτεία for Alexandrian Jews, which meant an inclusive desire to join the broad constitutional and political system of the Empire in Augustan times. Qumran, on the contrary, introduced the notion of *goral* ('individual lot'), by which it expressed its radical predeterminism. As a result of this exclusive principle, Judaism was limited to a 'remainder,' i.e. to the people of the Qumran Community. As far as Philo is concerned, the author first alludes in passing to the fact that, for Philo, the Mosaic *politeia* designates Judaism (p. 200). He then deals at greater length with his definition of Jewish identity in the diaspora, elaborated in connection with the events of 38 c.e. in Alexandria and reflected in *Flacc.* and *Legat.* This diaspora identity consists of four aspects: (1) the claim to legitimately belong to the city (*polis*) in which one is born, even when no formal Greek citizenship has been granted to the Jews; (2) the connection with the *politeia* of the Jews; (3) the connection with the Temple located in Jerusalem, the *metropolis* of the Jews; (4) the framework of the Roman empire, to which the Jews are loyal. (KB; based on the author's abstract)

P. Bilde, 'Philo as a Polemist and a Political Apologist: an Investigation of his Two Historical Treatises *Against Flaccus* and *The Embassy to Gaius*,' in G. Hinge and J. Krasilnikoff (edd.), *Alexandria: a Cultural and Religious Melting Pot* (Aarhus 2009) 97–114.

English translation of an article first published in Danish in 2007 and summarized in *SPhA* vol. 22, p. 214. (TS)

M. V. Blischke, ''Die Gerechten aber werden ewig leben (Sap 5,17)' : begrenzte und entgrenzte Zeit in der Sapientia Salomonis,' in R. G. Kratz and H. SPIECKERMANN (edd.), *Zeit und Ewigkeit als Raum göttlichen Handelns,* Beihefte zur Zeitschrift für die alttestamentliche Wissenschaft 390 (Berlin 2009) 187–212, esp. 202–206.

Philo's idea of death and dying is discussed as the book Wisdom's immediate theological and religious context. For Philo, the immortality of the soul is the only way to live beyond death (*Fug.* 199, *Opif.* 135, *Virt.* 9). This immortality is only given through the divine spirit (*Spec.* 1,32), by virtue of a life lived in righteousness (*Abr.* 33) according to God's will (*Fug.* 58–59). Death is not seen as negative, but as indifferent (*Praem.* 70), while dying is negative and a punishment (*Det.* 48–49, *Fug.* 55). Philo does not have any idea of a final judgment. Punishment is meted out in this life and serves to educate (*Det.* 144–146, *Praem.* 163). Even the eschatological scenario of a pilgrimage of the nations to Zion in Lev 26:14ff and Deut 30:1–7 is read in *Praem.* as an inner-worldly event. (JLB)

R. BLOCH, 'Von Szene zu Szene: das jüdische Theater in der Antike,' in M. KONRADT and R. C. SCHWINGES (edd.), *Juden in ihrer Umwelt: Akkulturation des Judentums in Antike und Mittelalter. Eine Publikation der Interfakultären Forschungsstelle Judaistik an der Universität Bern* (Basel 2009) 57–86, esp. 66–74.

Philo is an important source for Jewish attitudes towards the theatre. His evidence is ambivalent. On the one hand he describes that the arrested Jews in 38 C.E. were brought into the theatres and killed as in a performance (*Flacc.* 75, 84, 95), and the whole treatise uses the language of the theatre in a negative way (e.g. *Flacc.* 19). On the other hand, Philo also indicates that he was a frequent visitor of theatre performances (*Ebr.* 177), although he criticizes their excesses and myths (*Agr.* 35, *Legat.* 204, 368). (JLB)

M. BOCKMUEHL, 'Dead Sea Scrolls and the Origins of Biblical Commentary,' in R. CLEMENTS and D. R. SCHWARTZ (edd.), *Text, Thought, and Practice in Qumran and Early Christianity: Proceedings of the Ninth International Symposium of the Orion Center for the Study of the Dead Sea Scrolls and Associated Literature, Jointly Sponsored by the Hebrew University Center for the Study of Christianity, 11–13 January, 2004,* Studies on the Texts of the Desert of Judah 84 (Leiden 2009) 3–29.

This stimulating article aims to examine possible similarities and connections between the Qumran *pesharim* and contemporary Greco-Roman commentaries, and their connection to Jewish commentary, including the writings of Philo. Bockmuehl argues that Philo may be the most important connection—or 'bridge'—between Greco-Roman and Jewish commentary writing. In this context, commentary is defined as 'works consisting primarily of sequential, expository annotation of identified texts that are themselves distinguished from the comments and reproduced intact' (p. 4). Topics under discussion comprise: Greek and Roman commentaries; Qumran commentaries, focusing on 15 continuous *pesharim* written in Hebrew; and connections between the Dead Sea Scrolls and ancient commentary. As regards connections between Philo's writings and the *pesharim*, the following general points of connection are emphasized: the presence of Greek biblical texts among the Dead Sea Scrolls; the influence of Alexandrian literary criticism and commentary on works, including the Book of Jubilees, known from Qumran; evidence in some *pesharim* of knowledge of LXX text types or variants; evidence for contacts between Egyptian and Palestinian Jews, including exegetical connections; evidence for connections between the Essenes and the Therapeutae, both of whom Philo describes as engaged in allegorical interpretation; and the deeper sense of the biblical text. More specific possible points of connection include: that Philo's Essenes and Therapeutae may have taken up lemmata for interpretation in a very similar way to that employed by the authors of the Qumran *pesharim*; and that, apart from Philo and the *pesharim*, the Second Temple Period has produced no other known consecutive scriptural commentaries. In conclusion, Bockmuehl urges the need for further research 'because Qumran scriptural commentaries emerged in a context where Jewish scholars were aware of a thriving Hellenistic commentary tradition that bore certain analogies to their own concerns and techniques' (p. 27). (SJKP)

A. P. Bos, 'Philo on God as 'arche geneseôs," *Journal of Jewish Studies* 60 (2009) 1–16.

According to the author, Philo has an Aristotelian view with regard to the relationship between God and the cosmos. Philo's description of God as absolutely pure Intellect and as the first Cause and Unmoved Mover is Aristotelian. Bos discusses a number of important passages. In *Opif.* 7–8 Philo refers to people who regard the cosmos as ungenerated and eternal. Philo is here not criticizing Aristotle, as generally assumed, but rather the 'Chaldeans,' who see the universe as self-sufficient. A crucial passage is *Aet.* 14, where Philo refers to an interpretation of Plato's *Timaeus* that the cosmos does not have an ἀρχή γενέσεως. Usually this expression is interpreted as 'beginning of generation,' but Bos argues that it has to be understood as 'principle of generation.' This principle is of great importance in Aristotle's biological writings, for example at *Gen. anim.* 1.2 716a4–7. The article ends with a short overview of several passages where the expression *archê geneseôs* occurs. (ACG)

A. Bosch-Veciana, '«Els terapeutes» com a *Filósofs* en el «De vita contemplativa» de Filó d'Alexandria,' *Revista Catalana de Teología* 34 (2009) 167–188.

In the context of Pierre Hadot's thesis about ancient philosophy, the author attempts to analyze *Contempl.* to establish the distinctiveness of the community of Lake Mareotis, concluding that this community, known only from Philo's description, is a case of adherence to philosophy understood as a way of life. This is the 'true philosophy,' which has the following characteristics: it involves all aspects of life; occurs in a community which read a sacred text, a religious community which lives in a time that is part of eternity; and attempts the contemplation of the *causa prima*, the existent Being. (JPM)

A. Bosch-Veciana, 'La «filosofia» del judaisme alexandrí com a «manera de viure»,' *Revista Catalana de Teología* 34 (2009) 503–521.

By framing the inquiry in terms of sociology of religion following the example of Arthur Nock, Steve Mason and Joan Taylor, the author continues previous research about the Therapeutae portrayed in Philo's *Contempl.* Inquiring about the meanings of the word 'philosophy' at the beginning of our era, he concludes that Judaism in general and Alexandrian Judaism in particular must be considered as 'philosophy' understood as a way of life. Among the philosophical and religious streams that appeared in Greco-Roman society, *Ioudaïsmós*—the term first appears in 2 Macc—also indicates a way of life. Judaism is seen inside and outside the community as a philosophy, while also remaining a religion. The author bases his conclusions on texts from Hellenistic authors, and especially from Hellenistic Jews, such as the *Septuaginta*, the Letter of Aristeas, Aristobulus, Philo and Josephus. (JPM)

F. Calabi, 'Il re in Filone di Alessandria,' in S. Gastaldi and J.-F. Pradeau (edd.), *Le philosophe, le roi, le tyran,* Collegium Politicum 3 (Sankt Augustin 2009) 53–69.

This article discusses the characteristics of the (real) king in Philo: not any constitutional figure but the wise person who 'embodies' the Law of God (*nomos empsychos*). By following this Law he assimilates himself to God (*homoiôsis theôi*), is characterized by virtue and reason, and is a shepherd and model for his people. The opposite of the king is the tyrant, embodying *anomia* (lawlessness). The article highlights the aspects of Philo's view that are also found in other philosophers, notably the Stoics. For Philo, kings are represented by the figures of Moses, Melchizedek, Abraham, Adam, Samuel (not Solomon, David or Saul). Philo's idea of kingship is not determined by a specific form of government. If Philo is interested in monarchy, it is in monarchy as a symbol of monotheism, and also as an idea of virtue. Concerning real sovereigns of his time, Philo only speaks explicitly about Roman emperors: the emperor may be good in his role, but he is an *autokratôr*, not a king. Philo was politically active, as witnessed by his embassy to Rome, but did not have an over-arching political project. (HMK)

F. Calabi, 'Vita pratica e vita teoretica in Filone di Alessandria,' in C. Trottmann (ed.), *Vie active et vie contemplative au Moyen âge et au seuil de la Renaissance,* Collection de l'École Française de Rome (Rome 2009) 19–42.

The practical and the theoretical life for Philo are not mutually exclusive or opposed to each other, but represent different moments in human life. Paradigmatic of the alternation of the two are the days of the week, which is in turn based on God's activity as creator and his repose on the Sabbath. Contemplation is the study of the Scriptures, in order to know God (his existence, not his essence). Calabi demonstrates the different ways in which Therapeutai and Essenes realize a community life by combining the practical and theoretical life. She also touches upon themes of the desert and the city, discusses the dark and the light side of political activity (of which Joseph is a paradigm), and concludes with Moses, the king-legislator-priest-prophet in whom we find the practical and theoretical life intertwined in the best possible way. The article includes a rich bibliography. (HMK)

F. Calabi, 'La filosofia greca in Filone di Alessandria,' in R. González Salifero and M. T. Ortega Monasterio (edd.), *Fuentes clásicas en el judaís-mo: de Sophía a Hokmah* (Madrid 2009) 33–50.

The article analyzes the appropriation of traditional Greek philosophical material that Philo performs in the context of Alexandrian culture in order to present his reading of Moses. The exegetical method shows some traces of the Greek allegory about gods, particularly that of Chrysippus, although the author does not determine the extent to which Philo takes over or introduces each mode of allegory. To present the Bible as an expression of truth *in toto*, Philo draws upon nearly all the streams of Greek philosophy. A prominent place is occupied by Plato, who inspired the idea of two levels of creation of man and woman—an intelligible and a sensible—and also the idea of the invisibility and incomprehensibility of God. To bring God and the cosmos in relation, Philo often harmonizes Platonic and Aristotelian topics, anticipating Middle Platonism procedures. The issue of lifestyle, especially the distinction between the contemplative and the practical life, is related to Greek developments from the fifth century B.C.E. until the time of Hellenistic philosophy. The correlation of the law of nature with the creative Logos and ethical reason is a common topic among the Stoics. Philo's biblical exegesis shows knowledge of most of the philosophical schools, including that of Epicurus, although in his case the usage involves severe criticism. (JPM)

M. CANÉVET, *Philon d'Alexandrie: maître spirituel*, Initiations (Paris 2009).

This little book aims at providing an introduction to Philo's theological and spiritual teaching. It is not meant to be an academic book, even if its author is Professor Emeritus at the Catholic Faculty of Theology in Strasbourg. No references are made to secondary literature written by other scholars, but Philo's texts are quoted at length, to provide the reader with the opportunity to 'hear Philo's voice.' The book is divided into eight chapters on the following topics: Humanity and the Cosmos; Sin; Passions; Soundness of Judgment; Ascetic Life; Migrations; Virtues; God; God and the human being. Every chapter summarizes Philo's thought on these issues, which all deal with different aspects of the relationship of human beings to themselves, to God and to the world, and of the way humans can achieve their true calling, which is to know and to serve God with love, for which they receive divine joy in return. The author concludes that in spite of his Hellenistic culture, Philo was deeply rooted in his biblical and Jewish heritage, and that he was a religious and spiritual man who can be considered a master in this respect, too (and not only as far as philosophy and exegesis are concerned). His teaching on divine providence, for instance, not only reflects his knowledge of Stoicism, but also the notion of a personal as well as a universal providence of God towards his creatures. This notion of personal providence, and more generally Philo's representation of God as entering into a personal relationship with human beings and as sustaining them by his grace, is deeply indebted to Philo's Jewish culture. (KB)

J. CARITA, 'Uma utopia em Fílon de Alexandria,' *Sapiens: História, Património e Arqueologia* 2 (2009) 57–68.

In an overview of *Contempl.* the author states that the community of Lake Mariotis was a real community and not a literary utopia. Though few textual references are given, it is hypothesized that there was a historical communication between Philo's *Therapeutai*, Qumran and Jesus. (JPM)

M. CORIA, 'Paideía y Sophía en el itinerario del alma hacia Dios: Abraham, Sara y Agar en la exégesis filónica,' *Circe de clásicos y modernos* 13 (2009) 93–106.

The author emphasizes the important points of the approaches to virtue in the itinerary of the soul towards God in *Congr.* This ascent is achieved through what Philo considers to be the two most important levels of knowledge: education (παιδεία) and wisdom (σοφία) (*Spec.* 2, 29). The paper analyzes the special features of the different stages in the apprentice's journey towards wisdom by means of education, i.e., the spiritual union of Abraham (the intellect) and Sarah (virtue, wisdom), through the temporary mating with

Hagar (the preliminary studies, education). The significance of this particular triangle of biblical figures is discussed by Coria in terms of the confluence of Jewish and Greek ideas that characterizes Philo's thought. (JPM)

I. Costa, 'El dios creador del *Timeo* en Filón de Alejandría,' in A. Correa Motta and J. M. Zamora (edd.), *Eúnoia. Estudios de Filosofía Antigua, Un Homenaje a María Isabel Santa Cruz* (Bogotá 2009) 293–309.

Discusses the use that Philo makes of Plato's *Timaeus*, especially on the topics of supreme causes, world production and the attributes of the Demiurge. The treatise *Opif.* shows a large dependence on the Platonic dialogue, but also reveals the extent of the Philonic divergence from Plato. In that work, Philo, anticipating Middle Platonism and Christian thought, develops the idea of a supreme cause exempt from imperfection and need, a theory of ideas that ceases to involve contemplation of ideas but instead arrives at a divine conception of ideas, and a theology of an omnipotent and rational Demiurge. (JPM)

N. De Lange, 'The Celebration of the Passover in Greco-Roman Alexandria,' in C. Batsch and M. Vârtejanu-Joubert (edd.), *Manières de penser dans l'Antiquité méditerranéenne et orientale: Mélanges offerts à Francis Schmidt par ses élèves, ses collègues et ses amis*, Supplements to the Journal for the Study of Judaism 134 (Leiden 2009) 157–166.

This article investigates how Greek-speaking Jews in Alexandria celebrated the festival of Passover. The author discusses the references to the Passover in the Pentateuch, the *Exagoge* of Ezekiel, and the Wisdom of Solomon, but the fullest information is found in Philo, especially in *Spec.* 2.145–61. Philo calls the Passover τὰ διαβατήρια, which can denote sacrifices made before a crossing. It is allegorized as purification for the body and the passions. Philo states that the whole people sacrifice, and this makes clear that he considered the *Pascha* as a private sacrifice. Philo's interpretation of the Passover goes far beyond what we find in Ezekiel and Wisdom. Because Philo offers details that are not in the Pentateuch, it is very likely that Philo describes practices that he was acquainted with from the Jewish community. (ACG)

J. M. Dillon, 'Philo of Alexandria and Platonist Psychology,' in M. Elkaisy-Friemuth (ed.), *The Afterlife of the Platonic Soul: Reflections of Platonic Psychology in the Monotheistic Religions*, Studies in Platonism, Neoplatonism, and the Platonic Tradition 9 (Leiden 2009) 16–24.

The article focuses on Philo's psychology, an area in which he is indebted to Platonism. Usually the basic Platonic division of the soul into rational and irrational parts is offered, but in some texts the tripartite division (reason, spiritedness, desire) is found. Explaining the biblical statement that 'the soul is blood,' Philo distinguishes between the vital part and the rational part of the soul. The vital part (or life-principle) consists in blood, whereas the rational part is composed of *pneuma*. The true human being is to be identified with the rational part, which has been made by God himself. This rational soul is immortal, while the vital part (the lower soul, or the mortal part) disperses on death. (ACG)

L. H. Feldman, 'Philo and the Dangers of Philosophizing,' in S. L. Jacobs (ed.), *Maven in Blue Jeans: A Festschrift in Honor of Zev Garber* (West Lafayette, In. 2009) 147–159.

Against the background of the rabbinic and talmudic suspicion of philosophy, how should the uniqueness of Philo as a Jewish philosopher be evaluated? The author posits that Philo finds the highest expression of Greek wisdom in the thought of Plato. It is the synthesis of this wisdom with the Torah that he attempts and it is Plato's theory of ideas that is the starting-point of his philosophy. But he also demonstrates originality as a thinker, as demonstrated by Wolfson, for example in his distinction between the know-ability of God's existence and the unknowability of his essence, and his insistence on an individual Providence that can suspend the laws of nature. The key to his thought is the doctrine of the Logos which is his answer to the sheer remoteness of God and to the further problem of the origin of evil. It is surprising but true that philosophizing was no problem for Philo and his contemporaries. Perhaps there were apologetic reasons for Philo's mystical presentation of Judaism, but it should not be thought that he falls outside the mainstream of Jewish life and thought. In the final part of the article the effect of Philo's teachings and writings is examined and various reasons are postulated for his absence in the rabbinic writings. What is the difference, Feldman asks in conclusion, between the place of Maimonides and Philo in Jewish tradition? His answer: 'Maimonides read the Torah in the original and Aristotle in translation; Philo read Plato in the original and the Torah in translation' (p. 157). This interesting observation illustrates beautifully the ambivalent attitude towards Philo that pervades the entire article. (DTR)

R. Finn, *Asceticism in the Graeco-Roman World. Key Themes in Ancient History* (Cambridge 2009).

In Chapter Two, devoted to asceticism in Hellenistic and Rabbinic Judaism, some writings of Philo are discussed. In *Mos.*, Philo portrays Moses as a philosopher-king who subjects passions to reason, a process which involves asceticism in food, drink, and sexual pleasures. Moses also shows a disdain for wealth. This description shows a Platonic understanding of asceticism. The question is raised as to whether Philo's understanding of asceticism was shared by other Jews. He shows admiration for a group of Jewish men and women, the so-called Therapeutae whose ascetic way of life he reports in *Contempl.* It is unclear, however, whether Philo's report refers to a historical reality. The contemplative way of life of the Therapeutae is contrasted with the active life practised by another Jewish sectarian movement, the Essenes. Philo presents the movement in terms derived from Greek philosophy. Finally the author notes that in the first two centuries asceticism was part of the Christian faith and that Christians read Philo's writings with interest. (ACG)

D. Flusser, *Judaism of the Second Temple Period. Volume 2: The Jewish Sages and their Literature*, translated by D. Bivin (Grand Rapids 2009), esp. 216–220.

The second volume of the English translation of Flusser's collected essays in Hebrew on the second Temple period contains a brief but very interesting essay on Philo (pp. 216–220). Unfortunately the original context of this piece, which lacks all annotation, is not indicated. Flusser reports that, when he arrived in Jerusalem in 1939, his very first scholarly project under Hans Lewy was a study of daily life as reflected in Philo's writings. Philo shows us that by his time there was a robust and self-confident Jewish worldview.

This explains the similarity between Philo's commentaries and the rabbinic midrashim. Philo must be regarded as an authentic Jewish philosopher, in some ways not dissimilar to Martin Buber in the modern era. Both agree that Judaism is a spiritual and intellectual system that can successfuly compete with those of the non-Jewish world. Although we cannot learn much about the Bible from Philo, we can learn about the Jewish world he inhabited, and indirectly about the Judaism of the sages. (DTR)

S. Gambetti, *The Alexandrian Riots of 38 c.e. and the Persecution of the Jews. A Historical Reconstruction,* Supplements to the Journal for the Study of Judaism 135 (Leiden 2009).

This study offers a chronological reconstruction of the ethnic conflicts in Alexandria in 38 c.e., of which Philo was an eyewitness. His *Legat* and *Flacc.* are our only sources of the events. The author follows a political approach, seeing the conflict as the result of political and administrative measures taken by the Romans. She emphasizes three main points: (1) the Romans did not recognize the political and civic role of citizenship; (2) their politics favoured Roman interests at the expense of local interests; (3) they introduced a fiscal policy which served Roman interests, to a large extent in opposition to local governance. One measure of the Roman government was to force the Jews to live in a small part of quarter δ, the original Jewish quarter in Alexandria. The rights of the Jews were now territorial and not personal. An important role in Gambetti's study is taken by papyrus Yale II 107, which has many *lacunae* and is not easy to read. It is, however, clear that it reports a judicial hearing of two groups before the emperor Gaius. One group is named the Alexandrians, and Gambetti argues that the other group consists of Alexandrian Jews. In the papyrus a certain Isidorus is named, whom Gambetti identifies with the Isidorus referred to by Philo in *Flacc.* The text of the papyrus is given a close reading. According to the author the trial takes place in 37 and concerns illegal residence by a Jew. In the author's reconstruction of the events in 38, Agrippa went to Alexandria to bring Gaius' *mandata* (written instructions for a new governor) that ratified Flaccus' second appointment as the prefect of Alexandria. Flaccus' taking office was celebrated in the gymnasium. During the celebration Agrippa was vilified. According to Philo, the Alexandrian mob called for images of the emperor in the Jewish meeting-houses, but Gambetti argues that the setting up of Gaius' images was the carrying out of an imperial order. Next, violence against the Jews broke out, and in an edict Flaccus declares the Jews 'foreigners and immigrants.' According to Gambetti, this edict also arose from Gaius' *mandata*. In her concluding evaluation of Philo's description of the riots in *Flacc.* and *Legat.*, Gambetti concludes that he is selective and passes over important issues in silence. (ACG)

B. Garstad, 'Joseph as a Model for Faunus-Hermes: Myth, History, and Fiction in the Fourth Century,' *Vigiliae Christianae*, 63 (2009) 493–521, esp. 509–512.

Faunus–Hermes is one of the composite god-kings dealt with in the polemical Christian 'Picus-Zeus narrative' of the fourth century. The narrative of his life is based on the Biblical account of Joseph, along with the elaborations on Joseph's life in Hellenistic Jewish fiction. The author uses Philo's ambiguous interpretation of Joseph to show how a bad character can be developed out of his good character. (DTR)

P. VON GEMÜNDEN, 'Affektbeherrschung und Herrschaftsausübung: soziologische und psychologische Überlegungen zu dem in "Gegen Flaccus" geschilderten Judenpogrom,' in *Affekt und Glaube: Studien zur Historischen Psychologie des Frühjudentums und Urchristentums,* Novum Testamertum et Orbis Antiquus/Studien zur Umwelt des Neuen Testaments 73 (Göttingen 2009) 94–117.

The chapter summarizes Philo's account of the pogrom in 38 c.e. (*Flacc.*) and then studies the reasons Philo gives for the exclusion and persecution of the Jews in Alexandria. Situational influences on the behaviour of the individuals involved were Flaccus' insecure position after the accession of Gaius, and the Alexandrian Greeks' offer of support, motivated by their loss of influence under the Romans, against the Jewish support given to them by Rome. The Jewish-Greek tension is a structural factor which influences the psychology of both sides, resulting in prejudices and the projection of the Greek aggression onto the Jews. Both sides compete socio-culturally and economically with each other. The most important factor in the conflict, however, is individually psychological: it is Flaccus' inability to control himself and his emotions which causes him to fail in his duties as ruler; instead of restraining them like a ruler should, he tolerates their excesses. In conclusion, the author acknowledges the bias of the *Flacc.*; unlike the *Legat.*, where Philo as participant focuses on external influences, in the *Flacc.* he is an observer and focuses on internal factors. (JLB)

P. VON GEMÜNDEN, 'Jakob als Modell für den Umgang mit den Affekten bei Philo von Alexandrien,' in *Affekt und Glaube: Studien zur Histcrischen Psychologie des Frühjudentums und Urchristentums,* Novum Testamentum et Orbis Antiquus/Studien zur Umwelt des Neuen Testaments 73 (Göttingen 2009) 57–68.

Jacob is described in Philo as a positive character, the example of the wise man who progresses, not through learning, like Abraham, or by nature, like Isaac, but by patient practice (*Somn.* 1.169-170). Jacob's and Abraham's progress on their path is expressed by the change in their names. Jacob's progress occurs not by teaching but by effort. First he flees those caught in their passions (*Leg.* 3.15–20): Laban (*Fug.* 10–14), and those who are evil: Esau (*Leg.* 2.88–89; *Congr.* 61–62; *Fug.* 39–40). Then he fights the passions in order to obtain virtue: Esau in the womb (*Leg.* 2.89; 3.93) and the opponent at the Jabbok (*Migr.* 100). His victory crown is the vision of God, expressed in the change of his name to Israel (*Praem.* 27). But Jacob only sees that God is, not how he is (*Praem.* 44), and he only meets God's *Logos* (*Somn.* 1.62–70, 228–229). The other victory prize is a lame hip, as the hip represents pride and haughtiness (*Praem.* 47–48, *Somn.* 1.130). The first reward is theological, the vision of God, the second anthropological, the curbing of the passions. (JLB)

S. D. GIERE, *A New Glimpse of Day One. Intertextuality, History of Irterpretation, and Genesis 1.1–5,* Beihefte zur Zeitschrift fur die Neutestamentliche Wissenschaft 172 (Berlin 2009).

Revised edition of the author's University of St. Andrews PhD thesis summarized in *SPhA* vol. 23, p. 143. In this edition the discussion of Philonic texts relating to the account of Day One, Gen 1:1–5, is found in Chapter 5 under the heading 'Jewish texts': *Opif.* 26–35,

Somn. 1.72–76, *Gig.* 22–23, *Her.* 163b–164, *Deus* 58, *Aet.* 17–19. In each case the Greek text is first presented, followed by the author's own translation and a discussion of the contents. The selection of Christian texts that follows stops at Justin Martyr, so this does not discuss those Christian interpretations that were influenced by Philo. Among all the texts studied, Philo's account in *Opif.* 26–35 holds a special place. Its reading of the biblical text through the lenses of Middle Platonic philosophical categories 'is the closest thing to an exegetical commentary in the whole of this study' (p. 289). See further the review by C. Heard in *SPhA* vol. 23, pp. 184–187. (DTR)

G. S. GOERING, *Wisdom's Root Revealed. Ben Sira and the Election of Israel*, Supplements to the Journal for the Study of Judaism 139 (Leiden 2009), esp. 244–247.

This study of Ben Sira's doctrine of the election of the people of Israel includes a very brief comparative study of Philo as a means to deepen understanding of Ben Sira in the context of Second Temple period Jewish thought (pp. 244–247). Largely following Ellen Birnbaum's work, Goering sees Philo in general as tending towards a universal view according to which all may develop a close relationship with God by pursuing the philosophical goal of 'seeing God' (p. 20). Like Ben Sira, Philo inherited the biblical tradition of Israel's covenant with their God, and this tradition shaped Philo's particularist understandings of the relationship between the Jewish people and God. Both authors use Deut 32:8–9 as a foundational text for understanding Israel's election; but while Ben Sira reads the latter text as speaking of the election in terms of a divine initiative, Philo also emphasizes human initiative in the relationship between those elected and God (*Post.* 91–93). Ben Sira and Philo also agree in referring to the universal benefits of Israel's election and associate these with the role of the High Priest (*Spec.* 1.97). (SJKP)

M. GOFF, 'Genesis 1–3 and Conceptions of Humankind in 4QInstruction, Philo and Paul,' in C. A. EVANS and H. D. ZACHARIAS (edd.), *Early Christian Literature and Intertextuality. Volume 2: Exegetical Studies*, Library of New Testament studies 392 (London 2009) 114–125.

4QInstruction (1Q26, 4Q415–418, 423) from Qumran offers a dualistic understanding of humankind in terms of 'flesh' and 'spirit,' based on an interpretation of Gen 1–3. A similar view is found in Philo and Paul, and the author argues that these two authors were influence by Palestinian Jewish traditions that are attested in 4QInstruction. In *Opif.* Philo reads Gen 1–3 as indicating a double creation of man, making a distinction between a heavenly man and an earthly man. The former is associated with Gen 1:27, the latter with Gen 2:7. By way of contrast, 4QInstruction has no direct quotations from Genesis. Paul also makes a distinction between corporeal and spiritual types of people in the same way as 4QInstruction does. (ACG)

A. GRAFTON, 'From Roll to Codex : a Christian Initiative,' in P. VAN BOXEL and S. ARNDT (edd.), *Crossing Borders. Hebrew Manuscripts as a Meeting-place of Cultures* (Oxford 2009) 15–20.

This article, which introduces for a non-specialist readership the distinctive Christian adoption of the codex for book production, includes an interesting discussion about the Christian production of Philo's works in codex form, and the significance of Philo for

Christian thinkers. This discussion focuses on a comparison between Philo and Eusebius, another fundamental writer for the Christian tradition and whose works were also preserved in the codex form. Key points for comparison between Philo and Eusebius include their techniques for the interpretation of Scripture; their political role and their role as political models; and Eusebius' foundational role in constructing Philo as a figure worthy of great respect within the Christian tradition. (SJKP)

J. T. GREENE, 'The Balaam Figure and Type, Before, During, and After the Period of the Pseudepigrapha: 1 Enoch, Philo, NT, Josephus, Rabbinics, Islamics, and Modern Literature,' in J. H. ELLENS and J. T. GREENE (edd.), *Probing the Frontiers of Biblical Studies* (Eugene, Oreg. 2009) 223–238.

Although the title promises a consideration of Philo's treatment of Balaam, the author turns from 1 Enoch to the New Testament and does not discuss Philo at all. (DTR)

E. GRYPEOU and H. SPURLING, 'Abraham's Angels: Jewish and Christian Exegesis of Genesis 18–19,' in E. GRYPEOU and H. SPURLING (edd.), *Exegetical Encounter between Jews and Christians in Late Antiquity,* Jewish and Christian Perspectives Series 18 (Leiden 2009) 181–203.

The article is part of an edited collection examining the question of the relationship between Jewish and Christian exegesis of the book of Genesis in Late Antiquity. The essay focuses on rabbinic traditions and the work of Church Fathers on Genesis 18–19, but also considers wider material that may impact on the question of a possible 'exegetical encounter,' including Philo. The discussion is divided into three parts: the interpretation of Abraham's angelic visitors is examined in rabbinic (Spurling), followed by patristic (Grypeou) writings, with a comparative analysis of potential points of exegetical encounter in the remainder of the article. The authors argue for evidence of potential dialectic between rabbinic and Christian exegesis of Genesis 18–19 on the topics of angelology, the preincarnate Christ and the Trinity. The possible impact of Philonic ideas on rabbinic and patristic exegesis is a concern in the analysis. In particular, there is acknowledgement that the Christian Trinitarian interpretation of the episode at Mamre may have been influenced by the work of Philo. Reference is made to *Abr.* 121, in which the nature of Abraham's guests is debated, with the three figures understood to be the Father of the Universe, his creative power, and his royal power. Furthermore, when it comes to the nature of the different angelic visitors, the fact that they do not eat is recognized as a widely attested rabbinic and patristic tradition, but also found in Philo *QG* 4.9 and *Abr.* 118. A possible Philonic influence on rabbinic and Christian interpretations is not seen as a barrier to 'encounter,' as the essay argues for a fluid relationship between exegetical developments facilitated by the process of transmission. In other words, it is maintained that a particular tradition can be reused and developed over time for different needs, whether these be exegetical concerns internal to the respective interpretative traditions, or polemic or apologetic teaching. (SJKP)

J. GUNDRY, '"Or Who Gave First to Him, so that He Shall Receive Recompense?" (Rom 11,35): Divine Benefaction and Human Boasting in Paul and Philo,' in U. SCHNELLE (ed.), *The Letter to the Romans,* Bibliotheca Ephemeridum Theologicarum Lovaniensium 226 (Leuven 2009) 25–53.

In this study, the author deals with the issue of Gentile boasting in Rom 9-11, and uses Philo as an argument for her interpretation. Her main thesis runs thus: Paul closes his argument and discussion of Israel by depicting God as a Benefactor who is sovereign rather than one who reciprocates human beings. In this way Paul tries to counteract a Gentile Christian view of God which is based on a Greco-Roman reciprocity. According to the latter view, Paul's Roman Gentile readers may have assumed that God's benefaction was like the benefaction they were familiar with from Greco-Roman convention. Paul, however, argues that God is not a reciprocating God, but a sovereign one, who bestows favour in Christ to the unworthy. In the last part of this article, she deals with the subject of 'Divine benefaction and human clientism in Philo' (pp. 42–53). Here she argues that Philo makes a similar distinction between the two 'divine powers' and corresponding human dispositions, and that Philo's reasons for making the distinction overlap with Paul's reasons for distinguishing and judging between two types of benefactors and their social expression in interrelations with the 'other.' Hence, in this way, the author finds that Philo supports her interpretation of Paul. (TS)

G. GUTTENBERGER, '*Superstitio*: Facetten eines antik-religionstheoretischen Diskurses und die Genese des frühen Christentums als *religio*,' in W. KRAUS (ed.), *Beiträge zur urchristlichen Theologiegeschichte*, Beihefte zur Zeitschrift für die neutestamentliche Wissenschaft und die Kunde der älteren Kirche 163 (Berlin 2009) 183–227, esp. 196–202.

Philo is used along with Plutarch in this overview as evidence of the use of δεισιδαιμονία to describe illegitimate forms of religion. For Philo this means legitimate or illegitimate practice of religion within one's own religious community. He displays evidence of Peripatetic and Stoic influences, piety being the middle between impiety and superstition. Superstition is dishonest, harmful and impedes correct worship (*Deus* 102). It belongs to the passions and vices (*Sacr.* 15). Philo is an inner-Jewish equivalent to Strabo's perspective on Judaism: the Jewish religion becomes superstition if the rites are taken too literally and externally (*Praem.* 40; *Somn.* 1.230). (JLB)

U. HAGEDORN and D. HAGEDORN, 'P.Vindob. G 30531 + 60584: Fragmente eines Philon-Codex (De virtutibus),' *Archiv für Papyrusforschung und verwandte Gebiete* 55 (2009) 279–289.

P.Vindob. G 30531 = *P.Rainer Cent.* 36, a fragment of a Greek papyrus codex published in 1983 as an unidentified Christian text, can be recognized as belonging to Philo's treatise *Virt.* In fact, it comes from the same folio as P.Vindob. G 60584, another papyrus scrap of this treatise, which was published in 2002–03 (see summary at RRS 1831). The present article offers a new edition of the combined fragments, which derive from *Virt.* 62–70, and discusses their significance for our understanding of the medieval manuscript tradition of this specific work. The evidence of the papyrus suggests that it came from a text which had a different order than the sub-sections *De fortitudine* and *De humanitate* found in modern editions of the treatise. (DTR)

R. HAYWARD, 'What Did Cain Do Wrong? Jewish and Christian Exegesis of Genesis 4:3–6,' in E. GRYPEOU and H. SPURLING (edd.), *Exegetical Encounter Between Jews and Christians in Late Antiquity*, Jewish and Christian Perspectives Series 18 (Leiden 2009) 101–123.

This article deals with interpretations of the sacrifices of Abel and Cain (Gen 4:3–6) in the LXX , Philo, the New Testament, Josephus and Irenaeus. In the LXX Cain's offering is called a sacrifice, whereas Abel's offer is named gifts. Philo's translation of the names Cain and Abel as 'possession' and 'one who offers to God' respectively is derived from a traditional onomasticon. In Philo's exegesis the two brothers represent two different types of soul. Cain stands for vice, whereas Abel signifies virtue. Philo sees two faults in Cain's sacrifice. He did not offer at once, but only after some days, and his offering was 'from the fruits,' not from the choicest fruits. In *QG* 1.62 Philo discusses the difference between a gift and a sacrifice. Generally in Philo emphasis is laid upon Cain's bad character. (ACG)

C. B. HORN and J. W. MARTENS, *"Let the Little Children Come to Me": Childhood and Children in Early Christianity* (Washington D.C. 2009).

This co-authored volume aims to reconstruct ideas about and the reality of childhood within the first six centuries of the Christian world, looking specifically at questions about the construction of family, marriage and asceticism, discipline and education, play and work, violence and children, and the place of the child within the Christian community. Reflecting on the question 'How well did the early Church live up to Jesus' command: "Let the little children come to me" (Matt 19:14)?' (p. 346), the authors argue that, with the rise of Christianity, 'life for children began to change,' at least in some respects (p. 347). The study includes brief references to Philo's works as a resource for ideas about and the reality of childhood in the Jewish world of the first century in order to explain aspects of early Christian thought and practice. The main topics covered are as follows: Philo's accounts of human development, physical and spiritual (pp. 6–9); his terminology for 'children' (pp. 100–101); ideas about education (pp. 136–137) and sexual violence towards minors, focusing on pederasty (pp. 217–219); and Philo's account of the *Therapeutae* as a model of Jewish asceticism (p. 303). (SJKP)

F. HUDRY, *Le livre des vingt-quatre philosophes: résurgence d'un texte du IVe siècle*, Histoire des doctrines de l'antiquité classique 39 (Paris 2009).

In her study of this curious medieval Latin text, which gives 24 definitions of God, each followed by a brief commentary, the author sets out to demonstrate that it was originally written in the fourth century C.E. and is the work of the Christian rhetor and philosopher Marius Victorinus. She argues that various elements in the definitions and their explanations are derived from Philo and the sapiential books of the Bible (p. 84) and that this is an argument for an early date of composition (p. 87). (DTR)

S. INOWLOCKI-MEISTER, 'Le Moïse des auteurs juifs hellénistiques et sa réappropriation dans la littérature apologétique chrétienne: le cas de Clément d'Alexandrie,' in P. BORGEAUD, T. RÖMER and Y. VOLOKHINE (edd.), *Interprétations de Moïse: Égypte, Judée, Grèce et Rome*, Jerusalem Studies in Religion and Culture 10 (Leiden 2009) 103–131.

The article focuses on Clement of Alexandria's treatment of Moses in the *Stromata*. After a survey of Jewish Hellenistic presentations of Moses in the fragments of Judeo-Hellenistic authors, and a brief summary of Alexander Polyhistor's role in the transmission of these fragments, Clement's work on Moses and his indebtedness to Philo are analyzed in depth. In *Strom.* 1.23, different topics are at stake: (1) Moses' birth and childhood; (2) Moses' *paideia*; (3) the murder of the Egyptian (Exod 2:11–12); (4) Moses as shepherd and the so-called despoliation of the Egyptians by the Hebrews during the Exodus. The author argues that Clement wrote a small *vita* of Moses based on Philo's *Mos.*, to which elements taken from other Jewish Hellenistic authors were added. In contrast with previous studies of Clement's account, she argues that it does not have a mere narrative function, i.e., that the excerpts from the Hellenistic Jewish authors are mere embellishments, but that it plays a precise apologetic role. Not only does Clement defend Moses and the antiquity of his teaching, which influenced the Greeks, he also argues that the life of Moses represents a prelude or a preliminary stage in order to achieve an intimate knowledge of Christ. For Clement, Moses is still a θεῖος ἀνήρ, a man who spoke with God face to face and therefore represents a model for the gnostic, but he does not call him a high priest, as Philo did, because Christ is the only figure who may receive this title. (KB)

A. KAMENSKIKH, 'Syzygies in Philo of Alexandria [Russian],' *Schole: Ancient Philosophy and the Classical Tradition* 3 (2009) 445–449.

The article focuses on the problems of 'categorical interpretation' of matrimonial images in the Old Testament by Philo of Alexandria. The author proposes that Philo perceived female images as objectivized aspects of corresponding types of mind (represented by male images), draws parallels between this concept and the dialectic of emanation in Platonism, and proposes some analogies with Gnostic teaching about 'syzygies.' (DTR; based on author's summary)

A. KAMESAR (ed.), *The Cambridge Companion to Philo* (Cambridge 2009).

The volume dedicated to Philo in the distinguished Cambridge Companion series published by Cambridge University Press aims to be an up-to-date handbook which assists the reader in tackling the writings and thought of an author who is not only perplexing at times, but whose writings reveal a bulk and breadth that makes them difficult to navigate. Though not meant to be a substitute for reading the works themselves, the handbook 'endeavours to supply some essential introductory information in a clear and unassuming format that can turn that experience into less of a struggle' (p. 2 in the editor's introduction). Its chapters are also 'intended to provide not only a sense of recent progress in the scholarship on Philo, but also a certain vision of the topics under consideration' (ibid.). A further interesting feature of the volume is the geographical spread of the contributors, with three from the United States (including the editor), two from Italy, and the remainder from Australia, France, Germany and Israel. All the articles are, however, written in English. The chapters are summarized separately under the names of their authors in this bibliography. For a detailed review on the volume see the review article by G. E. Sterling summarized below. (DTR)

A. KAMESAR, 'Biblical Interpretation in Philo,' in A. KAMESAR (ed.), *The Cambridge Companion to Philo* (Cambridge 2009) 65–91.

This remarkably rich and learned essay aims to explain Philo's systematic approach to Scripture and its interpretation. Kamesar begins with a survey of Philo's ideas about the text and canon of Scripture, illustrating Philo's reliance on the Greek Pentateuch, which he took to be a divinely inspired translation of both the words and the sense of the words of the Hebrew original (cf. *Mos.* 2.37–40). Philo's view of the canon as basically confined to the Torah probably reflects earlier Alexandrian traditions. The second part of the chapter provides a detailed discussion of fundamental principles at work in Philo's exegesis. Firstly, Philo understands the Pentateuch as a literary work, i.e., comprising the literary genres of the cosmological, historical and legislative (cf. *Praem.* 1–2; *Mos.* 2.46–47), a scheme found in other Judeo-Hellenistic authors. These genres correspond to the didactic category of ancient Greek literature, as formulated in one strand of Hellenistic literary theory. Seen in this light, the Pentateuch is understood as non-mythical and non-fictional; as such, it does not require allegorical interpretation. This conception of the Pentateuch, which Philo inherits from Jewish predecessors, is represented in his *Exposition of the Law*, in which allegorical interpretation, while not absent, does not determine or dominate the structure of Philo's treatment of Scripture. In the second part of the essay, Kamesar explores Philo's reasons for using the allegorical method for interpreting Scripture. In the *Allegorical Commentary*, Philo's basic conception of the nature of the Pentateuch as a work that requires allegorical interpretation seems to differ from his approach to it in the *Exposition*. Two fundamental principles seem to be at work in Philo's insistence on the application of allegorical interpretation to the Pentateuch. First, following Greek theory and practice, Philo uses allegorical interpretation to make sense of texts which lack sense when interpreted literally, and to explain apparently mythical elements in the Pentateuch. Secondly, in contrast with Greek allegorical interpreters, Philo also often maintains both a literal and an allegorical level of interpretation, probably because he follows the Judeo-Hellenistic view (cf. 2 Tim 3:16) that every element of the Pentateuch's text, however trivial in appearance, is inspired by God and is 'beneficial,' intended as a source of divine instruction. For Philo, the literal interpretation is valid, but of limited value; the reader must move beyond the literal to the allegorical level of interpretation to arrive at the truly correct meaning, the higher level of instruction mediated through the words of the Pentateuch. In the final part of this essay, Kamesar argues that the primary orientation of Philo's allegorical interpretation of the Pentateuch in the *Allegorical Commentary* concerns the human soul and its ethical and spiritual progress. The systematic nature of this allegorical interpretation distinguishes Philo's work from that of his known predecessors, Jewish and non-Jewish; a comparable systematic approach in later Neoplatonist sources may indicate that both Philo and the Neoplatonists were inspired by a common source. Philo's treatment of the lives of the ancestors as moral exempla reflects a common view of history in his own time. His transformation of biblical characters from moral exempla into 'dispositions of soul' or 'mind' may be connected to late Hellenistic developments in Platonist thinking, according to which it is the soul or mind that is that part of the human being that engages in the quest for virtue, and that is therefore the model to be followed. Philo's development of the 'allegory of the soul' was also influenced by Platonist interest in the universal, not the particular; accordingly, Philo often emphasizes the significance of individual figures in Scripture as universal archetypes of virtue. (SJKP)

M. B. Kartzow, *Gossip and Gender: Othering of Speech in the Pastoral Epistles*, Beihefte zur Zeitschrift für die neutestamentliche Wissenschaft und die Kunde der älteren Kirche 164 (Berlin 2009).

This is the published version of a University of Oslo PhD, focusing on the themes of gossip and gender in the Pastoral Epistles, which looks specifically at their use of the notion that gossip is a kind of gendered speech, the construction of opponents as 'other' through labeling them as gossips, and the role of gender in the process of naming and blaming the 'other.' Kartzow concludes that the Pastoral Epistles draw on a widespread 'gossip discourse' among ancient authors, in which gossip is constructed as feminine speech and used to construct opponents as a negative 'other.' A chapter on 'Ancient representations of female gossipers' includes discussion of Philo, *Spec.* 3.171. Philo and Plutarch are seen as exceptional among ancient sources—Jewish and non-Jewish—which deal in 'gossip discourse,' in requiring a woman not to be a 'busybody' (πολυπραγμονέω, Philo, *Spec.* 3.171; cf. Plutarch's *Lycurgus and Numa* 3.5). The same requirement is found in the Pastoral Epistles. Philo differs from Plutarch, however, in his solution for keeping women from gossiping: by confining women to the household or other spaces that limit opportunities for exchanging information, with the exception of visiting the Temple. It should be noted that Philo uses πολυπραγμονέω and related words in a number of contexts not noted in this study, including examples of the gossipy male (esp. *Abr.* 20–21). (SJKP)

A. KERKESLAGER, 'Agrippa I and the Judeans of Alexandria in the Wake of the Violence in 38 C.E.,' *Revue des Études Juives* 168 (2009) 1–49.

This extensive and meticulously documented study argues that the Judean king Agrippa I can no longer be viewed as a champion for the Judeans of Alexandria. After his visit to the city in 38 C.E., Agrippa's behaviour repeatedly reveals an effort to avoid incrimination in the voilence that erupted during his visit. This is apparent from the various sources that give information on these events, including Philo's two treatises *Flacc.* and *Legat.* The author analyzes these sources in the order of the events they describe, beginning with the king's visit to Alexandria. In the final part of the analysis (pp. 35–45) he speculates that Philo's descriptions in the two treatises may have been influenced by the close relations between his family and that of the king. It is also highly likely that Josephus' knowledge of Philo's accounts was obtained in Rome. Indeed Rome may have played a key role in the early transmission of Philo's writings. The author concludes that at every stage Agrippa betrayed much more interest in the security of his own status in the Roman administration than in the plight of his fellow countrymen in Alexandria. It is proposed that this conclusion may help resolve numerous problems relating to the violence of 38 C.E., including the nature of the charges laid against the Roman governor Flaccus. (DTR)

C. KÖCKERT, *Christliche Kosmologie und kaiserzeitliche Philosophie. Die Auslegung des Schöpfungsberichtes bei Origenes, Basilius und Gregor von Nyssa vor dem Hintergrund kaizerzeitlicher Timaeus-Interpretation,* Studien und Texte zu Antike und Christentum 56 (Tübingen 2009), passim.

This impressive monograph is the published edition of a doctoral dissertation prepared at the University of Hamburg under the supervision of Prof. Christoph Markschies and Prof. Winrich Löhr. As the book's lengthy title and sub-title clarifies, its aim is to understand Patristic cosmology against the background of imperial philosophy, particularly as it engages with Plato's hugely influential cosmological dialogue, the *Timaeus.* 'Cosmology' here means not the study of the cosmos in any kind of scientific way, but rather through the exegesis of the scriptural account of creation in Gen 1 and other texts. The first part of the book gives an extensive account of Platonist cosmology based on the interpretation of the *Timaeus,* with separate chapters on Plutarch, Atticus, Numenius, Alcinous and Porphyry. The second part presents Christian cosmology based on the exegesis of Gen 1, with separate chapters on Origen, Basil and Gregory of Nyssa. The third and final part gives a thorough summary of the relation between Christian cosmology and Imperial philosophy. Although strangely there is no mention of Philo in the introductory section which sets out the book's methodology (and also not in the index of names and subjects), in fact the author is most conscientious in giving the Philonic background of the Patristic exegesis of the Genesis account and indicating how the Patristic authors appropriate, modify and sometimes reject his intepretations. For example, Origen uses Philo's exegesis of day one of creation in *Opif.* 17–20 but also substantially modifies it, rejecting the equation with the intelligible cosmos and preserving the unity of the created realm (p. 309). See further the index of Philonic passages utilized on pp. 604–605. (DTR)

M. Konradt, 'Tora und Naturgesetz: Interpretatio graeca und univer-saler Geltungsanspruch der Mosetora bei Philo von Alexandrien,' in M. Konradt and R. C. Schwinges (edd.), *Juden in ihrer Umwelt. Akkultura-tion des Judentums in Antike und Mittelalter. Eine Publikation der Interfakultären Forschungsstelle Judaistik an der Universität Bern* (Bern 2009) 87–112.

Philo's attitude to the Torah and the Law of nature is seen as a prime example of the acculturation of Jewish traditions to the surrounding culture. Philo's biography and his writings indicate his close link with the Jewish community in Alexandria. He is characterized mainly as an exegete; most of his writings are commentaries on the Torah. In these he identifies the Torah with the Law of nature, they are in harmony, as God is seen as the creator of both (*Opif.* 3, *Mos.* 2.45–52). The Exposition of the Laws presents the Patriarchs as personified Law, embodied virtue, a bridge between the natural and the written laws (*Abr.* 5). The written Laws therefore must follow a basic pattern: the Decalogue (*Decal.* 19, 30). Thus Philo's attitude to the Torah is based on Hellenistic principles, but he does not universalize it to the degree that the Torah as the focus of Jewish identity is sacrificed. The Law of nature is open to everyone, but the Torah guarantees the special status of the Jews in their relationship to the nations, as they are already governed by the perfect laws. (JLB)

D. Konstan, 'Le courage dans le roman grec de Chariton à Xénophon d'Éphèse, avec une référence à Philon d'Alexandrie,' in B. Pouderon, C. Bost-Pouderon and S. Montanari (edd.), *Passions, vertus et vices dans l'ancien roman: actes du colloque de Tours, 19–21 octobre 2006* (Paris 2009) 117–126.

In this contribution the representations of courage as a virtue in Philo's *Virt.* and in the Greek novels (particularly in the *Ephesiaca* of Xenophon of Ephesus) are examined and compared. According to Aristotle the concept of ἀνδρεία (courage) is essentially associated with war. Philo proposes a new interpretation of the idea of courage (already envisaged by Plato) as the capacity to resist sexual temptations. In this sense, ἀνδρεία is close to the concept of σωφροσύνη or ἐγκράτεια. Philo also broadly connects ἀνδρεία with knowledge (ἐπιστήμη), wisdom (σοφία) and humility (*Virt.* 1–4, 17). (KB)

R. A. Kraft, *Exploring the Scripturesque: Jewish Texts and their Christian Contexts*, Supplements to the Journal for the Study of Judaism 137 (Leiden 2009).

The volume contains a collection of published and unpublished studies on Jewish texts and their Christian contexts written during the author's long scholarly career from the mid 70s to the present. Part III entitled 'Some related studies' focuses primarily on Philo and his context of Alexandrian Judaïsm. Two brief half-chapters treat the themes 'Philo on Seth: was Philo aware of traditons that exalted Seth and his progeny?' and 'Philo (Josephus, Sirach and Wisdom of Solomon) on Enoch.' The next chapter presents an unpublished chapter on 'Philo's treatment of the number seven in *On Creation*.' The following two chapters are reprints of RRS 9137 and 9037 on the Sabbath crisis in Alexandria, in which an important role is postulated for Philo's nephew Tiberius Julius Alexander. (DTR)

R. Kritzer, 'Esau bei Philon und Josephus,' in G. Langer (ed.), *Esau — Bruder und Feind* (Göttingen 2009) 41–54.

Esau is mentioned in several of Philo's writings. In the allegorical interpretation, his hairiness stands in contrast to the nakedness of Adam and Eve and other biblical characters, which is seen as expression of virtue. Esau is not a citizen of virtue. Already in the womb he is predestined to servitude. Because of his ignorance he is subordinated to his younger brother, who displays good works. Jacob also represents the reasoning *Logos*, Esau brute force. The two thus represent the contrast between virtue and evil. Esau's blessing through Isaac is seen as a lesser form of blessing accessible even to the imperfect. Thus Philo reads the Esau narrative in terms of why he had to lose his right as firstborn son, a loss necessitated by the bodily, mental, spiritual, and moral differences between the two, which attribute all the negatives to Esau and all the positives to Jacob. (JLB)

J. Kügler, 'Das Ende der Kritik? Zur Funktion des Gebetes für die Herrschenden bei Philo von Alexandria und im 1. Timotheusbrief,' in J. Kügler and U. Bechmann (edd.), *Biblische Religionskritik. Kritik in, an und mit biblischen Texten. Beiträge des IBS 2007 in Vierzehnheiligen,* Bayreuther Forum Transit 9 (Berlin 2009) 111–130.

The paper uses Philo's *Legat.* and *Flacc.* as background for the attitude towards the rulers in 1 Tim. Philo's argument in both treatises moves along the lines of the traditional reasoning for the ruler cult, based on the *euergetes* concept as reaction to received favours, which the Jews could demonstrate they had not received from Gaius. The Emperor, in contrast, argues along an alternative idea of veneration due to divine blood. In the context of the argument in Alexandria and Rome, this clash of ideas meant that Philo's argument could not be successful. Kügler suggests that the reasoning in the treatises probably represents an attempt at influencing Claudius in the early days of his reign rather than an accurate depiction of Philo's argument in front of Gaius. There the tactic probably consisted of simple appeals for mercy, which were more promising in view of the Emperor's elevated self-image. Historically Kügler sees the problem as solved rather by the murder of Gaius than by any Jewish intervention. (JLB)

M. Landfester and B. Egger (edd.), *Dictionary of Greek and Latin Authors and Texts,* Brill's New Pauly Supplements 2 (Leiden 2009).

English translation of the German original summarized in *SPhA* vol. 22, p. 230, and reviewed in the same volume by J. R. Royse, pp. 272–276. (DTR)

M. LANG, 'Lebenskunst und Ethos. Beobachtungen zu Plutarch, Seneca, Philo von Alexandrien und dem 1. Petrusbrief,' in F. W. HORN and R. ZIMMERMAN (edd.), *Jenseits von Indikativ und Imperativ: Kontexte und Normen neutestamentlicher Ethik,* Wissenschaftliche Untersuchungen zum Neuen Testament 238 (Tübingen 2009) 57–74, esp. 65–68.

Philo's concept of a Jewish art of living is seen in the context of similar discourses in Plutarch and Seneca. Philo does not use the term itself, but a variation in *Leg.* 1.57. The idea occurs in *Migr.* 128–131 where Philo describes the perfect life which aims at virtue, a life according to God's will and word, which to Philo is identical to what the Greek philosophers teach as they in turn learnt from Moses. Virtue is the art of the whole life governed by philosophy (logic, ethics and physics) and expressed in deeds. Such nobility of living is not restricted ethnically, either to Greeks or Jews, but belongs to the virtuous of all backgrounds who do not live separately but serve as the backbone and support of humankind. (JLB)

C. LEBLOND, *À la croisée de deux mondes. Les relations entre maître et disciples selon quatre témoins d'époque impériale: deux grecs, le biographe Diogène Laërce et le philosophe Épictète; deux juifs, l'historien Flavius Josèphe et l'exégète Philon d'Alexandrie* (diss. Tours 2009).

This dissertation prepared under the supervision of Prof. Bernard Pouderon, analyzes different aspects of the relationship between a master and his disciples through the testimony of four ancient authors, Diogenes Laertius, Epictetus, Philo and Josephus. The first part focuses on the fundamental conditions required from the pupil: his good disposition, education, and training; special emphasis is placed on Philo's use of the biblical patriarchs Abraham, Isaac and Jacob as models for discipleship, and on Philo's notion of the self-taught or autodidact person. The second part examines the teachers' requirements, but also the ability of the teacher to adapt himself to the needs of the student. According to Philo, God provides the model of the patient teacher who makes such an effort. The third part attempts to define what a good relationship between master and disciples consists of, and asks whether the loyal pupil should be extremely faithful to the doctrine he receives from his master and hand it on to his own pupils, or whether the loyal pupil should adopt a critical attitude towards his master. Philo, for instance, praises Moses for considering the teaching of his masters in a critical way. The good and bad attitudes of the master are analyzed too. Philo adheres to the biblical sapiential tradition by stating that the master's benevolence can imply corporal punishment, but also puts forward the idea that the good master is allowed to use wrong notions, such as anthropomorphic language about God, for the sake of instruction. The fourth part deals with the different kinds of attachment that exist between a master and his disciples, considering that masters can also be parents, or lovers (an option Philo strongly condemns), or absolute ideals venerated by their pupils. Finally, the last part of the dissertation tackles the issue of the interaction of the master and his disciples with society at large and with wealthy and powerful people in particular, and the way master and disciples faced death. In the general conclusion of the dissertation it is emphasized that one of the main differences between the Greek approach and the Jewish one lies in the fact that within Judaism, a master can be someone who passed away a long time ago, whereas Greeks tend to consider a master as a person from whom one learns while he is alive. (KB)

F. Ledegang, 'The Interpretation of the Decalogue by Philo, Clement of Alexandria and Origen,' in G. Heidl and R. Somos (edd.), *Origeniana Nona. Origen and the Religious Practice of His Time* (Leuven 2009) 245–254.

The author argues that early Alexandrian interpretations of the Decalogue not only differ from the original context of the versions of the Decalogue in the Hebrew Bible, but that these interpretations also differ significantly from each other. Philo's treatment of the Decalogue emphasizes that its contents are identical with the Law of Nature. It follows that the Decalogue is to be regarded as representing a universal standard of ethical behaviour to be obeyed by all. It further follows that all should honour the God of the Jews, whose words are directly communicated in the Decalogue. Philo's interpretation of the Decalogue 'has a highly apologetic and missionary character,' aimed, at least in part, at non-Jews (p. 253; and see pp. 246–248). For Clement, by contrast, the Decalogue sets the moral standard for citizens of the Kingdom of God, but it is also directed towards the spiritual development of the 'gnostic.' Origen presents the moral significance of the Decalogue as intended for believers at the beginning of their spiritual development, while its mystical meaning is for more advanced believers. (SJKP)

J. Leonhardt-Balzer, 'A Case of Psychological Dualism. Philo of Alexandria and the Instruction on the Two Spirits,' in C. A. Evans and H. D. Zacharias (edd.), *Early Christian Literature and Intertextuality. Volume 2: Exegetical Studies*, Library of New Testament Studies 392 (London 2009) 27–45.

In the broad range of different dualisms, the *Instruction on the Two Spirits* (1QS 3.13–4.26) offers a combination of cosmic, ethical, and psychological dualism. In Philonic scholarship, the similarity of the passage to *QE* 1.23 has long been noted. The chapter provides a comparison of the two texts (based on the translation of the Armenian). The conclusion is that Philo indeed used a tradition similar to the Instruction on the Two Spirits, but he used it with a special focus on the psychological reading of the spirits. Different possibilities of the way in which it found its way to Philo are explored: did he meet Essenes? Did the Therapeutae transmit such a tradition? The most likely link is the Second Temple apocalyptic wisdom traditions. The migration of Jerusalem wisdom texts to Alexandria is established by Ben Sira, and Philo's knowledge of wisdom traditions is a well known fact. Philo's use of the Instruction shows that he was capable of using traditions which at first sight do not seem to be compatible with his philosophical outlook. (JLB).

J. Leonhardt-Balzer, 'Heilsgeschichte bei Philo? Die Aufnahme der Zweigeisterlehre in *QE* I 23,' in J. R. Frey, S. Krauter and H. Lichtenberger (edd.), *Heil und Geschichte* (Tübingen 2009) 129–148.

Philo does not have an idea of salvation history in the usual sense, as his idea of *pronoia* does not envisage an end of history. Yet it is not true, as has sometimes been stated, that he does not use apocalyptic traditions. This can be demonstrated by a comparison of *QE* I 23 (in Armenian) with the pre-sectarian *Instruction on the Two Spirits* in 1QS 3.13–4.26. The psychological, ethical and cosmic aspects of the two spirits in the *Instruction* are read psychologically and ethically by Philo. Philo's reading of the tradition is clearly influenced by Greek philosophy—he does not refer to 'spirits' but rather to 'powers,' and he drops any references to history—but the order of the individual thoughts is similar between the two texts, and almost all Philo's points have parallels in the *Instruction*. Possibly the version of the *Instruction* used by Philo included the insertion of an astronomical passage. Philo's motivation for using the *Instruction* is the idea of the victory of the angel of God against the angel of darkness, which he allegorizes and transfers onto the psychological processes inside the human being. Thus Philo's idea of salvation history is to read traditional myths morally, ethically, and psychologically for the present, not for some point in the future. (JLB)

J. R. LEVISON, *Filled with the Spirit* (Grand Rapids 2009), passim.

Inspired by Hermann Gunkel's pioneering work on pneumatology in the Jewish tradition, the author follows the theme of being 'filled with the spirit' through Israelite, Jewish, and early Christian literatures. Discussion of Philonic material, in which the author builds on earlier research, is found throughout the entire monograph. The main passages are on the exegesis of Gen 2:7 (pp. 145–150), the 'allure of ecstasy' and its escape (pp. 158–162, 178–180), inspiration and scriptural interpretation (pp. 189–196, 247–251), comparison with Paul (pp. 309–313), Acts and the theme of sober intoxication (pp. 332–335), and the presence of the spirit in comparison with the Johannine literature (pp. 391–398). (DTR)

C. LÉVY, 'Philo's Ethics,' in A. KAMESAR (ed.), *The Cambridge Companion to Philo* (Cambridge 2009) 146–171.

Philo is deeply interested in ethics, but the requirements of his biblical exegesis determine that he does not present his views systematically in the way of a philosopher. The chapter discusses five chief aspects of ethics in succession. (1) Philo rejects the Stoic doctrine of οἰκείωσις as the grounding of ethics, perhaps because as a Jew he could not accept that ethics had its root in an instinctive impulse common to human beings and animals. Instead he espouses the Platonist doctrine of ὁμοίωσις θεῷ, but also emphasizes the kinship between man and God. (2) For the doctrine of the virtues he often follows the philosophical tradition closely. Although he sometimes praises Aristotle's mild philosophy, his deeper adherence is to a more ascetic ethics. The virtues of μετάνοια (repentance) and εὐγένεια (nobility) are reinterpreted in line with biblical and Jewish thought. (3) Philo's views on the passions are particularly rich in contradictions and have given rise to a great diversity of interpretations. The author focuses on the various Philonic conceptions of the soul, the classification of the passions and the description of passion, how the passions can be healed and how, paradoxically, passion can be transcended by madness. (4) Although in this life it is not possible to avoid the passions and other evils, there is a moral itinerary consisting of three stages leading to perfection. Here Philo is indebted to the Stoicism of Panaetius and his successors. (5) In his political thought Moses is the example of true kingship, but Joseph illustrates the dangers of immersion in the world of politics. Lévy concludes his overview by arguing that the contradictions that Philo's ethical teachings contain 'are the result of two movements which in the dynamic line of his thought are contradictory only in appearance. It is necessary to flee from the world in order to come face to face with God, but also to deepen one's insertion into the world in order to experience a relationship with God through meeting others.' (p. 171) Philo's ethics are thus both transcendent and immanentist. (DTR)

B. C. LI, 'Dao-Logos. Lao Zi and Philo,' *Euntes docete* 62 (2009) 123–143.

While in Confucianism, Dao is employed to signify the way of heaven or humans, in Lao Zi (ca. 6th cent. B.C.E.) and Zhuang Zi (ca. 4th cent. B.C.E.), Dao acquires a metaphysical meaning. Dao is the ultimate reality as well as the first principle underlying form, substance, being and change. It is argued that there is a striking affinity between the role of Dao in Lao Zi and the role of the *Logos* in the thought of Philo of Alexandria. In spite of the use of Stoic terminology, Philo's thought is strongly influenced by Middle Platonism, and this provides a terrain for comparison between the two philosophers from east and west. (DTR; based on the author's abstract)

Y. LIEBES, 'The Work of the Chariot and the Work of Creation as Mystical Teachings in Philo of Alexandria,' in D. A. GREEN and L. S. LIEBER (edd.), *Scriptural Exegesis. The Shapes of Culture and the Religious Imagination: Essays in Honour of Michael Fishbane* (Oxford 2009) 105–121.

The author argues that Philo considered the Work of the Chariot (Ezek 1 and 10) and the Work of Creation (Gen 1) to be areas of esoteric knowledge that should be concealed. Regarding the 'Work of the Chariot' (pp. 107–112), it is suggested, based on a medieval addition to Josippon, that Philo wrote a treatise on the cherubim that dealt explicitly with the Chariot of Ezekiel (Philo's extant works do not cite Ezekiel). Moreover, even if this work did not exist, Philo's interpretation of the Chariot is 'concealed' within his interpretation of the cherubim, and especially in the treatise *Cher.* (detailed discussions of *Cher.* 11–20, 27). The author notes the close similarity of Philo's interpretations of the cherubim with those of medieval Jewish commentators, and the likely influence on his interpretation of the cherubim as symbols of the heavenly hemispheres of a Hellenistic allegorical tradition about the chariot of Hera and Athena preserved in the late antique collection of Demo. As to the 'Work of Creation' (pp. 112–116), it is argued that in Philo's treatise *Opif.* 12, contrary to other translations (with particular critique of the new Hebrew translation), he is expounding the name of the Book of Genesis, and speaks of 'a double Torah of Moses, one that is permissible to teach in public and one that must be concealed' (p. 113). The author emphasizes that Philo seems to relate the name Genesis here to the sensible world; however, the world that has not come into being, the imperceptible world, 'has no place in the Book of Genesis and Moses did not write about it' (p. 114). Overall, the author argues that rabbinic statements about the esoteric nature of the 'Work of Creation' and the 'Work of the Chariot' go back to traditions earlier than Philo, and that this study will help to develop research on connections between Philo and rabbinic literature, and even to show the continuity of Philo's teaching with Jewish mysticism and Kabbalah. (SJKP)

J. A. LOPEZ FEREZ, 'Filón de Alejandría: Obra y pensamiento. Una lectura filológica,' *Synthesis* 16 (2009) 13–82.

This lengthy article presents the *corpus philonicum* as a point of entry to the philological history of Judaism in Alexandrian culture, with emphasis on its rhetorical features. It examines the situation of the Jewish community in the context of Roman Alexandria, including the pogrom of year 38 C.E. and the relationship of this community with the Septuagint, which is considered to be the Bible in the 'language of communication.' In the main section of the article Lopez provides a summary of each of the treatises of Philo (with the exception of the *Quaestiones*), divided into four categories: 26 Exegesis of the Law (all regarded as a single series), 2 Apologetic, 2 Historical, and 3 Philosophical. The author then presents seven points on the thought of Philo within the Alexandrian context, outlining the number of quotations that Philo makes from classical Greek authors. Finally, the article highlights the position of Philo as a link that joins historically the thought of the Diaspora Jews and Christianity. (JPM)

E. D. MacGILLIVRAY, 'Re-evaluating Patronage and Reciprccity in Antiquity and New Testament Studies,' *Journal of Greco-Roman Christianity and Judaism* 6 (2009) 37–81.

According to this article, the notion of patronage as a voluntary, reciprocal relationship that pervaded Roman society has been widely adopted in New Testament scholarship without sufficient critical awareness of the shortcomings, as applied to antiquity, of models of patronage drawn from diverse cultures and contexts and treated as universally applicable. In particular, the author argues, it is not applicable to ancient Jewish culture. The author treats Philo and Josephus as key evidence for the lack of 'any large-scale presence of patronage or euergetism in Jewish society' (p. 55). In particular, Philo is seen as exceptional in the context of the Graeco-Roman world for his critical attitude towards a variety of practices involving reciprocity and patronage (pp. 56–62). Following a brief sketch of examples said to illustrate Philo's criticisms of euergetism and patronage (*Cher.* 122–123; *Agr.* 171; *Decal.* 2–4), the article argues that several passages in Philo's *Legat.* (148–152, 299–303) represent Greco-Roman reciprocal practices as foreign to the Jewish way of life. Philo's account of the hostility of Jews to Pilate's introduction of dedicatory shields into Jerusalem (*Legat.* 299–303) gives voice, alongside 2 Macc 4:15, to the idea that such honours were an objectionable foreign incursion. (SJKP)

S. D. MACKIE, 'Seeing God in Philo of Alexandria: the *Logos*, the Powers, or the Existent One?,' *The Studia Philonica Annual* 21 (2009) 25–48.

Philo frequently speaks about the vision of God, which is for him the ultimate goal in human life. It is, however, difficult to determine exactly what is seen. Sometimes God himself is seen, sometimes it is the divine *Logos* that is seen. It seems that Philo is conflicted about this matter, but this is a reflection of the complexity of the enterprise. The author discusses several passages on the *visio Dei*, taken from all three exegetical series. The most important passage is *QG* 4.2, 4–5, 8, where Philo treats God's manifestation to Abraham (Gen 18:2–7). In his conclusion the author states that there are four elements in Philo's description of *visio Dei* that occur in all three series. (1) The object of seeing varies but there are statements about the visibility of God himself. (2) Who is seen is determined by the spiritual level of the person who sees. The mystic philosopher is able to see τὸ ὄν (3) The *Logos* and the divine powers, who are intermediaries, operate as autonomous agents. They are distinct from τὸ ὄν. (4) In a few passages Philo underlines God's transcendence, and affirms that τὸ ὄν is 'non-visible.' The passages in which Philo speaks about seeing God without intermediaries are prevalent in the Exposition. This can be explained by the audience for which the Exposition is meant. The Exposition was intended for less sophisticated readers and therefore Philo rarely mentions the *visio Dei*, and, if he refers to it, a simple visual encounter with God is described. In the Allegorical Commentary the seeing of God is presented in a more complex way, including the vision of intermediaries. There are also other factors that account for the variety in Philo's treatment of the *visio Dei*. The most important is that Philo in his exegesis incorporates other exegetical traditions, which are not harmonized with his own view. (ACG)

A. MAGNANI, *Il processo di Isidoro: Roma e Alessandria nel primo secolo* (Bologna 2009).

In the context of a penetrating study of the *Acta Isidori* (those documents among the *Acta martyrum alexandrinorum* that deal with the juridical process and conviction of the

Alexandrian *gymnasiarchos* Isidorus in Rome in the presence of Claudius), much attention is given to the *Letter of Aristeas*, Philo, and Josephus, as the three most important witnesses for the relationship and growing tensions between the Greek and Jewish communities in Alexandria. Chapters are dedicated to the socio-political situation in Alexandria as part of the Roman empire, and to the views on the relationship and possible coexistence of Greek and Jewish culture as expressed by Philo in *Mos.*, *Ios.*, and of course *Flacc.* and *Legat.* (in which Isidorus is one of the protagonists), as well as by the author of the *Letter* and by Josephus in his *Against Apion*. Magnani offers an attentive overview of the contents of these works which shows Philo taking an intermediate position regarding Greek-Jewish socio-cultural relationships between the *Letter* (optimistic and rather unproblematic) and Josephus (hostile and polemical). It is suggested that two pairs of 'parallel lives' are represented by *Mos.* and *Legat.* (Moses as philosopher-king of universal value, beloved by God, contrasted with Caligula as monarch of the *oikoumene* precipitated in folly, vice and violence, and considering himself god), and by *Ios.* and *Flacc.* (Joseph as wise and provident administrator of Egypt contrasted with the Prefect of Egypt, Flaccus, opportunist and uncaring for the political and social disasters resulting from his doings). (HMK)

S. MARCULESCU-BADILITA, *Recherches sur la prophétie chez Philon d'Alexandrie* (diss. Sorbonne, Paris 2007).

This dissertation, prepared under the supervision of Prof. Monique Alexandre, addresses various aspects of prophecy in the works of Philo of Alexandria: the vocabulary connected with prophecy (Philo uses biblical terms like προφήτης or λόγιον, but also words that have a strong 'pagan' character, like χρησμός), the prophetic dimension of Abraham (especially his ecstatic experience in Gen 15), the relationship between Moses' prophecy and the three other functions he is attributed in *Mos.* (royalty, law-giving, and priesthood), the question of divine inspiration and the classification of Moses' oracles, the relationship between prophecy and interpretation as illustrated by the relationship between Moses and Aaron, prophetic dreams and their classification, and Philo's critique of divination, particularly through the example of the soothsayer Balaam. In addition, the comparison between biblical and post-biblical prophets in Philo's works is examined as well. In contrast to most previous studies, the present dissertation tackles the issue of prophecy by focusing on prophetical characters rather than on the theoretical aspects of prophecy. It addresses the question 'who is a prophet in Philo's eyes?' rather than 'what is prophecy for Philo?' It allows the author to reach the conclusion that prophecy in Philo's eyes is much more than the ability to foresee future events or a kind of moral or historical message delivered to the people of Israel alone. Prophecy is conceived of as a privileged relationship between the person who is *asteios* and God. Philo is more interested in the metaphysical aspects of prophecy—in terms of the relationship between God and the human spirit—than in its practical results. As far as Philo's own time is concerned, he considers that prophecy can be found in some kinds of inspired exegesis of the Bible and in the way of life of the *Therapeutae*. (KB; based on the author's abstract)

J. P. MARTÍN (ed.), *Filón de Alejandría Obras Completas Volumen I* (Madrid 2009).

This is the first volume of a Spanish-language edition of the complete writings of Philo. It is published by the distinguished publishing house of Trotta and is planned to occupy eight volumes. It contains an extensive general introduction to the entire work by the general editor, which gives an account of the life, family, and community of Philo; the structure of the Philonic corpus, literary genres and the Greek language; the thought of

Philo and his reception in the history of culture; and the transmission of the text (pp. 9–88). Francisco Lisi—expert on and translator of Plato's *Timaeus*—is responsible for the introduction, translation and commentary on *Opif.* (pp. 97–158), and Marta Alesso—specialist on the genre of Alexandrian allegory—is responsible for the introduction, translation and commentary on the three books of *Leg.* (pp. 159–301). Replacing the partial Spanish edition of J. M. Triviño in 1975–1976, which was based on the English translation of Colson-Whitaker, the new translation is based primarily on the Greek text of Cohn and Wendland and at times on input from other editors, such as Colson, Arnaldez, Mondésert and Radice. The volume concludes with indices of biblical and Philonic passages, of ancient and modern authors, and of Greek language and subjects. See further the review of this and the following volume by M. Alexandre, Jr. in *SPhA* vol. 22, pp. 276–280. (JPM)

J. P. Martín (ed.), *Filón de Alejandría Obras Completas Volumen V* (Madrid 2009).

The fifth volume of the Philo's complete works in Spanish translation is the second in order of publication. It contains five treatises which are considered to be historical in the sense that they contain narrative and interpretive elements about events of the past and present, but in a genre that can also be classified as historical-theological because it portrays a providential view of human history, in which Moses and Israel receive special functions as being chosen by God. The general editor discusses and translates the two treatises of *Mos.* (pp. 17–144), classified as a *bios*, but also as a manifesto of the Jewish Hellenistic culture. He also presents an introduction, translation, and notes of the treatise *Contempl.* (pp. 145–176). S. Torallas Tovar gives the same treatment to the two treatises *Flacc.* and *Legat.* (pp. 177–301), with copious references to the relevant source material from Roman and Alexandrian history in Philo's time, based on literary works, papyri, and archeology. The translations follow the Greek text established by Cohn and Wendland, and take into account previous translations. Several indices close this volume with the same criteria as in the first volume. For a review of this volume see the previous item. (JPM)

M. D. Matlock, *Traditions of Prose Prayer in Early Jewish Literature* (diss. Hebrew Union College—Jewish Institute of Religion (Ohio) 2009).

This dissertation, prepared under the supervision of Stephen A. Kaufman, examines extended prose prayers in early Jewish literature. Commencing with the investigation of one exilic and four post-exilic prayers in the Hebrew Bible and their translations in the Septuagint, it analyses approximately thirty prayers in the Apocrypha, Pseudepigrapha, Dead Sea Scrolls, Philo, Josephus, and Targum Jonathan with the aim of looking for rhetorical patterns and innovations that yield insight into the thinking of these Jewish communities and sponsors. Throughout the study, the author probes the structure, organization, and content of each prayer and explores the traces of ideology. The primary methods of analysis are narratology, rhetorical-criticism, discourse analysis, and a close reading of the literary and historical contexts. The specific prayers examined in Philo are the prayer of the people gathered for Yom Kippur (*Spec.* 2.198–199) and the prayer of Abraham in *Her.* 24–29. (DTR; based on author's summary in DA)

L. R. Miranda, '¿Cuál fue el pecado original?: traducciones e interpretaciones de Gn 3, 1–24,' *Circe* 13 (2009) 157–171.

The article analyses the interpretations of the Greek version of Gen 3:1–24 in Philo, in the Epistle to the Romans and in Ambrose's *On Paradise*. Concerning Philo, Miranda particularly points out that in *Leg.* 1.61 the soul, when it receives the impression of perfect virtue, becomes the tree of life, but when it receives the impression of vice, it becomes the tree of the knowledge of good and evil. This view is related to *Leg.* 2.1–2 and *Leg.* 2.24–25, where Philo says that after the creation of the mind it was necessary that the exterior senses should be created, as an assistant and ally of the mind. Thus God, having entirely perfected the first, proceeded to make the second, both in rank and in power. (JPM)

S. NADLER, and T. M. RUDAVSKY (edd.), *The Cambridge History of Jewish Philosophy From Antiquity through the Seventeenth Century* (Cambridge 2009).

This handsome multi-authored volume is 'conceived as part of the series of Cambridge Histories of Philosophy with the aim of presenting Jewish philosophy as part of an ongoing dialogue with the history of philosophy generally' (p. xi). The organization of the volume is thematic, but the individual chapters tend to follow a chronological sequence. Philo's philosophical views are briefly discussed in the following chapters: S. Pessin, "Matter, Form and the Corporeal World" (pp. 270–271); T. M. Rudavsky, "Time, Space, and Infinity" (pp. 398–400); C. Fraenkel, "God's Existence and Attributes" (pp. 564–572); L. E. Goodman, "Creation and Emanation" (pp. 600–602); S. Nadler, "Theodicy and Providence" (pp. 622–623); H. Tirosh-Samuelson, "Virtue and Happiness" (p. 717–721). For further references see the index p. 899. (DTR)

S. NORDGAARD SVENDSEN, *Allegory Transformed: the Appropriation of Philonic Hermeneutics in the Letter to the Hebrews*, Wissenschaftliche Untersuchungen zum Neuen Testament 2.269 (Tübingen 2009).

In this study, the author wishes to argue that Philo, or at least the tradition he was a part of, played a formative role for the author of the Letter to the Hebrews. While it has been contended in much research that a possible influence from Philo in this letter occurs primarily in the realms of language, cosmology, and theology, he argues that it also exists in the realm of scriptural exegesis. More specifically, he argues that both Philo and the author of Hebrews read the Old Testament allegorically, and that the author of the Letter drew on the hermeneutical tradition represented by Philo. The study is divided into three parts: Part 1, Allegory (pp. 9–52); Part 2, Preliminaries (pp. 55–80), and Part 3, Exegesis. In addition to the frequent references to the works and views of Philo, a special section is devoted to him in Part 1 (pp. 29–52), and in three excursusi (Philo and Divine Rest, pp. 112–120; Philo and the Tabernacle, pp. 162-167; and Philo and the High Priest, pp. 118–193). In the first and main section on Philo, the author first sets out his view of Philo's metaphysics, described primarily on the basis of *Opif.*, and then on Philo and allegory. The former he describes as basically operating within a Platonic framework of dualistic thought, but with the additional aspect that the link between the two levels was shaped by Stoic thinking. In the latter, he briefly discusses the view of S. Sowers and D. Dawson on why Moses used allegory, but finds them both defective. He sides, however, with Dawson in that Moses spoke in allegories because human language could not grasp what he wanted to convey; on the other hand, that does not mean that all propositional language is inaccurate. The totality of God's reason transcends what can be contained in human language. It can thus be said that Philo anchored his allegorical method in a comprehensive ontological theory. (TS)

R. A. NORRIS, 'Who is the Demiurge? Irenaeus' Picture of God in *Adversus haereses* 2,' in A. B. MCGOWAN, B. E. DALEY S.J. and T. J. GADEN (edd.), *God in Early Christian Thought: Essays in Memory of Lloyd G. Patterson,* Supplements to Vigiliae Christianae 94 (Leiden 2009) 9–36, esp. 16–19.

The formula 'enclosing and not enclosed' used by Irenaeus to describe God goes back to Philo, who developed the rabbinic doctrine that God is the 'place' of all things. (DTR)

T. NOVICK, 'Perspective, *Paideia*, and Accommodation in Philo,' *The Studia Philonica Annual* 21 (2009) 49–62.

This article deals with the notion of perspectival exegesis in Philo's writings. Perspectival exegesis can be described as an exegesis that attends to the point of view represented by a given proposition in a text. First, Novick discusses some examples of this phenomenon in Philo. Secondly, the author shows that Philo employs it in his view that mystical elements in the Bible have a paedeutic function. The perspectival approach draws together two different views on myth, a literalist one that myth has a paedeutic function, and a second view that plays it down by using allegory. In a perspectival way God is regarded as manifesting himself to souls in the way that they can see him. Finally, the author examines *Abr.* 107–132 as an example of a passage that illustrates how perspectival exegesis allows Philo to build a bridge between a literal and an allegorical reading. (ACG)

J. OPSOMER, 'M. Annius Ammonius, a Philosophical Profile,' in M. BONAZZI and J. OPSOMER (edd.), *The Origins of the Platonic System: Platonisms of the Early Empire and their Philosophical Contexts,* Collection des Études Classiques 23 (Leuven 2009) 123–186, esp. 164–170.

Brief discussion of the famous passage placed in the mouth of Plutarch's teacher Ammonius in his dialoge *De E apud Delphos* and the key parallel text in Philo, *Ios.* 126–129. The author concludes that the two passages go back to a common tradition that combines Pythagorean elements with ideas that are closer to the sceptical Academy. (DTR)

J. OTTO, *Reason, Revelation and Ridicule: Assessing the Criteria for Authoritative Allegorical Interpretations in Philo and Augustine* (M.A. thesis, McGill University 2009).

This thesis explores the interplay between reason and revelation in determining authoritative allegorical exegeses of Old Testament texts. Taking as its point of departure Augustine's ridiculing of Philo's exegesis of the Ark door in Genesis 6:16 as a human anus, this thesis examines the criteria by which Augustine is able to assert that the said door is correctly to be identified as the wounds of Christ. Both exegetes understand allegorical interpretation to be a rational exercise, following similar philosophically-derived exegetical principles. However, both Philo and Augustine agree that meaningful allegorical truths can only be discerned from texts whose divine provenance and authority are determined by revelation experienced either by the reader himself or by a reliable witness. The conceptualization of salvation both as understood rationally and as experienced beyond reason is a crucial point of divergence. Philo's exegesis—taken by Augustine as representative of contemporary Jewish praxis—is ridiculous not in its methodology but in its failure to recognize the salvific presence of Christ within the Genesis text revealed through the Incarnation. (DTR; based on author's summary)

E. PARKER, *Swiftly Runs the Word: Philo's Doctrine of Mediation in De Vita Moisis* (M.A. thesis, Dalhousie University 2009).

This thesis examines Philo of Alexandria's doctrine of mediation in *Mos.* Acting through his official roles as philosopher-king, legislator, high priest, and prophet, Philo's Moses is a divine mediator who reveals, completes, and fulfills the hierarchy of created beings, enabling the restoration of the human soul to a state of perfection beyond that of the pre-fallen human nature. Philo's interpretation of the Septuagint depends on philosophical elements drawn from Plato, the Stoics, and the Pythagoreans. Philo, like other Middle Platonists, develops the doctrine of Plato's *Timaeus* by locating the ideas in the mind of God, which enables him to posit an unbroken chain of created existents, hierarchically arranged from the creator to the creation, thereby making the constitution of Moses not just cosmic, but divine. Despite Philo's evident reliance on the Hellenic philosophical tradition, we have no evidence that any Hellene had articulated their roles with such precision and exactitude before Philo. (DTR; based on the author's abstract)

R. PASSARELLA, *Ambrogio e la medicina: le parole e i concetti*, Il Filarete 262 (Milan 2009).

In this voluminous and thorough examination of Ambrose's knowledge of medicine and use of medical terms, we regularly meet Philo as a source of which Ambrose made intensive use throughout his œuvre and regularly cites (albeit anonymously), e.g., on the subjects of digestion and the menstrual cycle. (HMK)

S. J. K. PEARCE, 'Egypt on the Pentateuch's map of migration in the writings of Philo of Alexandria,' *Jewish Culture and History* 11 (2009) 141–155.

For Philo, the journey narratives of the Torah constitute a kind of map of spiritual migration, a chart of the journey towards God under the direction of Moses. Indeed, it is this understanding of the centrality of the journey in Scripture that determines the fundamental place of migration in Philo's philosophical interpretation of Judaism. Through allegorical reading of the journeys of the ancestors, from Abraham to Moses, Philo points to the deeper meaning of these journeys, their starting points and destinations, and the waypoints in between. The land of Egypt is a central point of arrival and departure, culminating in the great Exodus under the leadership of Moses. This essay examines the particular significance of Egypt in Philo's reading of the Mosaic map of migration. What did Philo, an Egyptian Jew, make of the Torah's ambivalent construction of Egypt as home or waypoint on the ancestors' travels? Why did he consistently read the Torah's Egypt as the symbol, *par excellence*, of 'the land of the body'? This article suggests that two traditions seem to have been fundamental in generating this interpretation: the geographical imagination of the Torah, and the influence of Platonist exegesis of the world imagined by Homer. The article adapts, for the purposes of a broad-ranging conference volume on the idea of the journey in Jewish history and thought, material from the author's study *The Land of the Body: Studies in Philo's Representation of Egypt*; see summary in *SPhA*, vol. 21, pp. 136–137. (SJKP)

R. Penna, *Paolo e la chiesa di Roma* (Brescia 2009), Appendice 2 (p. 259–264), = reprint of R. Penna, 'L'immagine di Roma in Filone Alessandrino (*In Flaccum* e *Legatio ad Gaium*),' in P. Catalano and P. Siniscalco (edd.), *Roma fuori di Roma: istituzioni e immagini* (Rome 1994) 45–57.

As an appendix to Penna's book about Paul and the Church of Rome, an article is reprinted about 'the image of Rome in Philo of Alexandria,' first published in 1994. The article first analyzes the historical background of *Flacc.* and *Legat.* and of Philo's statements about Rome in these treatises. Philo's views on the politics of Rome with regard to the Jews are then described in three points. First, Philo fully recognizes a number of great benefits brought by the Roman empire. Second, he displays an unambiguous political loyalty towards Rome as a political and cultural entity. But third, he fiercely attacks officials representing this entity, if and inasmuch they are the cause of threats for the Jewish identity. (HMK)

M. Poljak, 'Filon Aleksandrijski kao spona izmedu antike i Srednjeg vijeka [Polish: Philo of Alexandria as a Link between Antiquity and the Middle Ages] (izmedu d crossed),' *Filozofska istraživanja (hatchet on second z)* 29 (2009) 657–668.

Introductory article in Polish with the aim of showing how Philo made a contribution to the understanding of the relation of revealed religion to philosophy and also how questions that appear in his philosophy but cannot be explicitly found in the Greek philosophy became dominant during the Middle Ages. (DTR; based on the author's abstract)

R. Radice, 'Philo's Theology and Theory of Creation,' in A. Kamesar (ed.), *The Cambridge Companion to Philo* (Cambridge 2009) 124–145.

Philo does not follow the usual philosophical method of speaking about God, but takes as his starting-point the exegesis of scripture, which is regarded as containing absolute truth, even if its language can often be obscure and requiring allegorical interpretation. For this reason Philo's chief ideas about God all lead to certain vacillations in his thought, e.g. on God's knowability, whether he is personal or impersonal, whether he is transcendent or immanent, whether he is absolutely unique, whether his power is finite or infinite, and so on. The chapter then goes on to discuss Philo's theory of creation, in which we find for the first time the doctrine of the Ideas as thoughts of God. The next section discusses the nature of the Powers and the Logos, as well as angels and divine pneuma, and ends with the Ideas, which for Philo are active causes in creation, not just objects of thought or models. In his conclusion the author returns to the relationship between God and the world. Philo espoused a mixed type of creation. For the creation of the noetic world we can speak of *creatio ex nihilo*, but for material reality matter is required. Yet Philo, unlike Plato, is nearly always positive about the cosmos. (DTR)

T. Rajak, *Translation and Survival. The Greek Bible of the Ancient Jewish Diaspora* (Oxford–New York 2009), passim.

Philo is a central figure in this wide-ranging, landmark discussion of the place of the Greek Bible in Jewish life and culture in the ancient world. In Chapter 1, 'The *Letter of Aristeas* between History and Myth,' Tessa Rajak argues that Philo's account of the translation of the Greek Torah (*Mos.* 2.26–44) illustrates the reality of acceptance among Alexandrian Jews of Aristeas' location of the translation event in Alexandria; Philo's account of the festival on the island of Pharos celebrates the translation as a real event and as 'a ritualized re-enactment of the collective memory of Alexandrian Jewry' (p. 35). Philo plays a foundational role in the evolution of the Aristeas tradition by introducing the idea that the translators were divinely inspired in their work, a theme developed by Christian authors though not shared, for example, by Josephus (pp. 36, 313). Philo figures prominently in Chapter 3, 'The Jewish Diaspora in Graeco-Roman Antiquity' (pp. 92–124, esp. 101–111): Rajak emphasizes that Philo, like Josephus, does not make a sharp conceptual divide between Jews in the land of Israel and those outside it; and that both make plentiful reference to an existing or longed-for homeland. In Chapter 4, 'Staying Jewish: Language and Identity in the Greek Bible,' there is an important discussion of Philo's view of the sanctity of the Greek translation of the Torah, based on *Mos.* 2.38–40 (pp. 139–140): Philo's theory of a one-to-one correspondence of the Hebrew with the Greek serves to strengthen his view of the inspired nature of the translation and the equality of the Greek with the Hebrew. In the same chapter, a rich discussion of ʟxx language used by ancient Jewish authors includes Philo's treatment of the word αἰών in *Mut.* 12 (p. 132). Regarding the question of Philo's knowledge of Hebrew, and his use of etymologies which rely largely on Hebrew meanings, Rajak argues that whether Philo knew Hebrew or not, 'he might reasonably have availed himself of a scholarly aid by way of a prepared name list...or of some kind of glossary' (p. 149); and that the use of etymologies from the Hebrew 'suggests that the Hebrew source remained a reference point, an object of respect, the perceived authority' (p. 150). Such expressions of profound respect for the Hebrew source probably reflect social reality. Evidence for Philo's knowledge of Palestinian exegetical traditions suggests that Alexandrian Jewish scholars might well have known Hebrew and must have acquired their knowledge of Palestinian traditions through the medium of the Hebrew language. Given how much uncertainty remains in this area, Rajak concludes, 'there is no room for building arguments about the total loss of Hebrew among the intellectual elite of Alexandrian Jewry, even in Philo's day' (p. 150). In Chapter 7, 'Parallels and Models,' Philo is also significant in Rajak's study of different models of text-based communities and of 'Bible-soaked' Jewish communities in particular (pp. 251–256). Philo's exegetical works exemplify the primary orientation of Hellenistic-Jewish authors towards 'bridge-building' between cultures, making connections between their Jewish lives and their Greek-speaking environment. For Jews like Philo, the Greek Bible proved 'an incalculable resource,' allowing them to live Jewish lives in Greek; immeasurable too was its contribution to that 'balancing act that they had to perform to ensure their continuity and survival as an ethnic and religious minority' (p. 256). (SJKP)

J. R. Royse, 'The Works of Philo,' in A. Kamesar (ed.), *The Cambridge Companion to Philo* (Cambridge 2009) 32–64.

This chapter, which was written in collaboration with the volume's editor, Adam Kamesar, gives an overview of the current scholarly consensus on how Philo's writings should be classified. They are divided into three main groups. (1) the three exegetical series: (a) the *Quaestiones,* (b) the Allegorical Commentary, and (c) the Exposition of the Law; (2) apologetic and historical works, among which *Mos.* is placed; (3) philosophical works. Some lost and spurious works are also listed. The question of chronology is also dealt with, and finally a brief discussion is devoted to the transmission of the Philonic corpus. The article also touches on many issues relating to the purpose and structure of Philo's writings, and esp. the three main corpora of exegetical writings. (ACG)

D. T. RUNIA, 'Philo and the Early Christian Fathers,' in A. KAMESAR (ed.), *The Cambridge Companion to Philo* (Cambridge 2009) 210–230.

It is a paradox that that the Philonic legacy was preserved by a group of whom he had never heard and who would later actively oppose his own religion. The chapter focuses on the question of why Philo's Christian successors adopted him and preserved his works. In the first part the author follows a largely chronological trajectory through the list of patristic authors who made use of Philo's writings, beginning with his Alexandrian successors Clement, Origen and Didymus, then moving to Eusebius, the Cappadocians and Theodore of Mopsuestia, and finishing with the fourth century Latin authors Ambrose, Jerome and Augustine. Mention is also made of three later compilations that contain valuable Philonica, the *Catenae on Genesis and Exodus*, Procopius of Gaza's *Commentary on the Octateuch*, and the *Sacra parallela* of John of Damascus, all of which preserve earlier material. In the second part the author then proceeds to outline three main reasons for Philo's survival and success in the Christian tradition. The first is his role as a historian and an apologist for the Jewish tradition, the second is his value as an exegete and interpreter of the Pentateuch, the third is his role as a theologian and philosopher. It is noted that by far the greatest number of explicit references occur in the second area of biblical interpretation, but that it would be a mistake to separate this usage too strictly from the other two. The chapter ends with a brief discussion on the role of Philo as a Jew in the Christian tradition. This was always recognized, but Philo had the posthumous good fortune of being taken up by the Christian tradition before the contentious anti-heretical and anti-Jewish atmosphere developed after the Council of Nicea in the fourth century. (DTR)

D. T. RUNIA, 'The Theme of Flight and Exile in the Allegorical Thought World of Philo of Alexandria,' *The Studia Philonica Annual* 21 (2009) 1–24.

The paper was originally presented at a conference on the subject of 'Exile in literature' organized by Prof. Chr. Riedweg (Zurich). It aims to describe the allegorical thought-world of Philo with specific reference to the theme of flight and exile in his writings. It starts with Philo's own experience which was not one of exile but of being the member of a minority group in a large city. Against this background Philo developed the method of allegorical exegesis and thus constructed an 'allegorical thought-world' which needs to be introduced before it can be entered into and understood. It is marked by four main features: (1) it is a form of textual hermeneutics; (2) it involves the relation and application of biblical texts to other conceptual frameworks which are thought to underlie the literal text; (3) it goes beyond the interpretation of single texts in order to situate them in larger networks of interpretation which form coherent systems in their own right; (4) the interpretation of a text also involves a 'performance' aspect which the reader experiences through reading the allegorical treatise in which it is contained. It is then pointed out that the term φυγή (flight) has a double aspect, both flight from and flight to. Against this background the author then treats the subject of flight and exile as an exegetical theme under ten headings which basically follow the trajectory of the Pentateuch: in the beginning, the banishment from paradise, the time that evil prevails, the first Patriarch, Isaac and Jacob, Joseph, the Exodus out of Egypt, the election of the Levites, the cities of refuge, and expulsion from the Mosaic polity. Analysis of this complex theme leads to the identification of three main lines of thought. The first is the exile from the city (or garden) of virtue, which in the spiritual sense is Israel, the people who are orientated towards God. The second is the flight from here to the higher realm, which is also linked to the theme of migration. Philo's thought here is certainly influenced by allegorical interpretations of Homer's *Odyssey* in terms of Platonic philosophy. The third line of thought is flight understood as taking refuge in God.

This conception has strong biblical roots and is closely linked to the advocacy of a Levitic spirituality. The paper concludes with some words on the relation between Judaism and Hellenism in Philo's thought-world. It may seem that Judaism triumphs, but it is Judaism of a very particular kind. The main aim of allegory is to interpret scripture in such a way that it is directly relevant to the life of the reader. In this task Hellenism still plays a vital role. In the final analysis the two must remain linked if Philo's real achievement is to be properly understood. (DTR)

D. T. RUNIA, 'Philo of Alexandria,' in G. OPPY and N. TRAKAKIS (edd.), *The History of Western Philosophy of Religion. Volume 1 Ancient Philosophy of Religion* (Durham 2009) 133–144.

Synoptic presentation of Philo's writing and thought in the context of the history of the Western philosophy of religion, with brief sections on his writings and method, epistemology, theology, the doctrine of creation, the nature of humanity, and ethics. The author concludes that, despite Philo's unquestioning loyalty to Judaism, his thought is 'a splendid illustration of the cultural and ideological power of Hellenism (p. 143). But the method of basing philosophy on the acceptance of a body of authoritative scripture was innovative and was to have a long future in the history of Western religious thought. (DTR)

D. T. RUNIA, E. BIRNBAUM, A. C. GELJON, H. M. KEIZER, J. P. MARTÍN, M. R. NIEHOFF, J. RIAUD, G. SCHIMANOWSKI, and T. SELAND, 'Philo of Alexandria: an Annotated Bibliography 2006,' *The Studia Philonica Annual* 21 (2009) 73–122.

The yearly annotated bibliography of Philonic studies prepared by the members of the International Philo Bibliography Project covers the year 2006 (99 items), with addenda for the years 1998–2005 (15 items), and provisional lists for the years 2007–09. This is the final year that is included in the new volume of the assembled Philonic bibliographies for the years 1997–2006 published in 2012 (= RRS2). (DTR)

D. T. RUNIA and G. E. STERLING (edd.), *The Studia Philonica Annual*, vol. 21 (Atlanta 2009).

The twenty-first volume of the Journal dedicated to Philonic studies contains three general articles, a review article, the usual bibliography section (see summary above), and six book reviews. These are followed by the customary News and Notes section, Notes on contributors and Instructions for contributors. The various articles are summarized elsewhere in this bibliography. (DTR)

P. SADHE, *The Motif of Mission in Philo of Alexandria: Philo and Jewish Proselytising* (diss. Hebrew University, Jerusalem 2009).

This paper attempts to demonstrate the ways in which Philo and the writers of 3 Maccabees, the Letter of Aristeas and the Wisdom of Solomon used the tools of Greek philosophy and Jewish culture. After a summary of the social and literary relationship of the Alexandrian community to Jerusalem and the Temple there, a close reading of the four authors' works reveals the ways which the idea of Temple ties the Jews to their fellow Jews in Palestine and to the Greek world which surrounded them. (DTR; based on author's summary)

K. O. SANDNES, *The Challenge of Homer: School, Pagan Poets and Early Christianity* (London 2009), esp. 68–78.

The present study by the Norwegian scholar Karl Olav Sandnes, Professor at the School of Theology, Oslo, is an investigation into the school system of antiquity and how the early Christians related to it. By focusing on the role of Homer in the processes of learning, it is also a study of the expression of Hellenistic culture through Greek language, mythology, sport, temples, theatres etc., and how the early Christians related to these aspects in their learning processes: 'The attendance of Christian boys (and presumably some girls) at these pagan schools became a hot issue among the Christians. It is the aim of this book to describe this challenge, and to present the debate and solutions sought throughout the first five centuries C.E.' (p. 7). The study is divided into two main parts: Part 1 School and Encyclical Education in Antiquity (pp. 1–80), and Part 2 The Christian Agôn over Encyclical Studies in the First Four Centuries C.E. (pp. 81–277). A brief section is devoted to Philo on his own because he is considered to be of particular interest as a figure who bridges the historical gap between the later Christian sources and the silence of the New Testament. Philo is also relevant because the early Christians found themselves in cultural situations very much like the Jews in relaton to the pagan culture. The section on Philo presents a brief review of important aspects of Philo's views on encyclical education, describing how he uses Sarah and Hagar to illustrate the relationship between encyclical studies and philosophy, and how he presents the former as a preparatory stage. In this way Philo demonstrates that he has accepted encyclical teaching as a natural part of the lives of at least the elite members in the Jewish community in Alexandria. In asking the question 'why Encyclical Studies' (pp. 74–77), Sandnes argues that although encyclical studies represented a danger, Philo did not abandon the pedagogical institutions in the pagan city. The real *paideia*, however, was the Law of Moses (pp. 77–78), while the encyclical *paideia* was a preparatory stage. (TS)

C. H. SAVELLE, 'Canonical and Extracanonical Portraits of Balaam,' *Bibliotheca Sacra (Dallas)* 166 (2009) 387–404.

The Hebrew Bible may be seen as preserving both positive and negative traditions about the non-Israelite prophet Balaam, called on by Balak, king of Moab, to curse the people of Israel. In Num 22–24, Balaam emerges as a figure inspired by the Spirit of God to bless Israel; in other traditions outside the Torah, Balaam is portrayed much more negatively. In this article, Philo's interpretation of Balaam (pp. 392–393) is seen as consistently negative, following the overall approach in the Hebrew Bible and most of the extracanonical sources reviewed, though Josephus is markedly less negative in his appraisal. Philo's evaluation of Balaam is consistent with Philo's exalted view of Moses, the opponent of Balaam: anyone who opposed Moses would emerge badly. (SJKP)

P. SCHÄFER, *The Origins of Jewish Mysticism* (Tübingen 2009), esp. 154–174.

In this volume the distinguished scholar of early Jewish mysticism has distilled the fruits of his research on the origins of Jewish mysticism in the pre-kabbalistic period. After chapters on Ezekiel, Enoch, apocalyptic Judaism, and Qumran, he turns his attention to

Philo in a chapter entitled Philo: the Ascent of the Soul (pp. 154–174). The argument moves in three steps. Firstly Schäfer sets out Philo's conception of God, starting with *Spec.* 1.32–50 and then turning to texts in the Allegorical Commentary. The Logos and Wisdom play a key role, since it is through them that God intervenes in our human world and it is through them that we can approach the higher divine world. The next section presents Philo's views on body and soul, senses and mind. Philo here is dependent on the philosophical distinction between body and soul which is alien to biblical Judaism. The true philosopher even during his life in the body can obtain a foretaste of the life his soul will lead when released from the body. In so doing it is possible to direct the mind to the invisible and eternal world above, and this is something that cannot be learnt, but springs up in the soul. In the final section the soul's vision of God is outlined. This occurs primarily through divine possession (*Her.* 264–265). The paragon of such a prophetic state is Moses and his ascent to Mount Sinai, where he passes from duality to unity (but this does not necessarily mean complete unification with the divine). Ultimately it is possible for any human soul to follow this route if it has been thoroughly purified. Occasionally, as in *Ebr.* 152, Philo does use the more biblical language of the vision of God. But usually he describes the ascent of the soul in terms of the ecstatic state of the mind, which is given by God as a gift. This ascent occurs in stages. Philo says little about the final stage, which is described in terms of tranquillity but is not attainable for human beings. He is more outspoken about the immediately preceding stage when the soul attains to the intelligible world of the divine Logos. Philo thus 'arrives at a completely new answer to the question of how God approaches his created world and how human beings in turn approach God' (p. 173). In so doing he goes far beyond the biblical and post-biblical concept of God revealing himself to the chosen seer or the human hero ascending to heaven. The key to this development is his splitting of the unity of body and soul, which enables him to focus on the fate of the soul as the better half of human existence. (DTR)

D. R. Schwartz, 'Philo, his Family, and his Times,' in A. Kamesar (ed.), *The Cambridge Companion to Philo* (Cambridge 2009) 9–31.

The purpose of the chapter is to provide background information on Philo and his historical milieu. It commences with a judicious discussion of the little we know about Philo's own life and the little more that we know about his family, including references to the sources on which this knowledge is based. The bulk of the chapter focuses on Philo's situation within the Judaism of his day. It is argued that as a diaspora Jew who was well established in the Alexandrian Jewish community, Philo tended to minimize the connection with Judaea and Jerusalem, and instead to favour a 'transcendental Judaism' which was furthermore combined with a pro-Roman (and anti-Alexandrian) stance. In his defence of the Alexandrian Jews and Judaism in general, however, Philo was not consistent, as is illustrated by his view of the Jamnia incident (*Legat.* 200–203). The article concludes with two striking speculations, namely (1) that it is hard not to sympathize with the Emperor Gaius when he was confronted by a Platonist thinker who was not prepared to accept the consequences of his own ideas, and (2) that if Philo had adopted a different attitude to the Jews of Jamnia, a process might have been set in motion that 'might have prevented the chain of events that was to bring his nephew, a generation later, to preside over the burning down of the temple his own father, Philo's brother, had so extravagantly funded' (p. 31). (DTR)

G. SELLIN, *Studien zu Paulus und zum Epheserbrief, edited by* D. *Sänger,* Forschungen zur Religion und Literatur des Alten und Neuen Testaments 229 (Göttingen 2009).

This collection of studies contains a number of articles pertaining to Philonic studies which have been summarized in earlier bibliographies and are now reprinted in an unaltered form except corrections of mistakes, updated orthography and unified quotations: 'Das "Geheimnis" der Weisheit und das Rätsel der "Christuspartei" (zu 1Kor 1–4),' first published in 1982 (pp. 9–36, = R-R 8248); 'Die religionsgeschichtlichen Hintergründe der paulinischen Christusmystik,' first published in 1996 (pp. 91–115, = RRS 9681); 'Hagar und Sara. Religionsgeschichtliche Hintergründe der Schriftallegorese Gal 4,21–31,' first published in 1999 (pp. 116–137, = RRS2 9976). (JLB)

G. SFARMENI GASPARRO, 'Scienza caldea e Dio unico in Filone Alessandrino. Una risposta giudaica alla teologia cosmica ellenistica,' in H.-J. GEHRKE and A. MASTROCINQUE (edd.), *Rom und der Osten im I. Jahrhundert v.Chr. (Akkulturation oder Kampf der Kulturen?),* Akten des Humboldt-Kollegs Verona, 19–21 febbraio 2005 (Hierà, 12–13) (Cosenza 2009) 337–391.

A study of Philo's views on 'Chaldean science,' or in other words, his position with regard to Hellenistic cosmic theology. With the help of many and ample quotations (in translation) from various Philonic treatises, the author illustrates how the intellectual and religious 'migration' of Abram, a Chaldean, from observation of the cosmos (Chaldean science) to perception of the existence of the One God and Creator, represents for Philo a way open for every human being. Fundamental for Philo is the intrinsic relationship between 'Chaldean science' or its counterpart, Hellenistic cosmic/astral theology, and polytheism, as well as the role of divine revelation on the way towards knowledge of (the existence, not the essence, of) the One God. While Philo is clear in his rejection of polytheism, he is at the same time open to a nuanced appreciation of a cosmic religion (with its potential polytheistic risks) which he identifies with the first phase of Abram/ Abraham's journey. Philo does not accept the apologetic tradition in Alexandrian Judaism that presents Abraham as the first astrologer or sees his migration as a way of continuity rather than of radical change. The article concludes with a survey of texts variously illustrating this tradition (*Testament of Orpheus,* Artapanus, *Book of Jubilees, Sibylline Oracles* Book 3, Josephus). (HMK)

F. SIEGERT, 'Philo and the New Testament,' in A. KAMESAR (ed.), *The Cambridge Companion to Philo* (Cambridge 2009) 175–209.

A comprehensive review of Philo and the New Testament is yet to be written; in this chapter of the Cambridge Companion (see above under the editor's name) Siegert provides an overview that by necessity must be brief, but nevertheless manages to provide a great deal of information. Taking his point of departure in the New Testament, he groups its writings as follows: The Epistle to the Hebrews; The Pauline Corpus; The Special case of 1 Corinthians; Luke, including the Pauline School; and The Gospel according to John. Each of these five sections is then divided into fourteen subsections, providing a topical focus as follows: Formalities, Literary Genres Employed, Specialized Language, Metaphors; Scripture and the Methods of Interpretation; Knowledge of God, Natural and Revealed, Secrets of the Divine Name; Wisdom and Eternal Torah, Angels, The Heavenly Realm; The Divine

Logos; Creation and Duality, The Two Powers; Freedom of Choice, Evil and Sin, Grace and Salvation; Man: Man and Woman; Sacred History: From the Patriarchs to Moses; The Exodus: Passover, Revealed Torah; The Commandments, Concrete Ethics; Cult, Prayer, Rites, and Holy Places; Eschatology. The chapter ends with a review of the main contrasts between these two bodies of writings, following the same set of fourteen topics. (TS)

F. Siegert, 'Philon Über die Vorsehung: ein Gespräch,' in J. Frey, S. Krauter and H. Lichtenberger (edd.), *Heil und Geschichte. Die Geschichtsbezogenheit des Heils und das Problem der Heilsgeschichte in der biblischen Tradition und in der theologischen Deutung*, Wissenschaftliche Untersuchungen zum Neuen Testament 248 (Tübingen 2009) 767–781.

Siegert presents an imaginary debate of early Christian, Greek and Roman philosophers (disciples of Apollos, Luke, the presbyter John, Plutarch, his brother Lamprias, the Stoic politician Flavius Euphanes and the Epicurean Boëthos) in Ephesus on the term *pronoia*, in which Philo's views appear via his reception by the Christian participants, especially the disciples of Apollos. Philonic themes mentioned are: (1) *Prov.* 2.102 with its view that providence only determines the broad context and focuses on the general good, so that it is not problematic that innocents get hurt occasionally with the guilty; (2) the treatise *Prov.* 2, addressed to Tiberius Iulius Alexander, may have encouraged him to embark on his Roman career; (3) *Legat.* and *Flacc.* 125f, 191, 170 present a more nuanced discussion of the divine providence focusing on the salvation of the Jews from oppression; here Philo remains silent with regard to the Alexandrian misbehaviour during the funerary rites for Gaius' sister Julia Drusilla. (JLB)

G. E. Sterling, 'How Do You Introduce Philo of Alexandria? The Cambridge Companion to Philo,' *The Studia Philonica Annual* 21 (2009) 63–72.

The author presents an informative and stimulating review of the recent introductory volume on Philo in the Cambridge Companion series (see above under Kamesar). He first outlines how it stands in a line of introductions by Goodenough, Sandmel and Schenck. In part one, the three essays on Philo's life and thought by Schwartz, Royse and Kamesar are excellent, but in each case they show that there remains more work to be done. For Philo's background we need more work on his family, for example inscriptions mentioning two 2nd century figures with the same name as his nephew Tiberius Julius Alexander. For his writings more work should be done on the internal cross-references in his *œuvre*. And for his allegorical method we need to understand more about his commentaries qua commentary. In part two, differences in the interpretation of his thought by the Italian scholars Termini and Radice show the difficulty of the task. For Sterling the key factors are that Philo wrote exegetically rather than systematically, and that he preserves different traditions at times. The chapter on his ethics (Levy) views him primarily against the background of Hellenistic philosophy. The final three essays explore his influence on the New Testament (Siegert) and the Church fathers (Runia), and address the question why later Jews failed to preserve his work (Winston). There remains work to be done, however, on pagan authors' knowledge of his work. Sterling concludes that this introductory work now sets the standard. The test of the volume will be whether it opens up Philo's world to those students who read his works. (DTR)

G. E. Sterling, 'Philosophy as the Handmaid of Wisdom: Philosophy in the Exegetical Traditions of Alexandrian Jews,' in R. Hirsch-Luipold, H. Görgemanns and M. von Albrecht (edd.), *Religiose Philosophie und philosophische Religion der fruhen Kaiserzeit* (Tübingen 2009) 67–98.

Informative and valuable survey of the use that Alexandrian Jews made of philosophical traditions in the context of a wide-ranging German research project investigating religious philosophy and philosophical religion in the early Imperial period. There can be little doubt that Hellenistic philosophy influenced Jewish thought, though the nature of that influence has been insufficiently researched. Sterling gives an outline of the major witnesses in the tradition of Alexandrian Judaism, focusing on their method, their understanding of philosophy and finally their theological views. The first two witnesses discussed are Aristobulus and the author of the *Letter of Aristeas*. Sterling then makes an interesting innovation by devoting a section to the 'Allegorists' as a separate group of exegetes and thinkers. For our knowledge of them we are wholly dependent on what Philo tells us, which is not always so easy to interpret. For example, we can be certain that they used differing philosophical frameworks, including Stoic and Platonist, but it is difficult to speak with confidence about their theology. The final section is devoted to Philo himself. After discussing the various series of writings that he produced, in which allegorical interpretation forms the heart of his enterprise taken as a whole, Sterling devotes attention to his view of the relationship between philosophy and wisdom (from which of course the title of the article is taken—based on *Congr.* 79) and the preeminent place of theology in his thought. In conclusion Sterling argues that there is evidence to suggest that these ideas were not the exclusive property of an intellectual elite, but also filtered down to the rank and file of Alexandrian Jews. When Philo says that Jews practice their ancestral philosophy by studying on the Sabbath (*Mos.* 2.26), we should give him some credence. (DTR)

G. J. Steyn, '"Perfecting Knowledge and Piety" (Philo, *Contempl.* 3, 25): Intertextual Similarities between Philo's Therapeutae and Lukan Early Christianity,' *Neotestamentica* 43 (2009) 424–448.

Following an introductory discussion of Eusebius' construction of the *Therapeutae* in Christian terms and of the similarities between the Qumran Community and Therapeutae, the article focuses on distinctive aspects of Philo's description of the Therapeutae in his treatise *Contempl.* and comparable elements in early Christian communities as described in the New Testament. No explicit connection is claimed between Philo's *Therapeutae* and Luke's account of Christianity, but comparative study of these sources is seen as revealing elements shared in common which may explain aspects of early Christianity in its Jewish context. Key areas for comparative discussion include: the art of healing; abandonment of property; abandonment of family and friends; contemplative way of life; approach to Scripture; style of worship (sermons, hymns and prayer); significance of the Sabbath (treated quite briefly) and Shavuot; social formation and community rules. (SJKP)

G. J. Steyn, *A Quest for the Assumed* lxx *Vorlage of the Explicit Quotations in Hebrews* (DLitt thesis, University of Stellenbosch 2009).

The Vorlage of the explicit quotations in Hebrews remains an unresolved question. In this thoroughly researched dissertation the author examines the question from a mainly historical and text-critical angle. On the basis of his investigations he reaches the noteworthy conclusion that almost all of the Torah quotations are already found in the works of Philo, and esp. in the book *Leg.* 3; see the table on p. 379. In addition, their readings agree with each other—both of them often against the LXX and MT versions, which might be an indication of another version (the Old Greek?) that was used by both. If the author of Hebrews did not use Philo directly, then they know and used the same literary and/or oral tradition. It is also observed that there are important parallel quotations in the early Christian writings by Clement of Rome and Justin Martyr. (DTR; based on author's summary)

H. SVEBAKKEN, *Philo of Alexandria's Exposition of the Tenth Commandment* (diss. Loyola University of Chicago 2009).

As part of a larger exposition on the Ten Commandments, Philo offers in *Spec.* 4.78b–131 a detailed exposition of both the Tenth Commandment, which he reads simply as 'You shall not desire,' and the Mosaic dietary laws, which he identifies as a distinct set of subsidiary laws designed to promote observance of the Tenth Commandment. Setting his exposition in the context of Middle-Platonic moral psychology, this dissertation, prepared under the supervision of Prof. Thomas H. Tobin, S.J., answers two fundamental questions. First, what, in Philo's view, does the Tenth Commandment prohibit? (All desire? A certain type? What type?) Second, how, in Philo's view, is the Tenth Commandment observed? (What are the mechanics of its observance? What role do the dietary laws play in its observance?) After an introduction to Philo's exposition of the Tenth Commandment and a review of previous research (chapter one), chapter two explains Philo's concept of desire, including its source, nature, function, and problematic malfunction. Chapter three explains Philo's concept of self-control, including his understanding of how the moral agent acquires self-control through practice, especially the practice of Mosaic precepts. Chapter four offers a new translation, with commentary, of Philo's exposition of the Tenth Commandment, explaining how Philo uses the conceptual nexus of desire, self-control, and practice as an overarching expository agenda for his work. Chapter five summarizes the results and suggests lines of further research. (DTR; based on author's summary)

C. TERMINI, 'Philo's Thought within the Context of Middle Judaism,' in A. KAMESAR (ed.), *The Cambridge Companion to Philo* (Cambridge 2009) 95–123.

This rich contribution commences with some remarks on how the scholarly paradigm of the first half of the 20th century, which distinguished between the normative Judaism of Palestine and the syncretistic Judaism of the diaspora, has now been abandoned in favour of a more unified view in which the Judaism of the Second Temple period, now perhaps best labelled as 'Middle Judaism' (Boccacini), is seen to display considerable diversity in both a synchronic and a diachronic perspective. The aim of the chapter is to place Philo within this pluralistic context and to highlight the rich network of links that exist between his work and contemporary Jewish literature. The topics discussed are systematically ordered in four parts. Part one treats Theology and examines the subjects of monotheism, the personified attributes of God (Logos, Wisdom, Powers), and angels. Part two moves on to the Theory of Man and deals with the creation of man and sin, salvation: retribution and eschatology, and messianism. Part three focuses on the Law and highlights circumcision, the Sabbath, and the dietary laws. The final part is devoted to Philo's views on Israel, in which the author expresses agreement with Ellen Birnbaum that the categories 'the Jews' and 'Israel' are not co-extensive. The author concludes: 'In Philo's vision of things, human merit and divine grace meet in synergy and his elitism retains an inclusive quality. If the

Jews, or at least some of them, have reached the ultimate objective by virtue of the excellence of their laws and traditions, it is not impossible for others to reach the same goal by means of the teachings of philosophy.' (p. 123) (DTR)

H. TERVANOTKO, 'Miriam's mistake: Numbers 12 renarrated in Demetrius the Chronographer, 4Q377 (*Apocryphal Pentateuch B*), *Legum Allegoriae* and the Pentateuchal Targumim,' in D. W. ROOKE (ed.), *Embroidered Garments: Priests and Gender in Biblical Israel* (Sheffield 2009) 131–148.

Of the seven appearances of the figure of Miriam in the Hebrew Bible, it is only in Num 12:1–15 that she is represented negatively. In that context, Miriam is presented as being in conflict with Moses, and punished, but the reasons given for the dispute are varied (cf. Num 12:1, 2), and the reason for her punishment is not given. Following a brief introduction to the story of the conflict between Miriam and Moses as represented in the Hebrew Bible, this article explores a range of Greco-Roman Jewish texts referring to this conflict (Demetrius the Chronographer, 4*QApocryphal Pentateuch B*, Philo's *Leg.*, and Targums Onqelos, Neofiti I and Pseudo-Jonathan). As regards Philo (pp. 137–139), focusing on *Leg.* 2.66–67 in which Philo quotes Num. 12, he presents the figure of Miriam as a symbol of 'irrational behaviour and the negative part of the soul' (p. 138). In this context, Philo describes by contrast the excellence of the 'Ethiopian woman' whom God married to Moses and who represents the soul's power of vision. In other contexts, however, Philo can treat Miriam—in her role as leader of the Song at the Sea (Exod 15)—as a positive symbol of the rational power of the soul. In Philo's interpretation, Miriam's mistake is to speak against Moses (Num 12), but when she works together with Moses (Exod 15), she becomes a positive symbol. (SJKP)

M. TILLY, 'Aus der Literatur zum antiken Judentum 1997–2008,' *Theologische Rundschau* 74 (2009) 147–178.

Monographs on Philo and themes relating to his thought are among the scholarly works discussed in a wide-ranging review of studies on ancient Judaism published in the years 1997–2008. Among the studies discussed are monographs by J. S. Allen (for summary see *SPhA* vol. 23, p. 98), P. Borgen (RRS2 9706), N. G. Cohen (*SPhA* vol. 22, p. 217), E. Koskenniemi (RRS 20539), D. T. Runia and H. M. Keizer (RRS 1214), A. T. Wright (RRS 20584). (JLB)

D. C. TIMMER, *Creation, Tabernacle, and Sabbath. The Sabbath Frame of Exodus 31:12–17; 35:1–3 in Exegetical and Theological Perspective*, Forschungen zur Religion und Literatur des Alten und Neuen Testaments 227 (Göttingen 2009), esp. 155–157.

This is the revised version of a PhD supervised by Richard E. Averbeck at Trinity International University (Deerfield), focusing on the significance of the material ('the sabbath frame') in Exod 31:12–17 and 35:1–3 which frames the story of the Golden Calf (Exod 32–34). The major part of the book deals with exegetical questions about the sabbath frame (chapter 2); hermeneutical and theological reflections on this material (chapter 3); the exegesis of Exod 32–34, focusing on the theme of divine presence (chapter 4); and the themes of divine presence and forgiveness in Exod 32–34, and of the relationship between the Tabernacle and the Sabbath in Exodus (chapter 5). The last main chapter (6) deals with the themes explored earlier in this study as they appear in later Jewish and Christian writings, including *Jubilees*, the Damascus Document, Philo, and Hebrews. With regard to Philo, the author restricts himself to a very brief overview (pp. 155–157) of Philo's treatment of the Sabbath, highlighting its universal significance. (SJKP)

R. Tomes, 'Educating Gentiles: Explanations of Torah in the New Testament, Philo and Josephus,' in M. Tait and P. Oakes (edd.), *The Torah in the New Testament: Papers Delivered at the Manchester-Lausanne Seminar of June 2008,* The Library of New Testament Studies 401 (Edinburgh 2009) 208–217.

This article aims to show what New Testament authors wanted non-Jews to know about Jewish Law and how it should be evaluated, and how far Philo and Josephus shared such views. Philo and Josephus agree with the New Testament authors that the Law was given by God, and that its purpose may be summarized in either the Decalogue or in duty to God and neighbour. New Testament references to the Law refer almost exclusively to the laws of the Decalogue or the commands to love God and neighbour, while for Philo and Josephus, the Law also includes the special laws found in the Torah and the customary traditions of observing them. Philo and Josephus are concerned with defending existing laws while New Testament authors focus on establishing ethical patterns of behaviour appropriate for converts from different cultural contexts. (SJKP)

F. Trabattoni, 'Philo, *De opificio mundi* 7–12,' in M. Bonazzi and J. Opsomer (edd.), *The Origins of the Platonic System: Platonisms of the Early Empire and their Philosophical Contexts,* Collection des Études Classiques 23 (Leuven 2009) 113–122.

The aim of the brief article is to reconstruct the philosophical meaning and the polemical targets of the introductory passage at *Opif.* 7–12. It raises three problems: who are the thinkers cited at the outset; are they the same ones who are charged with denying providence a little further on? and to whom can the metaphysical theory in §§8–9 be ascribed. The author takes issue with the views of A. P. Bos, who denies that the passage has Aristotle in mind and ascribes the views attacked to the Chaldeans (see RRS2 9824). He puts forward arguments (probably though not wholly decisive) to show that Philo does have Aristotle and his followers in mind in his polemics. As for the positive views put forward, they are not simply Platonic, but are the result of the attempt to reconcile Platonic and Mosaic philosophy. (DTR)

G. Veltri, *Renaissance Philosophy in Jewish Garb. Foundations and Challenges in Judaism on the Eve of Modernity,* Supplements to the Journal of Jewish Thought and Philosophy 8 (Leiden 2009), esp. 83ff.

This study is devoted to Jewish humanists and their ideas. One of the results of the study is that it was in the Renaissance that the adjective 'Jewish,' used in connection with philosophy, first took on the meaning that it has in the modern period. Chapter four deals with the writings of Azariah de' Rossi, who was the first Jewish writer since antiquity to deal with Philo's writings. This chapter is based on an article from 1995; see RRS 9588. (ACG)

H. DE VRIES, 'Philosophia ancilla theologiae. Allegory and Ascension in Philo's *On Mating with the Preliminary Studies (De congressu quaerendae eruditionis gratia),' The Bible and Critical Theory (Monash University ePress)* 5, no. 3 (2009).

English translation by Jack Ben-Levi of an article originally written in Dutch and published in 1987. See the summary at RRS 87100. It presents an analysis and evaluation of the allegorical method of interpretation as practised by Philo in *Congr*. The bibliography has been slightly updated. No mention is made of the Dutch original version. The journal in which the article is published is available online only. (DTR)

D. WESTERKAMP, *Die philonische Unterscheidung: Aufklärung, Orientalismus und Konstruktion der Philosophie* (Munich 2009), passim.

The book studies the reception of Philo's *Logos* idea in the context of the study of the distinction of 'Oriental,' 'Jewish' and 'Occidental' philosophy since the Enlightenment. The distinction between God and the *Logos*, 'substance' and 'subject,' 'principle' and 'person' in the absolute is called the 'Philonic distinction,' independenly of whether it is used with a conscious reference to Philo. In the early days Philo's thought was seen as part of the corruption of the *philosophia hebraeorum* since the patriarchs (Horn, 1620–1670). Philo was seen as a thoroughly Hellenized example of a *philosophia judaeorum*. Later on, Brucker (c. 1731–1736) regards Philo as influenced not just by Platonic but also by Jewish sources and his arithmology is seen as the origin of the Kabbalah. Particularly for Hegel, Philo is the precursor of the Christian bi- and trinitarian as well as Neoplatonic philosophy, carrying distinctions inside the deity and moving the absolute 'one' of Platonism into a development of personalization and subjectivation. Philo is criticized only for being too purely focused on thought, not on revelation. Jewish philosophy rejected Philo for the same reason. In the 19th century Philo was seen as soil for the Kabbalah, Gnosis and similar developments. Feuerbach inverted the Philonic distinction, reading the *Logos* as no longer a division inside God, but an aspect of mankind. See also the English language article summarized at *SPhA* vol. 23, p. 137. (JLB)

D. WINSTON, 'Philo and Rabbinic Literature,' in A. KAMESAR (ed.), *The Cambridge Companion to Philo* (Cambridge 2009) 231–253.

Scholars have been divided on why the Rabbis never mention, let alone engage with, Philo's writings and thought. Winston suggests it may have been caused by their disapproval of Philo's ignorance of the Hebrew scriptures and their lack of interest in his philosophical approach. There are, however, some echoes of his thought in rabbinic texts, for example Rabbi Hoshaia of Caesarea's image of the king building a palace in *Gen. Rabb.* 1.1. Certainly, the evidence for Philo's ignorance of Hebrew is overwhelming. On the other hand, there are clear similarities between Philo's exegesis and Palestinian rabbinic midrash. Winston argues that it is possible to prove his dependence on rabbinic material if an example can be found where he reads a doctrine into the biblical text that clashes with a fundamental philosophical principle that he holds dear. Such an example is the doctrine of repentance. In the remainder of the chapter a series of topics is dealt with in which similarities and contrasts between Philo and the Rabbis emerge. These are: God's transcendent immanence; the two types of Mosaic prophecy: predictive/ecstatic and noetic; the doctrine of natural law; various Philonic halakhah; and the doctrine of repentance already mentioned above. The chapter concludes with a brief remark on the further question of how we should interpret Philo: he is *both* Philo Judaeus and Philo philosophico-mysticus. (DTR)

K. WORST, *Regarding Women: Philo and Paul as Two Men in a Stoic World* (M.A. thesis, George Fox University, Oregon 2009).

We have not been able to procure a summary of this piece of research. (DTR)

A. YOSHIKO REED, 'The Construction and Subversion of Patriarchal Perfection: Abraham and Exemplarity in Philo, Josephus, and the Testament of Abraham,' *Journal for the Study of Judaism* 40 (2009) 185–212.

This article deals with the exemplarity of the patriarch Abraham in Philo, Josephus, and *The Testament of Abraham*. There is a special focus on how Hellenistic ideas about *exempla* were taken over and transformed by Jews and Roman writers. The idea of exemplarity, i.e., that figures from the past are examples to be imitated, was of great importance in Greek education. This notion has been taken over by Philo, who regards the Patriarchs as 'images' and 'archetypes.' Especially Abraham is regarded as an *exemplum*. For Philo, Moses as writer of the Torah is an authority comparable to that of Homer for the Greeks. In the writings of Josephus, too, Abraham is presented as a paradigmatic figure. Both Philo's and Josephus' treatment of the Patriarchs can be compared with the use of *exempla* in Roman historiography. By way of contrast, in *The Testament of Abraham* his deeds are described negatively, and this may seem to be a critique of the elevation of Abraham to the status of an ideal model. (ACG)

J. ZSENGELLÉR, 'Changes in the Balaam-Interpretation in the Hellenistic Jewish Literature (LXX , Philon, Pseudo-Philon and Josephus),' in H. LICHTENBERGER and U. MITTMANN-RICHERT (edd.), *Biblical Figures in Deuterocanonical and Cognate Literature*, Deuterocanonical and Cognate Literature Yearbook 2008 (Berlin 2009) 487–506, esp. 491–496.

The article deals with the interpretation of the figure of Balaam, as portrayed in Num 22–24, in the LXX , Philo, Pseudo-Philo, and Josephus. The LXX offers a messianic understanding of the prophecies given by Balaam. Philo, retelling the story in Mos., contrasts Balaam with Moses: Moses is the perfect and blameless man, whereas Balaam is self-interested and becomes disqualified. It is noteworthy that Balaam is never called προφήτης by Philo. He is an instrument used by the spirit to mediate the divine prophecy. Philo omits the detail of the speaking of the donkey and treats the contents of the prophecies rather freely. The author concludes that the figure of Balaam is useful for Philo in three ways: (1) He forms a sharp contrast with Moses; (2) as non-Israelite, he is the right person to interpret for non-Jews the notion of Israel as the chosen people; (3) he is a symbol of the fruitlessness of people arising against God and the Israelite people. In pseudo-Philo a positive picture of Balaam is given. Josephus stays closer to the biblical text than Philo. (ACG)

Extra items from before 2009

P. Ashwin-Siejkowski, *Clement of Alexandria: a Project of Christian Perfection* (London 2008).

This study focuses on an important theme in Clement's theology, viz. the attainment of perfection as the aim of Christian life. Though in this theology of perfection Clement is influenced by Greek philosophy, it is in fact the background of Jewish and Christian exegesis that is most crucial. Chapter two discusses Hellenistic Judaism as background. Philo was an important source for Clement, but Clement also refers to other Jewish Hellenistic writers, such as Aristobulus, Demetrius, and the poet Ezekiel. In addition, he has a profound knowledge of and admiration for the Hebrew scriptures. The author discusses two important Hebrew representations in Clement, the figure of Moses and the high priest. Both play a central role in Clement's theology of perfection. Philo inspired Clement to emphasize the role of Moses, Hebrew philosophy and the theme of Law as the original source of inspiration for the Greeks. For Clement, Moses is an example of the Christian sage who advances from visible reality to the invisible realm of God. As a Christian, however, Clement introduces the notion of the incarnated *Logos* to lead the Christian sage to an encounter with God. The second important Jewish theme in Clement is the figure of the high priest. He presents an allegorical interpretation of the entrance of the high priest into the sanctuary as the spiritual journey of the Christian sage into the divine realm. Philo's allegorical reading is present in the background of Clement's interpretation and makes its presence felt in his the identification of the high priest as the divine *Logos*, who of course is also Christ. (ACG)

A. Avidov, 'A Marginal Vision of Empire: Philo and Josephus on the Jews' Integration into Imperial Society,' in J. Pigoń (ed.), *The Children of Herodotus: Greek and Roman Historiography and Related Genres* (Newcastle upon Tyne 2008) 162–180.

The author applies the concept of marginality to the Jewish writers Philo and Josephus. Marginality is described as the phenomenon of a person or a people being part of a society and yet not fully integrated into it. It can thus be seen as a failure of social integration. Marginalization of the Jews in Roman times can be therefore best understood when set against a model of social integration of Roman society. Integration means access to the power and decision-making centres. The imperial cult was an important means for integration and a link to power. The peculiar character of the Jewish vision of empire and imperial cult comes out in Philo's *Legat*. In this treatise Philo contrasts two competing visions of the Roman social universe. One is the court of the lawless and unjust tyrant; the other is the just ruler. A just ruler allows the Jews to express their allegiance through their own religion. Avidov concludes that Philo and Josephus were marginal within a marginal culture. They had a foot in both cultures but were not at home in either one. They promoted a utopian vision of the Roman empire that was irrelevant to the interests of the Gentile addressees and incomprehensible to its Jewish ones. (ACG)

M. BERNETT, *Der Kaiserkult in Judäa unter den Herodiern und Römern: Untersuchungen zur politischen und religiösen Geschichte Judäas von 30 v. bis 66 n. Chr.*, Wissenschaftliche Untersuchungen zum Neuen Testament 1.203 (Tübingen 2007), esp. 194–202, 264–287.

Copious use is made of Philonic evidence in this detailed investigation of the Imperial cult in Judaea in the century from the Roman conquest of Egypt to the fall of Jerusalem. (DTR)

K. BERTHELOT, 'Jewish Views of Human Sacrifice in the Hellenistic and Roman Period,' in K. FINSTERBUSCH, A. LANGE and K. F. DIETHARD RÖMHELD (edd.), *Human Sacrifice in Jewish and Christian Tradition*, (Leiden 2007) 151–173.

This article investigates three aspects of Jewish views of human sacrifice: (1) the condemnation of human sacrifices, presented as a pagan abomination; (2) the 'demonization' of human sacrifices which can be found in some Qumran texts; and (3) the praise of self-sacrifice as illustrated through the interpretations of Jephthah's daughter and Isaac's near-sacrifice. In the first part it is argued that in *Spec.* 2.170 Philo implicitly alludes to the Canaanite practice of sacrificing children, as referred to in Deut 12:31, and that this allusion has an apologetic dimension (pp. 158–161). In the third part Philo's praise of Abraham's readiness to sacrifice his son in *Abr.* 170–207 and *Migr.* 140 is briefly examined (p. 169). (KB)

A. JÖRDENS, 'Judentum und Karriere im antiken Alexandria,' in A. JÖRDENS, H. A. GÄRTNER, H. GÖRGEMANNS and A. M. RITTER (edd.), *Quaerite faciem eius semper: Studien zu den geistesgeschichtlichen Beziehungen zwischen Antike und Christentum. Dankesgabe für Albrecht Dihle aus dem Heidelberger „Kirchenväterkolloquium,"* Studien zur Kirchengeschichte 8 (Hamburg 2008) 116–133.

The article studies Dositheos and Philo's nephew Tiberius Iulius Alexander as two Alexandrian career men who were regarded as apostates by the Jews. In the context of the latter, Philo is presented as a counter-example of a successful Jew who did not abandon his heritage. It is possible that Philo's warnings to young men not to be tempted by success to disregard their friends and families and to transgress their ancestral laws and customs (*Mos.* 1.31) were directed at Alexander. Philo never criticizes him explicitly, probably in order to avoid confrontation, and he even appreciates Alexander as partner in discussion (*Prov.; Anim.*), but Jördens does not see this as evidence that Philo supported Alexander's career. (JLB)

D. KUREK, *Making Scents of Revelation: The Significance of Cultic Scents in Ancient Judaism as the Backdrop of Saint Paul's Olfactory Metaphor in 2 Cor 2: 14–17* (diss. Leuven 2008).

In this Leuven disseration, prepared under the supervision of Reimund Bieringer, the author agrees that Paul's striking olfactory passage at 2 Cor 2:14–17 must be interpreted in sacrificial terms, but at the same time she argues that interpretations proposed hitherto have generally suffered from a flawed understanding of sacrifice. What distinguishes her approach is that she takes her cue from the insights furnished by the anthropology of the senses, i.e. how sensory experience is conceptualized in different societies. A section of chapter four is devoted to Philo. His treatment of odours largely differs from other writings discussed in the thesis, especially in his theoretical musings on sense perception. Despite his ambiguous attitude towards odours and sense of smell specifically, and even though he is wary about ascribing to God any sensory characteristics, Philo is nonetheless quite interested in cultic smells. This primarily includes incense offerings to which he ascribes multiple symbolisms. These encompass both the entire universe and the realm of the human soul. Allegorical interpretation, however, while bringing in a different dimension, does not disparage or call for the abandonment of literal cultic practice. (DTR; based on the author's summary)

L. H. Schiffman, 'The Prohibition of Judicial Corruption in the Dead Sea Scrolls, Philo, Josephus and Talmudic Law,' in L. H. Schiffman and F. García Martínez (edd.), *The Courtyards of the House of the Lord: Studies on the Temple Scroll* (Leiden 2008) 189–214.

Reprint of an article published in 1998 and summarized in *SPhA* vol. 13, p. 274. It forms part of a full collection of articles on the Temple scroll amounting to a 'full commentary' (F. G. Martínez) on this important text. (SJKP)

D. M. Searby, *The Corpus Parisinum. A Critical Edition of the Greek Text with Commentary and English Translation. A Medieval Anthology of Greek Texts from the Pre-Socratics to the Church Fathers, 600 B.C. – 700 A.D.*, 2 vols. (Lewiston, NY 2007).

The two volumes contain the landmark edition and English translation of the hitherto unpublished Corpus Parisinum, a Byzantine collection of sayings attributed to and derived from the works of Greek authors from 600 B.C.E. to 700 C.E. It includes a group of 31 excerpts from Philonic treatises (1.449–479). The other four texts attributed to Philo are spurious (see the index on p. 953). As the author acknowledges on p. 512, in dealing with these Philonica he has made extensive use of the 'carefully researched investigation' of James Royse in his study of the spurious fragments of Philo (= RRS 1823). It should be noted, however, that most of the 35 excerpts are authentic. (DTR)

SUPPLEMENT

A Provisional Bibliography 2010–2012

The user of this supplemental Bibliography of the most recent articles on Philo is reminded that it will doubtless contain inaccuracies and red herrings because it is not in all cases based on autopsy. It is merely meant as a service to the reader. Scholars who are disappointed by omissions or are keen to have their own work on Philo listed are strongly encouraged to contact the Bibliography's compilers (addresses in the section 'Notes on Contributors').

2010

S. AL-SUADI, 'Wechsel der Identitäten: Philos Therapeuten im Wandel der Wissenschaftsgeschichte,' *Judaica* 66 (2010) 209–228.

T. ALEKNIENÉ, 'L'«extase mystique» dans la tradition platonicienne: Philon d'Alexandrie et Plotin,' *The Studia Philonica Annual* 22 (2010) 53–82.

M. ALESSO, 'Qué es Israel en los textos de Filón,' *Circe, de clásicos y modernos* 14 (2010) 12–29.

L. ALEXIDZE, 'Imago et similitudo Dei (Platon–Philon von Alexandrien–Kirchenväter–Ioanne Petrizi,' *Phasis: Greek and Roman Studies (Ivane Javakhishvili Tbilisi State University)* 12 (2010) 48–72.

P. ASHWIN-SIEJKOWSKI, *Clement of Alexandria on Trial: The Evidence of 'Heresy' from Photius' Bibliotheca*, Supplements to Vigiliae Christianae 101 (Leiden 2010).

M. BARETTA, *Una biografia giudaico-ellenistica: il De vita Mosis di Filone Alessandrino* (diss. Pisa 2010).

C. T. BEGG, 'Moses' First Moves (Exod 2:11–22) as Retold by Josephus and Philo,' *Polish Journal of Biblical Research* 9 (2010) 67–93.

M. BELTRAN and J. L. LLINAS, 'Philo's Incomprehensible God and His Traces in Neoplatonism,' *Anales del Seminario de Historia de la Filosofía* 27 (2010) 49–61.

B. A. BERKOWITZ, 'Allegory and Ambiguity: Jewish Identity in Philo's *De Congressu*,' *Journal of Jewish Studies* 61 (2010) 1–17.

M. F. BIRD, *Crossing Over Sea and Land. Jewish Missionary Activity in the Second Temple Period* (Peabody, Mass. 2010).

E. BIRNBAUM, 'Exegetical Building Blocks in Philo's Interpretation of the Patriarchs,' in P. WALTERS (ed.), *From Judaism to Christianity: Tradition and Transition. A Festschrift for Thomas H. Tobin, S.J., on the Occasion of His Sixty-fifth Birthday* (Leiden 2010) 69–92.

A. Blasius, 'Zwischen Anpassung und Aufstand: Juden in der ägyptischen Diaspora vom 1. bis zum 3. Jh.,' *Welt und Umwelt der Bibel* 15 (2010) 43–47.

R. Bloch, *Moses und der Mythos: Die Auseinandersetzung mit der griechischen Mythologie bei jüdisch-hellenistischen Autoren*, Journal for the Study of Judaism Supplements 145 (Leiden 2010).

M. D. Boeri, 'Platonismo y estoicismo en el *De aeternitate mundi* de Filón de Alejandría,' *Études Platoniciennes* 7 (2010) 65–94.

D. Boesenberg, 'Philo's Descriptions of Jewish Sabbath Practice,' *The Studia Philonica Annual* 22 (2010) 143–163.

A. P. Bos, 'De uitleiding uit Egypte in de Openbaring van Johannes, bij Philo van Alexandrië en in de Hymne van de Parel,' in K. van der Ziel and H. Holwerda (edd.), *Het stralend teken. 60 jaar exegetische vergezichten van dr. D. Holwerda* (Franeker 2010) 18–27.

A. Bosch-Veciana, *Judaisme alexandrí i filosofia* (Barcelona 2010).

M.-O. Boulnois, 'Les péricopes de Sara 'sœur-épouse' (Gn 12, 10–20 et Gn 20, 1–18) chez les Pères grecs,' in M. Arnold, G. Dahan and A. Noblesse-Rocher (edd.), *La sœur-épouse (Genèse 12, 10–20)* (Paris 2010) 27–66.

G. Buch-Hansen, *"It is the Spirit that Gives Life": a Stoic Understanding of Pneuma in John's Gospel*, Beihefte zur Zeitschrift für die neutestamentliche Wissenschaft und die Kunde der älteren Kirche 173 (Berlin–New York 2010).

G. Buch-Hansen, 'The Emotional Jesus: Anti-Stoicism in the Fourth Gospel?,' in T. Rasimus, T. Engberg-Pedersen and I. Dunderberg (edd.), *Stoicism in Early Christianity* (Grand Rapids 2010) 93–114, esp. 106–112.

D. K. Burge, *First Century Guides to Life and Death in the Roman East: a Comparative Study of Epictetus, Philo and Peter* (diss. Macquarie University, Sydney 2010).

F. Calabi, *Storia del pensiero giudaico ellenistico* (Brescia 2010), esp. 39–94.

F. Calabi, 'Giuseppe e i sogni della folla in Filone di Alessandria,' *Études Platoniciennes* 7 (2010) 145–164.

J. J. Collins and D. C. Harlow (edd.), *The Eerdmans Dictionary of Early Judaism* (Grand Rapids 2010).

M. Cover, 'Reconceptualizing Conquest: Colonial Narratives and Philo's Roman Accuser in the *Hypothetica*,' *The Studia Philonica Annual* 22 (2010) 183–207.

M. DelCogliano, *Basil of Caesarea's Anti-Eunomian Theory of Names: Christian Theology and Late-Antique Philosophy in the Fourth Century Trinitarian Controversy*, Supplements to Vigiliae Christianae 103 (Leiden 2010), esp. 79–87.

J. DILLON, 'Philo of Alexandria and Platonist Psychology,' *Études Platoniciennes* 7 (2010) 165–172.

A. DINAN, 'Another Citation of Philo in Clement of Alexandria's Protrepticus,' *Vigiliae Christianae* 64 (2010) 435–444.

P. DRUILLE, 'Los Querubines, la espada flamígera y la Causa en Filón de Alejandría,' *Nova Tellus. Anuario del Centro de Estudios Clásicos* 28 (2010) 73–95.

L. DUPRÉE SANDGREN, *Vines Intertwined: a History of Jews and Christians from the Babylonian Exile to the Advent of Islam* (Peabody, Mass. 2010), esp. 217–224, 565–568.

D. M. FRIEDENBERG, *Tiberius Julius Alexander: a Historical Novel* (Amherst NY 2010).

A. C. GELJON, 'Philo's Interpretation of Noah,' in M. E. STONE, A. AMIHAY and V. HILLEL (edd.), *Noah and his Book(s)*, Early Judaism and its Literature 28 (Atlanta 2010) 183–191.

H.-G. GRADL, 'Kaisertum und Kaiserkult: ein Vergleich zwischen Philos Legatio ad Gaium und der Offenbarung des Johannes,' *New Testament Studies* 56 (2010) 116–138.

C. VON HEIJNE, *The Messenger of the Lord in Early Jewish Interpretations of Genesis*, Beihefte zur Zeitschrift für die alttestamentliche Wissenschaft 412 (Berlin 2010), esp. 192–234.

G. HERTZ, 'L'exégèse philonienne entre sacré et profane : Philon, un nouvel Aaron?,' in M. ADDA (ed.), *Textes Sacrés et Culture Profane : de la Révélation à la Création* (Bern 2010) 53–88.

G. HINGE and J. KRASILNIKOFF, *Alexandria: a Cultural and Religious Meltingpot* (Aarhus 2010).

P. W. VAN DER HORST, 'Philo and the Problem of God's Emotions,' *Études Platoniciennes* 7 (2010) 173–180.

F. JOURDAN, *Orphée et les Chrétiens: La réception du mythe d'Orphée dans la littérature chrétienne grecque des cinq premiers siècles. Tome I Orphée, du repoussoir au préfigurateur du Christ* (Paris 2010), esp. 284–286.

A. KLOSTERGAARD PETERSEN, 'Alexandrian Judaism: Rethinking of a Problematic Category,' in G. HINGE and J. KRASILNIKOFF (edd.), *Alexandria: a Cultural and Religious Meltingpot* (Aarhus 2010) 115–143.

N. KOLTUN-FROMM, *Hermeneutics of Holiness: Ancient Jewish and Christian Notions of Sexuality and Religious Community* (New York 2010).

D. KONSTAN, 'Of Two Minds: Philo On Cultivation,' *The Studia Philonica Annual* 22 (2010) 131–138.

E. KOSKENNIEMI, 'Philo and Greek Poets,' *Journal for the Study of Judaism* 41 (2010) 301–322.

W. Kullmann, *Naturgesetz in der Vorstellung der Antike, besonders der Stoa: eine Begriffsuntersuchung*, Philosophie der Antike Bd 30 (Stuttgart 2010).

J. Leonhardt Balzer, 'Philo und die Septuaginta,' in W. Kraus, M. Karrer and M. Meiser (edd.), *Die Septuaginta — Texte, Theologien, Einflüsse*, Wissenschaftliche Untersuchungen zum Neuen Testament 252 (Tübingen 2010) 623–637.

C. Lévy, 'À propos d'un rêve de puissance de Joseph (Philon, *Somn.* II, 17–109),' *Études Platoniciennes* 7 (2010) 133–144.

F. L. Lisi, 'Filón de Alejandría, ¿un judío platónico o un platónico judío?' *Études Platoniciennes* 7 (2010) 7–12.

F. L. Lisi, *Etudes platoniciennes VII: Philon d'Alexandrie* (Paris 2010).

N. E. Livesey, *Circumcision as a Malleable Symbol*, Wissenschaftliche Untersuchungen zum Neuen Testament 2.295 (Tübingen 2010).

S. Mancini Lombardi and P. Pontani, *Studies on the Ancient Armenian Version of Philo's Works*, Studies in Philo of Alexandria 6 (Leiden 2010).

J. P. Martín, 'Inmortalidad del alma y destino del cuerpo en la escatología de Filón,' *Études Platoniciennes* 7 (2010) 181–202.

J. P. Martín (ed.), *Filón de Alejandría Obras Completas Volumen II* (Madrid 2010).

M. W. Martin, *Judas and the Rhetoric of Comparison in the Fourth Gospel*, New Testament Monographs 25 (Sheffield 2010), esp. 61–63.

E. Matusova, 'Allegorical Interpretation of the Pentateuch in Alexandria: Inscribing Aristobulus and Philo in a Wider Literary Context,' *The Studia Philonica Annual* 22 (2010) 1–51.

A. M. Mazzanti, 'Fra superstizione ed empietà. La definizione intermedia di εὐσέβεια in Filone di Alessandria,' *Adamantius* 16 (2010) 193–205.

J. Mélèze Modrzejewski, 'Philo von Alexandrien. Jüdischer Exeget und Philosoph,' *Welt und Umwelt der Bibel* 55 (2010) 47ff.

E. Mena Salas, 'Publio Petronio, una aproximación a su imagen literaria e histórica,' *Estudios Bíblicos* 68 (2010) 185–218.

K. Metzler, *Origenes Die Kommentierung des Buches Genesis*, Origenes Werke mit deutscher Übersetzung 1.1 (Berlin 2010).

M. Mira, 'Philo of Alexandria,' in L. F. Mateo-Seco and G. Maspero (edd.), *The Brill Dictionary of Gregorius of Nyssa*, Vigiliae Christianae Supplements 99 (Leiden–Boston 2010) 601–603 and passim.

F. Morelli, 'Philo Vindobonensis restitutus. Non c'è due senza tre: P. Vindob. G 30531 + 60584 + 21649,' *Zeitschrift für Papyrologie und Epigraphik* 173 (2010) 167–174.

H. Najman, *Past Renewals: Interpretative Authority, Renewed Revelation and the Quest for Perfection in Jewish Antiquity*, Supplements to the Journal for the Study of Judaism 53 (Leiden 2010).

M. R. NIEHOFF, 'The Symposium of Philo's Therapeutae: Displaying Jewish Identity in an Increasingly Roman World,' *Greek, Roman, and Byzantine Studies* 50 (2010) 95–117.

M. R. NIEHOFF, 'Philo's Scholarly Inquiries into the Story of Paradise,' in M. BOCKMUEHL and G. G. STROUMSA (edd.), *Paradise in Antiquity: Jewish and Christian Views* (Cambridge 2010) 28–42.

M. R. NIEHOFF, 'Philo's Role as a Platonist in Alexandria,' *Études Platoniciennes* 7 (2010) 37–64.

V. RABENS, 'Geistes-Geschichte. Die Rede vom Geist im Horizont der griechisch-römischen und jüdisch-hellenistischen Literatur,' *Zeitschrift für Neues Testament* 25 (2010) 46–55.

R. RADICE, 'L'allegoria di Filone di Alessandria,' *Études Platoniciennes* 7 (2010) 95–114.

M. J. REDDOCH, *Dream Narratives and their Philosophical Orientation in Philo of Alexandria [electronic]*, OhioLINK Electronic Theses and Dissertations Center (Cincinnati, Ohio 2010).

E. REGEV, 'From "Enoch" to John the Essene: an Analysis of Sect Development – 1 "Enoch", "Jubilees" and the Essenes,' in E. G. CHAZON, B. HALPERIN-AMARU and R. CLEMENTS (edd.), *New Perspectives on Old Texts: Proceedings of the Tenth International Symposium of the Orion Center for the Study of the Dead Sea Scrolls and Associated Literature, 9–11 January, 2005* (Leiden 2010) 67–93.

J. R. ROYSE, 'Some Observations on the Biblical Text in Philo's *De Agricultura*,' *The Studia Philonica Annual* 22 (2010) 111–129.

D. T. RUNIA, 'The Structure of Philo's Allegorical Treatise *De Agricultura*,' *The Studia Philonica Annual* 22 (2010) 87–109.

D. T. RUNIA, '*Dogma* and *doxa* in the Allegorical Writings of Philo of Alexandria,' *Études Platoniciennes* 7 (2010) 115–132.

D. T. RUNIA, 'Early Alexandrian Theology and Plato's *Parmenides*,' in J. D. TURNER and K. CORRIGAN (edd.), *Plato's Parmenides and its Heritage: Volume II Reception in Patristic, Gnostic, and Christian Neoplatonic Texts*, Writings from the Greco-Roman World Supplements 3 (Atlanta 2010) 177–187.

G. SCHÖLLGEN (ed.), *Reallexikon für Antike und Christentum Band 23* (Stuttgart 2010).

T. SELAND, "'Colony' and 'Metropolis' in Philo. Examples of Mimicry and Hybridity in Philo's writing back from the Empire?' *Études Platoniciennes* 7 (2010) 13–36.

R. W. SHARPLES, *Peripatetic Philosophy 200 BC to AD 200: an Introduction and Collection of Sources in Translation*, Cambridge Source Books in Post-Hellenistic Philosophy (Cambridge 2010).

J. W. Smith, *Christian Grace and Pagan Virtue: the Theological Foundation of Ambrose's Ethics* (New York 2010).

G. E. Sterling, 'Philo's *De Agricultura*: Introduction,' *The Studia Philonica Annual* 22 (2010) 83–85.

G. E. Sterling, '*The Hypothetica*: Introduction,' *The Studia Philonica Annual* 22 (2010) 139–142.

H. Svebakken, 'Exegetical Traditions in Alexandria: Philo's Reworking of the Letter of Aristeas 145–149 as a Case Study,' in P. Walters (ed.), *From Judaism to Christianity: Tradition and Transition. A Festschrift for Thomas H. Tobin, S.J., on the Occasion of His Sixty-fifth Birthday* (Leiden 2010) 93–112.

F. Trabattoni, 'Y a-t-il une onto-théologie dans le platonisme antérieur à Plotin?' *Études Platoniciennes* 7 (2010) 203–220.

H. Vela, 'Philo and the Logic of History,' *The Studia Philonica Annual* 22 (2010) 165–182.

P. Walters (ed.), *From Judaism to Christianity: Tradition and Transition. A Festschrift for Thomas H. Tobin, S.J., on the Occasion of His Sixty-fifth Birthday*, Supplements to Novum Testamentum 136 (Leiden 2010).

D. Winston, 'Philo of Alexandria,' in L. Gerson (ed.), *The Cambridge History of Philosophy in Late Antiquity* (Cambridge 2010) 2.235–257.

2011

F. Alesse, '*Prohairesis* in Philo of Alexandria,' in B. Decharneux and S. Inowlocki (edd.), *Philon d'Alexandrie. Un penseur à l'intersection des cultures gréco-romaine, orientale, juive et chrétienne*, Monothéismes et philosophie (Turnhout 2011) 185–204.

F. Alesse, 'La 'radice alla mente' in Phil. Alex. *Quod deter.* 84–85. Breve analisi di una metafora astrologica,' *MHNH* 11 (2011) 218–228.

M. Alexandre Jr. (ed.), *Fílon de Alexandria nas origens da cultura ocidental*, Centro de Estudos Clássicos (Lisbon 2011).

M. Alexandre Jr., 'Fílon de Alexandria na Interpretação das Escrituras,' in idem (ed.) *Fílon de Alexandria nas origens da cultura ocidental*, Centro de Estudos Clássicos (Lisbon 2011) 9–22.

M. Alexandre Jr., 'Fílon entre os sofistas de Alexandria. A Sofística Alexandrina sob o olhar crítico de Fílon de Aenxandria,' in idem (ed.) *Fílon de Alexandria nas origens da cultura ocidental*, Centro de Estudos Clássicos (Lisbon 2011) 121–136.

M. Alexandre, 'Monarchie divine et dieux des nations chez Philon d'Alexandrie,' in B. Decharneux and S. Inowlocki (edd.), *Philon d'Alexandrie. Un penseur à l'intersection des cultures gréco-romaine, orientale, juive et chrétienne*, Monothéismes et philosophie (Turnhout 2011) 117–147.

C. A. ANDERSON, *Philo of Alexandria's Views of the Physical World*, Wissen-schaftliche Untersuchungen zum Neuen Testament 2.309 (Tübingen 2011).

S. BADILITA, 'Caïn, figure du mal cheze Philon d'Alexandrie,' in Y.-M. BLANCHARD, B. POUDERON and M. SCOPELLO (edd.), *Les forces du bien et du mal aux premiers siècles de l'Église: Actes du Colloque de Tours, septembre 2008*, Théologie historique 118 (Paris 2011).

T. BÉNATOUÏL, E. MAFFI and F. TRABATTONI, *Plato, Aristotle, or both?: Dialogues between Platonism and Aristotelianism in Antiquity*, Europaea memoria. Reihe 1, Studien, Bd 85. Diatribai, 4 (Hildesheim 2011).

K. BERTHELOT, 'Grecs, Barbares et Juifs dans l'œuvre de Philon,' in B. DECHARNEUX and S. INOWLOCKI (edd.), *Philon d'Alexandrie. Un penseur à l'intersection des cultures gréco-romaine, orientale, juive et chrétienne*, Monothéismes et philosophie (Turnhout 2011) 47–61.

E. BIRNBAUM, 'Who Celebrated on Pharos with the Jews? Conflicting Philonic Currents and Their Implications,' in B. DECHARNEUX and S. INOWLOCKI (edd.), *Philon d'Alexandrie. Un penseur à l'intersection des cultures gréco-romaine, orientale, juive et chrétienne*, Monothéismes et philosophie (Turnhout 2011) 63–82.

M. BROZE, 'L'Égypte de Philon d'Alexandrie: approches d'un discours ambigu,' in B. DECHARNEUX and S. INOWLOCKI (edd.), *Philon d'Alexandrie. Un penseur à l'intersection des cultures gréco-romaine, orientale, juive et chrétienne*, Monothéismes et philosophie (Turnhout 2011) 105–113.

F. CALABI, 'Le repos de Dieu chez Philon d'Alexandrie,' in B. DECHARNEUX and S. INOWLOCKI (edd.), *Philon d'Alexandrie. Un penseur à l'intersection des cultures gréco-romaine, orientale, juive et chrétienne*, Monothéismes et philosophie (Turnhout 2011) 185–204.

M. CEGLAREK, *Die Rede von der Gegenwart Gottes, Christi und des Geistes: eine Untersuchung zu den Briefen des Apostels Paulus* (Frankfurt am Main 2011).

J. T. CONROY JR., 'Philo's "Death of the Soul": Is This Only a Metaphor?' *The Studia Philonica Annual* 23 (2011) 23–40.

B. DECHARNEUX, 'Le Logos philonien comme fondation paradoxale de l'Évangile de Jean,' in B. DECHARNEUX and S. INOWLOCKI (edd.), *Philon d'Alexandrie. Un penseur à l'intersection des cultures gréco-romaine, orientale, juive et chrétienne*, Monothéismes et philosophie (Turnhout 2011) 317–333.

B. DECHARNEUX and S. INOWLOCKI (edd.), *Philon d'Alexandrie. Un penseur à l'intersection des cultures gréco-romaine, orientale, juive et chrétienne*, Mono-théismes et philosophie 12 (Turnhout 2011).

M. DUARTE, 'Λόγος ἐνδιάθετος e προφορικός na Formação da Cristologia Patrística,' in M. ALEXANDRE JR. (ed.) *Fílon de Alexandria nas origens da cultura ocidental*, Centro de Estudos Clássicos (Lisbon 2011) 47–79.

T. Faia, 'Embaixada de Calígula, Agustina Bessa-Luís e uma Memória de Fílon de Alexandria,' in M. Alexandre jr. (ed.) *Fílon de Alexandria nas origens da cultura ocidental,* Centro de Estudos Clássicos (Lisbon 2011) 37–467.

M. Fernandes, 'O Profetismo no Tratado De Iosepho de Fílon de Alexandria,' in M. Alexandre jr. (ed.) *Fílon de Alexandria nas origens da cultura ocidental,* Centro de Estudos Clássicos (Lisbon 2011) 81–90.

M. Fernandes, 'Φύσις no Tratado de Fílon de Alexandria De Iosepho,' in M. Alexandre jr. (ed.) *Fílon de Alexandria nas origens da cultura ocidental,* Centro de Estudos Clássicos (Lisbon 2011) 111–120.

A. C. Geljon, 'Philo's Influence on Didymus the Blind,' in B. Decharneux and S. Inowlocki (edd.), *Philon d'Alexandrie. Un penseur à l'intersection des cultures gréco-romaine, orientale, juive et chrétienne,* Monothéismes et philosophie (Turnhout 2011) 357–372.

M. Goodman, 'Philo as a Philosopher in Rome,' in B. Decharneux and S. Inowlocki (edd.), *Philon d'Alexandrie. Un penseur à l'intersection des cultures gréco-romaine, orientale, juive et chrétienne,* Monothéismes et philosophie (Turnhout 2011) 37–45.

N. Gupta, 'The Question of Coherence in Philo's Cultic Imagery: a Socio-literary Approach,' *Journal for the Study of the Pseudepigrapha* 20, no. 4 (2011) 277–297.

S. Inowlocki-Meister, 'Relectures apologétiques de Philon par Eusèbe de Césarée: le cas d'Enoch et des Thérapeutes,' in B. Decharneux and S. Inowlocki (edd.), *Philon d'Alexandrie. Un penseur à l'intersection des cultures gréco-romaine, orientale, juive et chrétienne,* Monothéismes et philosophie (Turnhout 2011).

R. S. Kraemer, *Unreliable Witnesses: Religion, Gender, and History in the Greco-Roman Mediterranean* (Oxford 2011), esp. ch. 3.

F. Ledegang, *Philo van Alexandrië Over de tien woorden, De Decalogo* (Budel, Netherlands 2011).

J. Leonhardt-Balzer, 'Priests and Priesthood in Philo: Could He Have Done without Them?,' in D. R. Schwartz and Z. Weiss (edd.), *Was 70 CE a Watershed in Jewish History? On Jews and Judaism Before and After the Destruction of the Second Temple,* Ancient Judaism and Early Christianity 78 (Leiden 2011) 121–147.

C. Lévy, 'La notion de signe chez Philon d'Alexandrie,' in B. Decharneux and S. Inowlocki (edd.), *Philon d'Alexandrie. Un penseur à l'intersection des cultures gréco-romaine, orientale, juive et chrétienne,* Monothéismes et philosophie (Turnhout 2011) 149–161.

C. Lévy, 'L'aristotélisme, parent pauvre de la pensée philonienne?,' in T. Bénatouïl, E. Maffi and F. Trabattoni (edd.), *Plato, Aristotle, or both? Dialogues between Platonism and Aristotelianism in Antiquity*, Europaea memoria. Reihe 1, Studien, Bd 85. Diatribai, 4 (Hildesheim 2011) 17–33.

D. Lincicum, 'Philo on Phinehas and the Levites: Observing an Exegetical Connection,' *Bulletin for Biblical Research* 21 (2011) 43–49.

W. Loader, *Philo, Josephus, and the Testaments on Sexuality: Attitudes towards Sexuality in the Writings of Philo and Josephus and in the Testaments of the Twelve Patriarchs* (Grand Rapids 2011).

E. Z. Lyons, *Hellenic Philosophers as Ambassadors to the Roman Empire: Performance, parrhesia, and power* (diss. University of Michigan 2011).

A. B. McGowan and K. Richards (edd.), *Method and Meaning: Essays on New Testament Interpretation in Honor of Harold W. Attridge* (Atlanta 2011).

W. Moon, *Your Love is Better than Wine: A Reading of Love in the Gospel according to John* (diss. The Claremont Graduate University 2011).

J. Moreau, 'Entre Écriture sainte et *paideia*: le langage exégétique de Philon d'Alexandrie. Étude sur la pistis d'Abraham dans le *Quis rerum divinarum heres sit* 90–95,' in B. Decharneux and S. Inowlocki (edd.), *Philon d'Alexandrie. Un penseur à l'intersection des cultures gréco-romaine, orientale, juive et chrétienne*, Monothéismes et philosophie (Turnhout 2011) 241–263.

O. Munnich, 'La fugacité de la vie humane (*De Josepho* § 125–147): la place des motifes traditionnels dans l'élaboration de la pensée philonienne,' in B. Decharneux and S. Inowlocki (edd.), *Philon d'Alexandrie. Un penseur à l'intersection des cultures gréco-romaine, orientale, juive et chrétienne*, Monothéismes et philosophie (Turnhout 2011) 163–183.

O. Munnich, 'Travail sur la langue et sur le texte dans l'exégèse de Philon d'Alexandrie,' in A. Balansard, G. Dorival and M. Loubet (edd.), *Prolongements et renouvellements de la tradition classique: en homage à Didier Pralon*, Textes et documents de la Méditerranée antique et médiévale (Aix en Provence 2011).

M. R. Niehoff, 'Recherche homérique et exégèse biblique à Alexandrie: un fragment sur la Tour de Babel préservé par Philon,' in B. Decharneux and S. Inowlocki (edd.), *Philon d'Alexandrie. Un penseur à l'intersection des cultures gréco-romaine, orientale, juive et chrétienne*, Monothéismes et philosophie (Turnhout 2011) 83–103.

M. R. Niehoff, *Jewish Exegesis and Homeric Scholarship in Alexandria* (Cambridge 2011).

M. R. Niehoff, 'Jüdische Bibelexegese im Spiegel alexandrinischer Homer-forschung,' *Biblische Notizen* NF 148 (2011) 19–33.

M. R. Niehoff, 'Philo's Exposition in a Roman Context,' *The Studia Philonica Annual* 23 (2011) 1–21.

F. Nobilio, 'Le chemin de l'Esprit dans l'œuvre de Philon d'Alexandrie en dans l'évangile de Jean,' in B. Decharneux and S. Inowlocki (edd.), *Philon d'Alexandrie. Un penseur à l'intersection des cultures gréco-romaine, orientale, juive et chrétienne,* Monothéismes et philosophie (Turnhout 2011) 283–315.

F. Petit, L. van Rompay and J. J. S. Weitenberg, *Eusèbe d'Émèse. Commentaire de la Genèse. Texte arménien de l'édition de Venise (1980), fragments grecs, avec traductions,* Traditio Exegetica Graeca 15 (Louvain 2011).

I. L. E. Ramelli, 'The Birth of the Rome–Alexandria Connection: the Early Sources on Mark and Philo, and the Petrine Tradition,' *The Studia Philonica Annual* 23 (2011) 69–95.

C. M. Rios, 'Exílio, Diáspora e Saudades de Jerusalém: Estudo em Jeremias 29:1–14 em Fílon de Alexandria,' in M. Alexandre jr. (ed.) *Fílon de Alexandria nas origens da cultura ocidental,* Centro de Estudos Clássicos (Lisbon 2011) 91–109.

P. Robertson, 'Toward an Understanding of Philo's and Cicero's Treatment of Sacrifice,' *The Studia Philonica Annual* 23 (2011) 41–67.

D. Roure, 'Forgiveness in Ben Sira and in Philo of Alexandria,' *Studia Monastica* 53 (2011) 7–19.

D. T. Runia, 'Why Philo of Alexandria is an Important Writer and Thinker,' in B. Decharneux and S. Inowlocki (edd.), *Philon d'Alexandrie. Un penseur à l'intersection des cultures gréco-romaine, orientale, juive et chrétienne,* Monothéismes et philosophie (Turnhout 2011) 13–33.

D. T. Runia, 'Ancient Philosophy and the New Testament: "Exemplar" as Example,' in A. B. McGowan and K. Richards (edd.), *Method and Meaning: Essays on New Testament Interpretation in Honor of Harold W. Attridge,* Society of Biblical Literature Resources for Biblical Study 67 (Atlanta 2011) 347–361.

L. Saudelli, 'Les fragments d'Héraclite et leur signification dans le *corpus philonicum*: le cas du fr. 60 DK,' in B. Decharneux and S. Inowlocki (edd.), *Philon d'Alexandrie. Un penseur à l'intersection des cultures gréco-romaine, orientale, juive et chrétienne,* Monothéismes et philosophie (Turnhout 2011) 265–280.

G. Schöllgen (ed.), *Reallexikon für Antike und Christentum,* Lieferungen 188–191 (Stuttgart 2011).

C. Tornau, art. Materie, 346–410, esp. 370–373 (Matter); M. Durst, R. Amedick, E. Enss, art. Meer 505–609, esp. 549–552 (Sea). (DTR)

G. Sellin, *Allegorie – Metapher – Mythos – Schrift. Beiträge zur religiösen Sprache im Neuen Testament und in seiner Umwelt,* edited by D. Sänger, Novum Testamentum et orbis antiquus 90 (Göttingen 2011).

F. Siegert, 'Philon et la philologie alexandrine. Aux origines du fondamentalisme chrétien,' in B. Decharneux and S. Inowlocki (edd.), *Philon d'Alexandrie. Un penseur à l'intersection des cultures gréco-romaine, orientale, juive et chrétienne,* Monothéismes et philosophie (Turnhout 2011) 393–402.

J. Smith, *Christ the Ideal King,* Wissenschaftliche Untersuchungen zum Neuen Testament 2.313 (Tübingen 2011).

G. E. Sterling, M. R. Niehoff, A. van den Hoek and D. T. Runia, 'Philo,' in J. J. Collins and D. C. Harlow (edd.), *The Eerdmans Dictionary of Early Judaism* 2011) 1063–1080.

T. H. Tobin SJ, 'Hellenistic Judaism and the New Testament,' in A. B. McGowan and K. Richards (edd.), *Method and Meaning: Essays on New Testament Interpretation in Honor of Harold W. Attridge,* Society of Biblical Literature Resources for Biblical Study 67 (Atlanta 2011) 363–380.

P. J. Tomson, 'Le temple céleste: pensée platonisante et orientation apocalyptique dans l'Épître aux Hébreux,' in B. Decharneux and S. Inowlocki (edd.), *Philon d'Alexandrie. Un penseur à l'intersection des cultures gréco-romaine, orientale, juive et chrétienne,* Monothéismes et philosophie (Turnhout 2011) 337–356.

S. Torallas Tovar, 'Orphic Hymn 86 "To Dream": On Orphic Sleep and Philo,' in M.H. de Jáuregui *et al.* (edd.), *Tracing Orpheus: Studies of Orphic Fragments* (Berlin 2011) 405–411.

S. Torallas Tovar, 'La lengua de Filón de Alejandría en el panorama lingüístico del Egipto Romano,' in M. Alexandre jr. (ed.) *Fílon de Alexandria nas origens da cultura ocidental,* Centro de Estudos Clássicos (Lisbon 2011) 23–36.

J. Weinberg, 'La quête de Philon dans l'historiographie juive du XVIᵉ s.,' in B. Decharneux and S. Inowlocki (edd.), *Philon d'Alexandrie. Un penseur à l'intersection des cultures gréco-romaine, orientale, juive et chrétienne,* Monothéismes et philosophie (Turnhout 2011) 403–432.

S. Weisser, 'La figure du progressant ou la proximité de la sagesse,' in B. Decharneux and S. Inowlocki (edd.), *Philon d'Alexandrie. Un penseur à l'intersection des cultures gréco-romaine, orientale, juive et chrétienne,* Monothéismes et philosophie (Turnhout 2011) 221–239.

W. T. Wilson, *Philo of Alexandria On Virtues. Introduction, Translation, and Commentary,* Philo of Alexandria Commentary Series 3 (Leiden 2011).

J. D. Worthington, *Creation in Paul and Philo,* Wissenschaftliche Untersuchungen zum Neuen Testament 2.317 (Tübingen 2011).

D. Zeller, *Studien zu Philo und Paulus*, Bonner Biblische Beiträge 165 (Göttingen 2011).

D. Zeller, 'Leben und Tod der Seele in der allegorischen Exegese Philo's. Gebrauch und Ursprung einer Metapher,' in idem (ed.), *Studien zu Philo und Paulus* (Göttingen 2011) 55–99.

2012

J. M. Dillon, *The Platonic Heritage. Further Studies in the History of Platonism and Early Christianity*, Variorum Collected Studies (Abingdon 2012).

E. L. Gallagher, *Hebrew Scripture in Patristic Biblical Theory*, Supplements to Vigiliae Christianae 114 (Leiden 2012).

S. D. Mackie, 'Seeing God in Philo of Alexandria: Means, Methods, and Mysticism,' *Journal for the Study of Judaism* 43 (2012) 147–179.

P. Martens, *Origen and Scripture: the Contours of Exegetical Life*, Oxford Early Christian Studies (Oxford 2012).

M. R. Niehoff (ed.), *Homer and the Bible in the Eyes of Ancient Interpreters*, Jerusalem Studies in Religion and Culture 16 (Leiden 2012).

D. T. Runia, 'Philon d'Alexandrie,' in R. Goulet (ed.), *Dictionnaire des philosophes antiques* (Paris 2012) 5.362–390.

L. Saudelli, *Eraclito ad Alessandria. Studi e ricerche intorno alla testimonianza di Filone*, Monothéismes et Philosophie 16 (Turnhout 2012).

A. Timotin, *La démonologie platonicienne: Histoire de la notion de daimôn de Platon aux derniers néoplatoniciennes*, Philosophia Antiqua 128 (Leiden 2012), esp. 100–112.

S. Weisser, 'Why Does Philo Criticize the Stoic Ideal of Apatheia in *On Abraham* 257? Philo and Consolatory Literature,' *Classical Quarterly* 62 (2012) 242–259.

BOOK REVIEW SECTION

MAREN R. NIEHOFF. *Jewish Exegesis and Homeric Scholarship in Alexandria*, Cambridge: Cambridge University Press, 2011. xiv + 222 pages. ISBN 978-1-1070-0072-8. Price £53, $85.

DIETER ZELLER. *Studien zu Philo und Paulus*. Bonner Biblische Beiträge 165. Göttingen/Bonn: Vandenhoeck & Ruprecht, 2011. 301 pages. ISBN 978-3-8997-1659-7. Price €43.90, $60.

"Ausgehend von der Bedeutung Alexandriens als *dem* Zentrum der Homer-Philologie in der hellenistischen Welt, habe ich erstmals jüdische exegetische Schriften analysiert im Licht der alexandrinischen Scholien zu Homer." Der Anspruch des Buches von Maren NIEHOFF (S. 186) ist hoch und die Originalität des Ansatzpunktes nicht zu bestreiten. Die Verfasserin, "Senior Lecturer in the Department of Jewish Thought in The Hebrew University of Jerusalem," ist bekannt durch *Philo on Jewish Identity and Culture* (Tübingen 2001) und anderes mehr zum nachbiblischen Judentum. Sie hat von einer Arbeitsgruppe an der Hebräischen Universität in Jerusalem profitiert, wo die Homer-Scholien gelesen wurden—im Original natürlich; Übersetzungen hat es nie gegeben, denn dies sind Texte für Kenner des Griechischen. Sie bezeugen den hohen Stand der alexandrinischen Philologie fast schon seit ihren Anfängen, genauer gesagt seit Aristarch. Ihre Prinzipien sind die noch heute gültigen; aristotelische Terminologie und Objektivität waltet in der Beschreibung sprachlicher Phänomene. Die damals rivalisierende Schule, die von Pergamon (hier nur zweimal unter diesem Namen erwähnt, sonst aber als "stoische Schule") ging bekanntlich anders vor: Sie nahm Sonderbares oder Veraltetes bei den klassischen Dichtern zum Anlass für die Vermutung, der Autor habe etwas anderes sagen wollen, als der Wortlaut hergibt,[1] er habe Rätselrede (bald sagte man

---

[1] In die "pergamenische" Exegese (die der Stoiker) hat die Autorin sich leider nicht völlig eingearbeitet, sonst würde sie nicht behaupten (S. 143), das Fragen nach der Autorenabsicht sei erst mit Philon aufgekommen. "The roots of this approach cannot be traced to the Stoics" (143): Aber ja! Siehe Heraclitus Stoicus, *Quaestiones Homericae* 3,1 u.ö. Die schöne Ausgabe dieses Textes durch Félix Buffière (Coll. Budé, Paris 1962) bleibt unerwähnt.

auch: Allegorie)² gebraucht. Gezeigt wird nun, dass Philon auf beiden Seiten kompetent war.

In seinem Gesamtduktus erhebt dieses Buch für Philon den Anspruch, er habe die historisch-kritische Methodik (um sie mit heutigem Ausdruck so zu benennen) überwunden und lasse sie hinter sich zugunsten einer Synthese. Ungenannt bleibt das Problem, dass er damit für lange Jahrhunderte christlicher Bibelauslegung, in Schüben sogar bis heute, der geistige Vater dessen wurde, was im Christentum—wo seine Wirkung anderthalb Jahrtausende lang ausschließlich lag—als Biblizismus, ja Fundamentalismus bekannt ist. Typisch hierfür ist bis heute, dass Texte mythischen Charakters (mit den ihnen eigenen Verstehensschwierigkeiten, die damals schon den Intellektuellen Alexandriens bewusst wurden) "als nicht-mythisch deklariert werden" (so 178 über Philons letzte Phase). Philon ist somit ein Vertreter "nachkritischer Naivität," wie ein christlicher Bibelwissenschaftler es treffend genannt hat.³ Philons Art von Fundamentalismus hat immerhin ein philosophisches Gewand, und zwar in der Loslösung des Interesses von der Geschichte (wo ja fast alles sich wandelt) zugunsten "unwandelbarer" Wahrheiten (97 u.ö.). Eine platonisierende Tora-Theologie platziert Gott außerhalb der Geschichte, um desto ungestörter die Tora als ewige Weisheit darstellen zu können. Ein Stück weit gibt die Gesamtüberschrift des dritten und letzten Teils (S. 131ff) den Preis für Philons Erfolge zu: "The inversion of Homeric scholarship by Philo." Auf S. 155 wird schon zu den *Quaestiones* "Philo's move from a more dialogical to a more orthodox position" vermerkt, eine Entwicklung, die in der *Expositio Legis* zu ihrem Abschluss kommt.

Um wieder aus dem Epilog (S. 186) zu zitieren: "Jüdische Bibelgelehrte leisteten die ersten kritischen Studien des kanonischen Textes, womit sie der modernen Forschung um mehr als 2000 Jahre voraus waren." Dass Philon diesen Vorsprung nicht nur verschenkt, sondern kritisches Fragen durch moralische Verdächtigungen der Frager nachhaltig blockiert hat (um wieder an seine Rezeption zu denken), wird nicht zum Problem erhoben. Dem Judentum, wo die Tora für unveränderlich gilt und gelten muss, ist die alexandrinische Kritik auf Dauer doch fremd geblieben.⁴

---

² Hier ist auf S. 144 ein wortgeschichtlicher Fehler störend: "Significantly" habe Aristotle den Ausdruck "Allegorie" nicht benutzt. Das heißt aber nichts, wenn man bedenkt, dass dieses Wort zu seiner Zeit noch nicht gebildet war.

³ Hans-Peter Müller (Münster) mündlich.

⁴ Was in der Kirche "alexandrinische" Exegese heißt, ist in Philons Nachfolge das Allegorisieren. Kritisches Fragen blieb der weniger einflussreichen "antiochenischen" Exegese eigen.

"Jeder von den drei Teilen dieses Buches hat eine separate Kategorie alexandrinischer Bibelauslegung behandelt. Der erste prüfte die frühen Quellen aus der ptolemäischen Zeit; auf jede von ihnen warf er völlig neues Licht (ebd.)." Der *Aristeasbrief* gilt der Autorin zu Recht als "konservative Reaktion auf kritische Forschung (S. 19ff)." Größere Nähe zum aristotelischen Forschungsziel findet sie bei Demetrios (S. 38ff), dessen von Elias Bickermann vorgeschlagene Frühdatierung sie nicht übernimmt. Aristobul sodann (S. 58ff) ist das überzeugende Beispiel eines jüdischen Aristotelikers—der freilich im Judentum überhaupt nicht reüssierte; nur einige christliche Zitate gibt es von ihm noch. Hier wäre es übrigens gut gewesen, die Nummerierung der Fragmente, die Nikolaus Walter vorgeschlagen hat, nicht nur bei Aristobul zu verwenden, sondern auch bei Demetrios. Es handelt sich bei letzterem um Fragment 5 (S. 39ff), Fragment 2 § 14f. (S. 46ff) und Fragment 3 (S. 53f.). Sehr aufschlussreich sind in diesem Teil des Buches, wie auch sonst, die Zitate aus den Homerscholien, auch die Kontrastierung von deren Verfahrensweise zu jener des Midrasch (z.B. auf S. 56f); hier hätte mit Nutzen auf die *Encyclopedia of Midrash* von J. Neusner und A. Avery-Peck hingewiesen werden können.[5]

"Der zweite Teil des Buches hat Fragmente anonymer jüdischer Exegeten in Philons Werken identifiziert. Aufgrund einer Lektüre seiner Polemik gegen solche Kollegen im Licht der Scholien habe ich eine neue Rekonstruktion anonymer Bibelexegese in Alexandrien geboten (ebd.)." Hier ist der Stolz der Autorin berechtigt. In sehr genauen und überzeugenden Analysen bestätigt sich, was die Philon-Forschung des letzten Vierteljahrhunderts mehr und mehr betont, dass nämlich Philon im Judentum seiner Zeit keineswegs isoliert zu sehen ist. An Spuren vor- und nebenphilonischer alexandrinisch-jüdischer Exegese werden vorgestellt: *Conf.* 1–13 (S. 77–91), *Gig.* 7 (S. 92–95), *Abr.* 178–183 (S. 95–111) sowie im Weiteren (bis S. 129) *Deus* 140ff, *Congr.* 178, *QG* 4, 168, *Conf.* (erneut) 142, *Her.* 101, *QG* 4, 90f. und *Mut.* 60–62. Man sieht dort, über die Beweisabsichten der Autorin hinaus, was alexandrinisch-jüdische Exegese hätte werden können, hätte Philon kritisches Fragen nicht als unmoralisch bezeichnet.

"Im letzten Teil des Buches habe ich Philon gewürdigt im Kontext seiner Kollegen und Vorgänger. Er erweist sich mehr oder weniger als konservativer, der literarische Techniken mit beträchtlicher Vorsicht anwendet, weil er auf der Einheit und Authentizität des biblischen Textes besteht.

[5] Leiden/Boston: Brill 2005. Der ursprüngliche, chronologisch angelegte Plan dieses Werkes hätte zutage treten lassen, dass selbst der Midrasch seine ältesten Belege nicht im hebräischen Judentum hat, sondern im griechischsprachigen. Der Plan wurde geändert zugunsten einer unhistorischen, nämlich alphabetischen Anordnung.

Zugleich aber war ich in der Lage zu zeigen, dass Philon eine neue Synthese geschaffen hat zwischen wörtlicher Auslegung in aristotelischer Art und platonischer Allegorie (ebd.)." Nun, die pergamenische Exegese, die von den Stoikern zum Altersbeweis ihrer Lehren freudig übernommen worden war, ist ja zu Philons Zeiten vom Platonismus (sofern er nicht Skepsis wurde) seinerseits angeeignet worden; es war griechischen Intellektuellen einfach nicht möglich, auf Homer zu verzichten. Philon selbst, das kriegt man hier vorgeführt, wurde im Alter mehr und mehr Platoniker. Das heißt aber auch: Analysen, die nicht auch einer Synthese dienten, werden unwillig beiseite geschoben. Zu Beginn dieses Teils (S. 133) sagt die Autorin: "Ich werde zeigen, dass er sie nicht ignorierte, wie man erwarten könnte, sondern dass er sie auf eine raffinierte und hochgradig innovative Art sich zu Diensten machte *to construct a separate discourse of Jewish hermeneutics*—um eine spezifisch jüdische Hermeneutik zu erschaffen." Das Glück an dieser Schöpfung sei denen überlassen, die es empfinden.

Was aber gerade an diesem Teil des Buches ohne alle Reserve gerühmt werden muss, ist die Exaktheit, mit welcher die drei großen Einheiten in Philons schriftstellerischem Werk voneinander geschieden und gegeneinander differenziert werden: Der *allegorische Kommentar* (sc. zur Genesis) ist eine an ein jüdisches Auditorium (doch wohl Alexandriens) gerichtete Tora-Unterweisung mit allen Raffinessen zeitgenössischer alexandrinischer Gelehrsamkeit—Vorsicht allerdings: die Genesis ist kaum schon Tora; eher handelt es sich um eine Selbstvergewisserung im Judentum allgemein. Die Verf.in unterscheidet hiervon klar die *Queastiones*, die schon sehr deutlich von der Philologie "abheben" ins Allegorische; auch stellen sie insgesamt weniger Anforderungen an den Bildungsgrad der Hörerschaft. Diese beiden Reihen können, wie schon länger vermutet wird, durchaus parallel entstanden sein. Besonders interessant ist nun aber die Zuordnung der *Expositio Legis*: Hier verstärken die gebotenen Analysen die derzeit sich festigende Forschungsmeinung (Dieter Zeller z.B. gehört ihr an), wonach Philon sich hier an ein paganes Auditorium wendet. Das führt auf die spannende Frage, wo Philon denn wohl ein solches hatte. Antwort: in Rom (S. 170 u.ö.), wo Philon wohl oder übel (weil Caligula ihn nicht hören wollte) sich zwei Jahre, wo nicht länger, auszuhalten hatte (S. 15: i.J. 38–40, "vielleicht" bis 41). Entwicklungslogisch ist es jedenfalls gegenüber den anderen die "fortgeschrittenere" Reihe (so S. 164) und dürfte also später begonnen worden sein.

Auffällig ist für diese Reihe (welcher nach heutigem Konsens auch der Traktat *De opificio mundi* zuzurechnen ist), dass Philon so gut wie keine Bibelkenntnis voraussetzt. Aus alledem gewinnt sein allzu unbekannter Lebenslauf neue Konturen: Man kann sich gut denken, dass er in Rom, dessen Judenheit kein hohes Bildungsniveau aufwies (und auch lange Zeit kein Schriftdenkmal hinterließ), wieder und wieder in die Lage kam, von einem intellektuellen Standpunkt aus darzulegen, was Judentum überhaupt ist. Er mag, so denken wir uns nun, diese Vorträge damals schon oder in der Folge zu Papier (Papyrus) gebracht haben. Einer seiner Hörer, so erlaubt sich der Rez. zu vermuten, war dann wohl der für uns anonyme Autor des *Hebräerbriefs.*[6] Wir überlassen es jedoch dem zweiten in dieser Rezension vorzustellenden Autor, die Berührungen Philons zum Christentum, namentlich zu dessen berühmtesten Romreisenden, Paulus, näher ins Auge zu fassen.

Zu rühmen ist die ästhetisch perfekte Aufmachung des Buches: bestes Papier, schöne Typen, scharfer Druck, ein sehr ansprechender Umschlag, vorbildliche Register (auch Griechisch). Das Englisch, soweit der Rez. es zu beurteilen vermag, ist vorzüglich und idiomatisch.—Was dem Buch noch gut getan hätte, wäre eine Durchsicht unter altphilologischem Gesichtspunkt. Im Latein: S. 2 *numerus verbum* lies *numerus verborum*. Der Buchtitel *De anima procreatione*, soll er denn Sinn haben, muss heißen *De animae procreatione* (S. 72). Philons Neffe heißt in römischer Reihenfolge der Namen Tiberius Julius Alexander (zu S. 164); der *Venetus Codex* von S. 81 wäre ein *Codex Venetus*. Griechisch ist zu bemerken (hier nur jeweils die korrigierten Formen): διδασκαλεῖα (5), Ἑβραϊκοῖς (31, viersilbig), μερίς (46), θεῖον (68), σφαγιάζω (101), ὧν (ebd.), Ἰλλύριοι (104), ἐπ᾽ ἐκδικίᾳ (106), μέν τισιν (114), πτῶσιν (ebd.), ἐξῆλθεν (115), διασώζω (127), εὐτελῆ (128), ᾧ (134), ὑπόμνημα (136), οὐδὲν (146), τῷ ἐνεργεῖ (147), γραφή (158); οἳ (167) ist zu tilgen, denn es gehört nicht zum Syntagma, sondern zum Rahmensatz. Und schließlich Armenisch (dieser Sprache hat sich die Autorin um der *Quaestiones* willen befleißigt hat): *ew* (154), *yaytni* (158), *a(stowa)cayin* (158). —Öfters ist unklar, aus welcher Philon-Ausgabe oder -übersetzung die Verf.in zitiert. Im Literaturverzeichnis fehlt A.Y. Collins (genannt auf S. 62, Anm. 25). Die *Fragmente der Griechischen Historiker* von Jacoby haben weit mehr als 7 Bände (S. xiv).

Insgesamt hat dieses Buch, reich an philologischen Nachweisen und Entdeckungen, gute Chancen, ein Klassiker in seinem Fach zu werden. Die Fehler im Detail, die wir bemerkt haben, sind dabei weniger störend als das in jedem Kapitel spürbare Bestreben der Autorin, sich in den Vordergrund zu spielen. *My argument* (S. 13), *my argument* (ebd.) dient auch für längst Bekanntes. Im Literaturverzeichnis zitiert sie sich mit 18 Titeln, ein Drittel davon noch nicht veröffentlicht. Derzeit wird ja den Verfassern von

---

[6] So der Rez. in: A. Kamesar (Hg.): *The Cambridge Companion to Philo,* Cambridge 2009, 177.

Qualifikationsschriften nahe gelegt, sich möglichst selbstbewusst darzustellen und sich als Erfinder ihres Wissensgebiets zu geben—war das noch nötig? Von Lesepublikum aus gesehen, hätte ein Buch von solcher Kennerschaft diesen Aufputz weniger nötig gehabt als vielmehr eine geduldige Durchsicht von altphilologischer Seite.

Der bekannte Neutestamentler (und, als die katholische Kirche ihm den Lehrstuhl nahm, Religionsgeschichtler) Dieter ZELLER hat in seinen *Studien zu Philo und Paulus* eine stattliche Sammlung von Aufsätzen zu diesen seinen beiden Forschungsschwerpunkten vorgelegt. Um hier mit dem Formalen zu beginnen: Es handelt sich um die Veröffentlichungsform der *books on demand*, die also auf Bestellung Stück für Stück gefertigt werden, ohne die Kosten einer Lagerung. Auch so entsteht ein robuster, ansprechender Pappband, dessen Leimbindung freilich dem Öffnen widerstrebt.[7] Editorisch sind die Beiträge aufeinander abgestimmt und mit einem kurzen gemeinsamen Literaturverzeichnis versehen (S. 295–300), leider ohne Register, auch ohne Abkürzungsverzeichnis;[8] bei AK z.B. soll man wissen: *Allegorischer Kommentar*. Gelegentliche Zusätze zu den Erstfassungen stehen in eckigen Klammern. Der Hinweis auf die Erstveröffentlichung findet sich jeweils in Fußnote 1. Altsprachliche Fehler muss man hier mit der Lupe suchen: Dem Rez. ist nur aufgefallen ἡγημών (statt ἡγεμών, S. 22 zweimal); S. 25 ποῖον lies ποιόν (indefinit). Auch im Deutschen ist sehr gründlich Korrektur gelesen worden. Vorgänger war der Sammelband *Neues Testament und hellenistische Umwelt* (BBB 150, 2006). Eine Monographie im Voraus war *Charis bei Philon und Paulus* (SBS 142), Stuttgart 1990.

Im Folgenden soll das Augenmerk vor allem auf dem philonischen Teil des Buches liegen (S. 13–138), wobei auch die sich anschließenden Beiträge nicht selten auf Philon bzw. auf die von ihm angeschlagenen Themen und angewendeten Methoden zurückgreifen. Der Verf. verbindet seine meisterhafte Kenntnis der Antike mit einer hohen Sensibilität für philosophische und theologische Fragestellungen.

Gleich der erste Beitrag zielt in die Mitte: "Gott bei Philo von Alexandrien" (2003, hier S. 13–135). Er setzt ein mit einer Frage, welche die religionswissenschaftliche Aufgeschlossenheit der gesamten Aufsatzsammlung verdeutlicht: "Wie kommt der Mensch zum Gottesbegriff?" Vom Standpunkt des heutigen deutschen Sprachgebrauchs ist hier allenfalls das Titelstichwort in Frage zu stellen und einzuwenden, dass Ausdrücke wie

---

[7] Typographisch ist noch zu bemerken, dass das ö in den Kapitälchen zu fehlen scheint; es ist durch einen Fettbuchstaben ersetzt.

[8] Stattdessen wird auf S. 38, Anm. 4 verwiesen auf *LThK³*.

"Vorstellung von Gott" oder "Gotteserkenntnis" weniger angreifbar wären; "Begriff" meint inzwischen eher etwas Wohldefiniertes.—Zeller referiert hier das, was seit Aristoteles als das Argument *e consensu gentium* bekannt ist. Eine Klammer hierzu bildet der Aufsatz "Theologie der Mission bei Paulus" (1982) gegen Ende des Bandes, wo der Verf. folgende Voraussetzungen seiner Arbeit mitteilt (S. 267): "Ich gehe von zwei religions-philosphischen Vermutungen aus:

- Religion beruht auf der Erfahrung des Absoluten im Relativen.
- Ihre Gefahr ist die Verabsolutierung des Relativen unter dem Denkmal des wahrhaft Absoluten."

Nachdem nun, was Philon betrifft, dessen Gotteslehre sich als Abstraktion aus verschiedenen griechischen Gotteslehren erweist, fragt der Verf. nunmehr zu Recht, ob dies noch der Gott Israels sei. S. 28: "Was hat dieser abstrakte, beziehungslose Gottesbegriff noch mit dem in der Bibel bezeugten Gott zu tun, der sich an menschliche Verheißungsträger, ja an ein konkretes Volk bindet?" Antwort gibt bei Philon die Vorzugsstellung Israels, auch wenn sie nicht über den Bundesbegriff ausgedrückt wird. S. 35: "Der auf dem Weg über den Kosmos gewonnene philosophische Gottesbegriff scheint schwer vereinbar mit dem biblischen, wonach sich Gott in der Geschichte selbst engagiert. Dass Gott immer der Gott von jemand ist, stellt ein religionswissenschaftliches Primärphänomen dar. Bedeutet Relationalität auch Relativität, wie das Philo insinuiert? (...) Dass Gott auch der Gott eines bestimmten Volkes, hier: der Gott Israels ist, erscheint ambivalent." M.a.W.: Philon bringt seine eigene Tradition nur schwer in den griechischen Begriffen unter, die zugleich seine Wertbegriffe sind.

S. 37 bis 54: "Schöpfungsglaube und fremde Religion bei Philo von Alexandrien" (2008) setzt ein bei Jan Assmanns Kritik, Monotheismus sei eine Ursache von Intoleranz, und verfolgt in Bezug auf Philon die Frage: "Hat der Schöpfungsglaube bei ihm inkludierende oder exkludierende Funktion?" Zunächst jedenfalls letzteres; Schöpfungsglaube ist ein "Mittel der Abgrenzung," sofern nämlich Polytheismus als Anbetung von Geschöpfen abgelehnt wird (S. 43ff), ein jüdisches Grundbekenntnis. Jedoch: "Der kämpferische Impetus richtet sich auch nach innen" (S. 53), und philosophische Gotteserkenntnis wird anerkannt. Im Übrigen steht es ja—hier ist Philon mit Josephus einig—jedem Menschen frei, Proselyt zu werden.

Der dritte Beitrag ist in *SPhA* 7, 1995, 19–55 bereits auf Englisch erschienen; hier findet er sich auf Deutsch auf S. 55-99. Der Verf. spürt hier der Metapher vom "Tod der Seele" nach (die auch Niehoff auf S. 138-141 wiedergibt, mit eigenen Belegen). Anders als der Vulgärplatonismus glaubt—selbst Wolfson, *Philo* I, 407–410 muss sich hier korrigieren lassen—, ist die menschliche Seele, in Philons Augen jedenfalls, nur potentiell unsterblich (*Post.* 73 u.ö.; S. 70). Der Verlust des Kontaktes zu Gott könnte ihr Ende bedeuten. In geradezu johanneischer Sprache empfiehlt Philon, im Umsetzen mosaischer Weisheit "das wahre Leben" zu erwerben (*Migr.* 21; S. 72; andere antike Belege auf S. 91). "So werden die philosophischen Lehren von der unsterblichen und tugendhaften Seele als dem wahren Leben des Menschen ein stückweit korrigiert und gerahmt durch Philo's religiöses Denken, das wiederum in der überlieferten jüdischen Frömmigkeit seine Wurzeln hat" (S.99).

S. 101–118: "Philo's spiritualisierende Eschatologie und ihre Nachwirkungen bei den Kirchenvätern" (1997) bleibt auf dieser Spur: Leben und scheinbares Leben, Tod und scheinbarer Tod werden philonisch unterschieden. "Die schönste Definition des unsterblichen Lebens ist: von unfleischlicher, unkörperlicher Liebe und Freundschaft zu Gott besessen zu sein"—so *Fug.* 58, mit anschließendem Bezug auf das "Heute" von Dtn 4,4. Im weiteren Aufsatz geht es sodann um die christlichen "Versuche, die platonische Unsterblichkeit der Seele mit der christlichen Auferstehungslehre zu vermitteln," u.z. bei Clemens von Alexandrien, Origenes, Ambrosius und Augustin. Anonyme, fast wörtliche Philonauszüge und -übersetzungen werden bei Ambrosius in *De paradiso* 1,6; 14,70; *de Cain* 2,9,31 identifiziert. Die Anklänge bei Augustin hingegen dürften nicht auf eigenständige Lektüre zurückgehen, sondern auf Ambrosius.

Die beiden Folgebeiträge (S. 119–128: "Philonische Logos-Theologie im Hintergrund des Konflikts von 1Kor 1–4?" und 129–141: "Die angebliche enthusiastische oder spiritualistische Front 1Kor 15") richten sich gegen Interpretationen vor allem Gerhard Sellins, der in den von Paulus abgelehnten Auffassungen gewisser Christenlehrer in Korinth einen ziemlich direkten Einfluss Philons vermutet hatte, vermittelt nämlich durch den Alexandriner Apollos (Apg 18,24; 1Kor 1,12; 3,6.22; 4,6; 16,12; vgl. Tit 3,13)—eine Auffassung, die auch dem Rez. schon gefallen hat.[9] Die Attraktivität dieser Hypothese ist vor allem eine historische: dass wenigstens einmal ein Übermittlungskanal philonischen Denkens hinein ins Christentum näher benannt werden könnte. Dem hält Zeller entgegen: Zu vieles muss an Philon abgebogen werden, bis eine Heilslehre wie die in Korinth vermutete entsteht. Auch ist die von Paulus bekämpfte Gegenpartei eher ein Sammelbecken für vielerlei auch sonst nachweisbare Auffassungen.

---

[9] In A. Kamesar (Hg.): *The Cambridge Companion to Philo*, 2009, 190f.

Aus den weiteren, sich auf das Neue Testament konzentrierenden Beiträgen sei hervorgehoben S. 189–218: "Zur neueren Diskussion über das Gesetz bei Paulus" (1987). Das ist ein früher Versuch, Ausfälle des Paulus gegen seine eigene jüdische Gesetzesfrömmigkeit (etwa in 1Kor 15,56f) abzufangen, ohne daraus christliche Vorurteile gegen das Judentum abzuleiten. Paulus sieht keinen Sinn in der Empfehlung der Torapraxis *für Nichtjuden*—darin dürfte er sich mit manchem nachmaligen Rabbi einig sein. Andererseits ist Christus für ihn nicht einfach das "Ende" des Gesetzes, sondern durchaus dessen "Ziel" (Röm 10,4)—wobei dann freilich *nomos* im Sinne der ganzen darin bezeugten Offenbarung genommen wird (S. 201).

Ähnliche Überlegungen folgen auch auf S. 209–218: "Tyrann oder Wegweiser? Zum paulinischen Verständnis des Gesetzes" (1993). Ganz zu Recht behält sich auch hier der Verf. eine gewisse Kritik vor: "Den Darlegungen des Apostels über das Gesetz fehlt die letzte Schlüssigkeit, weil er sie selbst immer wieder durchlöchert; so führt er etwa Heiden ein, die das Gesetz halten (Röm 2,16ff.26–29), um einen Kontrast gegen die gesetzesbrüchigen Juden aufzubauen" (S. 215). —"Die pragmatische Ausrichtung der paulinischen Argumentation schließt aber nicht aus, dass diese sich als relativ kohärent herausstellt, wenn man den jeweiligen Kontext beachtet, und dass sich darin echte Erfahrungen niederschlagen können" (ebd.). Ganz ähnlich hatte der Verf. auch bei Philon die Tendenz festgestellt, "Streit zu vermeiden" (S. 50), also die Absicht einer "Schadensbegrenzung" (ebd.), was jedenfalls klug ist in einer Minderheitensituation. Bei dieser Gelegenheit sei noch angemerkt, dass in Philons Selbstwahrnehmung das jüdische Volk das größte ist auf der ganzen Welt (*Virt.* 64, wörtlich: das "menschenreichste"; S. 50).[10] Erst drei Jahrhunderte nach ihm konnte die Kirche sich so wahrnehmen.

S. 225–245: "Christus, Skandal und Hoffnung. Die Juden in den Briefen des Paulus" (1979) nimmt in ähnlichem Geiste Stellung zu solch anstößigen Passagen wie 1Thess 2,14–16 oder Gal 6,16. Es folgt eine Betrachtung zu Röm 9–11. In "Theologie der Mission bei Paulus" (1982, hier S. 247–268) finden sich die oben zitierten religionsphilosophischen Prämissen der Arbeit Zellers ausgesprochen. Faktisch (S. 268) ist das Christentum heute eine eigene Religion, abweichend von dem, was Paulus einst erwartet hatte. "Lässt sich diese Entwicklung—etwa im Gespräch mit dem Judentum—zurückdrehen? Wie weit kann man sich hierbei auf Paulus berufen? Sicher gibt er unserem theologischen Denken auf, dass Israel einen eigenen Heils-

---

[10] Auch heute gibt es Vermutungen, wonach ein Siebtel der Bevölkerung des römischen Reiches jüdisch war.

grund hat: Gottes Verheißungen an die Väter. Aber der konkrete Heilsweg, den er in Röm 11,11–32 in Aussicht nimmt, scheint doch durch die tatsächlichen Ereignisse überholt (S. 268)." Dem lässt sich höchstens hinzufügen, dass der Ausdruck "Heilsweg," beheimatet im Calvinismus neuerer Zeiten, dort einem paulinischen, aber nicht philonischen Rückgriff auf die Exodustradition (1Kor 10 < Ex 13–14) entspricht;[11] bis heute passt er auf das Selbstbewusstsein der jüdischen Seite sehr wenig. Was dieses betrifft—da man als Jude und als Glied des Bundes ja schon geboren wird—, kommt nicht erst Franz Rosenzweig, sondern schon Philon vom Heil her. Er muss nicht erst auf es zugehen; die Gefahr wäre höchstens, es zu verlieren ("Tod der Seele").

All das sind Fragestellungen, die sich aus einer nicht nur philologischen, sondern auch theologischen Philon-Lektüre ergeben. Sie als Gegenwartsbezüge im Rahmen historisch-kritisch argumentierender Aufsätze aufgewiesen zu haben, ist nicht das geringste Verdienst der hier neu vorgelegten Beiträge.

Folker Siegert
Westfälischen Wilhelms-Universität Münster

CHARLES A. ANDERSON, *Philo of Alexandria's Views of the Physical World.* Wissenschaftliche Untersuchungen zum Neuen Testament 2.309. Mohr Siebeck: Tübingen, 2011. xii + 299 pages. ISBN 978-3-16-150640-6. Price €74.

The study under review began as a Cambridge dissertation under the supervision of Prof. Markus Bockmuehl. Originally the author set out to study the ethical appeals that Paul made to creation in 1 Corinthians, for which he needed to take a quick look at Philo. The Philonic aspect of the research soon gained hold and in the end it took over completely. But the original purpose of the research still comes through clearly in the final product. The aim of the study is to determine the "ethical status" of the physical and sense-perceptible world in Philo's thought. How does Philo evaluate the world in which we live and what does this mean for human action in relation to that world and the God who created it?

The method that Anderson uses to formulate an answer is primarily lexical. He takes six key terms for Philo's description of the world and its

---

[11] Der Begriff „Heil" (σωτηρία) ist bei Philon ebenso stark schöpfungstheologisch gefüllt wie bei Paulus eschatologisch.

creation—οὐσία, ὕλη, γένεσις, γενητός, κόσμος, φύσις—and gives a thorough analysis of their contextual use in the entire Philonic corpus, taking into account their background in the LXX , Jewish literature and Greek philosophy. It emerges that the first four are predominantly negative, the latter two highly positive. The task is then to resolve this apparent ambivalence in Philo's views. A first step is to examine higher and lower approaches to God. There are indirect and direct ways to see God and there are lower and higher categories of people engaged in that search. Philo's pronouncements depend on the perspective that he takes on a question, as revealed in the very different kinds of commentaries he wrote. Anderson aptly calls this Philo's "multi-perspectivalism" (p. 167) and regards it as the key to understanding the many apparent contradictions in his pronouncements.

In the final chapter our author reaches his conclusions. Philo's ambivalence about the ethical status of the sense-perceptible world runs very deep. At a more superficial level the world is praised and it can lead to recognition of the creator. At a deeper level, however, to know and have communion with God is to reject the world completely. Although the passages indicating this view are much fewer in number than the positive ones, they represent his deepest and truest thought. In reaching this view Philo takes a more negative stance than scripture (both the LXX and Paul) and Greek philosophy, particularly Plato and the Stoa. If he is to be compared to anyone, then it would be the pessimistic Middle Platonist thinkers such as Plutarch or Numenius, or even the Gnostics (though his recognition of God the good creator makes him at most a pre-Gnostic). The source of his pessimism is a strong mystical-ascetic impulse, which operates at an underlying level in his psyche and leads to strong condemnation of all that has to do with the body and its impulses.

In many regards this study is an excellent piece of research, representing the state-of-the-art in current Philonic scholarship. The author is extremely well-read and acutely aware of methodological problems. He follows recent scholarship in taking account of the differences between Philo's various kinds of writings, both exegetical and other. He has worked astonishingly hard to sift through all the cases of Philo's use of the six main terms he has studied. In adopting his lexical approach he is careful to contextualise the use of the terms, as indicated by his emphasis on Philo's perspective in utilizing them. The book has a well-thought through and systematic structure, in which the evidence provided leads logically to the conclusions reached.

Despite all these virtues the study reaches conclusions that in my view are not convincing. I am not persuaded that in the final analysis Philo reaches a more negative stance on the physical world than almost any other thinker in the Jewish or the Greek world before the advent of Gnosticism and Neoplatonism. Yet, as I just said, the book proceeds systematically from the evidence to its conclusions. Where have things gone wrong?

Nearly sixty years ago the great American Platonic scholar Harold Cherniss wrote a short but profound article on "the sources of evil according to Plato" (*Selected Papers*, pp. 23–30). He pointed out that there are levels of evil in the Platonic worldview. The entire world of sense-perceptible reality cannot match the perfection of the ideal world, and so it is tainted with a weak sense of evil. This is what Philo refers to in *Opif.* 151 when he says that mutability is an ineradicable element of the world of γένεσις (the locus classicus in Plato for this view is *Tht.* 176a, a text which is underutilized in Anderson's study). A stronger kind of evil is represented by the body, since it obstructs purposeful rational change and movement. But the strongest kind of evil is moral, when the soul, living in the world of sense-perceptible reality and distracted by the body, goes astray, makes mistakes and leads the wrong kind of life. Only this level is comparable to the biblical notion of "sin." When Anderson states that "evil belongs to the essence of γένεσις as concrete creation," he fails to distinguish clearly enough between these different levels of imperfection and evil.

There can be no doubt that at its deepest level Philo's thought is profoundly influenced by Platonism and particularly by its dualism of matter and mind. In that sense Anderson is right that Philo is more negative than, for example, Paul, for whom the cosmos and the body have the eschatological perspective of transformation into sinless perfection. Yet at the same time Philo surely has a much more positive view of the cosmos and its powers, including the heavenly bodies and nature, than Paul does. I fully agree with Anderson that perspective is the key. But I am not persuaded that he follows this insight through correctly. Naturally references to matter, becoming, and the body are going to be especially negative in the Allegorical Commentary, because in that work Philo is describing the journey of the soul, which is in danger of making the wrong decisions due to the distractions that the realm of body and becoming represent. Anderson makes much of a text at *Her.* 160 in which "Philo interprets Gen 1:31 so it praises God's creative skill in what he has made and not the stuff from which it is made" (p. 188, cf. pp. 174–175). But this is not exact. What Philo says is that God did not praise the material that he had used for his work (ὕλη, i.e. Platonic dualism) but the works of his own skill (τὰ ἕαυτοῦ τεχνικὰ ἔργα). The physical world, *qua* divine creation through the divine Logos, is praiseworthy and human beings do well to follow the divine example.

At heart the argument of this study follows a simple syllogistic logic. Philo is ambivalent about the world of physical reality and, in his interpretation of scripture, makes both optimistic and pessimistic pronouncements about it (of which the former are much more numerous than the latter). The optimistic statements belong to what he states to be the lower approach to reality, the pessimistic to the higher approach. Therefore, despite appearances, the pessimistic pronouncements represent his deepest and truest thought. In response to this conclusion I would argue that Philo is deeply influenced by Platonic philosophy in his reading of scripture and as a result he displays the same *tension* (not contradiction) between a negative view of physical reality expressed in *Tht.* 176a and a positive view given full expression in the *Timaeus*. The positive view has the strong overhand and is integral to Philo's view of creation, which ultimately has biblical roots. The negative view is strongly contextual because it almost always occurs when Philo wants to explain how the soul goes astray, focusing on the body and distracted by the passions from seeking God.

But the reader might say to me: you wrote your dissertation on Philo's use of the *Timaeus* and through the years you have conditioned yourself to privilege Philo's positive evaluation of the world of God's creation at the expense of the passages that express his negative view. To such a reader I would say: read this well-crafted and thought-provoking piece of research for yourself. You will learn a great deal and not regret taking the trouble to do so.

David T. Runia
Queen's College
The University of Melbourne

JONATHAN D. WORTHINGTON, *Creation in Paul and Philo*. Wissenschaftliche Untersuchungen zum Neuen Testament 2.317. Tübingen: Mohr Siebeck, 2011. xiii + 260. ISBN 978-3-16-150839-4. Price €64.

This book is a revision of a Ph.D. dissertation at Durham University directed by Francis Watson. It began with the author's reflections on Paul's soteriology. Paul stresses humankind's plight arising from Adam's fall and the salvation offered in Christ. But what about *before* the beginning of sin in the world? Eschatology is a well-known feature of Paul's theology, but it is usually not noticed that protology plays an important role as well. This book is intended to fill that gap in Pauline scholarship. It also serves as an important study of protology in the biblical commentaries produced by Paul's near-contemporary, Philo of Alexandria.

The book focuses on three of Paul's letters: 1 and 2 Corinthians and Romans, where most of Paul's references to Genesis are found, and serves as a kind of commentary on Paul's theology of creation. Worthington argues that by placing Paul's references to creation next to the formal commentary on Gen 1–2 written by Philo (*De opificio mundi*) more can be discerned about Paul's reading of creation. He argues that a broad hermeneutical similarity can be discerned between the two interpreters, based on the authority of the biblical text for both. He organizes his book around the following proposal: "Paul's interpretation of creation, like Philo's in his commentary, contains three interwoven aspects: the beginning of the world, the beginning of humanity, and God's intentions before the beginning (p. 3)."

The first chapter is entitled, "Before the Beginning?" and treats what God was doing or thinking before he began to create. For both Paul and Philo God's creative acts are preceded by his thoughts. While Gen 1–2 are central texts for both Philo and Paul, Prov 8:22–31 is also an important text for both. That text explicitly deals with "pre-protology," but also evokes Gen 1.

In this chapter Worthington first deals extensively with Philo's "Before." He notes that, for Philo, the existence of God's Ideas according to which creation unfolds is a necessary prerequisite for the world's beginning. Philo describes God's pre-creational plan under the strong influence of Plato's *Timaeus*. What is described in Gen 1:1–5 is the "incorporeal" heaven and "invisible" earth, i.e. the "ideas" of the world in Plato's terminology.

Paul's "Before," in contrast, has to do with God's pre-creation deliberation centered in the cross of Christ. The key text here is 1 Cor 2:7, God's "wisdom" centered in the cross of Christ decreed "before the ages for our glorification." Whereas for Philo God's pre-deliberations have an "ontic structural focus," for Paul they have what Worthington terms a "historical redemptive focus" (p. 76). I would suggest that "eschatological" would be a better term. "Philo is confident that due to God's intentions *before* creation the physical world would turn out structurally 'good,' Paul is confident that due to God's intentions before creation all things in history (even suffering) will turn out 'for good' and 'for glory' for those who love God (ibid.)." I would add "in the end-time," stressing Paul's eschatological focus.

Chapter two is entitled "The Beginning of the World." Both for Philo and for Paul God's creation of light is something special. Of course, they read Gen 1:2–5 quite differently. For Philo, the "light" of those verses "was an invisible light that would serve as a paradigm for all light-bearing bodies in Gen 1:14–19" (p. 83). Paul, on the other hand, sees in God's creation of light a motif for describing the personal illumination experienced by

Christian believers. The key text here is 2 Cor 4:6. The "face" of Christ shines his "glory" into the hearts of believers. Whereas Philo relates the shining of Gen 1:2–5 paradigmatically to the subsequent shining of the heavenly bodies, Paul relates the same text to "the historical shining in the hearts of believers who recognized God's glory in the risen body of Jesus" (p. 96).

As for the following verses in Gen 1, i.e. 6–31, Philo and Paul have very different interpretations. Philo understands these verses to mean that God granted an ontological "immortality" to the world, and prepared the cosmos for humanity according to his previous purpose. Paul's interpretation of Gen 1:6–31 can be found in 1 Cor 15:35–41. "Paul looks up and sees 'bodies' in the two cosmic realms: in heaven and on earth." The two realms "are not only distinguishable but also appropriate for their own kinds of bodies" (p. 128). Of course, Paul's arguments here occur in the larger context of his discussion of the resurrection of the dead in the end-time. Even so, "Paul's End still does not leave behind either the Beginning or the Before, for Paul casts the End in the language and conceptuality of both" (p. 135).

The third and final chapter is entitled "The Beginning of Humanity." Worthington treats first Philo's and Paul's readings of Gen 1:27 and the "image of God." He notes that Philo has two very different readings of that verse. In the first reading (*Opif.* 69–88) Philo treats the human as corporeal and composite, a "human body" and a "mind." The "image of God" in humankind is "the mind, which rules the soul" (*Opif.* 69.7–8, p. 144). Philo argues that humanity was created last because God was preparing the world for the best and most perfect of created beings. "The Beginning of the world is intimately related to the Beginning of humanity, even to the 'earth-born' human of Gen 1:27, and this is so because of the pre-creational divine design, i.e. the Before (p. 147)."

Philo's other reading of Gen 1:27 occurs in the context of his discussion of Gen 2 (*Opif.* 131ff.) Philo now finds the beginning of the sense-perceptible world in Gen 2:6, rather than 1:6, the sensible world taking shape in accord with the noetic. In the case of humanity, Philo finds in Gen 2:7 two humans, the man of 1:27 as bodiless. "Philo has re-construed the human of 1:27 as the 'incorporeal,' 'noetic' 'idea' of humanity (p. 151)."

Worthington also finds two readings of Gen 1:27 in Paul, one in 1 Cor 11:7 and the other in 2 Cor 4:4. In the former Paul combines Gen 1:27 and Gen 2 to explain "certain aspects of bi-gendered anthropology and therefore worship-practice" (p. 152). Paul considers the initial human, Adam, as "a visible reflector of God's glory," unlike Eve who was "from man" (Gen

1:21–23); so men and women "perform their shared worship in different manners" (156–57).

In the second passage, Paul refers to Christ as "the image of God," whose "glory" shines into hearts of darkness. In that passage the humans blinded by darkness are the progeny of the fallen Adam into whose hearts the light shines. While Gen 1:3 is reflected in that passage, the emphasis is on the redemptive work of Christ, the "image of God."

Worthington takes up next Philo's interpretation of Gen 2:7. As already noted, the corporeal human of Gen 2:7 is contrasted with the incorporeal human of Gen 1:27. But the noetic human comes into the corporeal human through God's inbreathing. "When God breathes into the human face the sensory human 'becomes' an 'image' and 'copy' of God's 'word'... . Since the Adam of 2:7 has 'the ruling mind in the soul' he can here be identified as an 'image' (*apeikonisma*) of God's word" (p. 172).

Paul, too, has two portrayals of the first-created Adam, one negative and the other positive. Paul's positive reading is found in his references to Adam's "glory" prior to the fall in 1 Cor 11:7–9, 12:12–30, and 15:39–40. The "inglorious" Adam appears in 1 Cor 15:44b–47, where Paul shifts from the Beginning to the End. Paul sees in Gen 2:7 a reference to two Adams, one earthly and the other heavenly, a "life-giving spirit." Worthington argues that Paul considers "the first Adam to have been created perfect" (i.e. "flawless") but not the "perfect (i.e. full) human" because he "lacked what God pre-intended for the eschatological age of Jesus' resurrection and Spirit" (pp. 183–84). But in 1 Cor 15:42ff. Paul's references to the bodies "sown" into the ground are not to Adam's originally created body, but to the bodies of the fallen Adam and his progeny.

The last passage in Genesis discussed in this book is 5:3, where it is said that Seth was born in Adam's "image." Philo's reading of that passage is completely positive. As for Paul's treatment of the "image" of Adam, Worthington sees Gen 5:3 reflected in three passages: 1 Cor 15:49, 2 Cor 3:18, and Romans 8:29. In the first passage Paul contrasts the image of the "earthly" Adam which is borne by all humans with the image of the "heavenly" Adam (the resurrected Christ) which will be borne by all believers. As for 2 Cor 3:18, I am not able to follow Worthington in seeing in that passage a reflection of Gen 5:3. In Romans 8:29, Paul refers to God having predestined the believers' being conformed to the image of his resurrected son, thus making of the risen Christ "the first-born of many brethren." God's children "were marked out before creation to receive glory through the pre-creationally marked out method which God subsequently initiated in Gen 5:3" (p. 202).

Chapter 3 is followed by a short "Conclusion" (pp. 205–210), plus an extensive bibliography and indices.

While I have some minor disagreements with Worthington on his interpretation of Paul, I consider his book to be a major contribution to scholarship on Paul, and on Philo as well.

Birger A. Pearson
Emeritus, University of California, Santa Barbara

WILLIAM LOADER, *The Pseudepigrapha on Sexuality: Attitudes towards Sexuality in Apocalypses, Testaments, Legends, Wisdom, and Related Literature.* Attitudes Towards Sexuality in Judaism and Christianity in the Hellenistic Greco-Roman Era 3. Grand Rapids, Mich.: Eerdmans, 2011. xiii + 571 pages. ISBN 978-0-8028-6666-0. Price $65.

The third volume in a series on attitudes toward sexuality in Judaism and Christianity in the Hellenistic Greco-Roman era, *The Pseudepigrapha on Sexuality* by William Loader, investigates sexuality in all Second Temple Jewish literature apart from Philo, Josephus, early Enochic literature, and the Dead Sea Scrolls (the foci of other volumes in the series). Thus, despite the main title, the book covers not only texts commonly identified with the term pseudepigrapha but also material from the Septuagint and elsewhere. Loader defines "sexuality" broadly to include marriage, childbearing and rearing, infanticide, circumcision, attitudes toward women, women's roles in marriage and society, and women as metaphors. Loader's analysis interacts on occasion with the writings of Philo, accessible through an index of ancient sources. As he intends to investigate each text "in its own integrity" (p. 1), he proceeds text by text, dividing the literature into three major categories. Nevertheless, the book helpfully concludes with a preliminary synthesis, anticipating a more comprehensive assessment upon conclusion of the five-volume series.

Part one investigates apocalypses, testaments, and related writings. In the *Parables of Enoch*, Loader finds the topic of sexuality incidental rather than central. Sexual wrongdoing has indirectly contributed to the current chaos and is a sign of it, but the primary ethical critique is directed not against sexual behavior but rather against violence and social injustice. Loader finds even less interest in sexuality in *2 Enoch*, which he concludes does not condemn human sexuality in general. Similarly, while *2 Baruch* denounces the sexual violence of Roman oppression, it appears to assume sexual activity in the new age. Despite the concern of *4 Ezra* for the evil heart of humankind, it never points to sexual wrongdoing as evidence of this evil.

Fourth Ezra is also "remarkable in its use of the imagery of child-bearing" (p. 98), and like *Baruch*, depicts Jerusalem as mother and wisdom as female. *The Testament of Moses* uses mothering images to describe leadership, also showing concern for issues of intermarriage and circumcision. Whereas a number of interpreters have argued that *The Testament of Job* depicts women negatively, Loader concludes that because nothing in the text devalues women for their sexuality or their involvement in the processes of birth, "sexuality as such plays a relatively minor role" (p. 132).

By contrast, the *Apocalypse of Abraham* identifies sexual desire as an impetus for sin, while the *Testament of Solomon* portrays human desire in general as "having demonic origins" (p. 140). Similarly, Books 1–2 of *The Sibylline Oracles*, by suppressing the sexuality of the garden story in Genesis and anticipating that there will be no marriage in paradise, seems to limit sex in marriage to procreation. (However, Loader views the section on paradise as possibly a Christian interpolation.) The *Sibylline Oracles* also strongly condemn what the authors view as abnormal or unnatural sex, such as pederasty, male prostitution, adultery, same sex relations, etc. The *Letter of Jeremiah* censures sacral prostitution, and *The Testament of Abraham* decries the sin of adultery (but when Abraham calls down judgment on adulterers, a patient God intervenes, giving sinners time to repent).

Part two analyzes histories, legends, and related writings. "The Tale of Three Youths" (1 Esd 3:1–5:6) offers a relatively positive view of the traditional "role of women in the patriarchal household" and of romantic love in the context of marriage, alongside "boy's humour" depicting women's sexuality as dangerous and men as unable to resist their attraction: a "tacit espousal of sexual irresponsibility" (pp. 144–45).

Tobit shows much interest in marriage, including fidelity, warnings against fornication, the place of marriage within one's extended family, and divine selection of one's spouse. The marriage of Tobit and Anna is characterized by respect and love despite their problems. By comparison with Anna, Edna is more subservient, and her marriage with Raguel would likely be seen by the original audience as proper and normal. The union of Tobias and Sarah depicts desire positively and also provides useful information about marriage practices that might have occurred in the real world.

The book of Judith affirms a woman as an agent of divine will and as a symbolic representation of Israel. Countering feminist interpretations, Loader argues that Judith's return to her estate at the end of the story is not an attempt by the author to subvert the picture of female authority. If Judith affirms a woman's authority, Susanna affirms female sexuality and attacks the corrupt sexual behavior of men in authority, as well as any who condone their behavior. In both texts, as in the "Tale of Three Youths," male sexuality has the potential to cause men to look foolish. Like Judith, *Joseph and Aseneth* elevates its female protagonist to representative status, a "path for future proselytes" (p. 328). Championing marriage between proselytes and Jews, it also affirms sex within marriage and hints at an egalitarian relationship. (However, in agreement with feminist interpreters, Loader views Aseneth's depiction as more subservient in the longer recension.) The *Additions to Esther* presents Esther as a victim of sexual exploitation, having been forced into service to the king.

In *LAB*, licit sexual relations (in marriage) feature regularly as a normal part of human life, governed by the mandate to multiply. As such, celibacy is viewed negatively. Intermarriage is strongly condemned, but the "loophole" of Joseph and Aseneth is not treated by the author. While *LAB* gives particular attention to women, female characters appear primarily in the context of childbearing and motherhood. The text's depiction of paradise as a sanctuary suggests an absence of sex in the new age. First and Second Maccabees condemn illicit sexuality near the temple and depict some men's shame about their circumcisions, but surprisingly, these books do not deal much with sexual issues that must have resulted from Hellenization. Like *T. Sol.*, the *Life of Adam and Eve* and the *Apocalypse of Moses* view passion negatively, associating sex with the devil and accepting it only as necessary for procreation.

Part three examines psalms, wisdom writings, and fragmentary works. Sexuality appears in the *Psalms of Solomon* in the context of crisis and community. Related to crisis, illicit sex is viewed as characteristic of Gentiles yet tragically, practiced by Jews, leading to Pompey's conquest. Community instruction includes both condemnation of officials and judges who use their positions to engage in adultery and a concern that men cannot resist wicked women (as in Judith, Susanna, and "Tale of Three Youths"). In contrast to *Jos. Asen.*, *Pss. Sol.* condemns marriage between proselytes and Jews but seems to view positively desire within licit marriage.

The section on Sirach, contributed by Ibolya Balla, compares the Hebrew manuscripts with the Greek translation, concluding that Ben Sira's grandson toned down the erotic content of the original. Ben Sira is more concerned with the sexuality and marital qualities of women than of men. He shares the view that women's sexuality is dangerous for men yet views desire within marriage positively. The wisdom poems, depicting personified wisdom with her lover, most clearly show that "Ben Sira is not shy about sexuality" (p. 392).

The Wisdom of Solomon addresses the wrong sexual behavior of wayward Jews and pagan idolaters but ignores sexual wrongdoing in its recital of Jewish history. While offering a less erotic depiction of wisdom as lover, by comparison with other texts, it is nowhere negative toward sexuality in general. *Pseudo-Aristeus* condemns male homosexual prostitution and incest with mothers and daughters. Fourth Maccabees intends sexual desire to conform to the requirements of Torah and Augustan law and shows a remarkable interest in the processes of childbearing and rearing, which provides a context for the author's encomium of the manly courage of the mother of seven sons. *Pseudo-Phocylides* emphasizes the link between sexuality and procreation, perhaps reflecting Stoic ideals.

Overall, the volume provides a wealth of data on the subject of sexuality in a variety of texts in Second Temple Judaism. Its strengths are the consistently careful, thorough, and scholarly analyses of individual texts, prefaced by short introductions on textual issues and provenance and informed by relevant secondary literature. The expertise resulting from Loader's wider project produces many thought-provoking observations. He also regularly explores not only instances where sexuality is present in a text but also where it might logically have appeared but did not, drawing tentative conclusions from these silences. The in-depth analyses of individual texts invite comparison and synthesis. While the final chapter begins to answer this call by arranging conclusions into categories, readers may hope for a more thorough synthesis upon the conclusion of the series, along with a subject index to the five volumes.

Kindalee Pfremmer De Long
Pepperdine University, Malibu, Calif.

WILLIAM LOADER. *Philo, Josephus, and the Testaments on Sexuality: Attitudes towards Sexuality in the Writings of Philo and Josephus and in the Testaments of the Twelve Patriarchs*. Attitudes towards Sexuality in Judaism and Christianity in the Hellenistic Greco-Roman Era 4. Grand Rapids: William B. Eerdmans, 2011. Pp. xii + 476. ISBN 978-0-8028-6641-7. Price $65.

This is the fourth volume in William Loader's survey of texts dealing with sexuality in Jewish and Christian works in the Hellenistic and Roman worlds. It is the final volume covering Jewish sources. The first addressed

Enochic traditions, Aramaic Levi, and *Jubilees*;[12] the second surveyed the Dead Sea Scrolls;[13] and the third explored Jewish pseudepigrapha.[14] Loader plans to turn to the Christian material in a fifth volume (pp. xii, 437), but has already published several volumes laying the groundwork.[15]

Loader organizes this volume into three parts, one part devoted to each author or text: Part One, the most extensive section, deals with Philo (pp. 2–258); Part Two explores the writings of Josephus (pp. 259–367); and Part Three works its way through the *Testaments of the Twelve Patriarchs* (pp. 368-435). The goal of each part is to provide a comprehensive survey of the material related to sexuality. Loader has worked through the writings of each author/text and identified the references—including metaphorical references—to sexuality. He has read the scholarly literature that deals with each author's/text's references to sexuality and engaged them in his own reading. The one major lacuna is that Loader only points to parallels in the larger Greco–Roman world *en passant* when citing the analyses of others. This has the advantage of highlighting the texts of Philo, Josephus, and the *Testaments*, but the disadvantage of minimalizing the context of their *Umwelt*.

Loader prefaced his analysis of Philo in Part One with a *status quaestionis* on Philo's views on women and sexuality (pp. 2–10). The summary set up a fundamental tension that surfaces repeatedly in his analyses of Philo's discussions: the negative statements—often drawing on Platonic or Stoic philosophy—that Philo makes about the feminine and the qualities associated with the feminine (e.g., sense perception) versus Philo's more positive statements about specific women and creation. Loader recognizes the tension and handles it by pointing to the rhetorical nature of Philo's negative statements and argues that they should not be made absolute but

---

[12] William Loader, *Enoch, Levi, and Jubilees on Sexuality: Attitudes towards Sexuality in the Early Enoch Literature, the Aramaic Levi Document, and the Book of Jubilees* (Attitudes towards Sexuality in Judaism and Christianity in the Hellenistic Greco-Roman Era 1; Grand Rapids: Eerdmans, 2007).

[13] William Loader, *The Dead Sea Scrolls on Sexuality: Attitudes towards Sexuality in Sectarian and Related Literature at Qumran* (Attitudes towards Sexuality in Judaism and Christianity in the Hellenistic Greco-Roman Era 2; Grand Rapids: Eerdmans, 2009).

[14] William Loader, *The Pseudepigrapha on Sexuality: Attitudes towards Sexuality in Apocalypses, Testaments, Legends, Wisdom, and Related Literature; with a Contribution by Ibolya Baila on Ben Sira/Sirach* (Attitudes towards Sexuality in Judaism and Christianity in the Hellenistic Greco-Roman Era 3; Grand Rapids: Eerdmans, 2011). See the review in this volume.

[15] William Loader, *The Septuagint, Sexuality, and the New Testament: Case Studies on the Impact of the* LXX *in Philo and the New Testament* (Grand Rapids: Eerdmans, 2004); idem, *Sexuality and the Jesus Tradition* (Grand Rapids: Eerdmans, 2005); and idem, *Sexuality in the New Testament: Understanding the Key Texts* (Louisville, KY: Westminster John Knox, 2010).

must be weighed within the framework of Philo's thought, e.g. pp. 45–55, 87, 230. The result is a balanced approach that—in my judgment—correctly captures the basic views of Philo on women, sexuality and pleasure.

Loader explores Philo's comments by following the lead of the biblical text as Philo understood it in the Exposition of the Law: he opens with creation (Gen 1–3), considers allusions and images beyond the fall (Gen 4–11, 12–50; Exodus); and then the laws in the Exposition using *Decal.* and *Spec.* as keys. This echoes the three parts of the Law in Philo's presentation of the Pentateuch in *Praem.* 1–3: creation, the historical, and the legislative (see p. 10).[16] Loader should be saluted for recognizing the exegetical nature of Philo's work and following his basic approach to the biblical text. Further, Loader recognizes the fact that Philo wrote three separate commentaries and that they should be treated separately. He helpfully points differences in the views that Philo takes as a result of the different orientations of the commentary series. Unfortunately—in my judgment—he works through them in the order of the Exposition, the *Questions and Answers*, and then the Allegorical Commentary, e.g., pp. 76–84, 91–99, 110–17. He would have done better to have taken them in chronological order: the *Questions and Answers*, the Allegorical Commentary, and the Exposition—although I recognize that the relationship among the series is not without dispute.[17]

Loader's assessment of Philo is that the Alexandrian viewed sexuality positively but narrowly. The Alexandrian criticized excess in pleasure which led to unacceptable sexual practices. For Philo, sexuality should be for procreative purposes in a heterosexual marital relationship. Within this framework it is not only acceptable, but can be pleasurable. In this general assessment and in his specific judgments about a wide range of Philonic texts, I think that Loader offers solid analyses and draws reasonable conclusions. In such a wide range of texts, differences in judgment are inevitable. Specialists will also think of things that one might have mentioned but Loader did not, e.g., he might have drawn from Adam Kamesar's recogni-

---

[16] Philo provided summaries in *Abr.* 2–5 and *Mos.* 2.45–47 as well. There are significant differences. *Abr.* has two parts: creation and the laws. *Mos.* has two parts as well, but considers them the historical part followed by commands and prohibitions.

[17] On the relationship between the Allegorical Commentary and the Exposition of the Law see my forthcoming "'Prolific in Expression and Broad in Thought': Internal References to Philo's Allegorical Commentary and Exposition of the Law," *Euphrosyne* (in press). See also Jenny Morris, "The Jewish Philosopher Philo," in Emil Schürer, *The History of the Jewish People in the Age of Jesus Christ* (3 vols.; rev. by Geza Vermes, Fergus Millar, and Martin Goodman; Edinburgh: T&T Clark, 1973–86), 3:841–44 and Maren Niehoff, *Jewish Exegesis and Homeric Scholarship in Alexandria* (Cambridge: Cambridge University Press, 2011), 133-51.

tion about the function of characters to serve as *exempla* for virtues or vices[18] or have addressed the issue of intention in his treatment of a text like *Migr.* 225 (pp. 175–76) or referred to Erwin R. Goodenough when he suggested that Philo's treatments of the laws might reflect experience in a Jewish court (p. 257).[19] These comments do not detract from the impressive collection of Philonic material and Loader's basic evaluation of them.

Loader follows a similar structure in Part Two when he treats Josephus's writings: he opens with an introduction that sets out some of the basic issues in treating the Josephan corpus, works through the narratives of the *Antiquitates Judaicae* and *Bellum* by selecting those that deal with sexual issues in chronological order, summarizes the law codes that Josephus gives, synthesizes Josephus's statements on relevant issues, and finally provides a summary. Again, Loader's control of Josephus and the scholarly literature is impressive. He uses the secondary literature, but forms his own judgments in very responsible ways, e.g., see his discussion on Ezra and intermarriage on pp. 299–300. Josephus shares the same basic views on sexuality as Philo, only he lacks the depth of rationale that Philo offers for many of his judgments. He summarized his view in *CA* 2.199: "the Law recognizes sexual union only in the natural relation with a woman, and this if it is for the procreation of children." Like Philo, he recognized that a man and woman could have pleasure in such a relationship (*AJ* 2.251–52).

The scope of the treatment once again means that those who are familiar with Josephus and Josephan scholarship will have differences and think of issues that might draw more attention, e.g., Loader notes that Josephus knew *Jubilees* when retelling creation, but fails to recognize his debt to Philo—more specifically Philo's *De opificio mundi*;[20] similarly, he recognizes the need to point to a possible source behind Moses's marriage to an Ethiopian but only cites Feldman's commentary (p. 285 n. 11). While this list could be expanded, it does not detract from the impressive grasp that Loader demonstrates in handling Josephus's texts.

The third and final part deals with the *Testaments of the Twelve Patriarchs*. Loader recognizes that the text as we now have it is a Christian

---

[18] Adam Kamesar, "Biblical Interpretation in Philo," in *The Cambridge Companion to Philo* (ed. Adam Kamesar; Cambridge: Cambridge University Press, 2009), 88–89.

[19] See Erwin R. Goodenough, *The Jurisprudence of the Jewish Courts in Egypt: Legal Administration by the Jews under the early Roman Empire as described by Philo Judaeus* (New Haven: Yale University Press, 1929) and idem, *The Politics of Philo Judaeus: Practice and Theory* (New Haven: Yale University Prss, 1938).

[20] See my "Recherché or Representative? What is the Relationship between Philo's Treatises and Greek-speaking Judaism?," *SPhA* 11 (1999): 27–29.

text; however, he argues—quite responsibly—that it has Jewish roots. He works through each of the testaments, but appropriately devotes the lion's share of his attention to the *Testament of Reuben* (pp. 371–90), the *Testament of Levi* (pp. 392–400), and the *Testament of Judah* (pp. 400–411). The major contribution made by these testaments is their psychological exploration of sexual immorality and its consequences, e.g., the role of sight and desire. He notes that the testaments recognize the presence of external demonic forces, but argues that humans are still responsible (e.g., pp. 376–79, 408–09). There are far fewer texts in the *Testaments of the Twelve Patriarchs* and Loader is able to deal with them more fully.

This is an impressive collection of texts from three major bodies of literature in Second Temple Judaism/Early Christianity. One of its greatest strengths might also be seen as a weakness. The comprehensive collection of relevant texts means that this can be used as a reference work by others looking for assistance on a particular issue or passage in these three corpora; at the same time, it feels like one is reading a reference work. The result is that it may prove to be more useful as a work to consult than as a monograph to read. It should be a standard "go to" source for those working on sexuality in Second Temple Judaism and Early Christianity. We are in Loader's debt for providing such a work.

Gregory E. Sterling
Yale University

Sara Mancini Lombardi & Paola Pontani, eds., *Studies on the Ancient Armenian Version of Philo's Works*. Studies in Philo of Alexandria 6. Leiden, Brill, 2011. viii + 222 pages. ISBN 978-90-04-18466-4. Price €86, $123.

This volume, aimed at acquainting scholars with studies on the Armenian version of Philo, a version that preserves several works the Greek originals of which have been lost and which has a rather distinctive reception history in medieval Armenian literature, accomplishes its purpose in a most impressive way.

In nine articles in English, including an introduction by Gabriella Uluhogian that sums up the contents (pp. 1–6), the various authors touch on a variety of subjects dealing with the Armenian corpus of Philo's works. The volume may best be described as a scholarly venture by six contributors from Italy (three women and three men) with mostly linguistic/philological interest in Armenian renditions from Greek, and three contributors from Armenia (all women) with interest mostly in the history of

Philonic interpretation in the Armenian tradition. Uluhogian rightly describes the volume in the opening page as follows: "This collection of essays is emblematic of the contribution of the Italian school of Armenian Studies—as it is now widely known—on this major Alexandrian author within the panorama of studies devoted to Armenian translations of Greek texts over the last fifty years." She, along with a colleague at the Catholic University of Milan, the late Giancarlo Bolognesi, were responsible in preparing a cadre of scholars devoted to deciphering the translation techniques behind such works rendered from Greek originals. While Bolognesi devoted much of his attention to the Armenian text of Philo (a sample of his studies, translated from a previously published article in Italian, appears as the second essay in this volume: "Marginal Notes on the Armenian Translation of the *Quaestiones et Solutiones in Genesin* by Philo," pp. 45–50), Uluhogian gave her attention to Patristic works rendered by the same school of Armenian translators, who were collectively known as the "Hellenizing School" for typically maintaining the Greek syntax.

For Philonists, perhaps the most informative of the essays is Anna Sirinian's "'Armenian Philo': a Survey of the Literature" (pp. 7–44), in which she updates earlier surveys by Folgert Siegert (1989) and the reviewer of this volume (1995). She errs, however, in stating that "Siegert's 1989 essay was the last attempt at a *status quaestionis*" (p. 10). She begins with some interesting history of the Lvov manuscript donated to the Venetian Mekhitharists (MS 1040, the preferred Armenian manuscript of the works of Philo) and the scholarly interest it generated even before Aucher's edition of the works that survive in Armenian only (published in two volumes in Venice, 1822 and 1826). She concludes her survey with six *desiderata*, foremost of which is the need for a critical text of the Armenian *corpus Philonicum*, assuming that "the new text will certainly be an improvement upon the precious, but largely obsolete, Mechitarist editions" (p. 38). I am not so sure about the estimated certainty of the anticipated outcome of such an undertaking, judging from Hans Lewy's work on the text of the pseudo-Philonic *De Jona* (1936) and Maurizio Olivieri's 2000 dissertation, *Il secondo libro del* De Providentia *di Filone Alessandrino: i frammenti greci e la tradizione armena* (Università degli Studi di Bologna), in which a collation of the known Armenian manuscripts is provided for the text of *Prov.* II (pp. 127–227). Other *desiderata*, partially fulfilled in this volume, include study of the formation of the corpus; comparative study of translated works of other authors; study of the indirect tradition of the Armenian Philo text through such witnesses as commentaries and scholia; the influence of Philo on medieval Armenian authors; and, finally, the enhancement of digitized resources, including Gk.-Arm. indices and lexica, such as the Leiden

Armenian Lexical Textbase (LALT). Her classified bibliography in three appendices (pp. 40–44) preempts the need for a separate bibliography at the end of the volume.

Although the subsequent articles are alphabetically arranged following the respective authors' names, there is a remarkable degree of logical continuity in their sequence. In "The Armenian Version of Philo Alexandrinus: Translation Technique, Biblical Citations" (pp. 51–85), Gohar Muradyan compares the translation technique in this corpus of works with similar translations from Greek. In addition to pointing out the recurring and long known lexical, morphological, and syntactical anomalies one encounters in these translations by the "Hellenizing School," she invites attention to these peculiarities within biblical citations, dwelling especially on periphrastic renditions where varieties of doublets are used to render a Greek word. "Philo's *De Providentia:* a Work between Two Traditions" (pp. 87–124) by Maurizio Olivieri is a revised and translated version of the introduction to his dissertation mentioned above. Of special interest here are the author's stemmata of the Greek and Armenian manuscripts of Philo and their textual relatedness. Paola Pontani's "Saying (Almost) the Same Thing: On Some Relevant Differences between Greek-Language Originals and Their Armenian Translations" (pp. 125–146) illustrates the linguistic difficulties that plague the Armenian translation of Philo and the extended difficulties besetting its modern translators. Romano Sgarbi's "Philo's Stylemes *vs* Armenian Translation Stylemes" (pp. 147–154) complements Muradyan's article on the problem of doublets in the Armenian Philo. Sgarbi shows how the complexity becomes compounded since Philo often pairs synonyms together, and that his Greek suffers from a tortuous style full of redundancies and awkwardness reflected in Armenian reduplications. To illustrate this, Sgarbi draws on several passages from *De vita contemplativa,* a work extant in both languages.

In "Philo and the *Book of Causes* by Grigor Abasean" (pp. 155–189), Manea Erna Shirinian underscores the extent to which the Armenian author, who thrived at the turn of the thirteenth century, drew on Philo's works for the curricular compendia that comprise *The Book of Causes*. Lastly, in "The 'Armenian Philo': a Remnant of an unknown Tradition" (pp. 191–216), Olga Vardazaryan takes up the subject of how Philo came to the Armenian milieu and what became of his writings once they were translated into Armenian. Beginning with those early authors familiar with his works, whom Aucher mentions in the preface to his edition, she proceeds to twelfth–fourteenth-century authors who elaborate on the familiar Philo Christianus legend by associating Philo with Peter, John, James, and Paul respectively. However, she points out how the Armenian authors' fascination with allegorical interpretation (variously called "secre-tive," "subtle," or "spiritual") was conditioned by their admiration of Cyril of Jerusalem's catechetical lectures as moral teaching. More interestingly, she shows how they took over Eusebius of Caesarea's recommendation of Philo's *De Providentia* as a viable means to reach catechumens who were as yet incapable of exegetical understanding of Scripture (p. 214).

Two indices, "Index of Modern Authors" (pp. 217–220) and "Index of Philonic Passages" (pp. 221–222) mark the end of the volume.

In conclusion, the rather artificial syntax and grammar that characterize the Armenian translations by the "Hellenizing School" provide ample material for comparative studies, especially for those with mostly philo-logical and linguistic interests. Nonetheless, the contributors, all of whom are established scholars in their respective fields, offer fresh insights and remarks as they recapitulate long known observations made on the Armenian version of Philo; they review the history of research with its attendant methodology as they proceed to their commendable considera-tions with utmost clarity, all of which makes this volume a welcome guidebook for present and future scholars utilizing the Armenian Philo.

Abraham Terian
St. Nersess Armenian Seminary

DAVID T. RUNIA, editor. *Philo of Alexandria: An Annotated Bibliography 1997–2006, with Addenda for 1987–1996.* Supplements to Vigiliae Christianae 109. Leiden: Brill, 2012. Pp. xxvi + 492. ISBN 978-9004210806. Price €155, $212.

It is imperative for researchers to know the literature of the field in which they are working. This requires the presence of bibliographies, especially in fields where research is extensive. There are a significant number of biblio-graphies and bibliographical essays for Philo;[21] however, there are a few standard works that are indispensable. The first was the work of Howard L. Goodhart and Erwin R. Goodenough, who compiled a comprehensive list of manuscripts, translations, and titles of works devoted to Philo arranged in thirty-three subject categories up to 1937.[22] Two subsequent efforts have

---

[21] An important example is Peder Borgen, "Philo of Alexandria. A critical and syn-thetical survey of research since World War II," *ANRW* 21.1:98–154.

[22] It was published in Erwin R. Goodenough, *The Politics of Philo Judaeus: Practice and Theory* (New Haven: Yale University Press, 1938), 125–321.

taken their *point d'appui* from this bibliography. Louis Feldman extended the work to 1962 with a critical bibliography in which he both summarized the contents and assessed the importance of the works he included.[23] With the launch of the Philo Institute, Earle Hilgert recognized the need to update both the Goodhard/Goodenough and the Feldman bibliographies. He began to do so annually by publishing lists of titles devoted to Philo in the *Studia Philonica*[24] and then a comprehensive "Bibliographia Philoniana 1935–1981" arranged in twenty-one categories in the *Aufstieg und Niedergang der römischen Welt* volume devoted to Philo and Josephus.[25] In addition, a team of members of the Institute published abstracts of the most important recent works on Philo in all but one issue of the *Studia Philonica*.[26]

The second effort that took its cue from the Goodhart/Goodenough blbliography is the direct forerunner of Runia's bibliography. The noted Italian Philonist, Roberto Radice, decided to build a comprehensive bibliography that included abstracts. He elected to be as comprehensive as possible by including works that devoted at least three pages to Philo or made a significant contribution if they were more condensed. He began with the year that the Goodhart and Goodenough volume ended and brought the entries down to 1982.[27] David Runia quickly recognized the value of Radice's work and proposed that it be translated into English and brought up to 1986 to round off a half century of work. In order to carry out this task, Runia formed a team to assist with the collection and annotation of works, in particular a team of Israeli scholars led by David Satran to assist with works published in Hebrew. The result was a volume that collected 1,666 separate scholarly works, a significant increase over the 1,120 that Goodhart and Goodenough compiled.[28] The bibliography included works published in seven languages: Dutch, English, French, German, Hebrew, Italian, and Spanish. Runia recognized that a bibliography is out of date as soon as it is released. He suggested that if the *Studia Philonica* were restarted, he would continue the practice that Hilgert had

---

[23] Louis Feldman, *Studies in Judaica: Scholarship on Philo and Josephus (1937–1962)* (Studies in Judaica; New York: Yeshiva University, n.d.), esp. 1–26.

[24] Earle Hilgert, "A Bibliography of Philo Studies," *SPh* 1 (1972): 57–71; 2 (1973): 51–54; 3 (1974–75): 117–25; 4 (1976–77): 79–85; 5 (1978): 113–20; 6 (1979–80): 197–200.

[25] Earle Hilgert, "Bibliographia Philoniana 1935–1981," *ANRW* 21.1:47–97.

[26] The abstracts appear in *SPh* 1 (1972): 72–91; 2 (1973): 55–73; 4 (1976–77): 87–108; 5 (1978): 121–36; and 6 (1979–80): 201–22.

[27] Roberto Radice, *Filone di Alessandria: Bibliografia generale 1937–1982* (Elenchos: Collana di testi e studi sul pensiero antico; Naples: Bibliopolis, 1983).

[28] Roberto Radice and David T. Runia, *Philo of Alexandria: An Annotated Bibliogrpahy (1937–1986)* (VCSup 8; Leiden: Brill, 1988).

begun.[29] This became possible when the *Studia Philonica* was relaunched as *The Studia Philonica Annual*. In the first year, Runia and his team published a list of works from 1981–1986 based on the Radice/Runia bibliography but supplemented and without annotations.[30] Beginning with volume 2, Runia and the international team began publishing annotated bibliographies.[31] Three years later the team dropped the linguistic restriction to the seven languages—although coverage was restricted for some European languages (Greek and Russian) and almost all non-European languages—[32] and two years after this began to describe the team effort as the International Philo Bibliography Project.[33] Each volume of the Annual since then contains an annotated bibliography for the year three years prior to the publication date of the annual and a provisional bibliography for the three intervening years.[34] After a decade, the editor has collected the annual annotated bibliographies with additions into a comprehensive volume and added indices: Runia and his team published the bibliographies for 1987–1996 in 2000[35] and now the bibliographies for 1997–2006 in 2012. The 1987–1996 volume contains 953 abstracts to which an additional forty were added in the 1997–2006 production. The 1997–2006 volume contains 1,082 annotations.

The format of the bibliography has remained largely the same since the initial Radice/Runia bibliography. The first part consists of annotated bibliographies for Philonic *instrumenta* and reference works in eight categories. The 2000 and 2012 bibliographies added internet sites to the seven categories in the 1988 volume. The second part is devoted to summaries of critical studies arranged by year. Each entry is arranged alphabetically by the author's last name and numbered with numerals that mark the year. So, for example, works published in 2004 are numbered 20401, 20402, 20403, etc. The system makes it very easy to find the work(s)

[29] Runia, *Philo of Alexandria: An Annotated Bibliography (1937–1986)*, xxi–xxii.

[30] "David T. Runia, Roberto Radice, and David Satran, "A Bibliography of Philonic Studies 1981–1986," *SPhA* 1 (1989): 95–123.

[31] Runia provides the principles for the project which have remained largely in place in *SPhA* 2 (1990): 141–42.

[32] David T. Runia in *SPhA* 5 (1993): 180.

[33] The first reference that I have found to this is David T. Runia in *SPhA* 7 (1995): 186.

[34] David T. Runia et al., "Philo of Alexandria: An Annotated Bibliography," *SPhA* 2 (1990): 141–75; 3 (1991): 347–74; 4 (1992): 97–124; 5 (1993): 180–208; 6 (1994): 122–159; 7 (1995): 186–222; 8 (1996): 122–54; 9 (1997): 332–66; 10 (1998): 135–75; 11 (1999): 121–60; 12 (2000): 148–91; 13 (2001): 250–90; 14 (2002): 141–79; 15 (2003): 109–48; 16 (2004): 235–80; 17 (2005): 1612–214; 18 (2006): 143–204; 19 (2007): 143–204; 20 (2008): 167–210; 21 (2009): 73–123; 22 (2010): 209–68; 23 (2011): 97–159.

[35] David T. Runia, *Philo of Alexandria: An Annotated Bibliography (1987–1996), With Additions for 1937–1986* (VCSup 57; Leiden: Brill, 2000).

of a known scholar in any given year. The 2000 and 2012 bibliographies have a third part consisting of additional items and corrections to the preceding bibliography. The works all conclude with indices: six in the 1988 bibliography and seven in the 2000 and 2012 bibliographies: authors, reviewers, biblical passages, Philonic passages, subjects, Greek terms, and the contributors—the final is the additional index. The most important of these indices are the biblical passages, Philonic passages, and subjects. The last is the most challenging to compile. Fortunately, the indexer has made it fuller rather than thinner. The result is that it is almost always possible to find the relevant works quickly.

This bibliography is a *sine qua non* for students of Philo. The three bibliographies (1988, 2000, 2012) should serve as the first stop for anyone who wants to conduct a literature review on a text or a topic in Philo. There is simply no other place where someone can access Philonic scholarship comprehensively. The current volume maintains the same principles and high quality of the two preceding volumes. The abstracts are straight-forward rehearsals of the contents without value judgments. The abstracts are typically a paragraph in length but range in scope from a single sentence[36] to approximately a page[37]—two pages in one exceptional case.[38] In cases where a member of the team was not able to see and read the work personally, the source of the information is noted. The team has varied through the years, but this volume has consisted of fourteen scholars plus the editor. The international nature of the team allows them to gather material from throughout the world in many different languages. It is doubtful that any single scholar would know all of the languages involved in the project. The English summaries give all of us access to works in Arabic, Chinese, Japanese, and Russian languages that are not commonly known to those trained in the disciplines that draw on Philo in the US or Western Europe.

While it would be possible to quibble about small particulars at times, the bibliography is an impressive scholarly work. The editor and team members are to be congratulated and thanked for an invaluable contribution to Philonic scholarship. I hope that the project will continue for decades. My wish—like that of others—is that it would be possible to put all three volumes and the abstracts into a searchable digital data base. The editor is aware of this need, but has not been able to raise the resources to

---

[36] E.g., 9986, 20202, 20501, 20513, 20613, 20636, 20660.
[37] E.g., 9706, 2029.
[38] 20694.

make this possible.[39] Until this happens, we will have to rest content with the old-fashioned way of using a bibliography in the form that maintains the etymology of the word bibliography itself.

Gregory E. Sterling
Yale University

DANIEL M. GURTNER, ed. *This World and the World to Come: Soteriology in Early Judaism*. Library of Second Temple Studies 74. London: T&T Clark International. A Continuum imprint, 2011. xix + 364 pages. ISBN 978-0-567-02838-9. Price £ 70, $130.

Did authors of Second Temple texts concern themselves with "salvation"? If so, on what terms? What does one need "salvation" from? Are the parameters of who is included in or excluded from "salvation" defined? What is the "content" of salvation? These are some of the questions the various contributors in this book deal with. The volume consists of a total of seventeen contributions; each dealing with some selected works and authors from Second Temple Judaism.

The concept of soteriology is notoriously slippery. Its content may vary from author to author, from tradition to tradition even within the same religion; and of course from religion to religion. There are a variety of understandings present in the Jewish writings of the Second Temple Period, as well in early Christian texts. A search for issues like individual salvation vis-à-vis a collective understanding is relevant; terms and issues like salvation, messianism or messianic delivery, resurrection, after-life, eschatology, Kingdom of God, etc., would likely pop up in many educated minds when confronted with the word "soteriology." In this volume, however, each contributor was asked to work in such a way as to understand the issue of soteriology on his (no female authors involved!) respective book's or author's own terms.

The focus and scope of the book is to pick up where various texts from the Hebrew Bible leave off with respect to the topic of soteriology, broadly conceived. Hence, with the exception of the Book of Daniel, no texts from the Hebrew Bible/Old Testament are dealt with. However, the Book of Judith and the Psalms of Salomon, both present in the Septuagint, are also included. Not only single books, but also a range of books from a particular author (Philo), or from specific milieus and/or traditions (Dead Sea Scrolls;

---

[39] See his comments, *Philo of Alexandria: An Annotated Bibliography (1997–2006)*, p. xv.

Rabbinics) are investigated. In addition to these, we find chapters on several more. The books/authors dealt with are divided into six groups: I) Narratives (Judith, 3 Maccabees, Pseudo-Philo's *Biblical Antiquities*); II) Apocalypses (Book of Daniel; Apocalypse of Abraham; 4 Ezra; 2 Baruch; 2 Enoch); III) A set of some Psalms (Psalms of Solomon); IV) Philosophical texts (Philo of Alexandria; Wisdom of Solomon); V) Dead Sea Scrolls (Pescharim; Jubilees; 1QS/4QS), and VI) Rabbinic texts (Targum Jonathan to the Former and Later prophets; Restoration of Israel in Rabbinic Judaism). No clear-cut arguments for the choice of these particular books and authors are given. One might wonder why an author like Josephus is left out? And while some later books from the Hebrew Bible/Septuagint are included, one might ask if it would have been useful to have included some more from the Hebrew Bible/Septuagint as a kind of comparative background for studying these later Jewish works.

The particular chapters dealing with specific books or authors are framed by an introductory chapter by the editor, Daniel M. Gurtner (pp. 1–11), and by a final summarizing and synthesizing chapter by George W.E. Nickelsburg (pp. 299–314). In the first, Gurtner discusses the complexity of the main topic, and then summarizes the various contributions. Nickelsburg, somewhat surprisingly, also summarizes the various chapters, and then offers a brief synthesis that brings together some of the similarities and differences involved.

I shall not comment on all the chapters in this book, but in light of the focus of the present Annual, a focus on the three works from the Jewish Diaspora are included: the 3 Maccabees, Wisdom of Solomon, and especially the chapter on Philo. Though the distinction between Palestine and the Diaspora has been highly problematized in the last decades, in some cases it might nevertheless be useful to uphold a distinction without postulating too wide or too diverse of views on the topic; this world and the world to come–as is the book's main title.

In his chapter on 3 Maccabees (pp. 31-49), J. R. C. Cousland finds that the concept of salvation is in many ways summed up in the term "deliverance." God delivers his people in several ways; in 3 Macc especially in providing deliverance from earthly crises and in giving his people a good earthly life. Salvation does not extend beyond Israel, and is manifested in God's deliverance and restoration. There is no mention of an after-life; salvation is to be found in the present world among those who abide by God's Law. According to Cousland, this "message of salvation is designed to legitimate and sustain the diaspora Jews of Egypt" (p. 48).

Daniel J. Harrington, S.J., deals with the Wisdom of Solomon (pp. 181–190) under the heading "Saved by Wisdom" (Wis 9:18). After a brief introduction, he rephrases and reflects on the theology of salvation in the various sections of the book (1:1–6:11; 6:12–9:18; 10:1–19:22). I can do no better than cite Harrington's brief, but pointed final summary: "He (the author) urged his readers to live righteously and wisely, in fidelity to the God of Israel. He also wanted them to enjoy immortality in the form of eternal life with God, and believed that to do so they had to pass the scrutiny of divine judgement. For help along the way they could rely on the God of Israel as 'the savior of all' (16:7) as well as his surrogates or mediators—wisdom and the word of God (p. 190)." This then paves the way for our review of the article on Philo.

Philo is dealt with by Ronald Cox under the heading "Travelling the Royal Road: The Soteriology of Philo of Alexandria" (pp. 167–180). Philo's writings are not a systematic presentation of the various aspects of his theology, but his ideas are presented in writings belonging to various genres, contexts and audiences; hence trying to systematize his views might therefore lead to over-systematization resulting in distortions of his thoughts and ideas. Nevertheless, paying attention to these caveats, Cox here focuses on what Philo writes about the journey of the soul heavenward. This is certainly a central concern in Philo's works; the question is if it is broad enough to capture his soteriology. It also leads Cox to pay primary attention to Philo's allegorical works. Be that as it may, Cox provides an informative and lucid exposition of Philo's views concerning the ascent of the soul. The soul, being of heavenly origin, is longing for its return. Or, phrased differently, the means of the soul to achieve its salvation is to "become like God." The remedy of the souls in their earthly existence is described as the practice of dying to self in the body, and the attainment of God. According to Cox, Philo's view of salvation, in nuce, is the soul's death to its material body and ascent back to its heavenly origins (p. 171). Furthermore, as Cox argues, this road goes via the attainment of the virtues, a process not the least achieved through the allegorical exegesis of the Scriptures. In the Scriptures we have not only the Law, but also the examples of the patriarchs, of which the laws of the Torah are copies. Thus Scripture reveals the path of virtue, and the qualities needed for moving from the earthly/bodily existence to the heavenly/rational one. Cox then emphasizes that the attainment of this salvation is not simply a human work, but is a result of God's providence and help through his intermediaries. Among these, the *Logos* is the primary means as it has a distinctive relationship with both God and humanity. In short, as Cox summarizes his view on salvation in the works of Philo, he says that for Philo, salvation "is the return of the soul to its heavenly home, and the divine *Logos*, the image of God and source for the soul's reasoning, serves as both means and goal in the journey" (p. 180).

I find this exposition by Cox both pertinent and reliable. My problem with his article is not so much what he says and presents, as what he does not take into consideration. It should be admitted that he of course is aware of (p. 169) the fact that Philo seems to hold an eschatology of some sort, but he leaves that out of consideration. However, Philo is a Hellenized Jew; that is, both Hellenized and a Jew. While there is not much of a personal and national eschatology (cf. however *Praem.* 94–95; 160–172; *Mos.* 1.288–291; 2.43–4), what there nevertheless is might be of greater importance for Philo's soteriology than is granted in this otherwise well-informed study.

This volume, dealing with so many Jewish works and authors, will certainly both raise questions and inform its readers. The topic is well chosen, and should be of interest to both students of Second Temple Judaism and of early Christianity. The book also has twenty-one pages of bibliography, in addition to an index of references (pp. 337–356), an index of authors (pp. 357–362), and an index of subjects (pp. 363–364).

Torrey Seland
School of Theology and Mission
Stavanger, Norway

Ross Shepard Kraemer. *Unreliable Witnesses: Religion, Gender, and History in the Greco-Roman Mediterranean.* Oxford: Oxford University Press, 2011. xv + 322 pages. ISBN 978-0-19-974318-6. Price $74.

In *Unreliable Witnesses*, Kraemer reflects upon the central questions that she has investigated for over thirty years. Kraemer began her career "interested in the recovery and accurate description of what women themselves did and thought within contexts that could be labeled 'religious'" (p. 4), but over the years, she became more aware of the complications in examining women's engagement in religious practice. Not only are women's experiences difficult to extract from ancient texts, obscured by the ideological intentions of male authors (as Elizabeth Clark and others have notably discussed as well), but also scholarly understandings of key terms (e.g., "women," "gender," and "religion") and their relation to the examined evidence require further scrutiny. Kraemer sets out to provide this kind of analytical precision in revisiting issues she has written about in the past (altering some of her former positions) and by examining new topics in light of contemporary theoretical models.

In chapter one, Kraemer reviews theoretical developments regarding the terms "women," "gender," and "religion," and she outlines her operating assumptions about them. Her work focuses on women of adult status who, broadly speaking, would be identified as women today (in anatomical and genetic terms); and she understands gender as produced by humans, ascribed to biological status yet seen as "natural," and existing in relational terms (feminine and masculine). She especially advocates the use of cognitive theory to better explain religion and its associated practices, and she promotes Stanley Stowers' recent definition of "religion"[40] which resonates a great deal with her focus on "religion as the product of human thought, agency, and activity" (p. 25). Kraemer also addresses the interpretive issues around the terms *Ioudaios* and *Judeus*, and she decides to translate these terms as "Judean" for usages prior to the second century C.E., mostly "Judean" but sometimes "Jew" for references from the second to the fourth centuries C.E., and "Jew" for usages post-fourth century C.E.

In chapter two, Kraemer then presents four case studies that are meant to demonstrate the fundamental concerns of her work. Her examples primarily discuss the societal underpinnings of gender constructions in narratives and how these constructions offer little about how real women engaged in religious practice. For example, concerning the Roman senate's ban of certain Bacchic rites in the second century B.C.E. and Livy's later account of it, the limited information provided by the *Senatus Consultum* inscription and the rhetorical use of gender in Livy's portrayal do not, in the end, render much about actual women's engagement in those practices. The most productive approach is to analyze Livy's feminization of the Bacchic rites as a form of slander. So too, we learn much about the ideals promoted by the murdered woman's report from hell in the *Acts of Thomas* and how these ideals relate to Christianity as construed by the narrative, but we discover little about women and their involvement in Christian practices. The rabbis' discussion about whether or not their daughters should be taught Torah is best understood as a way of creating conformity

[40] "*Religions* are the often linked and combined practices (i.e., doings and sayings) of particular human populations (e.g., imagined as cultures, societies, ethnicities, groups, global movements) that involve the imagined participation of gods or other normally nonobservable beings in those practices and social formation and that shade into many kinds of anthropomorphizing interpretations of the world. *Religion* is the unfolding activity (including thinking and believing) involving those practices that postulate participation with and make reference to gods, normally nonobservable beings and anthropomorphizing interpretations of the world." "Theorizing the Religion of Ancient Households and Families," in *Household and Family Religion in Antiquity* (ed. J. Bodel and S. M. Olyan; Oxford: Blackwell, 2008), 8–9.

to particular gendered norms and not so much as a reflection of the "fact" that some daughters engaged in Torah study. Yet Kraemer does not wish to discard the possibility of ancient evidence referring to actual women, no matter how vaguely discerned. Justin Martyr's account about a Roman Christian matron and her struggles with the Roman legal system fundamentally promotes the superiority of Christianity, but his rhetorical use of gender in the story (e.g., the dichotomy between the woman's moral fortitude and the irrationality of male authority) raises suspicion about the accuracy of his tale. Nonetheless, for Kraemer, it seems possible that Justin embellished a real case of such a matron, even though the historical case may be irretrievable. The crux of Kraemer's book resides in this problem of what can be gleaned from ancient written evidence—how much do gendered constructions reflect the writers' (or culture's) worldviews *and* how much do these constructions reflect the activity (cognitive and otherwise) of actual women.

The following four chapters ultimately emphasize that, when examining the epigraphical and literary evidence, it is far more productive and reliable to investigate ancient perceptions of gender and their relation to societal ideals and structures than it is to discern the activities of real women. Regarding Philo's Therapeutae, Kraemer revises her original position (i.e., that they represented an historical group) and concedes that it is more productive to examine *De vita contemplativa* in terms of Philo's gender constructions and how they relate to his ideal picture of such a group. His exegesis of particular biblical passages (especially Exod 15) influenced his representation of the community, and his description of the *Therapeutrides* (who take on masculine ideals) corresponds to that of the *Therapeutae* (who are more 'feminine' in their activity). Whereas Kraemer had once posited that female characters like Thecla in the *Apocryphal Acts* reflected "actual social experiences and practices of women in ascetic Christian communities" (p. 122), she now agrees that these fictional women were created to persuasively demonstrate the moral and pious superiority of Christianity. Women functioned "generally in antiquity to index the presence or absence of [morality and piety] in any particular social group" (p. 147), and the female characters in these narratives serve to promote Christian ideals. Even more so do female figures serve a completely fictional and rhetorical purpose in Severus' account of the mass conversion by the fifth century (c.e.) Jewish community in Minorca. In his *Letter on the Conversion of the Jews*, Severus narrates the resistance of several elite Jewish women, who, Kraemer argues, "serve as the ultimate exemplars of Jewish stubbornness in the face of the reasonableness and truth of Christianity" (p. 165). With *De vita contemplativa*, the *Apocryphal Acts*, and Severus' letter, Kraemer concludes that it is more productive to explore the cultural assumptions and structures that underlie written works and feed writers' arguments when examining gender issues.

At the same time, however, Kraemer adamantly argues against the scholarly decision to erase real women out the picture altogether. Except for Severus' account, she leaves open the possibility that the ancient evidence reflects religious activities of actual women. There may have been women like the *Therapeutrides*, and Thecla's activities could allude to leadership activity of women in Christian communities (such as teaching, as Paul instructs Thecla to do). Although clouded by the ideological motivations behind much of the evidence, some of the activities of actual women in antiquity remain reasonably discernable. But even when the evidence names actual women (as in epigraphical evidence), Kraemer cautions that particular terms associated with these women may not imply what scholars tend to suppose.

In her final case study, Kraemer qualifies what we can detect about elite women associated with "Judean" religious practices. She argues against the position that more women than men converted to Judaism during the Roman period, and she identifies scholars' use of the terms "God-fearing" and "conversion" as problematic. More is needed to dissect whether or when "God-fearing" referred to "ordinary acts of piety" or actual accep-tance of Judean religious practices by polytheists (p. 187), let alone whether the term was attributed more to men than to women. We cannot tell much, therefore, about what exactly *theosebēs* means in the Aphrodisias inscrip-tions, or, more importantly, whether there was a universal understanding of the term in antiquity. The term "conversion" implies exclusivity that does not adequately describe ancient religious practice, and Kraemer redefines the term as "reconfigured kinship" affiliation (p. 187) to better explain the designation of female "proselytes" in several inscriptions. The low percentage of proselyte inscriptions in general, however, makes it futile to draw conclusions about whether more women than men "converted" to Judaism. More intriguing for Kraemer are the social implications inherent in the act of a woman changing kinship affiliation as opposed to that of a man. Whether or not it appears that women "converted" more than men did, the evidence may instead reflect cultural conditions that determined or explained how women supported "Judean" practices as opposed to how men did. What is at issue, then, is how ancient theories of gender defined possible activity of Gentile women in Judean practices. Narratives about Gentile women "adopting" and/or supporting Judean practices (e.g., according to Josephus) are best examined for their manipulation of these ancient gender theories and less so for providing information about the actual activity of Gentile women. To conclude the chapter, Kraemer challenges recent arguments about female office holders mentioned in synagogue inscriptions (especially those referred to as *archisynagōgos*). Kraemer contends that such leadership positions could have existed for women, but obviously within gendered norms and structures that likely yielded leadership activity for women that differed from that of men.

This book well illustrates the rich contribution that Kraemer continues to offer to the study of women and religious practice in the ancient world. With most of the examples that she discusses, Kraemer urges more precision in the scholarly analysis of how ancient gender constructions relate both to the evidence and to what we can say about it. Her discussion about the scholarly application of the term "conversion" is particularly compelling on this matter. She also provides detailed insights regarding specific interpretative issues and scholarly discussions (noteworthy are her chapters on Philo's *De vita contemplativa*, Thecla in the *Apocryphal Acts*, and the term *theosebēs* in the epigraphical evidence). The direction of her discussion, however, is not always clear (as in chapter two, for example), and some readers may wish that Kraemer had more explicitly resolved the issues that she discusses. Kraemer certainly intends to problematize much of what scholars have unquestionably found to be plausible, but it can be difficult to follow her argument while keeping in mind all of her qualifications. Despite these limitations, Kraemer offers fruitful analysis of ancient evidence and raises significant methodological questions in the study of women and their religious activity that require attention.

Patricia Ahearne-Kroll
Ohio Wesleyan University

ABRAHAM TERIAN, *Opera Selecta Teriana: a Scholarly Retrospective*, edited by Roberta R. Ervine. St. Nersess Theological Review vol. 13, New Rochelle, N.Y. 2008. v + 434 pages. ISSN 1086-2080. Price $30.

In a career that has spanned nearly four decades, Professor Abraham Terian has served the Academy, the Church, and his own Armenian community with devotion and distinction. It is highly fitting that the institution of which he was Dean from 1997 to 2008, St. Nersess Armenian Seminary (New York), has published a selection of his scholarly articles to mark the occasion of his retirement.

After a preliminary section that contains a complete bibliography of Terian's scholarly publications compiled by Edward G. Mathews, Jr., the volume is divided into two main parts. The first, entitled Armeniaca, contains fourteen articles on ancient and medieval Armenian literature. The first two articles on the Hellenizing school of Armenian translation are of particular relevance to Philo, since it was this school that produced the Armenian translations that have proved so important for our knowledge of Philo. The second part, entitled Philonica, reprints thirteen articles which have the writing, thought and intellectual context of Philo as their subject.

The following list gives the titles and year of publication of the articles contained in this part (for fuller references see R-R, RRS and RRS2):

I "Philo and the Stoic Doctrine of εὐπάθειαι: a Note on *Quaes. Gen.* 2.57" (with John Dillon) (1976–77); II "The Implications of Philo's Dialogues on His Exegetical Works" (1978); III "A Critical Introduction to Philo's Dialogues" (1984); IV "A Philonic Fragment on the Decad" (1985): V "Some Stock Arguments for the Magnanimity of the Law in Hellenistic Jewish Apologetics" (1985); VI "The Priority of the *Quaestiones* among Philo's Exegetical Commentaries" (1991); VII "Strange Interpolations in the Text of Philo: the Case of *Quaestiones in Exodum*" (1991); VIII "Two Unusual Uses of aṙn in the Armenian Version of Philo's *Quaestiones*" (1993); IX "Creation in Johannine Theology" (1993); X "Had the Works of Philo been newly Discovered" (1994); XI "Notes on the Transmission of the Philonic Corpus" (1994); XII "Inspiration and Originality: Philo's Distinctive Exclamations" (1995); XIII "Back to Creation: The Beginning of Philo's Third Grand Commentary" (1997).

Since quite a few of these articles are not so easily accessible, it is most valuable to have them collected together in this way. It also allows us, as the book's sub-title indicates, to obtain a retrospective overview of an important body of research.

Most, but not all, of the articles focus on the Armenian Philo. The first draws attention to a passage in QG, in which Philo provides interesting evidence on the Stoic terminology for their doctrine of rational emotions (I). Two articles focus on the philosophical dialogues preserved only in Armenian translation. They can be considered by-products of Terian's work on the splendid edition of *De animalibus* published in 1981 (II–III). During this time he also noticed an arithmological fragment in one of Aucher's editions which had up to then been overlooked by Philonic scholars. He concluded that it was most likely a remnant of Philo's lost work Περὶ ἀριθμῶν (IV). Three articles are the result of his work on the *Quaestiones in Exodum* which he produced for the celebrated Lyon French translation of Philo's complete works (VI, VII, VIII). Ever since his work on the Dialogues Terian has been interested in what we can discover about the chronology of Philo's many writings. These interests led to two further important articles (VI, XIII). Two articles explored some of the background to Philo's work in Hellenistic Judaism and Early Christianity (V, IX). A further article makes comments on the Philonic heritage in the early Christian and especially the Armenian tradition (XI). It is perhaps to be regretted that Terian has not published more on this subject, on which he is a world expert. It was no doubt during his research on this subject that he reflected on the value of the Philonic legacy and how it is often taken for granted. This reflection led to a piece that combines popularization and originality in a most attractive way (X). Finally there is what is perhaps his most original article on Philo, a piece of detective work in which he discovered that there is a correlation between Philo's appeal to his mind or soul (ὦ διάνοια, ὦ ψυχή) and what he presents as his own exegetical insights (XII). It should also be noted that four of the articles were written as tributes to scholars with whom he has had a special relationship: Samuel Sandmel, Earle Hilgert, his *Doctorvater* Bo Reicke, and David Winston (IV, VII, IX, XIII).

Philonic scholarship is greatly indebted to Abraham Terian for the penetrating and often highly original research that he has carried out over a period of more than two decades. It seems that his onerous duties as Dean did not allow him the leisure to do further work on Philo, for since 1997 he has not published in this field. It is to be fervently hoped that in his retirement he will be able to return to his beloved Philo and resume his research, including work on the English translation and commentary on the *De Providentia* that would be such a valuable instrument for further scholarship.

St. Nersess Armenian Seminary and the editor of the volume, Roberta Erskine, are to be warmly thanked and congratulated on this superb publication. It is a most fitting tribute to one of its great teachers and scholars.

David T. Runia
Queen's College
The University of Melbourne

The Studia Philonica Annual 24 (2012) 283–285

NEWS AND NOTES*

Philo of Alexandria Group of the Society of Biblical Literature

At the 2011 Annual Meeting of the Society of Biblical Literature in San Francisco, the Philo of Alexandria Group met for three sessions. The first session (20 November) was devoted to a review of Maren Niehoff's recent monograph on *Jewish Exegesis and Homeric Scholarship in Alexandria* (Cambridge University Press, 2011), and comprised responses by Teresa Morgan (University of Oxford), John Collins (Yale University), Gregory Sterling (University of Notre Dame), Steven Fraade (Yale University), and Maren Niehoff (Hebrew University, Jerusalem), with Ellen Birnbaum (Cambridge, Mass.) presiding. A second session (21 November) focused on the new translation and commentary on Philo's treatise *De Confusione Linguarum (On the Confusion of Tongues)*, currently in preparation by Ronald Cox. Speakers included Ronald Cox (Pepperdine University), "The Logos as Consolation Prize: Sample Commentary on Philo, *De Confusione*," with responses by James Royse (Claremont, California) and Thomas Tobin, S.J. (Loyola University Chicago), and a further paper by Peter Martens (Saint Louis University), "Origen's Allegory of the Tower of Babel," with Sarah Pearce (University of Southampton) presiding. This was followed on the same day by a final session in which speakers presented on a varied range of topics, responding to the Philo Group's open call for papers relating to Philonic studies: Abraham Terian (National Academy of Sciences, Armenia), "From Monologue To Trialogue: *De Providentia* I–II and the Culmination of Philo's Apology for the Law"; Gabriele Cornelli (Universidade de Brasilia) and Luiz Felipe Ribeiro (University of Toronto), "Who Needs a Philosophical Way of Life? Ancient Koinonia in the Therapeutae 'Pythagorean Life': Notes From Iamblichus' *De Vita Pythagorica*, Porphyry's *Vita Pythagorae*, and Philo's *De Vita Contemplativa*"; René Bloch (Universität Bern), "Alexandria in Pharaonic Egypt: Projections in *De Vita Mosis*"; Trent Rogers (Loyola University Chicago), "Philo's Universalization of Sinai in *De Decalogo*"; Brian C. Dennert (Loyola University of Chicago), "The Exegetical Basis of Philo's Exposition of the Sabbath Command in *De Decalogo* and *De*

---

* Items of general interest to Philo scholars to be included in this section can be sent to the editor, David Runia (contact details in Notes on Contributors below).

Specialibus Legibus"; and Jason Reddoch (University of Cincinnati), "Enigmatic Dreams and Onirocritical Skill in *De Somniis* 2," with David Runia (University of Melbourne) presiding. A number of these papers will be published in either this year's or next year's issue of *The Studia Philonica Annual*.

The Philo of Alexandria Group will convene again in November 2012 at the SBL Annual Meeting in Chicago. The program will include a panel devoted to the topic of "Philo's Greco-Roman Readers" and two sessions focusing on a new translation and commentary on Philo's *Legum Allegoriae* Books 1-3, being prepared for the PACS series by Thomas Tobin, S.J.

Ellen Birnbaum and Sarah Pearce
Co-Chairs, SBL Philo of Alexandria Group

Philo Conference in Lisbon

In March 2011 the Project "Fílon de Alexandria nas Origens da Cultura Ocidental," integrated in the Center of Classical Studies, University of Lisbon, and coordinated by Manuel Alexandre Jr., held a Colloquium on the theme of Philo of Alexandria at the Origins of Alexandrian Culture. Its purpose was to emphasize the importance of Philonic Studies for the Portuguese academic community, especially in the areas of Jewish philosophy, theology and literature, as well as in classical literature and Hellenistic culture in general. This colloquium was preceded a few weeks before by a lecture on "Language and Culture in Philo of Alexandria," given at the same University by Sofía Torallas Tovar, one of the editors and translators of *Filón de Alexandría: Obras Completas* in Spanish.

All the papers given in this colloquium were edited by Manuel Alexandre Jr. in a book entitled *Fílon de Alexandria nas Origens da Cultura Ocidental*, Lisboa, Centro de Estudos Clássicos, 2011. The contributions provided in this book include nine articles: two by leading Philonists in Europe, Sarah Pearce, "Philo of Alexandria on Jewish Law and Jewish Community" (137–154), and Sofía Torallas Tovar, "La Lengua de Filón de Alexandría en el Panorama Lingüístico del Egipto Romano" (23–36); and seven by members of the Portuguese project, Manuel Alexandre Jr., "Fílon de Alexandria na Interpretação das Escrituras" (9–22); Tatiana Faia, "Embaixada a Calígula, Agustina Bessa–Luís e uma Memória de Fílon de Alexandria" (37–46); Rui Miguel Duarte, "Λόγος ἐνδιάθετος e προφορικός na Formação da Cristologia Patrística" (47–80); Maria Fernandes, "O Profetismo no Tratado *De Iosepho* de Fílon de Alexandria" (81–90); Cesar Motta

Rios, "Exílio, Diáspora e Saudades de Jerusalém: Estudo em Jeremias 29:1–14 em Fílon de Alexandria" (91–110); Maria Fernandes, "Φύσις no Tratado de Fílon de Alexandria *De Iosepho*" (111–120); Manuel Alexandre Jr., "Fílon entre os Sofistas de Alexandria: A Sofística Alexandrina sob o Olhar Crítico de Fílon de Alexandria" (121–135).

The translation of Philo's work in Portuguese is a debt we owe to the Portuguese speaking peoples and their culture. It is a main purpose of the Philo Project in our Center of Classical Studies to fulfil this debt. Four treatises have already been translated. But its objectives transcend translation, as seen in the articles listed above. A fine group of young researchers is emerging. Two of them are working on Philo in their postgraduate studies, and one of them, Tatiana Faia, has already completed her Master's degree on "Fílon de Alexandria – Flaco & Embaixada a Gaio: Tradução, Introdução e Notas." She is now doing research work at Oxford University for a doctorate on Philo's *De Vita Mosis*.

The perspectives for Philonic studies in Portugal are promising.

Manuel Alexandre Jr.
University of Lisbon

NOTES ON CONTRIBUTORS

PATRICIA AHEARNE-KROLL is Associate Professor of Religion at Ohio Wesleyan University. Her postal address is: Department of Religion, Ohio Wesleyan University, 61 S. Sandusky St., Delaware, OH 43015, USA; her electronic address is pdahearn@owu.edu.

KATELL BERTHELOT is Researcher at the National Center for Scientific Research (France), currently appointed at the French Research Center in Jerusalem. Her postal address is: CRFJ, PB 547, 3 Shimshon St., 91004 Jerusalem, ISRAEL; her electronic address is katell.berthelot@crfj.org.il.

RENÉ BLOCH is Professor of Jewish Studies at the University of Bern. His postal address is: Institut für Judaistik, Universität Bern, Länggassstrasse 51, 3012 Bern, SWITZERLAND; his electronic address is: rene.bloch@theol.-unibe.ch

RONALD R. COX is Associate Professor in the Religion Division, Pepperdine University. His postal address is Religion Division, Pepperdine University, Malibu, CA 90263-4352, USA; his electronic address is ronald.cox@pepperdine.edu.

KINDALEE PFREMMER DE LONG is Associate Professor in the Religion Division, Pepperdine University. Her postal address is Religion Division, Pepperdine University, Malibu, CA 90263-4352, USA; her electronic address is kdelong@pepperdine.edu.

ALBERT C. GELJON teaches classical languages at the Christelijke Gymnasium in Utrecht. His postal address is Gazellestraat 138, 3523 SZ Utrecht, THE NETHERLANDS; his electronic address is geljon@ixs.nl.

ERICH S. GRUEN, is Gladys Rehard Wood Professor of History and Classics, Emeritus at the University of California, Berkeley. His postal address is 1045 Mariposa Ave., Berkeley, CA 94707, USA; his electronic address is gruene@berkeley.edu

HELEEN M. KEIZER is Dean of Academic Affairs at the Istituto Superiore di Osteopatia in Milan, Italy. Her postal address is Via Guerrazzi 3, 20900 Monza (MB), ITALY; her electronic address is h.m.keizer@virgilio.it.

JUTTA LEONHARDT-BALZER is Lecturer in New Testament at the University of Aberdeen. Her postal address is School of Divinity and Religious Studies, King's College, University of Aberdeen, Aberdeen AB24 3UB, UNITED KINGDOM; her electronic address is j.leonhardt-balzer@abdn.ac.uk.

PETER W. MARTENS, is an Assistant Professor of Theological Studies at Saint Louis University. His postal address is Department of Theological Studies, Saint Louis University, 3800 Lindell Blvd., Saint Louis, MO 63108, USA; his electronic address is pmarten1@slu.edu.

JOSÉ PABLO MARTÍN is Professor Consultus at the Universidad Nacional de General Sarmiento, San Miguel, Argentina, and Senior Research fellow of the Argentinian Research Organization (CONICET). His postal address is Azcuenaga 1090, 1663 San Miguel, ARGENTINA; his electronic address is philonis@fastmail.fm.

SARAH J. K. PEARCE is Ian Karten Professor of Jewish Studies, Department of History, University of Southampton, Southampton SO17 1BF, UNITED KINGDOM; her electronic address is sjp2@soton.ac.uk.

BIRGER A. PEARSON is Emeritus Professor of Religious Studies at the University of California, Santa Barbara. His postal address is 27345 Vine Ave., Escalon, CA 95320, USA; his electronic address is bpearson@thevision.net.

TRENT A. ROGERS is a Ph.D. student in New Testament and Early Christianity at Loyola University Chicago. His postal address is: 124 N CR 580 W, Frankfort, IN, 46041; his email address is trent.alan.rogers@gmail.com

JAMES R. ROYSE is a Visiting Scholar at the Claremont School of Theology. His postal address is P.O. Box 567, Claremont, CA 91711-0567, USA; his electronic address is jamesrroyse@hotmail.com.

DAVID T. RUNIA is Master of Queen's College and Professorial Fellow in the School of Historical and Philosophical Studies at the University of Melbourne. His postal address is Queen's College, 1–17 College Crescent,

Parkville 3052, AUSTRALIA; his electronic address is runia@queens. unimelb.edu.au.

DANIEL R. SCHWARTZ, is Professor of Jewish History at the Hebrew University of Jerusalem. His postal address is: Dept. of Jewish History and Contemporary Jewry, The Hebrew University of Jerusalem, Mt. Scopus, Jerusalem 91905, Israel; his electronic address is danielr.schwartz@ mail.huji.ac.il.

TORREY SELAND is Dean of Studies and Professor in New Testament Studies at the School of Mission and Theology, Stavanger, Norway. His postal address is MHS, Misjonsmarka 12, 4024 Stavanger, NORWAY; his electronic mail address is torreys@gmail.com.

FOLKER SIEGERT has recently retired as Professor of Judaism and New Testament at the Westfälischen Wilhelms-Universität Münster and Director of the Institutum Judaicum Delitzschianum. His postal address is Wilmergasse 1, 48147 Münster, DEUTSCHLAND; his electronic address is siegert@uni-muenster.de

GREGORY E. STERLING is the Lillian Claus Professor of New Testament and the Reverend Henry L. Slack Dean of the Yale Divinity School. His postal address is 409 Prospect Street, New Haven, CT 06511, USA; his electronic address is gregory.sterling@yale.edu.

ABRAHAM TERIAN retired in 2008 as Professor Emeritus of Early Christianity and Armenian Patristics at St. Nersess Armenian Seminary. His postal address is 5478 N. Ferger Ave., Fresno, CA 93704; his electronic address is terian@stnersess.edu.

THOMAS H. TOBIN, S.J. is Professor of New Testament and Early Christianity at Loyola University Chicago. His postal address is Department of Theology, Loyola University Chicago, 1032 West Sheridan Road, Chicago, IL 60660-1537, USA; his electronic address is ttobin@luc.edu.

JOSHUA YODER, recently completed the Ph.D. in Christianity and Judaism in Antiquity at the University of Notre Dame. His electronic address is jyoder4@nd.edu.

The Studia Philonica Annual 24 (2012) 289–295

INSTRUCTIONS TO CONTRIBUTORS

Articles and Book reviews can only be considered for publication in *The Studia Philonica Annual* if they rigorously conform to the guidelines established by the editorial board. For further information see also the website of the Annual:

http://www.nd.edu/~philojud

1. *The Studia Philonica Annual* accepts articles for publication in the area of Hellenistic Judaism, with special emphasis on Philo and his *Umwelt*. Articles on Josephus will be given consideration if they focus on his relation to Judaism and classical culture (and not on primarily historical subjects). The languages in which the articles may be published are English, French and German. Translations from Italian or Dutch into English can be arranged at a modest cost to the author.

2. Articles and reviews are to be sent to the editors in electronic form as email attachments. The preferred word processor is Microsoft Word. Users of other word processors are requested to submit a copy exported in a format compatible with Word, e.g. in RTF format. Manuscripts should be double-spaced, including the notes. Words should be italicized when required, not underlined. Quotes five lines or longer should be indented and may be single-spaced. For texts in Greek only Unicode fonts can be accepted. For Hebrew the font provided on the SBL website is recommended. In all cases it is **imperative** that authors give **full details** about the word processor (if it is not Word) and foreign language fonts used. Moreover, if the manuscript contains Greek or Hebrew material, a PDF version of the document must be sent together with the word processing file. If this proves difficult, a hard copy can be sent by mail or by fax. No handwritten Greek or Hebrew can be accepted. Authors are requested not to vocalize their Hebrew (except when necessary) and to keep their use of this language to a reasonable minimum. It should always be borne in mind that not all readers of the Annual can be expected to read Greek or Hebrew. Transliteration is encouraged for incidental terms.

3. Authors are encouraged to use inclusive language wherever possible, avoiding terms such as "man" and "mankind" when referring to humanity in general.

4. For the preparation of articles and book reviews the Annual follows the guidelines of *The SBL Handbook of Style for Ancient Near Eastern, Biblical, and Early Christian Studies*, Hendrickson: Peabody Mass., 1999. For members of the Society of Biblical Literature, a downloadable PDF version of this guide is available on the SBL website, www.sbl-site.org (if non-members need a copy, they are asked to contact the editors). Here are examples of how a monograph, a monograph in a series, an edited volume, an article in an edited volume and a journal article are to be cited in notes (different conventions apply for bibliographies):

> Joan E. Taylor, *Jewish Women Philosophers of First-Century Alexandria—Philo's 'Therapeutae' Reconsidered* (Oxford: Oxford University Press, 2003), 123.
> Ellen Birnbaum, *The Place of Judaism in Philo's Thought: Israel, Jews, and Proselytes* (BJS 290; SPhM 2; Atlanta: Scholars Press, 1996), 134.
> Gerard P. Luttikhuizen, ed., *Eve's Children: The Biblical Stories Retold and Interpreted in Jewish and Christian Traditions* (Themes in Biblical Narrative 5; Leiden: Brill, 2003), 145.
> Gregory E. Sterling, "The Bond of Humanity: Friendship in Philo of Alexandria," in *Greco-Roman Perspectives on Friendship*, (ed. John T. Fitzgerald; SBLRBS 34; Atlanta: Scholars Press, 1997), 203–23.
> James R. Royse, "Jeremiah Markland's Contribution to the Textual Criticism of Philo." *SPhA* 16 (2004): 50–60.

Note that abbreviations are used in the notes, but not in a bibliography. Numbers should be given in full for texts, e.g. *Aet.* 107–110; in references to modern publications the conventions of the *SBL Handbook of Style* should be followed (see p. 16). When joining up numbers in all textual and bibliographical references, the n-dash should be used and not the hyphen, i.e. 50–60, not 50-60. For publishing houses only the first location is given. Submissions which do not conform to these guidelines will be returned to the authors for re-submission.

5. The following abbreviations are to be used in both articles and book reviews.

(a) Philonic treatises are to be abbreviated according to the following list. Numbering follows the edition of Cohn and Wendland, using Arabic numbers only and full stops rather than colons (e.g. *Spec.* 4.123). Note that *De Providentia* should be cited according to Aucher's edition, and not the LCL translation of the fragments by F. H. Colson.

Abr.	*De Abrahamo*
Aet.	*De aeternitate mundi*
Agr.	*De agricultura*
Anim.	*De animalibus*
Cher.	*De Cherubim*
Contempl.	*De vita contemplativa*
Conf.	*De confusione linguarum*
Congr.	*De congressu eruditionis gratia*

Decal.	*De Decalogo*
Deo	*De Deo*
Det.	*Quod deterius potiori insidiari soleat*
Deus	*Quod Deus sit immutabilis*
Ebr.	*De ebrietate*
Flacc.	*In Flaccum*
Fug.	*De fuga et inventione*
Gig.	*De gigantibus*
Her.	*Quis rerum divinarum heres sit*
Hypoth.	*Hypothetica*
Ios.	*De Iosepho*
Leg. 1–3	*Legum allegoriae* I, II, III
Legat.	*Legatio ad Gaium*
Migr.	*De migratione Abrahami*
Mos. 1–2	*De vita Moysis* I, II
Mut.	*De mutatione nominum*
Opif.	*De opificio mundi*
Plant.	*De plantatione*
Post.	*De posteritate Caini*
Praem.	*De praemiis et poenis, De exsecrationibus*
Prob.	*Quod omnis probus liber sit*
Prov. 1–2	*De Providentia* I, II
QE 1–2	*Quaestiones et solutiones in Exodum* I, II
QG 1–4	*Quaestiones et solutiones in Genesim* I, II, III, IV
Sacr.	*De sacrificiis Abelis et Caini*
Sobr.	*De sobrietate*
Somn. 1–2	*De somniis* I, II
Spec. 1–4	*De specialibus legibus* I, II, III, IV
Virt.	*De virtutibus*

(b) Standard works of Philonic scholarship are abbreviated as follows:

G-G   Howard L. Goodhart and Erwin R. Goodenough, "A General Bibliography of Philo Judaeus." In *The Politics of Philo Judaeus: Practice and Theory* (ed. Erwin R. Goodenough; New Haven: Yale University Press, 1938; repr. Georg Olms: Hildesheim, 1967), 125–321.

PCH   *Philo von Alexandria: die Werke in deutscher Übersetzung,* ed. Leopold Cohn, Isaac Heinemann *et al.,* 7 vols. (Breslau: M & H Marcus Verlag, Berlin: Walter de Gruyter, 1909–64).

PCW   *Philonis Alexandrini opera quae supersunt,* ed. Leopoldus Cohn, Paulus Wendland et Sigismundus Reiter, 6 vols. (Berlin: Georg Reimer, 1896–1915).

PLCL   *Philo in Ten Volumes (and Two Supplementary Volumes),* English translation by F. H. Colson, G. H. Whitaker (and R. Marcus), 12 vols. (Loeb Classical Library; London: William Heinemann, Cambridge, Mass.: Harvard University Press, 1929–62).

PAPM   *Les œuvres de Philon d'Alexandrie,* French translation under the general editorship of Roger Arnaldez, Jean Pouilloux, and Claude Mondésert (Paris: Cerf, 1961–92).

R-R   Roberto Radice and David T. Runia, *Philo of Alexandria: an Annotated Bibliography 1937–1986* (VCSup 8; Leiden: Brill 1988).

RRS   David T. Runia, *Philo of Alexandria: an Annotated Bibliography 1987–1996* (VCSup 57; Leiden: Brill 2000).

RRS2   David T. Runia, *Philo of Alexandria: an Annotated Bibliography 1997–2006* (VCSup 109; Leiden: Brill 2012).

SPh   *Studia Philonica*

SPhA   *The Studia Philonica Annual*

SPhM   Studia Philonica Monographs

PACS   Philo of Alexandria Commentary Series

(c) References to biblical authors and texts and to ancient authors and writings are to be abbreviated as recommended in the *SBL Handbook of Style* §8.2–3. Note that biblical books are not italicized and that between chapter and verse a colon is placed (but for non-biblical references colons should not be used). Abbreviations should be used for biblical books when they are followed by chapter or chapter and verse unless the book is the first word in a sentence. Authors writing in German or French should follow their own conventions for biblical citations.

(d) For giving dates the abbreviations B.C.E. and C.E. are preferred and should be printed in small caps.

(e) Journals, monograph series, source collections, and standard reference works are to be be abbreviated in accordance with the recommendations listed in *The SBL Handbook of Style* §8.4. The following list contains a selection of the more important abbreviations, along with a few abbreviations of classical and philosophical journals and standard reference books not furnished in the list.

ABD   *The Anchor Bible Dictionary,* 6 vols. New York, 1992

AC   *L'Antiquité Classique*

ACW   Ancient Christian Writers

AGJU   Arbeiten zur Geschichte des antiken Judentums und des Urchristentums

AJPh   *American Journal of Philology*

AJSL   *American Journal of Semitic Languages*

ALGHJ   Arbeiten zur Literatur und Geschichte des hellenistischen Judentums

ANRW   *Aufstieg und Niedergang der römischen Welt*

APh   *L'Année Philologique*

BDAG   Bauer, W., F. W. Danker, W. F. Arndt, and F. W. Gingrich. *A Greek-English Lexicon of the New Testament and Other Early Christian literature.* 3^d ed. Chicago: University of Chicago Press, 1999

BibOr	Bibliotheca Orientalis
BJRL	*Bulletin of the John Rylands Library*
BJS	Brown Judaic Studies
BMCR	*Bryn Mawr Classical Review* (electronic)
BZAW	Beihefte zur Zeitschrift für die alttestamentliche Wissenschaft
BZNW	Beihefte zur Zeitschrift für die neutestamentliche Wissenschaft
BZRGG	Beihefte zur Zeitschrift für Religions- und Geistesgeschichte
CBQ	*The Catholic Biblical Quarterly*
CBQMS	The Catholic Biblical Quarterly. Monograph Series
CC	Corpus Christianorum, Turnhout
CIG	*Corpus Inscriptionum Graecarum.* Edited by A. Boeckh, 4 vols. in 8. Berlin, 1828–77
CIJ	*Corpus Inscriptionum Judaicarum.* Edited by J. B. Frey, 2 vols. Rome, 1936–52
CIL	*Corpus Inscriptionum Latinarum.* Berlin, 1862–
CIS	*Corpus Inscriptionum Semiticarum.* Paris, 1881–1962
CPh	*Classical Philology*
CPJ	*Corpus Papyrorum Judaicarum.* Edited by V. Tcherikover and A. Fuks, 3 vols. Cambrige Mass., 1957–64
CQ	*The Classical Quarterly*
CR	*The Classical Review*
CRINT	Compendia Rerum Iudaicarum ad Novum Testamentum
CPG	*Clavis Patrum Graecorum.* Edited by M. Geerard, 5 vols. and suppl. vol. Turnhout, 1974–98
CPL	*Clavis Patrum Latinorum.* Edited by E. Dekkers. 3rd ed. Turnhout, 1995
CSCO	Corpus Scriptorum Christianorum Orientalium
CWS	Classics of Western Spirituality
DA	Dissertation Abstracts
DBSup	*Dictionnaire de la Bible,* Supplément. Paris, 1928–
DPhA	R. Goulet (ed.), *Dictionnaire des philosophes antiques*, Paris, 1989–
DSpir	*Dictionnaire de Spiritualité*, 17 vols. Paris, 1932–95
EncJud	*Encyclopaedia Judaica*, 16 vols. Jerusalem, 1972
EPRO	Études préliminaires aux religions orientales dans l'Empire romain
FrGH	*Fragmente der Griechische Historiker.* Edited by F. Jacoby et al. Leiden, 1954–
GCS	Die griechischen christlichen Schriftsteller, Leipzig
GLAJJ	M. Stern, *Greek and Latin Authors on Jews and Judaism*, 3 vols. Jerusalem, 1974–84
GRBS	*Greek, Roman and Byzantine Studies*
HKNT	Handkommentar zum Neuen Testament, Tübingen
HNT	Handbuch zum Neuen Testament, Tübingen
HR	*History of Religions*
HThR	*Harvard Theological Review*
HUCA	*Hebrew Union College Annual*
JAAR	*Journal of the American Academy of Religion*
JAOS	*Journal of the American Oriental Society*
JAC	*Jahrbuch für Antike und Christentum*
JBL	*Journal of Biblical Literature*
JHI	*Journal of the History of Ideas*
JHS	*The Journal of Hellenic Studies*
JJS	*The Journal of Jewish Studies*

JQR	*The Jewish Quarterly Review*
JR	*The Journal of Religion*
JRS	*The Journal of Roman Studies*
JSHRZ	Jüdische Schriften aus hellenistisch-römischer Zeit
JSJ	*Journal for the Study of Judaism in the Persian, Hellenistic and Roman Periods*
JSJSup	Supplements to the Journal for the Study of Judaism
JSNT	*Journal for the Study of the New Testament*
JSNTSup	Journal for the Study of the New Testament. Supplement Series
JSOT	*Journal for the Study of the Old Testament*
JSOTSup	Journal for the Study of the Old Testament. Supplement Series
JSP	*Journal for the Study of the Pseudepigrapha and Related Literature*
JSSt	*Journal of Semitic Studies*
JThS	*The Journal of Theological Studies*
KBL	L. Koehler and W. Baumgartner, *Lexicon in Veteris Testamenti libros*, 3 vols. 3rd ed. Leiden, 1967–83
KJ	*Kirjath Sepher*
LCL	Loeb Classical Library
LSJ	*A Greek-English Lexicon.* Edited by H. G. Liddell, R. Scott, H. S. Jones. 9th ed. with revised suppl. Oxford, 1996
MGWJ	*Monatsschrift für Geschichte und Wissenschaft des Judentums*
Mnem	*Mnemosyne*
NCE	*New Catholic Encyclopedia*, 15 vols. New York, 1967
NETS	New English Translation of the Septuagint. Edited by Albert Pietersma and Ben Wright, New York: Oxford University Press, 2007
NHS	Nag Hammadi Studies
NT	*Novum Testamentum*
NTSup	Supplements to Novum Testamentum
NTA	*New Testament Abstracts*
NTOA	Novum Testamentum et Orbis Antiquus
NTS	*New Testament Studies*
ODJ	*The Oxford Dictionary of Judaism.* Edited by R.J.Z. Werblowsky and G. Wigoder, New York 1997
OGIS	*Orientis Graeci inscriptiones selectae*
OLD	*The Oxford Latin Dictionary.* Edited by P. G. W. Glare. Oxford, 1982
OTP	*The Old Testament Pseudepigrapha.* Edited by J. H. Charlesworth. 2 vols. New York–London, 1983–85
PAAJR	*Proceedings of the American Academy for Jewish Research*
PAL	*Philon d'Alexandrie: Lyon 11–15 Septembre 1966.* Éditions du CNRS, Paris, 1967
P G	Patrologiae cursus completus: series Graeca. Edited by J. P. Migne. 162 vols. Paris, 1857–1912
PGL	*A Patristic Greek Lexicon.* Edited by G. W. H. Lampe. Oxford, 1961
PhilAnt	Philosophia Antiqua
P L	Patrologiae cursus completus: series Latina. Edited by J. P. Migne. 221 vols. Paris, 1844–64
PW	Pauly-Wissowa-Kroll, *Real-Encyclopaedie der classischen Altertumswissenschaft.* 49 vols. Munich, 1980
PWSup	Supplement to PW
RAC	*Reallexikon für Antike und Christentum*
RB	*Revue Biblique*

REA	*Revue des Études Anciennes*
REArm	*Revue des Études Arméniennes*
REAug	*Revue des Études Augustiniennes*
REG	*Revue des Études Grecques*
REJ	*Revue des Études Juives*
REL	*Revue des Études Latines*
RGG	*Die Religion in Geschichte und Gegenwart*, 7 vols. 3rd edition Tübingen, 1957–65
RhM	*Rheinisches Museum für Philologie*
RQ	*Revue de Qumran*
RSR	*Revue des Sciences Religieuses*
Str-B	H. L. Strack and P. Billerbeck, *Kommentar zum Neuen Testament aus Talmud und Midrasch*, 6 vols. Munich, 1922–61
SBLDS	Society of Biblical Literature Dissertation Series
SBLMS	Society of Biblical Literature Monograph Series
SBLSCS	Society of Biblical Studies Septuagint and Cognate Studies
SBLSPS	Society of Biblical Literature Seminar Papers Series
SC	Sources Chrétiennes
Sem	*Semitica*
SHJP	E. Schürer, *The History of the Jewish People in the Age of Jesus Christ*. Revised edition, 3 vols. in 4. Edinburgh, 1973–87
SJLA	Studies in Judaism in Late Antiquity
SNTSMS	Society for New Testament Studies. Monograph Series
SR	*Studies in Religion*
STAC	Studies and Texts in Antiquity and Judaism
SUNT	Studien zur Umwelt des Neuen Testaments
SVF	*Stoicorum veterum fragmenta*. Edited by J. von Arnim. 4 vols. Leipzig, 1903–24
TDNT	*Theological Dictionary of the New Testament*. 10 vols. Grand Rapids, 1964–76
THKNT	Theologischer Handkommentar zum Neuen Testament, Berlin
TRE	*Theologische Realenzyklopädie*, Berlin
TSAJ	Texte und Studien zum Antike Judentum
TU	Texte und Untersuchungen zur Geschichte der altchristlichen Literatur, Berlin
TWNT	*Theologisches Wörterbuch zum Neuen Testament*, 10 vols. Stuttgart 1933–79.
TZ	*Theologische Zeitschrift*
VC	*Vigiliae Christianae*
VCSup	Supplements to Vigiliae Christianae
VT	*Vetus Testamentum*
WMANT	Wissenschaftliche Monographien zum Alten und Neuen Testament
WUNT	Wissenschaftliche Untersuchungen zum Neuen Testament
YJS	*Yale Jewish Studies*
ZAW	*Zeitschrift für die alttestamentliche Wissenschaft*
ZKG	*Zeitschrift für Kirchengeschichte*
ZKTh	*Zeitschrift für Katholische Theologie*
ZNW	*Zeitschrift für die neutestamentliche Wissenschaft*
ZRGG	*Zeitschrift für Religions- und Geistesgeschichte*

www.ingramcontent.com/pod-product-compliance
Lightning Source LLC
Chambersburg PA
CBHW020404100426
42812CB00001B/199